S0-ACH-907

Offshore
Cruising
Navigation
Racing

*Other Publications:*

THE GOOD COOK
THE SEAFARERS
THE ENCYCLOPEDIA OF COLLECTIBLES
THE GREAT CITIES
WORLD WAR II
HOME REPAIR AND IMPROVEMENT
THE WORLD'S WILD PLACES
HUMAN BEHAVIOR
THE ART OF SEWING
THE OLD WEST
THE EMERGENCE OF MAN
THE AMERICAN WILDERNESS
THE TIME-LIFE ENCYCLOPEDIA OF GARDENING
LIFE LIBRARY OF PHOTOGRAPHY
THIS FABULOUS CENTURY
FOODS OF THE WORLD
TIME-LIFE LIBRARY OF AMERICA
TIME-LIFE LIBRARY OF ART
GREAT AGES OF MAN
LIFE SCIENCE LIBRARY
THE LIFE HISTORY OF THE UNITED STATES
TIME READING PROGRAM
LIFE NATURE LIBRARY
LIFE WORLD LIBRARY
FAMILY LIBRARY:
- HOW THINGS WORK IN YOUR HOME
- THE TIME-LIFE BOOK OF THE FAMILY CAR
- THE TIME-LIFE FAMILY LEGAL GUIDE
- THE TIME-LIFE BOOK OF FAMILY FINANCE

# Offshore

Cruising
Navigation
Racing

By the Editors of
TIME-LIFE BOOKS

The

TIME-LIFE Library of Boating

TIME-LIFE BOOKS/ALEXANDRIA, VIRGINIA

**The TIME-LIFE Library of Boating**

**Editorial Staff for Offshore:**
*Text Editors:* Philip W. Payne, Bryce S. Walker
*Picture Editor:* Nancy Shuker
*Designer:* James Eisenman
*Associate Designer:* Edward Frank
*Staff Writers:* Lee Greene, Wendy Buehr Murphy, John von Hartz
*Chief Researcher:* Myra Mangan
*Researchers:* Starr Badger, Jane Colihan, Holly C. Evarts, Stuart Gannes, Monica O. Horne, Trish Kiesewetter, James B. Murphy, Joyce Pelto, Carolyn Stallworth
*Design Assistants:* Rosi Cassano, Deanna Lorenz
*Editorial Assistant:* Lisa Berger McGuirt

Editorial Production
*Production Editor:* Douglas B. Graham
*Operations Manager:* Gennaro C. Esposito, Gordon E. Buck (assistant)
*Assistant Production Editor:* Feliciano Madrid
*Quality Control:* Robert L. Young (director), James J. Cox (assistant), Michael G. Wight (associate)
*Art Coordinator:* Anne B. Landry
*Copy Staff:* Susan B. Galloway (chief), Charles Blackwell, Edward B. Clarke, Celia Beattie
*Traffic:* Jeanne Potter

**The Cover:** Near sunset, an offshore mariner adjusts his sextant while sighting the first star of twilight. He will quickly make similar sightings of two more stars, then use the data indicated on the sextant's scale to help calculate the exact position of his vessel.

**The Consultants:** Halsey Herreshoff is a naval architect and boatman of 25 years' experience. He was the navigator for *Courageous* in her successful defense of the America's Cup in 1974 and is a veteran of many ocean races, including the Fastnet, Bermuda and the S.O.R.C. competitions.

John Rousmaniere, a small-boat sailor and an avid ocean racer, is an editor of *Yachting* magazine.

**Correspondents:** Elisabeth Kraemer (Bonn); Margot Hapgood, Dorothy Bacon, Lesley Coleman (London); Susan Jonas, Lucy T. Voulgaris (New York); Maria Vincenza Aloisi, Josephine du Brusle (Paris); Ann Natanson (Rome). Valuable assistance was also provided by: Helga Kohl (Athens); Gayle Rosenberg (Los Angeles); Carolyn T. Chubet, Miriam Hsia (New York).


Third printing. Revised 1979.
Published simultaneously in Canada.
Library of Congress catalogue card number 76-417.

# Contents

# The Challenge of Blue Water

# The Challenge of Blue Water

by David M. Parker

I have, on occasion, felt less than ecstatic about offshore voyaging. I vividly recall, for instance, a moment in a passage with a friend named Jim Barbour in my elderly sloop, *Laguna*. For 12 miserable June days we had been outbound from San Diego to Hawaii. At that time of year we should have been reaching smoothly along on the wings of the northeast trades and under sunny skies. Instead, an unseasonable tropical depression to the south had brought us strong north winds, a dense overcast and incessant swells that battered us abeam, straining *Laguna's* stout old timbers.

Heeled down about 20°, we were making 160 miles or so a day but were also taking aboard large and regular quantities of cold Pacific Ocean. Salt water drenched the cockpit, invaded the cabin and sprayed into the galley through a skylight I had tried in vain to caulk, occasionally dousing the stove and briefly splashing burning alcohol hither and yon. Jim and I fell into the habit of humming Wagner's "Magic Fire" music as an incantation before starting to cook. It was one of our few moments of levity. We cooked, ate and worked in our oilskins—even slept in them on our sodden bunks. My hands were raw from keeping tremendous pressure on the tiller at all times to combat *Laguna's* weather helm, and at the end of every three-hour trick at the wheel there were pink splatters of blood on the deck from my broken blisters.

To keep our frustrations at the situation from flaring into squabbles between us, Jim and I had virtually stopped speaking. With my thoughts turned inward, I had plenty of time to wonder why a couple of otherwise intelligent, responsible men would endure such misery, take risks that would appall their insurance agents, and lavish time and money on a trip they could make by air in four hours at a fraction of the cost.

I got my answer on the 13th day, when the trade winds arrived, the swell subsided and the sun came out. We spread *Laguna's* sails to a fair wind, opened the hatches, dried our bedding and feasted on fresh-caught dolphinfish. The answer was plain: I was there because, on balance, I simply cannot imagine anything better to do than to sail the ocean.

My father was a Navy man and I have lived with the sea most of my life. As a boy in Samoa I sailed in outrigger canoes, Navy whaleboats and the tub-like tin coracles that local children built and paddled around the harbor to the amusement or horror of their elders. As our family moved from one naval station to another, I learned the ways of pirogues and shrimp seiners in New Orleans, and of skipjacks and bugeye ketches on Chesapeake Bay. After World War II, I settled in San Diego where I worked on tuna boats, got a doctorate in physiological psychology and became a college professor. I also began sailing with anyone who would take me along, logging nearly 20,000 miles on other people's boats before acquiring my own offshore vessel. It was all marvelous preparation for that exhausting, rejuvenating, exasperating and hugely rewarding way of life that is called offshore voyaging—the ultimate form of cruising or racing.

In the years since then, I have done both, with some frequency. I ocean-raced every weekend, and often during the week, for eight or nine years, mostly in faithful old *Laguna,* a French-built, 35-foot cutter-sloop in which I won more than 30 races, including the Newport Beach, California-to-Ensenada race. I have also spent most of my summers in blue-water cruising, and I still can't decide which of the two activities I like best. In some respects, they are very different. Ocean racing involves a crew that is fairly large in relation to the size of the boat. A racing sailor follows a well-known course, often in sight of his rivals and sometimes in radio contact with shore, since the rules of a number of races require a daily report of each boat's position. The racer sleeps and eats when he can, wolfing a peanut-butter sandwich and gulping a can of beer before springing forward to set a staysail or a blooper. By con-

*Veteran offshore voyager David M. Parker of Los Angeles, California, stands at the companionway of Dawn Treader II, a 42-foot fiberglass cutter that he and his wife built themselves. A professor of psychology, Parker specializes in the study of motion sickness. He also teaches his own simplified version of celestial navigation, and writes books and articles on deepwater cruising and racing.*

trast, the cruising sailor ships a minimal crew—sometimes consisting only of himself. He dictates his own course, conserves his equipment and energy, and usually does not care if anyone else knows where he is until he gets there.

Every cruiser sets his own pace. For example, my friend Dave Irvine, who runs Samoa's educational TV system, likes to fish, play cards and do ropework while sailing with his wife Pidge from Los Angeles to Samoa in their Tahiti ketch, *Matthew*. I, too, prefer to sail with only my wife as crew and I tend to treat every voyage—whether a 30-mile jaunt to Catalina Island or a 2,200-mile haul to Hawaii—as a chance to beat my best previous time, a passion that has cost me a lot of broken rigging and blown-out sails.

No matter how it is done, sailing out of sight of land offers gratifications that are to me all but unique. Nowhere else have I felt such personal contact with nature. I have spent hours talking to dolphins playing in my bow wave, and over a period of days have learned to recognize individuals among them. I have marveled at the grace of a Pacific albatross hanging nearly motionless 20 feet off my weather bow, riding air currents thrown up by the swell—and I have also marveled at the same bird's clumsiness as, with folded wings, it paddled awkwardly alongside. As an amateur meteorologist, I have spent days happily observing clouds, squalls and wave patterns, and pondering their varying relationships. I have sailed through blood-red waves toward sunsets that defy ready description.

Some of life's simplest physical pleasures can become almost overpoweringly delightful on a long offshore haul. A hot cup of coffee after a freezing watch is bliss. A dry bunk, though only 20 inches wide and too short, can provide rest unmatched by a bed in the finest hotel. I remember greeting with rapture one of those sudden, vicious black squalls that sometimes invade the shifting, ocean-girdling region of dead air called the doldrums. My crew and I were short of fresh water and so salt-encrusted and goaty that we ignored the danger of the squall in our haste to break out the soap and enjoy the luxury of a pelting fresh-water bath.

The protracted solitude of ocean voyaging can take a toll, to be sure —sometimes causing the mind to play unpleasant tricks. After a few days at sea, I have been assailed by recurring, senseless dreams or by tunes that I could not get out of my head. And on lonely night watches a thousand miles from land, I have seen the sudden loom of lighthouses and heard voices that were not there. But under the same conditions, I have also had flashes of insight so deep and keen as to be in the nature of revelation.

Then, too, there is the profound emotional satisfaction of succeeding entirely on one's own. The offshore man must accept and ride out whatever weather he finds, since safe harbors are seldom handy in times of crisis. It is my belief that a man can learn more about his limitations and abilities in a long offshore passage than in years of psychoanalysis, if only because all the usual measures of status ashore—bank accounts, honors, degrees—are utterly worthless when the gale is up and it's time to turn to and bail for hours, or to rig a jury mast, or to go about and rescue a man overboard.

In some ways, the greatest dividend of all is the thrill of making a good landfall after 20 or 30 days at sea. This is the moment that marks the payoff of all the offshore voyager's seamanly skills, particularly that of celestial navigation, the way-finding technique based on sextant sightings of the sun, stars or planets. Although celestial navigation has a reputation for daunting mathematical complexities, it is really quite simple. One need only be able to add, subtract, read English and carry along the right implements—a good timepiece, a current almanac giving the positions of heavenly bodies and a couple of sight reduction tables. These are thick volumes of precomputed solutions to the navigator's mathematical problems, and they substantially reduce the amount of calculating he must do.

A navigator must also carry with him the courage of his calculations. I had only recently taught myself celestial navigation when Jim Barbour and I took *Laguna* to Hawaii. Bad weather prevented taking sights for the first 12 days or so, but when the sun finally appeared, my first fix showed an error in our dead reckoning of only about 18 miles. Greatly encouraged, we sailed on until the day when, by my reckoning, we were to sight the city of Hilo at 5 p.m. I took one more sight to double-check our longitude and got a set of figures placing us 600 miles east of Tokyo. Alarmed, I took another sight that located us on the outskirts of Chicago. As Jim collapsed with laughter, I furiously recalculated and found I had used the wrong month in the almanac. My previous observations were confirmed, and at exactly 5 p.m., Kamukahi Point loomed out of a rain squall just as predicted.

Like so many other offshore skills, celestial navigation can be very useful not only during long ocean passages but also on shorter trips, such as a week's run from Miami to Bermuda or an overnight cruise from San Diego to Ensenada. For any boatman would do well to learn how to fix his position in the absence of landmarks—since there is always the possibility that he may someday be forced by a gale to head out to sea to avoid a lee shore.

Moreover, the challenges and satisfactions of offshore voyaging are as available to the powerboater as to the sailing man, and the advantages of a power yacht are undeniable. My old friend Spec Rolley, who has given up his 40-foot ketch for a 40-foot trawler yacht, can travel the 700 or so miles from San Diego's Silvergate Yacht Club to Cape San Lucas at the tip of Baja California and return without refueling—and without being frustrated by the morning and evening calms that beset sailors in that area. However, a powerboat has drawbacks, too. Because it is dependent on a single source of propulsion, its skipper needs a host of spare parts and the ability to install them. In order to accommodate big fuel tanks, the powerboat must be larger in total cubic capacity than a sailboat with comparable living space. Yet over a long haul it will generally not be much faster than the sailboat because of the way sea conditions limit speed. Personally, I prefer wind power. I find sailboats, in the main, more stable and responsive than powerboats. And by planning a cruise to fit prevailing winds and currents, I can be reasonably sure of making port within a previously calculated time.

Almost any yacht that is of seaworthy design and construction can cross oceans if it is properly prepared, suitably provisioned and sailed in a solid, seaman-like manner. Dozens of small yachts are at this moment cruising the oceans of the world with crews of one, two or three people—some young, some elderly, many of them not particularly notable for their strength or endurance. The successful offshore sailor survives more by his wit and experience than by sheer muscle.

Luck helps, too. In 1963, a 61-year-old house painter and real-estate salesman named Felix J. Novel set out from San Diego for Hawaii in an 8-by-15-foot life raft—christened *Felix III*—with an old bathtub for a cockpit, two five-horsepower outboards for auxiliary power and a boy of 18 for crew. He was 24 days out when his rudder broke. The crew of a passing Japanese fishing boat helped him to fix it but also took off his young companion, who had become disheartened. Novel continued on alone, survived storms and a heart attack, and arrived in Hawaii after 76 days at sea.

Rather than relying on luck like Novel's, a prospective offshore sailor should invest time and effort in properly readying himself and his boat for the open ocean. To get a sense of what lies ahead, it is a good idea to begin by serving as crew on somebody else's boat—if you have the opportunity. Then, when you have bought your own boat, be sure to acquire an intimate knowledge of its anatomy and workings on coastwise cruises. Some people ensure this close acquaintance by actually building their own boats. And though such a prospect suggests the need for an uncommon amount of energy, spare time and manual dexterity, in reality it is not so formidable a prospect as it may sound.

Good, seaworthy kit boats of up to 50 feet are available today in a variety of configurations. In 1970 my wife Joanne and I designed and built *Dawn Treader,* a light (4,400 pounds), cheap ($6,000) 27-foot fiberglass cutter with no engine, no brightwork and no electrical system. I felt more independent while sailing her than in any other yacht I had ever owned. She was so satisfactory that we decided to apply her principles to a larger boat, which was what we really wanted. The next year, working for six months and only on weekends, we built our equally successful 42-foot *Dawn Treader II* *(pages 26-29)* along the same lines.

If you already own a boat, you can gain much the same familiarity with it in the course of modifying and fitting it out, since virtually no stock sailboat now on the market is suited for extended offshore sailing as it comes from the manufacturer. If possible, seek out a boat like your own that has been sailed offshore and note what reinforcements its skipper has found necessary. Do as much of the refitting job yourself as you can: watching a professional do the work is instructive, but if the work fails at sea, only you will be there to make repairs.

Strengthening the rigging and chain plates, beefing up the rudder tube, and perhaps changing the mast will give you a firsthand knowledge of vital skills and a good idea of what spares you will need. Have the yacht surveyed before you leave—but be sure to pick a surveyor with offshore experience. Finally, take a shakedown cruise before starting a long voyage. I always test my boat on a few 100-to-200-mile hitches to weather, staying within range of a good shipyard in case any of the equipment proves inadequate.

Once you have prepared yourself and your boat for every foreseeable contingency, you can set forth with the assurance that inevitably something will go wrong. I relearned this lesson recently at 2 o'clock on a dark June morning. My wife and I had set out from Los Angeles four days earlier, bound for Hawaii in *Dawn Treader II,* the cutter we had just spent six months building. We were, as usual, equipped with everything that experience had trained us to bring along for an emergency. We had plenty of cable and clamps (both had come in handy some years before when *Laguna's* shrouds parted in a squall), spare halyards, engine parts and sails. And if worst came to worst, we had a rubber raft, a fiberglass dinghy, an automatic position-reporting radio, and a good survival kit with water, rations, knives, gaff and fishing tackle.

We were charging along at a solid eight knots under working jib and single-reefed main, delighted with the boat's fine turn of speed and with the new self-steering system I had devised, when we hit some underwater object with a jarring shock that hurled both of us to the bottom of the cockpit.

Down below, water began rising above the cabin sole. Joanne grabbed the pump handle and began the backbreaking chore of clearing the yacht of water while I looked for the leak. Anyone who was less familiar than we were with the intimate details of the boat's construction and workings would probably have broken out the survival gear and then, in any remaining time, tried to save the yacht.

As it was, I quickly found the leak, a one-inch hole in the lower reaches of the bilges where the floating log—or whatever it was—had knocked off the depth-sounder transducer. I had built a small hatch above the installation so that it could be replaced, but hadn't counted on doing the job at 2 a.m. in 20 or 30 knots of wind and a lumpy sea. I had also neglected an elementary precaution: always carry a plug of the proper size and shape to fit any hole that has been drilled through the hull, even one normally fitted with a seacock—and especially when, as in the case of our transducer, the fitting includes no seacock. As it was, I had to substitute ingenuity for anticipation. I whittled a plug from a mop handle—to the accompaniment of acid comments from the pump brigade—and stopped the leak securely enough to allow us to make for port and complete more permanent repairs.

This was just one more reminder from the sea that it will not tolerate incompetence, laziness or foolishness for long; nor will it give many second chances to those who take foolish ones. But if one is confident, prepared and prudent, success is practically assured in what is, for me, the greatest challenge and the most gratifying achievement left to most of us.

1

There is much that is wrong about venturing out onto great waters in a small cruising boat. And one evening, remonstrating with his longtime friend, the naval hero and obdurate ocean sailor Commander William King, Winston Churchill summed it all up in his characteristically succinct fashion: "It's perilous, uncomfortable and unremunerative." And, he advised King, "Stop it." Of course, Sir Winston was right. And, of course, Commander King went right on doing it, as has almost every other person who has had the ultimate satisfaction of setting forth on an ocean passage with nothing before him but his own mast, his own horizon and his own guiding stars. The act of heading offshore for a week or

# STRATEGIES FOR OCEAN VOYAGING

more, beyond the sight of land and beyond the reach of immediate help, is both a testing and an exhilarating experience. Many people never dare it; yet a sea voyage, for all of its awesome problems and perils, is well within the capacities of any able sailor.

The key to success in blue-water boating is careful planning. And nothing reflects the quality and care of an offshore voyager's preparations so much as the vessel he sails. A sampling of superbly fitted deepwater craft appears on the following pages. Like the people who planned and sail them, they differ widely in many respects, yet they share the common denominator of special seaworthiness. One of the boats, David Parker's 42-foot *Dawn Treader II,* reflects her owner's spartan practicability: there are no frills or extra fixtures to tear loose or break down under the stress of a gale; Parker even eschews the use of electricity, making do with kerosene cabin lights and icebox refrigeration. Another vessel, Bruce and Alexandra Crabtree's 50-foot *Crabby Too,* is a year-round home afloat that shows a taste for more civilized maritime living; her main cabin is carpeted, hung with framed pictures and bright curtains, and lined with bookshelves. Yet whatever their degree of comfort, all these boats, with their extra measure of ballast, heavy fittings and rigging, and other modifications, have been equipped to outlast virtually any punishment the ocean may hand out.

Another requisite for safe, comfortable deepwater sailing is scrupulous analysis of the itinerary of a voyage. Although to the novice the ocean appears as a trackless waste, veteran seamen know it is crosshatched with very definite and advantageous routes *(pages 38-53)* that have been mapped out over the centuries with all the care and precision of the landsman's superhighways. The locations of these high-seas highways are determined by the direction and strength of prevailing winds and currents, and by the seasonal patterns and frequencies of storms, such as the Indian Ocean cyclones that brew winds of 125 knots.

In addition, the seagoing skipper must have a very clear idea of the basic stores that any boat, regardless of the owner's taste, must have aboard before venturing for any length of time beyond sight of land. These include such essentials as a minimum of 10 gallons of fresh water per month for every person on board; spares for all vital engine and rigging parts; a meticulously stocked medical kit; and, of course, adequate food. (It is also not a bad idea to see a dentist before embarking.)

With such preparations well in hand, a competent skipper can, like Commander King, ignore Sir Winston's advice with no consequences save pleasure and satisfaction. But the mariner must always remember the latent power of the sea, which can, with no warning or reason *(pages 62-75),* do in the most well-found vessel. At such rare and unavoidable moments, the able seaman's all-round preparedness, for emergencies as well as for everyday sailing, can be the margin of survival for both skipper and crew.

*A deepwater cruiser approaches Oahu, Hawaii, after a voyage from San Francisco. Gliding before the northeast trades, she flies a mainsail and two jibs boomed out wing and wing.*

*The modified sloop Starboard Hiller ghosts past the Los Angeles shoreline shortly after her return home from a 4,400-mile round-trip voyage to Hawaii. As altered by her three owners, the boat provides enough space for 30 grocery bags of provisions, outsized water tanks holding 75 gallons and two fuel tanks holding a total of 45 gallons. Fully stocked, she can cruise for more than a month without docking.*

## Building Up from Stock

At the time deepwater veterans Darryl and Ruth Ann Johnston and their partner Dan Higgins set out to find an ideal ocean-going craft, their basic requirement was a compact, easy-handling vessel capable of taking them on a 2,200-mile Pacific trek from their home port in California to Hawaii. They began by buying for $3,500 the bare decked-over hull of a brand-new, stock Islander 32 Mark II. They liked its fin keel and slim hull of low-maintenance fiberglass. However, as with other mass-produced boats, the basic Islander was not set up for extended voyaging offshore. Working after hours, the partners spent 18 months and an additional $16,000 to build in deepwater modifications.

Higgins and the Johnstons made three basic alterations of structure and rig. The first was to extend the cabin three feet aft—using heavy-duty three-quarter-inch plywood bulkheads and fiberglass-coated plywood cabin roofing to provide extra space. This space is carefully utilized for storage, living area and galley facilities.

The expanded cabin area, along with the huge quantity of supplies required for long-distance cruising, added so much weight that the boat, christened *Starboard Hiller,* needed an extra-large sail plan to keep her moving, particularly in light to moderate air. Consequently, her owners enlarged the foretriangle by splicing on a three-foot bowsprit. This bowsprit also serves to anchor a dual headsail rig, one of the additional features *(page 17)* built into *Starboard Hiller* to make her easier to handle during the extended downwind sailing that is a major part of open-water cruising.

Finally, the owners installed a heavy-duty mast and rigging strong enough to match any foreseeable Pacific gale. The 45-foot mast of extruded aluminum is supported by a taut cat's cradle of one-quarter-inch stainless-steel shrouds and five-sixteenth-inch stays. All halyards are prestretched Dacron, which, though vulnerable to chafing, is much easier to handle than wire. And the gooseneck fitting connecting the boom to the mast is of stainless steel, providing greater durability than the common brass variety.

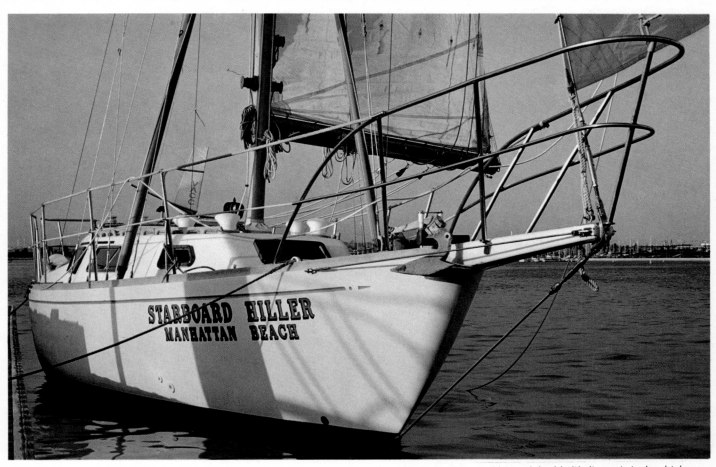

For added security, a webbing of double life lines, six inches higher than on the standard production model, encircles Starboard Hiller. The lines are of three-quarter-inch rope rather than conventional plastic-covered wire—which can be hard to grasp, and even dangerous if a frayed strand pops through the plastic. The life lines are anchored to an oversized pulpit mounted on a strong, stubby bowsprit secured by a heavy-duty bob stay and two bowsprit shrouds.

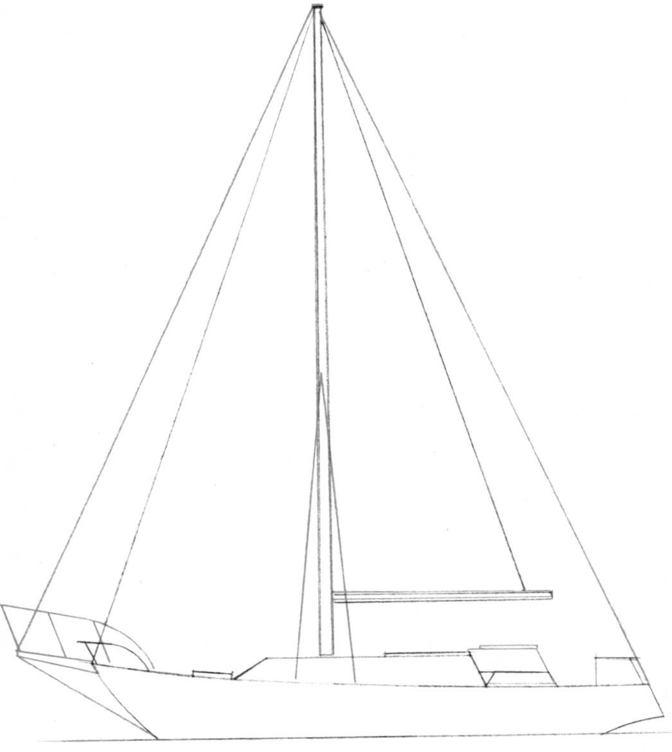

The major custom alterations that changed a production-line 32-footer into a specialized deepwater cruising vessel are indicated in blue at left, superimposed on an outline of the original stock model. They include the three-foot cabin extension, the bowsprit and pulpit, and extra-heavy rigging. These adaptations, along with some structural strengthening such as adding nine layers of mat and cloth on certain key bulkheads, resulted in a weight gain for the boat of 1,700 pounds —and a gain in seaworthiness that allowed the vessel to sail for 7,000 miles with no major structural failures in her first four years.

*Starboard Hiller's steering rig is typical of one kind of device installed by offshore skippers to save themselves countless hours at the helm. It consists of a wind vane that steers an auxiliary rudder to keep the boat on course. To engage the rig, the skipper puts the boat on the desired heading and then, using a worm gear (below), sets the vane so that it points into the wind. Any change in the boat's heading —and consequent shift in apparent wind—causes the vane to pivot. As the vane turns, its motion is transmitted via a tube, bell crank and link to a trim tab (dark blue) on the auxiliary rudder, creating pressures that turn the rudder and bring the boat back on its proper heading.*

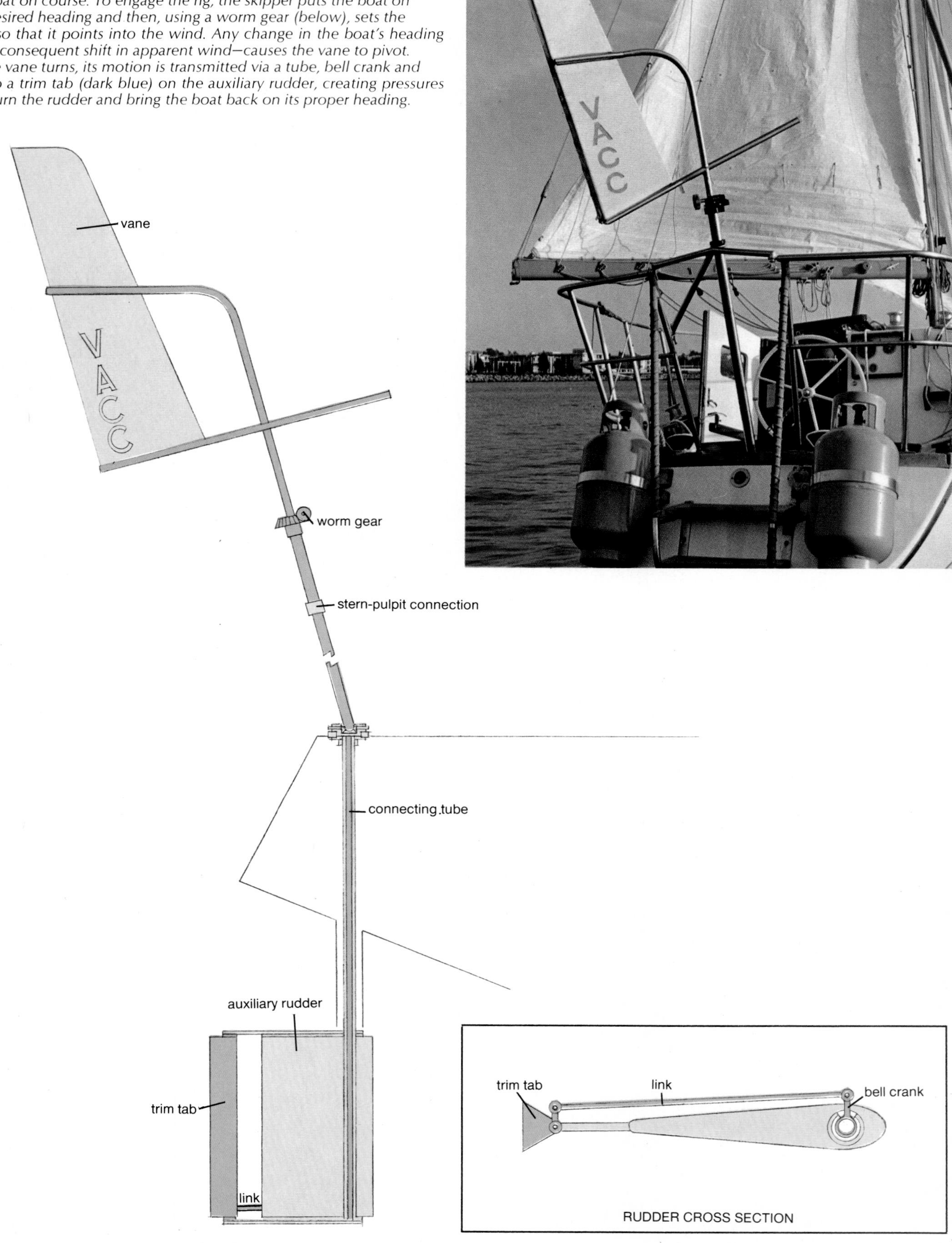

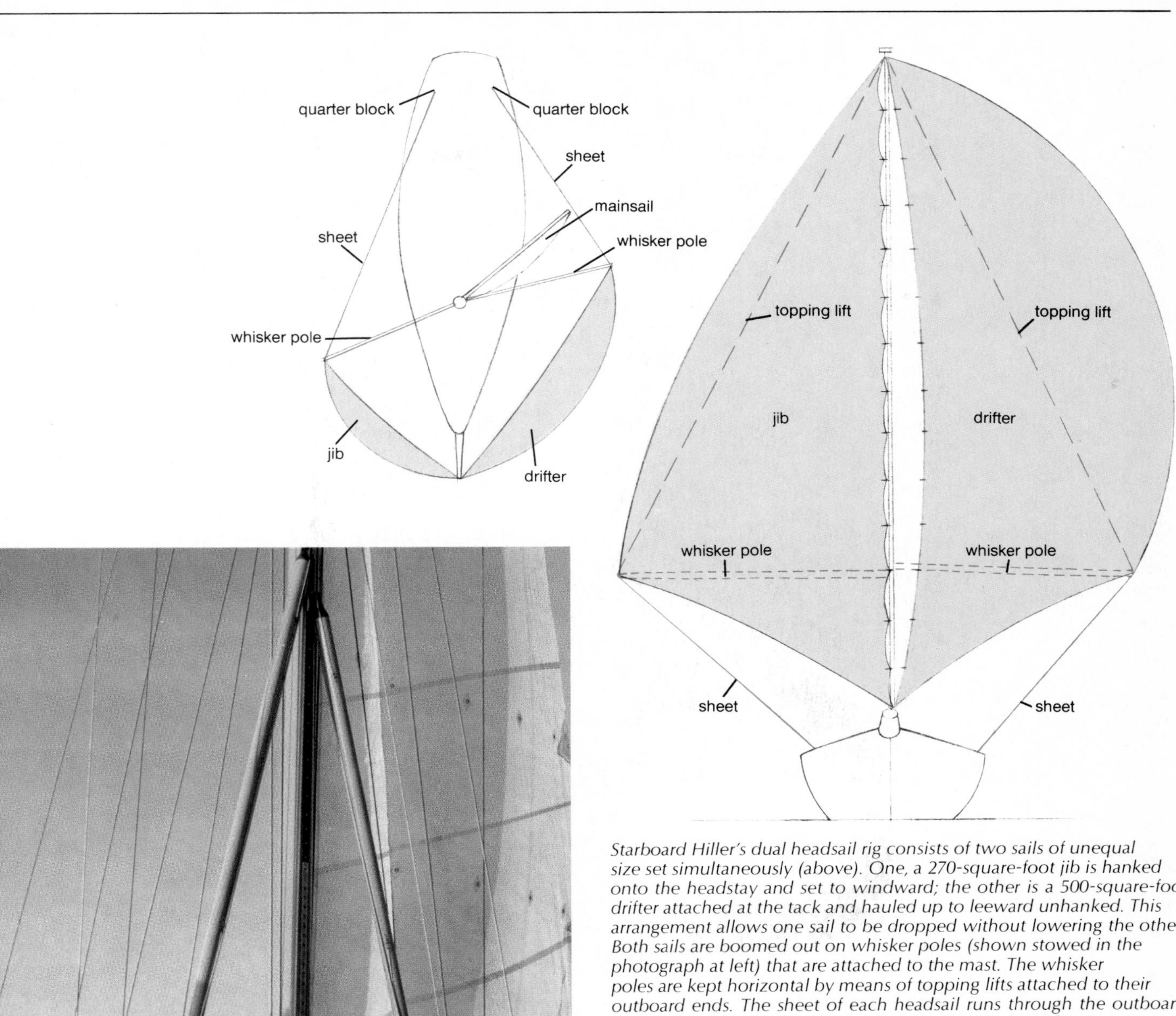


*Starboard Hiller's dual headsail rig consists of two sails of unequal size set simultaneously (above). One, a 270-square-foot jib is hanked onto the headstay and set to windward; the other is a 500-square-foot drifter attached at the tack and hauled up to leeward unhanked. This arrangement allows one sail to be dropped without lowering the other. Both sails are boomed out on whisker poles (shown stowed in the photograph at left) that are attached to the mast. The whisker poles are kept horizontal by means of topping lifts attached to their outboard ends. The sheet of each headsail runs through the outboard end of the respective whisker pole, then to a block on the quarter.*

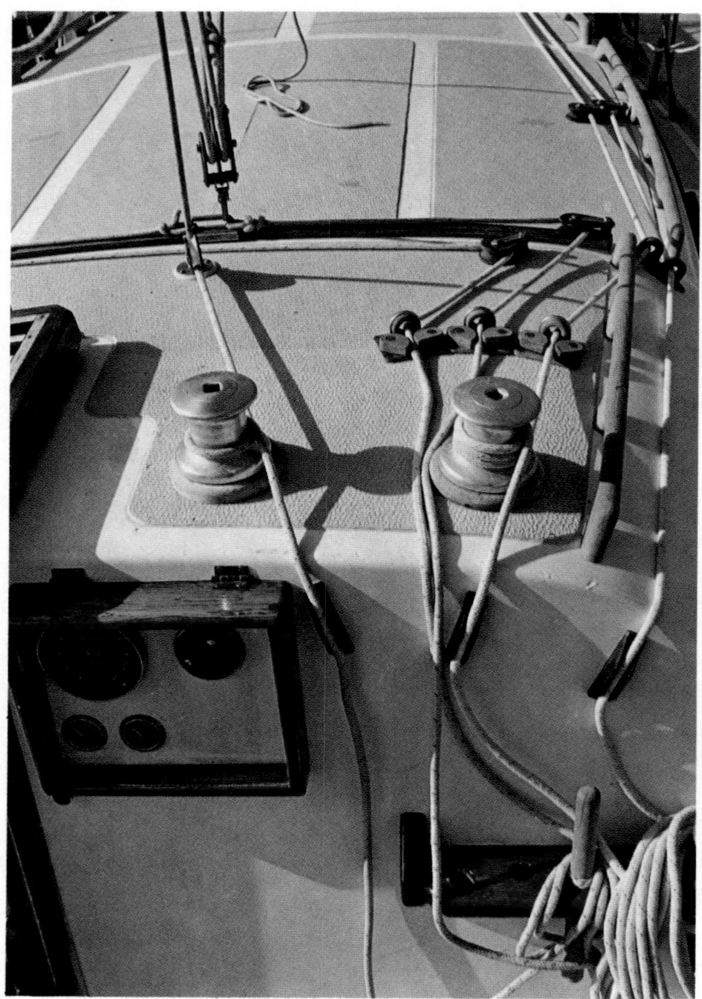

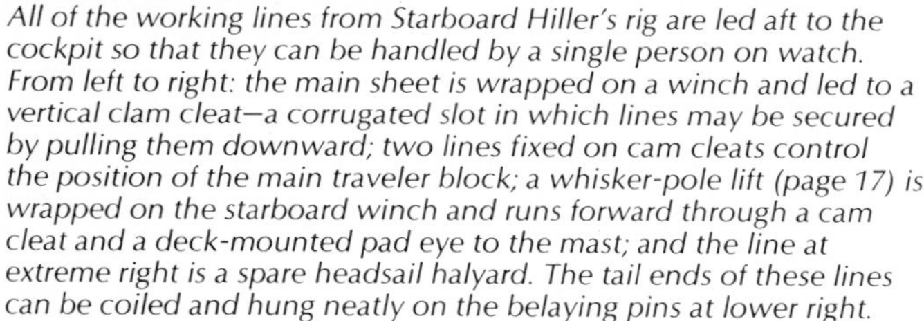

*All of the working lines from Starboard Hiller's rig are led aft to the cockpit so that they can be handled by a single person on watch. From left to right: the main sheet is wrapped on a winch and led to a vertical clam cleat—a corrugated slot in which lines may be secured by pulling them downward; two lines fixed on cam cleats control the position of the main traveler block; a whisker-pole lift (page 17) is wrapped on the starboard winch and runs forward through a cam cleat and a deck-mounted pad eye to the mast; and the line at extreme right is a spare headsail halyard. The tail ends of these lines can be coiled and hung neatly on the belaying pins at lower right.*

*A twist-on swaging bolt—a fitting that grips the end of a wire shroud or stay and attaches it to a turnbuckle—allows quick at-sea repairs of the standing rigging. Unlike conventional eyebolt swages, which must be put on ashore with a special machine, this fitting can be installed by slipping the upper sleeve over the wire and then tightening it with an ordinary wrench. The bolt in the lower section then threads into the turnbuckle.*

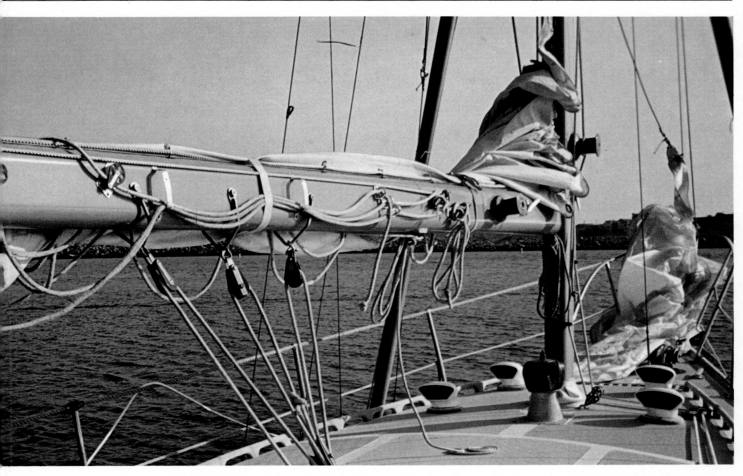

*Jiffy reef lines draped along the boom are a prime convenience for shortening sail with a minimal crew. The lines run through blocks on the boom and up to reef cringles in the leech of the main. The line looped through the aft block leads to the lowermost cringle for a single reef, the forwardmost line to the upper cringle for a triple reef. Then the lines are made fast to eye straps on the other side of the boom. When the time comes to reef, a line is hauled in and its cringle is strapped to the boom. The halyard is then eased to lower the sail's tack, which is made fast with a hook. Then the foot of the sail is quickly furled, and the reef is secure.*

*A set of running lights mounted at either end of the spreaders serves as a safety measure for Starboard Hiller at night—a sensible precaution on a boat this small, since running lights in their standard position on the bow cannot readily be seen amid ocean swells by helmsmen on commercial vessels. In heavily traveled waters, the skipper may also flick on the spreader lights (nearer the mast). Normally used for on-deck work at night, these lights, reflecting off the sails, warn larger vessels of Starboard Hiller's presence.*

*Starboard Hiller's custom-extended main cabin, seen here from the companionway steps, offers a spacious 70 square feet of living space. The galley, at near left, consists of a butane stove, refrigerator and a sink with foot-pump-operated faucets (page 28). At center rear is a wood-and-charcoal-burning stainless-steel stove to warm the cabin on dank, mid-ocean nights. Coat hooks on the brick facing behind the stove can hold clothing for drying. The cabin table in front of the stove doubles as a cover for the engine. To its right are a settee berth and a chart table with a pencil rack above. A quarter berth with stowage space beneath (below, right) completes the cabin layout.*

*A stowage locker beneath the mattress of the quarter berth (bottom right-hand corner of picture above) is divided into cubbyholes for essential items of gear. Clockwise from right center, the compartments hold spare winch handles, the boat's 12-volt batteries, spare engine belts, cleaner for the teak deck and rust preventive, extra blocks and a manual bilge pump. The last of these, a backup for an electrical pump set in the bilge, is activated by a lever inserted into its socket and, with vigorous cranking, will expel 25 gallons of water a minute.*

A two-cylinder diesel engine is carefully tucked away inside the cabin's center table—a position that makes it particularly accessible for difficult repairs in a seaway. The boat's two fuel tanks hold 45 gallons of fuel oil that provide over 250 hours of running time at idle for charging the batteries, or 180 miles of propulsion at 1,600 rpm's.

This neatly ordered fuse box, located on the aft bulkhead near the companionway, is the heart of Starboard Hiller's complex 12-volt DC electrical system. Each wire is numbered at its terminals so that problems in any individual circuit can be easily traced; the number key is posted on the fuse-box door. The system feeds off the boat's two batteries, which can be kept charged by running the engine for 30 to 60 minutes each day while underway.

*The organized clutter of her superstructure marks Crabby Too as an offshore cruiser. The 15-foot mast and boom will lower any of the vessel's four auxiliary craft to the water. Mounted on the mast are two radar receivers —one a backup. Aerials for the boat's radios and radio direction finder reach skyward on either side of the canopied bridge.*

## Push-Button Posh

While long passages under sail can mean hard physical work for days on end, cruising offshore in a properly adapted powerboat can be positively opulent. Moving independently of the wind, the owner of a well-found powerboat enjoys near-total control over his itinerary and speed. Furthermore, with the engine to generate both electrical and mechanical power, he can hook up all kinds of push-button devices—from air conditioners to toasters.

There are, however, certain problems associated with venturing any distance under power. Since all powerboats tend to roll and pitch in a seaway, an offshore cruiser's hull must be carefully designed to minimize motion. And every important power-driven device must have a dependable backup in case of a breakdown at sea.

With these considerations in mind, former *Yachting* magazine editors Bruce and Alexandra Crabtree commissioned naval architect Arthur DeFever to create *Crabby Too,* the 50-foot trawler shown on these pages. Built in Yokosuka, Japan, in 1970, she incorporates an awesome assortment of original adaptations that solve the problems and increase the comforts of powering offshore.

At the vessel's heart, a 400-horsepower diesel—with 1,750-gallon fuel tanks—can push *Crabby Too* more than 2,800 miles at a cruising speed of eight knots without refueling, while also providing power for the main generator. A backup diesel of 26 horsepower provides emergency power and turns an auxiliary generator. A butane stove can stand in for the electric one; and five different radios ensure a successful SOS in case of trouble.

*Crabby Too's* blue-water hull design keeps her on a relatively even keel in any reasonable sea. The welded steel body has a sharp, deep forefoot to part ocean combers, with the aft sections flattened off to help prevent lateral roll. The design is so successful that the vessel needs none of the stabilizing devices—such as fins or outrigger poles—that are standard on many offshore power cruisers.

A model of seagoing safety, *Crabby Too* has four watertight bulkheads in case the hull is punctured by collision or grounding on rocks. In addition, she carries handy and efficient lifesaving gear *(left)* and no less than four lifeboats—a six-man life raft, an inflatable dinghy, a dory and an outboard-powered tender.

*A flag-tipped lifesaving pole cradled on deck alongside the flying bridge can be quickly lifted free and heaved overboard, along with the orange horseshoe life ring visible at upper left. This rig, which can mark a man's position during a rescue operation, is commonly seen on ocean-racing sailboats, but constitutes a rare—and prudent—addition to a power craft.*

*Crabby Too's main control center, located forward in the main cabin, includes an automatic pilot that can be engaged and turned by means of the switches on the vertical panel at lower right. On the counter directly above the autopilot, bright colored lights electronically monitor a fresh-water maker (below, left) located in the engine room. The two black iron balls on either side of the compass correct magnetic interference from the boat's steel hull. Interspersed among these offshore modifications are standard instruments and controls, such as switches for lights, wipers and horn (upper center).*

*To supplement Crabby Too's on-board 500-gallon water supply, this fresh-water maker—capable of producing as much as eight gallons an hour—occupies a niche in the engine room. The water maker runs on the vessel's 110-volt power supply and uses the heat of the engine to distill sea water, which is pumped in from the ocean, vaporized and then conveyed to a water tank beside the engine room.*

*The view forward from the galley into Crabby Too's spacious main cabin shows the utility-minded care with which an offshore vessel should be laid out. The helmsman's seat faces the control console and backs up against a comfortable settee on the starboard side. Above the settee, mounted on a bulkhead, is a depth finder that gives a graphic rendition of the bottom up to a depth of 200 feet. To the left of the helm stands a cabinet containing electronic and navigational gear (below, right). Large windows forward provide the helmsman with maximum visibility; their unbreakable safety-glass panes are sealed shut for total waterproofing in a storm.*

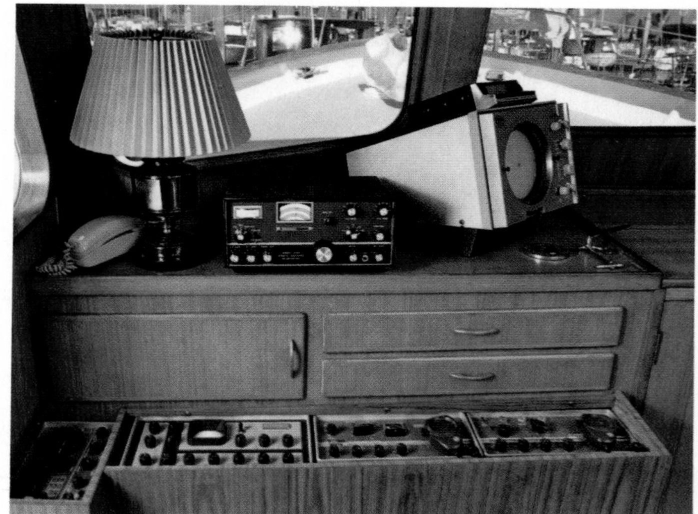

*Inside the low cabinet on the forward port side of the control area is an awesome collection of electronic gear. From left to right on the bottom row the console contains a radio direction finder, a loran-A receiver and two ship-to-shore radios. Atop the cabinet, which also holds two chart drawers and a locker for navigational tools, stands a telephone that can be connected to outside lines at a marina, a ham radio and a radarscope—the last of these surmounted by a tape deck that is hooked to a stereo system. A fifth radio, not visible here, allows VHF-FM receiving. And for added safety, the Crabtrees have yet another radio, this one in a cabinet on the flying bridge.*

*Looking aft from the helm, Crabby Too's main cabin is the image of teak-trimmed comfort, complete with such amenities as a television, framed pictures on the bulkheads, indoor-outdoor carpeting and well-stocked bookshelves. But amid the homey touches are more refinements for long-range ocean cruising. All tables and flat surfaces are rimmed with fiddle rails to catch straying objects when the boat rolls. A central charcoal-burning brass space heater warms the cabin, and below the TV set is a refrigerator-freezer capable of holding provisions for two passengers for over two weeks. Crabby Too even has a backup for the electric coffeepot, should power fail.*

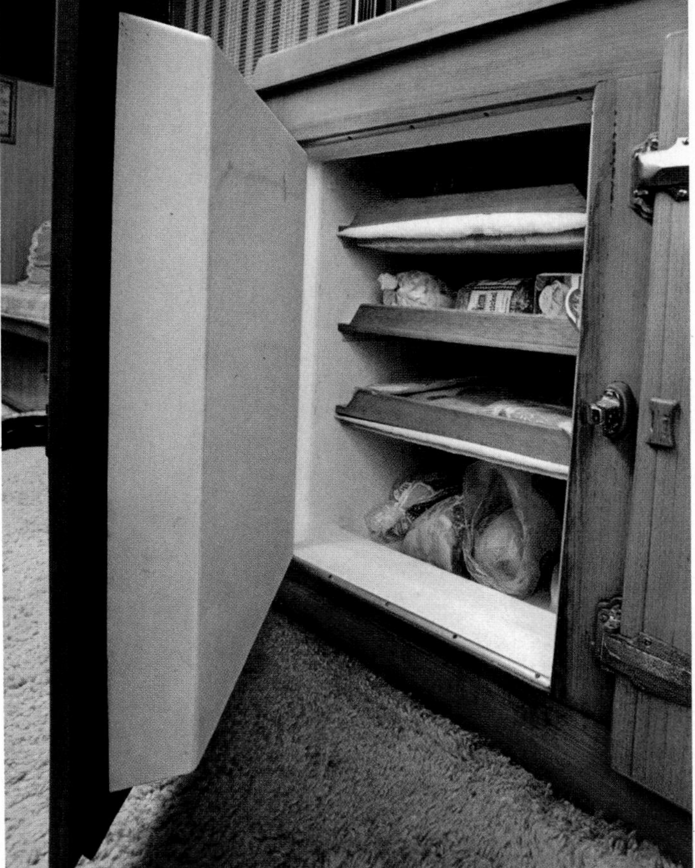

*A glance into the freezer section of Crabby Too's refrigerator reveals half of the unit's 16 cubic feet of storage space, partitioned by shelves rimmed with fiddle rails. A supplementary freezer—of eight cubic feet capacity—is installed above decks on the fantail, where it can be easily stocked with fish hauled aboard by the Crabtrees' battery of a dozen custom-made fishing poles.*

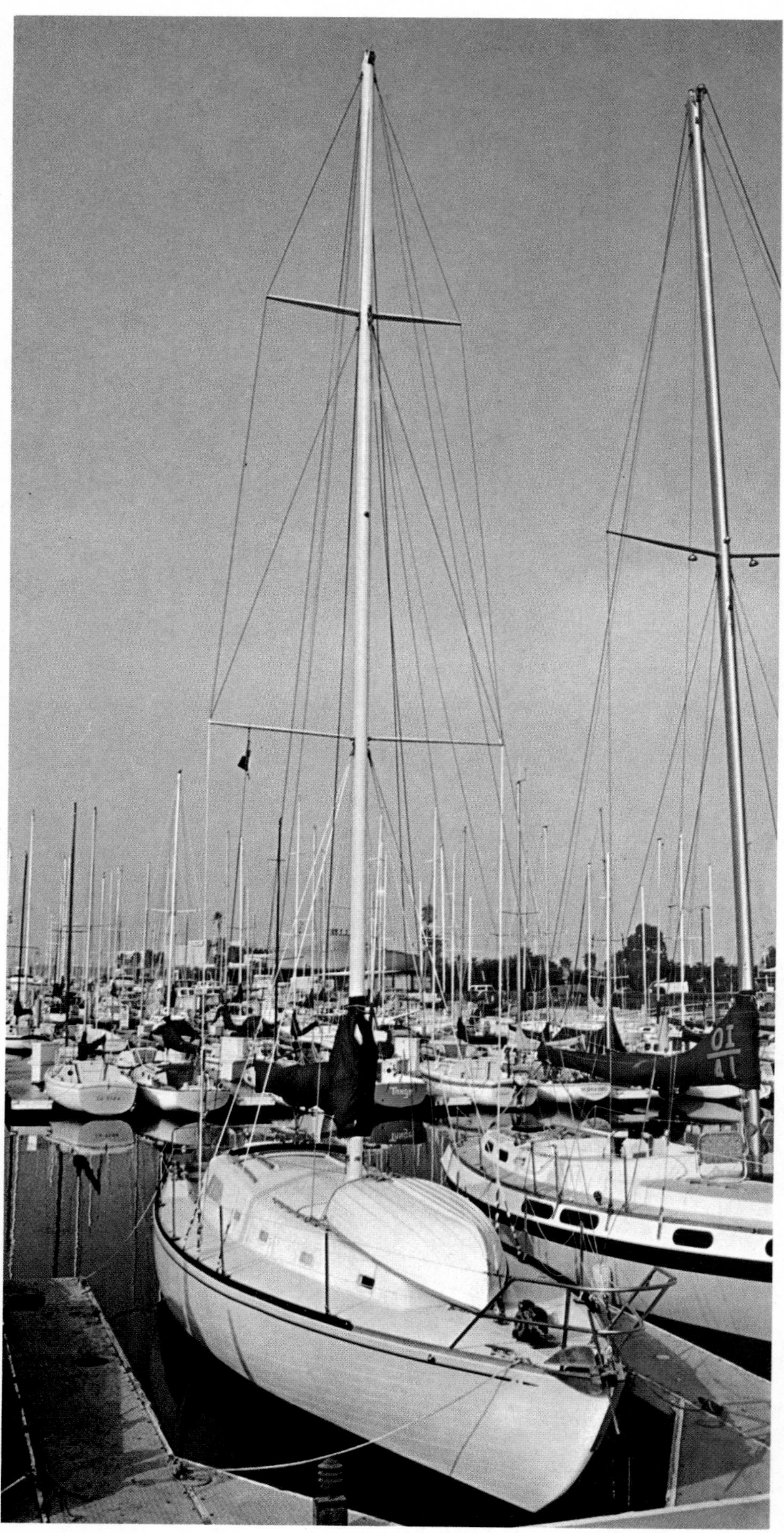

## Styled for Independence

The trim 42-foot cutter *Dawn Treader II,* owned by seagoing author David Parker *(page 9),* represents the essence of rugged self-reliance at sea. She is laid out with a bare minimum of power-driven gear, thereby eliminating the need for complex electrical systems and backup devices—and for frequent port visits for fuel or repairs. Her storage lockers will keep Parker and his wife provisioned for six months at a stretch.

Like the small sloop *Starboard Hiller (pages 14-21),* Parker's boat is essentially built up from a modified fiberglass hull. However, *Dawn Treader II's* hull was cast to order, to provide the strength and stability that Parker felt to be just right for his seagoing purpose. This custom hull also incorporates some special reinforcing. The bottom includes four more layers than normal of fiberglass roving, for a total thickness of one quarter inch; other fiberglass strips reinforce the stress areas around the chain plates. Supplementary floor timbers are set into the bilge, and all bulkheads are bonded with double the standard amount of fiberglass. In addition, Parker added an extra ton of ballast to the boat's four-ton lead keel to keep her on her feet in an extreme gale.

Having beefed up the hull, Parker cut back severely on gadgetry. The bilge pump is operated manually rather than by electricity; so is the water system *(page 28).* Electronic navigational gear is kept to a minimum, and each item except the log *(page 28)* runs on its own battery; indeed, Parker dispenses with both RDF and ship-to-shore radio, reasoning that neither is effective at a range of more than several hundred miles from land. The 20-horsepower engine, intentionally small and seldom used, generates only enough power for close maneuvering when entering a harbor. Because the ship's batteries supply enough electricity to start the engine and operate the running lights, Parker illuminates the cabin when he is at sea only with kerosene lamps.

*Snugged down for a rare layover in a California marina, Dawn Treader II displays a stout, versatile cutter rig ideal for offshore sailing conditions; the large foretriangle allows the skipper to set either a jib, a staysail, or both, depending on the strength of the wind. The mast is bolstered with shrouds 20 per cent stronger than standard. The dinghy is atop the forecabin, where it is unlikely to be dislodged in heavy seas.*

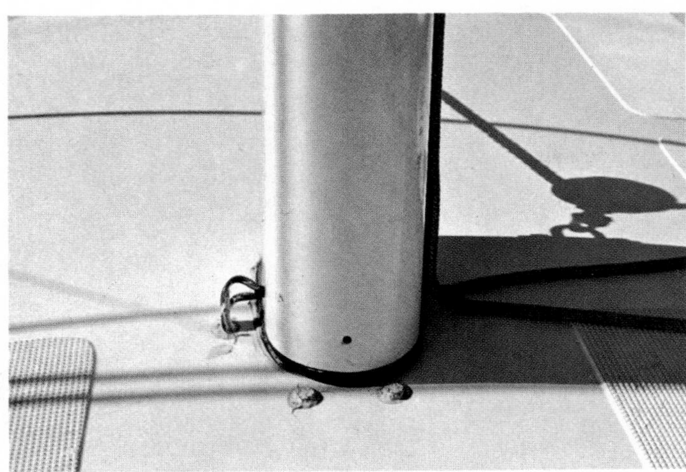

Dawn Treader II's mast is stepped flush on the cabin top rather than extending belowdecks to the keel—the normal arrangement on most large boats. Should a freak wave carry away the mast, there is thus less danger that the falling spar will wrench open the cabin, leaving a gash where water could slosh in and swamp the boat.

Belowdecks bracing for the mast is supplied by this seven-foot length of steel boiler tubing whose upper end is bolted to the cabin top directly beneath the mast step. The lower end of the tube, stress-tested for pressures up to 3,800 pounds per square inch, is bolted to a two-foot length of I-beam fiberglassed to the vessel's keel.

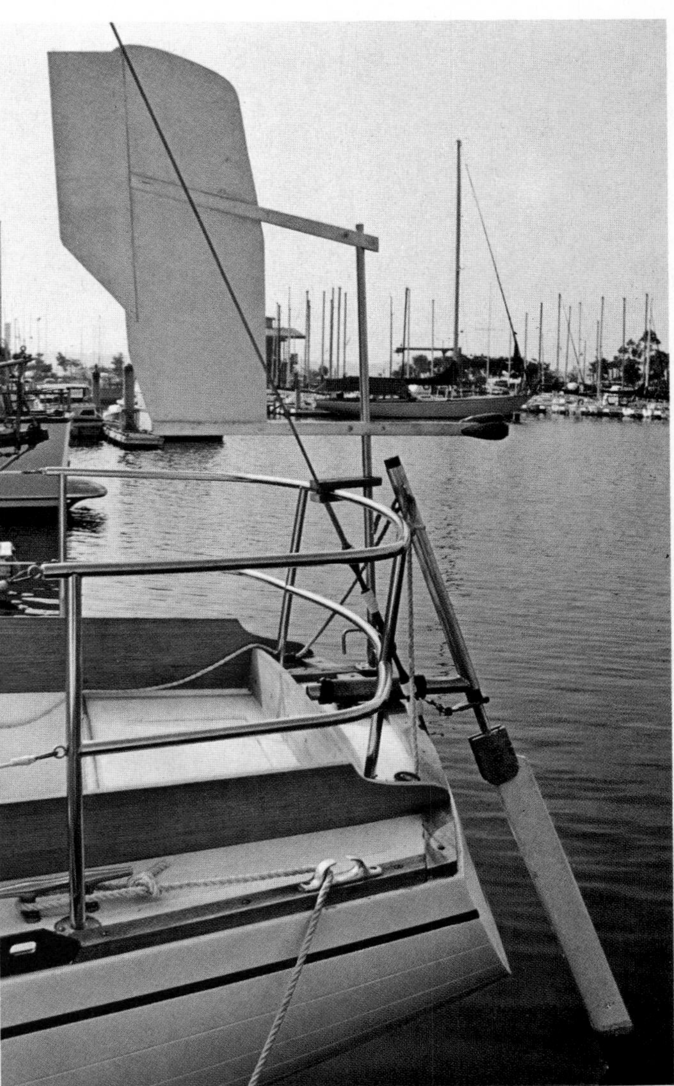

Dawn Treader II's self-steering device, designed by the owner, is a variation on the vanes commonly used in singlehanded ocean sailing. With Parker's rig, when the boat strays off course and the vane turns, the movement is transmitted to the vessel's own rudder rather than to an auxiliary rudder of the type shown on page 16. But since this turning motion must be amplified to be effective, it passes first to a so-called servomechanism—a thin blade hanging aft of the transom. As the blade turns obliquely in the water, it generates a powerful turning force. Lines from the top of the blade apparatus then convey this force to the tiller—and thence to the rudder.

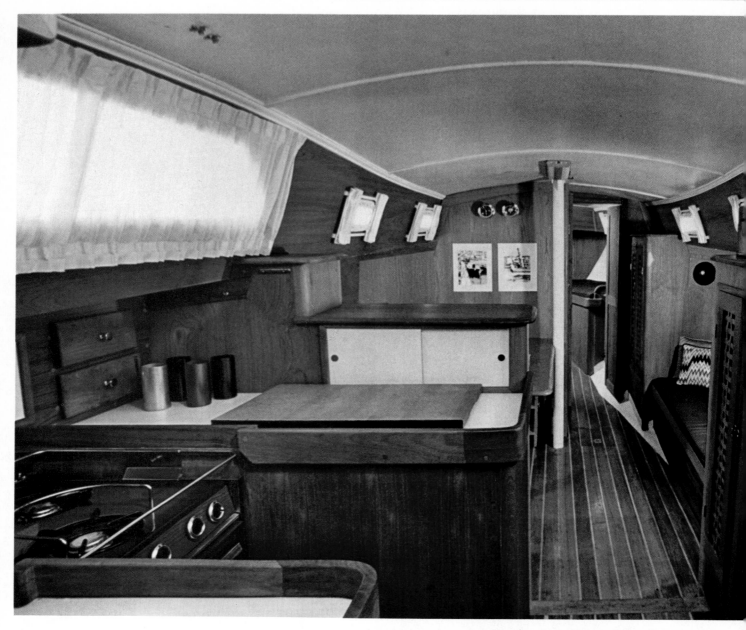

*The trim, utilitarian cabin of Dawn Treader II contains a compact galley at near left, with a U-shaped counter arrangement so that the cook can brace in a seaway. On either side of the starboard settee are lockers with latticed doors that allow air to circulate, combating mildew. At near right, the chart table is surmounted by navigational instruments: the large dial is a speedometer; to its right are a log for tolling up accumulated mileage and the ship's chronometer; below the speedometer is a dinometer for measuring heeling angle and a small auxiliary compass. A depth finder mounted on the hanging locker completes the navigational gear.*

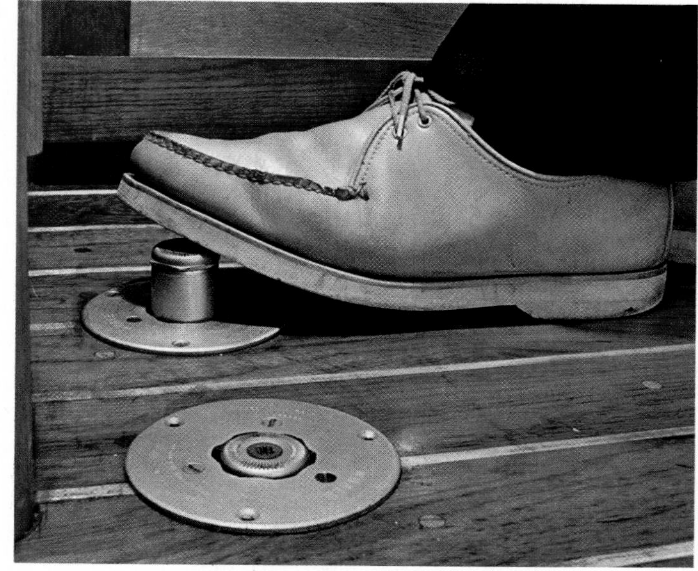

*Two recessed foot pumps, one for fresh water, the other for salt water, provide a simple and reliable alternative to an electrically pressurized water system. The pedal is extremely durable—unlike the more conventional hand pump, which might tear off if used in a heavy sea. The pedals also allow a crewman a free hand to hang on in rough weather; on calmer days he can wash both hands at once, thus saving water.*

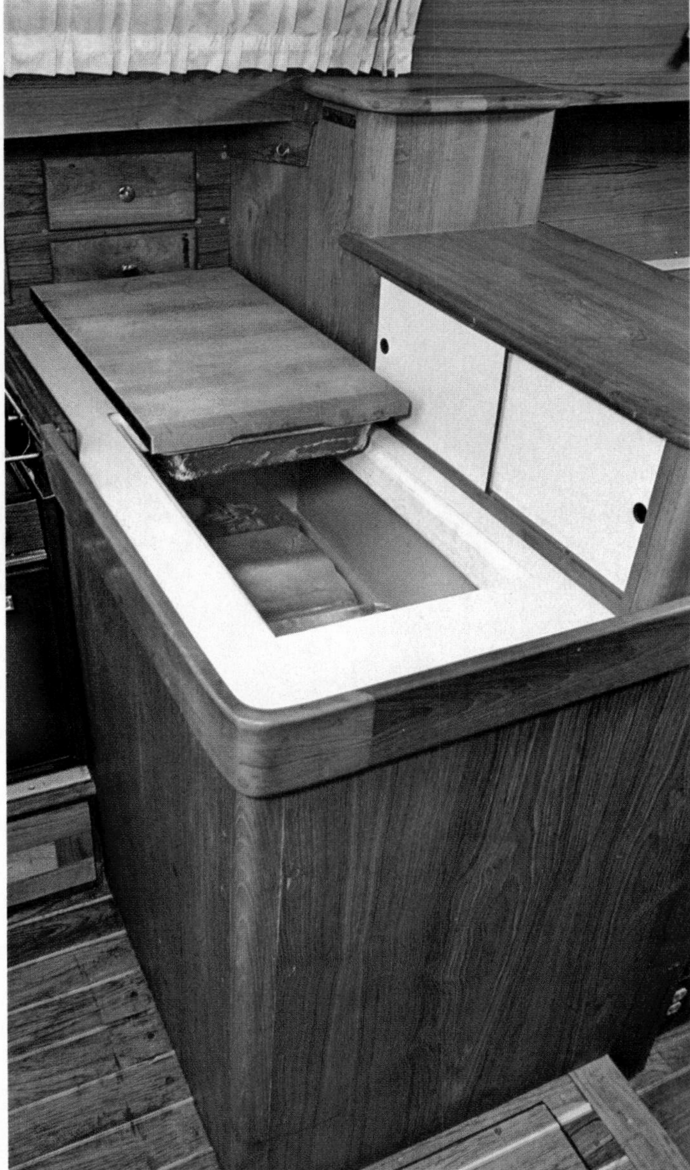

*For long-term storage of perishables, a specially designed icebox protects 75 pounds of block ice so well that it can last up to three weeks. The box is lined on three sides with Freon foam six inches thick; the side nearest the hull has a full two feet of foam sheathing to prevent conductive losses in warm waters. Skipper Parker considers the box superior to an electric refrigerator for an offshore sailing craft. Not only would a malfunction in the boat's electrical system cause spoilage in a refrigerator, but the drain on the boat's batteries would require that the engine be run four hours a day for recharging.*

*Along with the unique advantages of her three-part hull design, Bacchanal incorporates many key features common to deep-keel offshore cruisers. Encircling her broad deck area is a one-eighth-inch wire life line with a test strength of more than half a ton that connects to a bow and a stern pulpit. The vessel's cutter-rigged 45-foot mast is held fast by heavy five-sixteenths-inch shrouds run through double spreaders. A self-steerer hangs from the stern.*

## A Three-Way Bonus

One of the most exciting and innovative developments in deepwater design is the trimaran—a triple-hulled version of the catamaran day sailers and ocean cruisers that began to capture boatmen's attention in the early 1960s. Like the cats, trimarans have at least three important advantages over conventional deep-keeled vessels, the most striking of which is speed—as demonstrated by the 37-foot cutter *Bacchanal* on these pages. Owned by California yacht-plan broker John Marples, she swept to victory in the 1972 Transpacific Race for multihulls, completing the 2,200-mile course in 10½ days at an average speed of almost 10 knots—two knots or more faster than conventional keelboats her size.

Interestingly enough, Marples had built *Bacchanal* not primarily as a racing machine but as a long-distance cruiser. He did the carpentry himself in his backyard in San Jose. Working from plans provided by multihull designer Jim Brown of National City, California, he fashioned the three hulls and connecting decks, or wings, from molded plywood, which he then coated with fiberglass.

The project took four years to complete and produced a vessel that was not only superfast but stable in a blow and remarkably comfortable to live on. When the breeze pipes up hard enough to put a keelboat's rail down by as much as 40°, *Bacchanal's* buoyant side hulls, or pontoons, keep her at a mere 8° to 10°. Besides providing stability, the pontoons serve as emergency flotation chambers should the center hull puncture. Furthermore, they offer an enormous amount of storage space, so that the main cabin can be left open and uncluttered for commodious on-board living.

During her first four years in commission, *Bacchanal* logged over 20,000 miles of trouble-free ocean passages, including her dash to Honolulu in the Transpac race. For long-distance voyaging of this kind, however, the multihull configuration possesses one potentially dangerous weakness. Unlike a keelboat, which will always right itself even if completely pitchpoled *(pages 68-69)*, a flipped-over trimaran will stay flipped. Marples admits to this menacing possibility, and as a precaution he has provided *Bacchanal* with the unique double-access life-raft compartment that is shown on page 33.

*Bacchanal's cockpit is placed amidships between two cabin areas—a main living section aft and a bunk area in the fo'c'sle. The midships position brings the wheel close to the mast and halyards; all sheets are led here, too, so that a helmsman alone on deck can change and trim sail unaided. The cockpit placement also provides a clear view of the bow and stern of each of the boat's three hulls for tight maneuvering. And it allows the centerboard trunk to be tucked away between the cabins where it will not clutter up living quarters.*

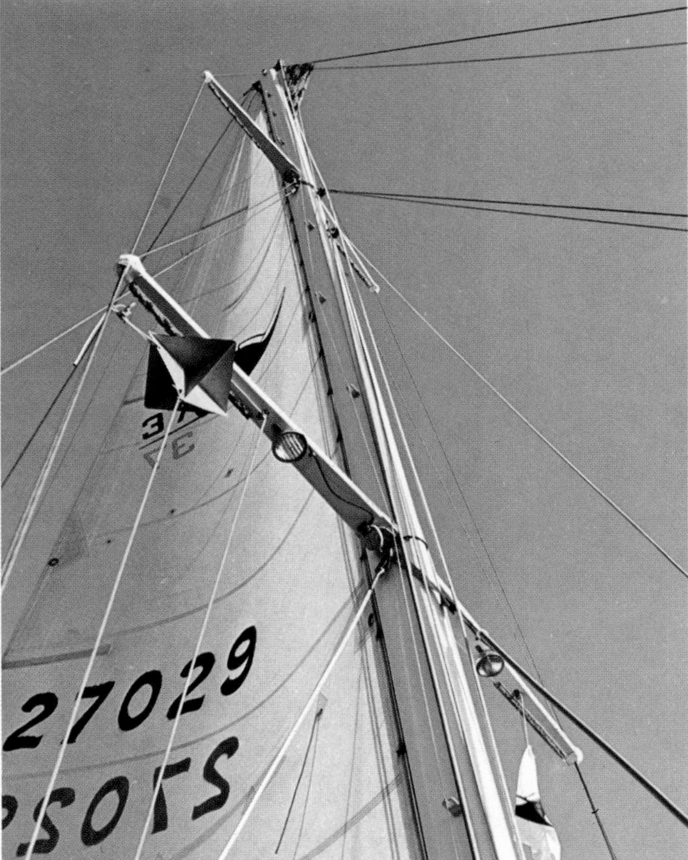


*An aluminum radar reflector hangs from Bacchanal's lower starboard spreader as a precautionary measure for traveling in waters with commercial traffic. The spreaders themselves are buffered on their after sides with antichafe insulation to reduce friction on the mainsail. And to help the skipper climb aloft for repairs when underway, the mast is studded with angle irons that serve as steps. These are connected with a length of cord to keep the climber from slipping.*

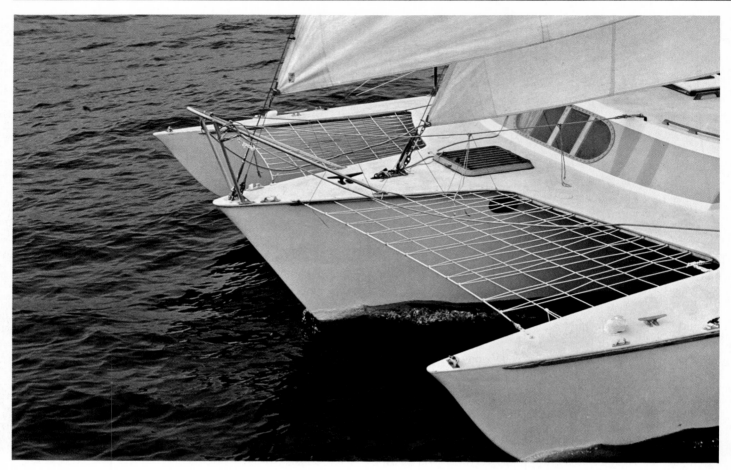

*When the crew is handling sail or anchor, during normal cruising, strong nylon safety nets fill the spaces between Bacchanal's central hull and her pontoons, whose forward portions are the only on-deck areas not surrounded by life lines. The nets may also be used for drying sails and clothing, and even for sunbathing. When Bacchanal races, however, they are stowed to cut down wind and water resistance, and the crew must wear safety harnesses clipped to the life line from the main hull's pulpit to the deckhouse.*

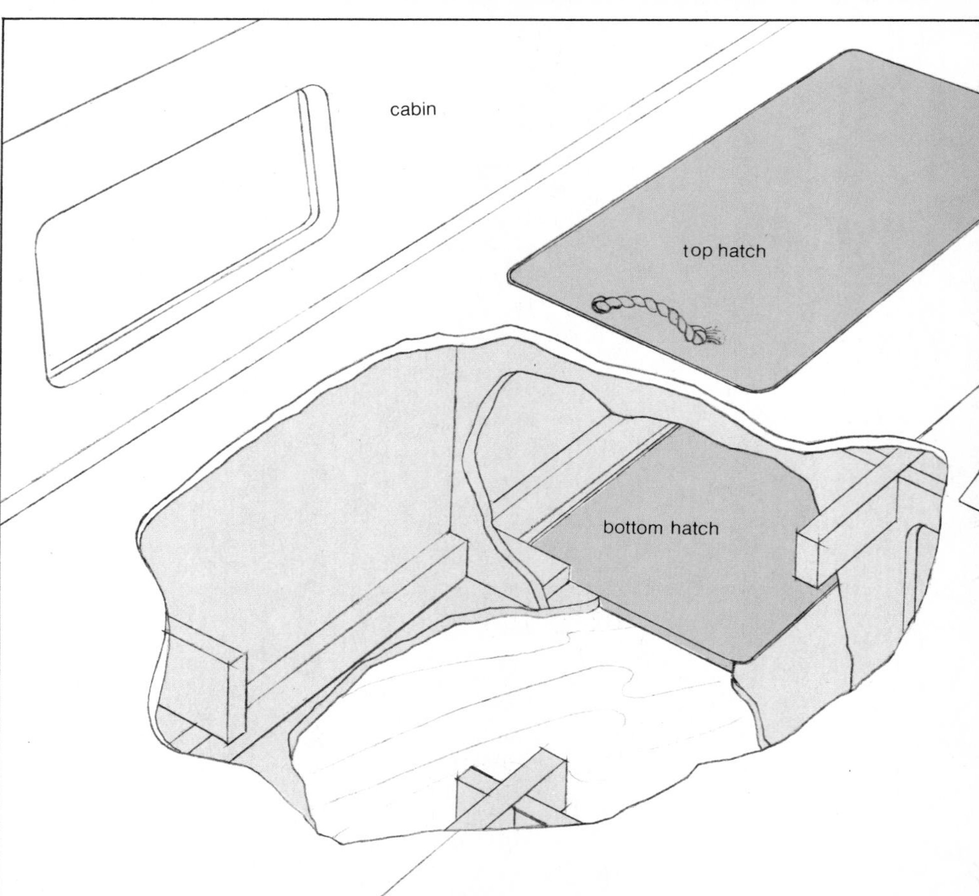

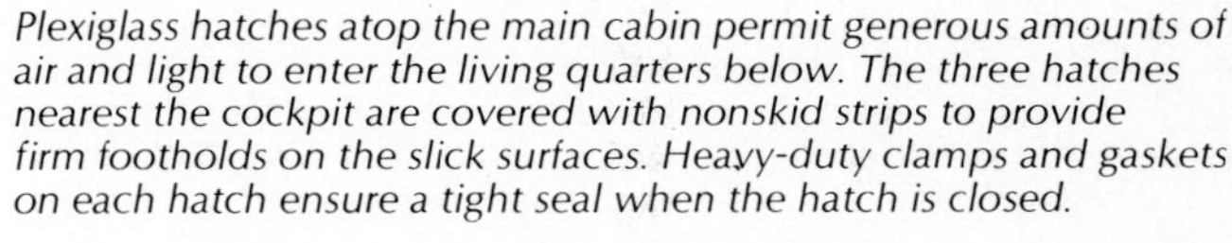

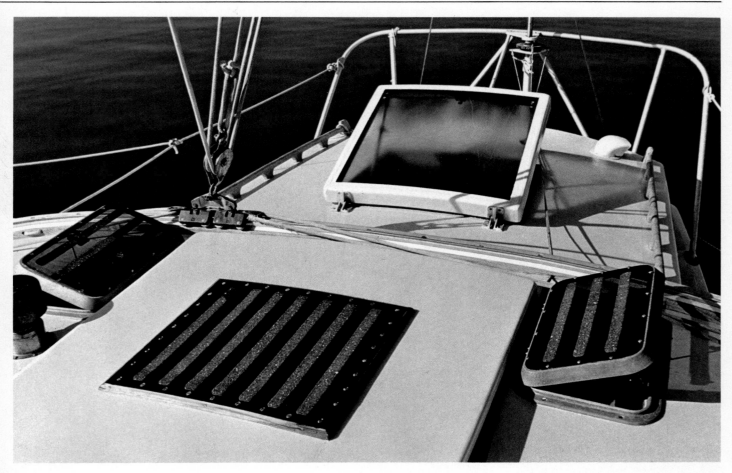

*Plexiglass hatches atop the main cabin permit generous amounts of air and light to enter the living quarters below. The three hatches nearest the cockpit are covered with nonskid strips to provide firm footholds on the slick surfaces. Heavy-duty clamps and gaskets on each hatch ensure a tight seal when the hatch is closed.*

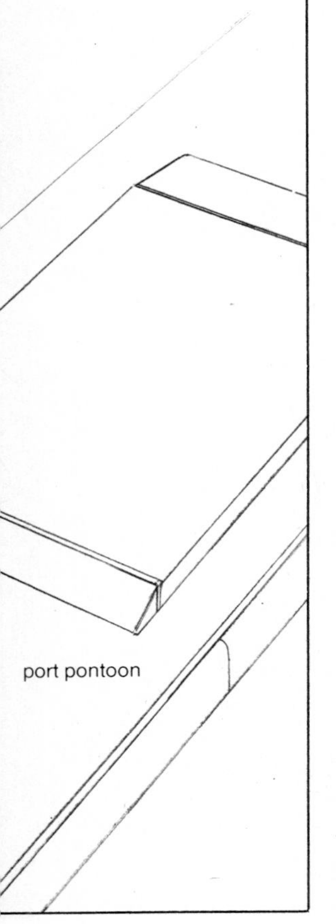


*An emergency double-entry compartment in the port wing between the hull and pontoon allows Bacchanal's inflatable raft to be reached from above under normal conditions—and from below if the boat capsized. Owner-builder Marples is convinced that, if the trimaran flipped over, air trapped in the cabin and pontoons would not only keep the vessel afloat long enough for the crew to launch the raft, but might hold the boat on the surface for as long as two weeks.*

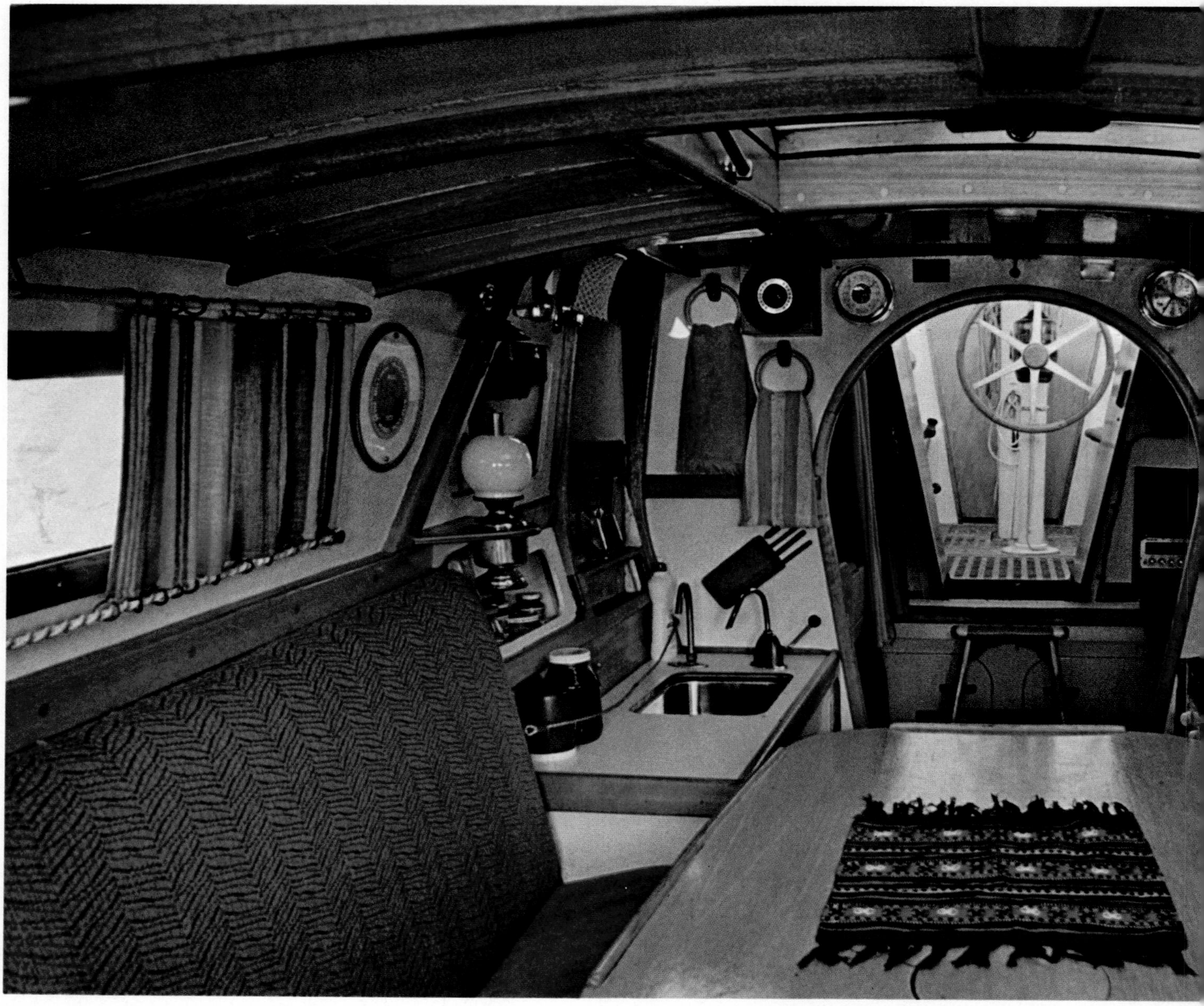

*Bacchanal's aftercabin, seen from the stern, is dominated by a dinette (foreground) that seats five comfortably. On the starboard side of the carefully arranged galley is a butane stove; to port is a sink with a manual raw-water pump and a foot pump for fresh water. Fitted into the bulkhead behind the sink are storage cubbyholes and a five-cubic-foot slide-out icebox that holds 25 pounds of ice. At the far end of the cabin, mounted overhead on the bulkhead, are (left to right) towel rings, a stereo speaker for the boat's tape deck, a barometer, a clock, a charcoal-burning heater, and racks for a toaster and a kettle.*

*Looking forward through the galley entryway, a small compartment adjacent to the cockpit contains a quarter berth (left) and the navigation station (right). A fold-out plywood extension in the navigation station provides extra counter space for chart reading. On the bulkhead above, mounted at top from left to right, are the vessel's fuse box, a hand bearing compass and a storage rack. Beneath these are a radio direction finder and a portable TV.*

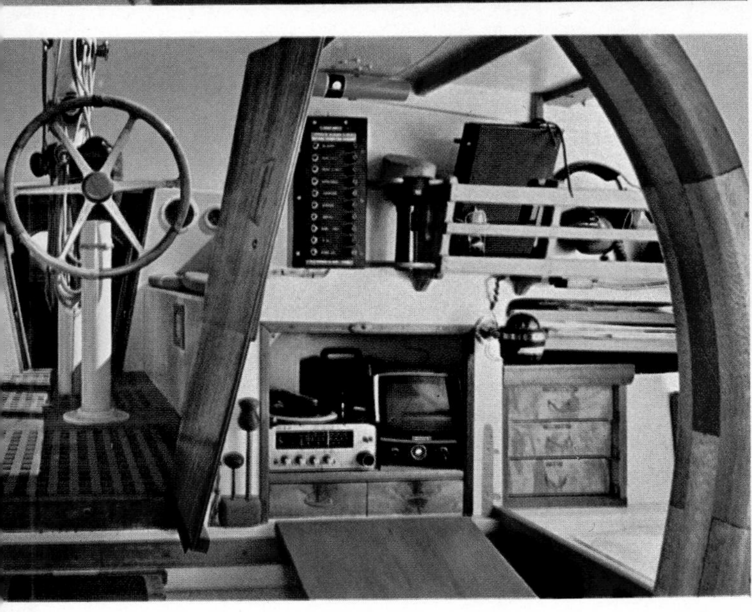

*Bacchanal's head fits snugly into the forward cabin just beyond the two-man fo'c'sle (the foot of one bunk can be seen at near right). The sink in the head is provided with dual raw- and fresh-water spigots, operated by hand and foot pumps respectively. At left is a portable shower that generates pressure by means of a hand-pumped cannister. (The cannister can double as an auxiliary fire extinguisher.) Extra sails are stowed in the forepeak, just beyond the toilet.*

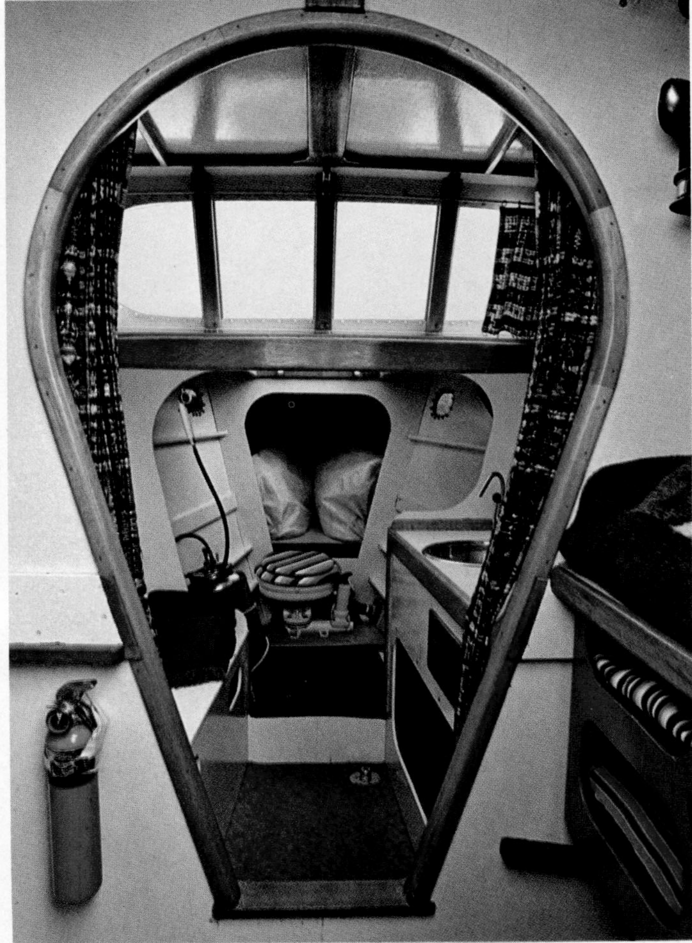

*At sunset on the Atlantic, a member of the three-man crew of a Europe-bound ketch stands his watch while the others rest below. To break up the two-month, 5,000-mile voyage from Florida to the French Riviera, the boat's navigator charted a course that included layovers at Bermuda, the Azores, Gibraltar and Majorca.*

# THE LOGISTICS OF A SEA PASSAGE

Successful blue-water voyaging is as dependent on thorough planning as it is on a well-found boat. Indeed, experienced mariners may spend as many weeks plotting a pleasant, practical and safe itinerary as they do on the cruise itself.

With the help of pilot charts and a few basic publications *(pages 44-45)*, first rough out a scheme for completing each leg of the trip during periods of good weather and favorable winds and currents. Then collect all navigation charts needed for every phase of the voyage—including approaches to foreign ports. If this list includes materials that are more easily and cheaply available from overseas than from domestic sources, allow plenty of time to send away for them. For example, a harbor chart for Papeete, Tahiti, which is most readily available from a chart agent in France, might take eight weeks to arrive. While refining the itinerary, allow time in every port of call for impromptu side trips, sightseeing ashore, repairs and resupply.

To ensure that all useful planning data is in hand, seek out such knowledgeable sources as the consuls and naval attachés of countries to be visited and, if possible, try to get several opinions on any doubtful points. For example, these sources might provide a warning of recent increases in port charges, reports of congested conditions in some ports or advice against taking firearms into a particular area. (Few veteran offshore sailors keep weapons aboard on any trip, and those who do seldom carry expensive arms, since these are most likely to invite confiscation by covetous port officials.)

Brush up on weather lore so as to be able to relate such portents as barometric readings or cloud changes to forecasts and warnings received by short-wave radio. Since the radio will be the prime source of weather information at sea, make sure that the unit is capable of picking up English-language broadcasts from any point along the proposed route. Before departure, practice tuning the radio to various frequencies, and review Morse code if you plan to make use of Morse weather broadcasts *(page 58)*.

Financial planning is an important aspect of offshore travel. A wise voyager computes in advance his various operating expenses and the probable cost of whatever life style he intends to maintain abroad, then adds a prudent reserve for emergencies. Yachtsmen planning to earn money at odd jobs in ports along the way should take care not to fall afoul of local labor laws—and the skipper should remember that in this matter, as in all others, the captain is held responsible for actions on the part of any crewman.

Cash carried aboard can be limited to a small reserve of one-dollar bills—the form of U.S. currency most generally accepted in foreign ports. Major transactions are best accomplished with travelers checks, international credit cards or funds deposited in local banks.

Some banks will agree to hold mail until called for, as will some foreign shipping agents and yacht clubs. Almost any such arrangement is better than having mail from home addressed to general delivery at scheduled ports of call. Most post offices hold such mail only for short periods, and they may have already returned it by the time the yacht arrives.

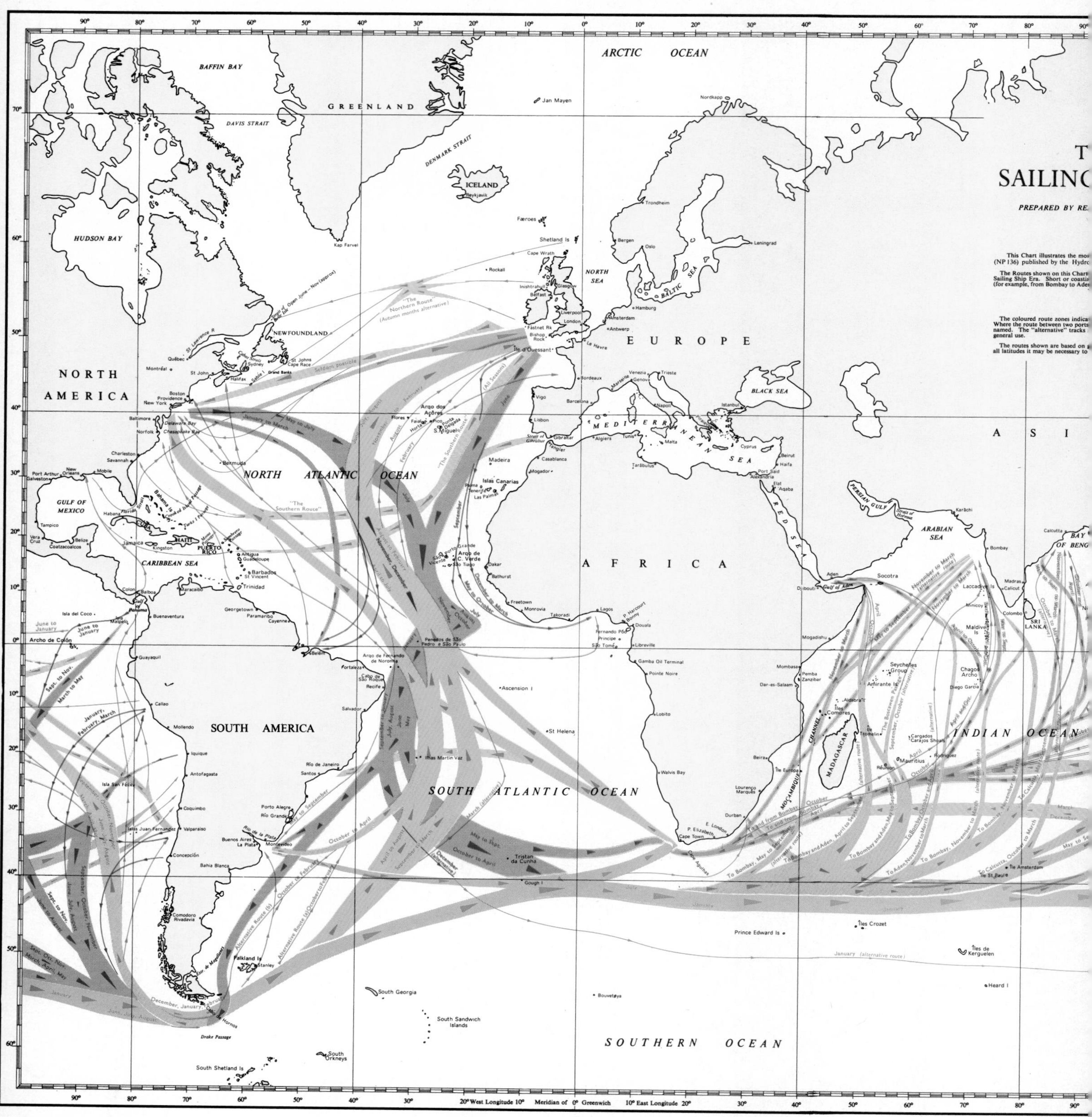

ARCTIC OCEAN
BAFFIN BAY
GREENLAND
DAVIS STRAIT
DENMARK STRAIT
ICELAND
Reykjavik
Jan Mayen
Nordkapp
HUDSON BAY
Kap Farvel
Færoes
Shetland Is
Cape Wrath
Rockall
Trondheim
Bergen
Oslo
Leningrad
NORTH SEA
BALTIC SEA
Hamburg
Amsterdam
Antwerp
London
Liverpool
Glasgow
Belfast
Inishtrahull
Fastnet Rk
Bishop Rock
Île d'Ouessant
Le Havre
EUROPE
NEWFOUNDLAND
St Lawrence R
Québec
Montréal
St John
Sydney
St Johns
Cape Race
Grand Banks
Halifax
Sable I
NORTH AMERICA
Boston
Providence
New York
Baltimore
Delaware Bay
Norfolk
Chesapeake Bay
Charleston
Savannah
Mobile
New Orleans
Port Arthur
Galveston
GULF OF MEXICO
Tampico
Vera Cruz
Coatzacoalcos
Belize
Habana
Bahama Is
Bermuda
"The Northern Route" (Autumn months alternative)
"The Southern Route"
NORTH ATLANTIC OCEAN
Flores
Faial
Horta
Pico
Ponta Delgada
São Miguel
Arqo dos Açores
Madeira
Islas Canarias
Las Palmas
Tenerife
Palma
Bordeaux
Vigo
Lisbon
Barcelona
Marseille
Genova
Venezia
Trieste
Napoli
Gibraltar
Tangier
Algiers
Tunis
Malta
Casablanca
Mogador
Tarābulus
MEDITERRANEAN SEA
BLACK SEA
Istanbul
Cyprus
Beirut
Haifa
Port Said
Alexandria
Elat
Aqaba
RED SEA
PERSIAN GULF
Karāchi
ARABIAN SEA
Bombay
Calcutta
BAY OF BENG
Aden
Gulf of Aden
Djibouti
Socotra
Madras
Calicut
Laccadive Is
Minicoy
Colombo
SRI LANKA
Maldive Is
Chagos Archo
Diego Garcia
ASI
AFRICA
Jamaica
Kingston
CUBA
HAITI
PUERTO RICO
Antigua
Guadeloupe
Barbados
St Vincent
Trinidad
CARIBBEAN SEA
Colon
Balboa
Gulf of Panama
Maracaibo
Georgetown
Paramaribo
Cayenne
Buenaventura
Isla del Coco
Isla Malpelo
Archo de Colón
Guayaquil
Callao
Mollendo
SOUTH AMERICA
Iquique
Antofagasta
Isla San Felix
Coquimbo
Valparaiso
Islas Juan Fernandez
Concepción
Bahia Blanca
Buenos Aires
La Plata
Montevideo
Rio de la Plata
Porto Alegre
Rio Grande
Rio de Janeiro
Santos
Salvador
Recife
Cabo de São Roque
Fortaleza
Belém
Arqo de Fernando de Noronha
Penedos de São Pedro e São Paulo
Arqo de C Verde
São Tiago
Dakar
Bathurst
Freetown
Monrovia
Takoradi
Lagos
P. Harcourt
Bonny
Douala
Fernando Póo
Principe
São Tomé
Libreville
Gamba Oil Terminal
Pointe Noire
Lobito
Ascension I
St Helena
Ilhas Martin Vaz
Walvis Bay
SOUTH ATLANTIC OCEAN
Tristan da Cunha
Gough I
Cape Town
Cape Agulhas
P. Elizabeth
E. London
Durban
Lourenço Marques
Beira
Île Europa
MOÇAMBIQUE CHANNEL
MADAGASCAR
Mogadishu
Mombasa
Pemba
Zanzibar
Dar-es-Salaam
Seychelles Group
Amirante Is
Aldabra
Îles Comores
Tromelin
Cargados Carajos Shoals
Mauritius
Réunion
Rodriguez
INDIAN OCEAN
Île Amsterdam
Île St Paul
Îles Crozet
Prince Edward Is
Îles de Kerguelen
Heard I
Comodoro Rivadavia
Falkland Is
Stanley
Str. de Magallanes
Hornos
Drake Passage
South Georgia
South Sandwich Islands
South Orkneys
South Shetland Is
Bouvetøya
SOUTHERN OCEAN
January (alternative route)
20° West Longitude 10° Meridian of 0° Greenwich 10° East Longitude 20°

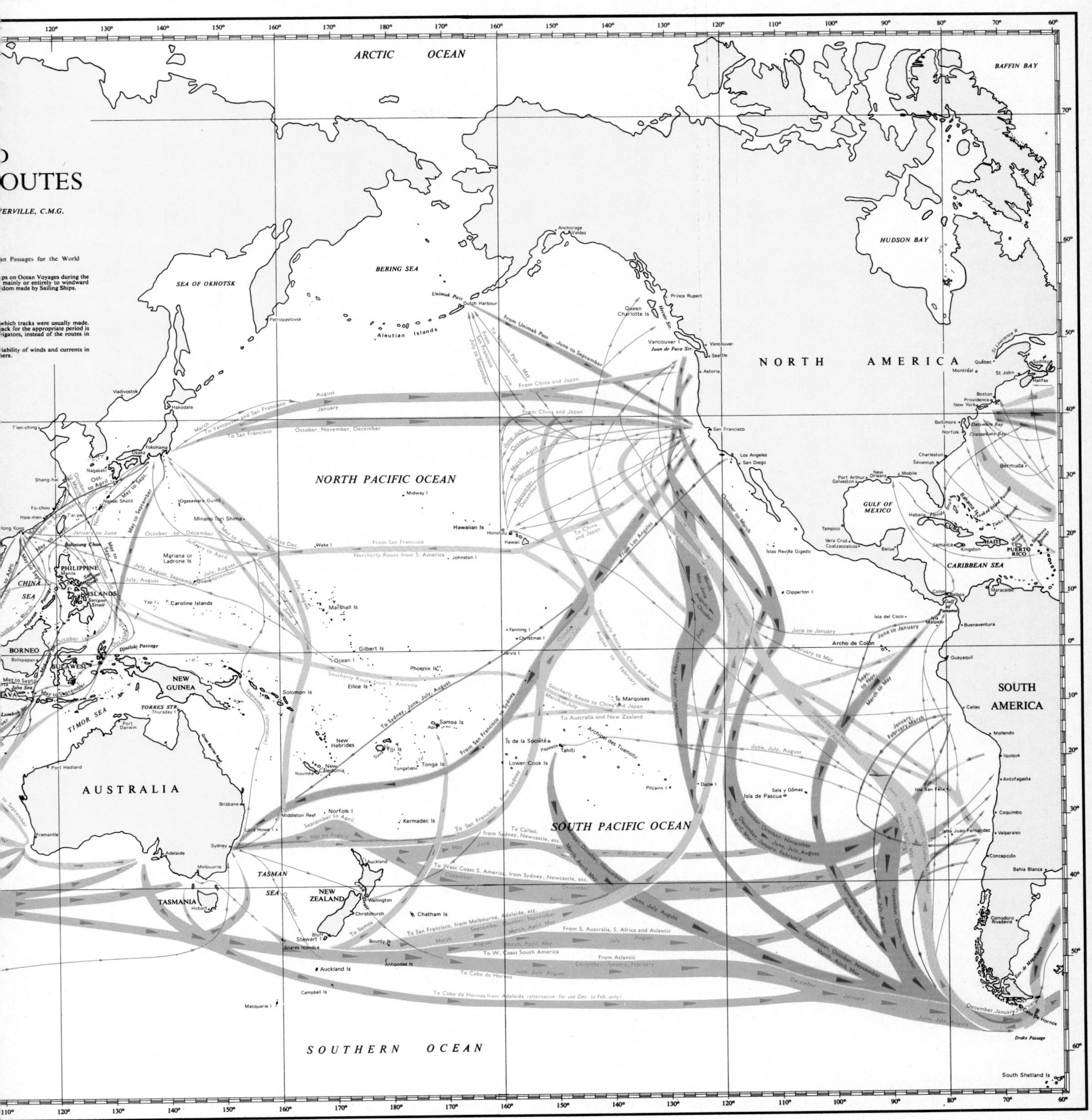


*The world's principal sailing routes crisscross this map in the British Admiralty's guidebook entitled Ocean Passages for the World. The chart is based on data culled from the logs of hundreds of voyages over more than a century; colors indicate directions—brown for north, purple for south, blue for east and magenta for west. The routes take into account seasonal variations in winds and currents. Thus, depending on the time of year, both a northern route and a southern route from England to New York are recommended; the direct route is succinctly labeled "seldom possible."*

## Winds and Currents

Any offshore voyage, whether under sail or power, should be planned so as to take advantage of the prevailing ocean winds and currents shown on the maps here and on pages 42-43, and to avoid the calms that plague sailing craft and the seasonal storms that menace even large vessels.

The major winds follow the same easterly or westerly directions throughout the year, but as the maps at right show, some of the zones in which they operate shift north or south with the changing seasons. The steadiest of the air currents—and the friendliest to mariners—are the trade winds, named for the trade routes that followed their tracks in the era of sail. Blowing northwest and southwest through 1,200-mile belts of ocean on either side of the equator, the balmy trade winds are separated by a narrow belt of doldrums, areas of light, shifting winds where a luckless sailing vessel can be becalmed for days—or suddenly buffeted by the squalls and thunderstorms that are typical of these regions.

Almost as hated by sailing men as the doldrums are the variables. These areas of light and uncertain breezes lie along the northern edge of the Tropic of Cancer and the southern border of the Tropic of Capricorn. The variables include the infamous horse latitudes—which were named, according to legend, for the floating carcasses of livestock that were jettisoned in these latitudes in order to conserve drinking water for the crews of becalmed windjammers.

But beyond the variables are the broad belts of dependable westerlies, counterparts of the trade winds for eastbound vessels. Unlike the milder trade winds, however, the westerlies can be tempestuous. In the Southern Hemisphere they encompass latitudes that are aptly named the roaring forties.

Besides planning to keep out of the doldrums and variables, the prudent skipper uses the calendar to avoid the widely scattered areas where, at certain times of the year, fierce seasonal storms are spawned. Each year these areas give birth not only to the rain-laden winds of the monsoons—from an Arabic word meaning "seasons"—but to as many as 40 tropical storms that generate winds of from 73 to 200 miles an hour. Called hurricanes in the Caribbean, cyclones in the Indian Ocean, typhoons in the western Pacific and willy-willies in the seas northwest of Australia, these storms have in common the ability to destroy even the sturdiest vessels caught in their paths.

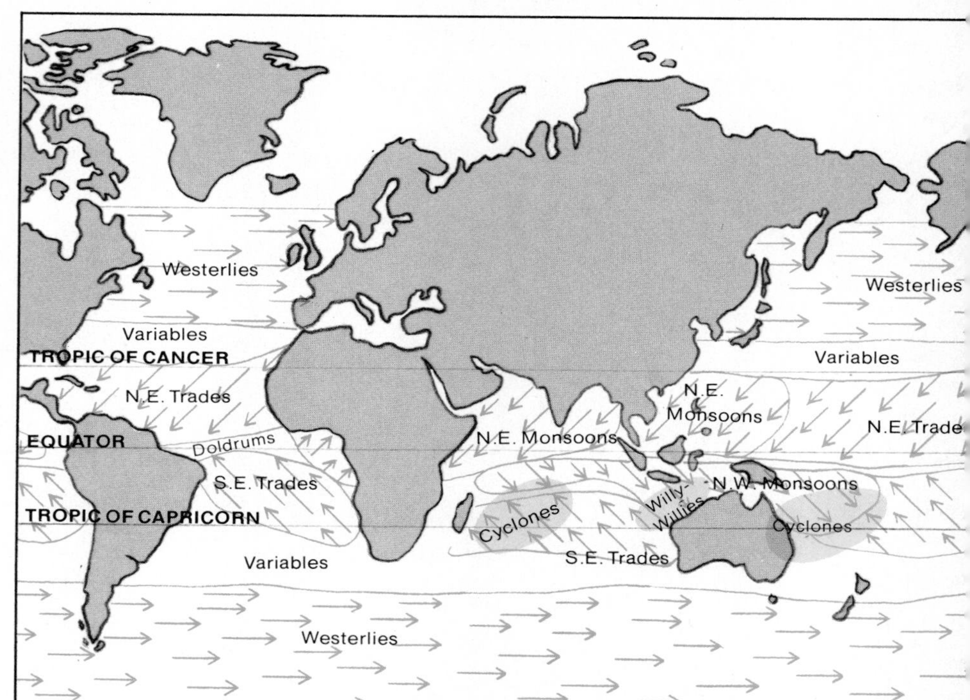


January to March

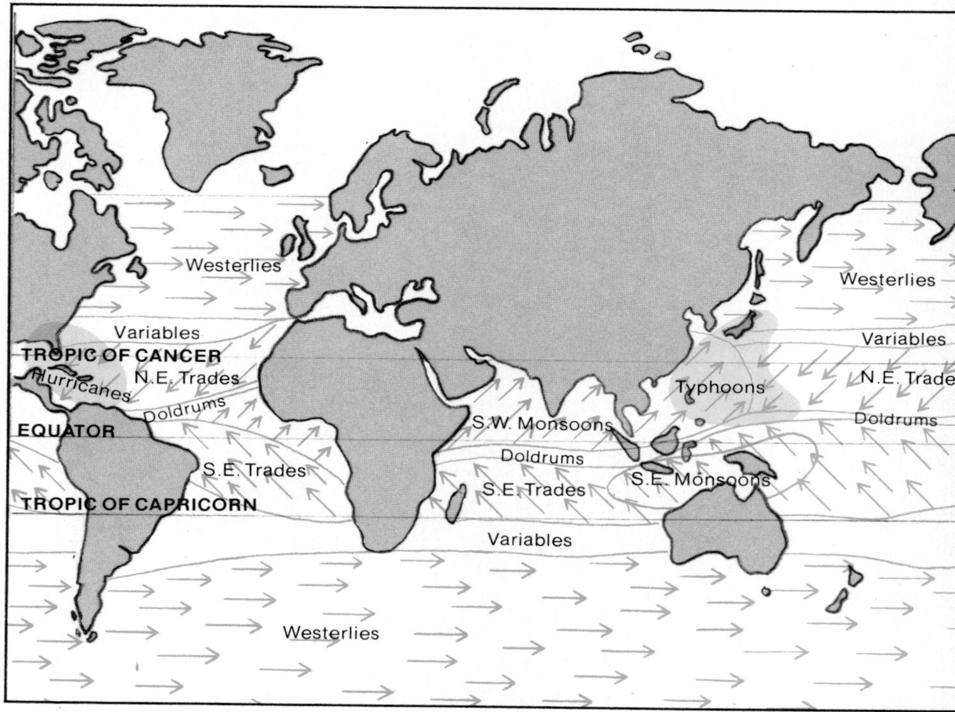


July to September

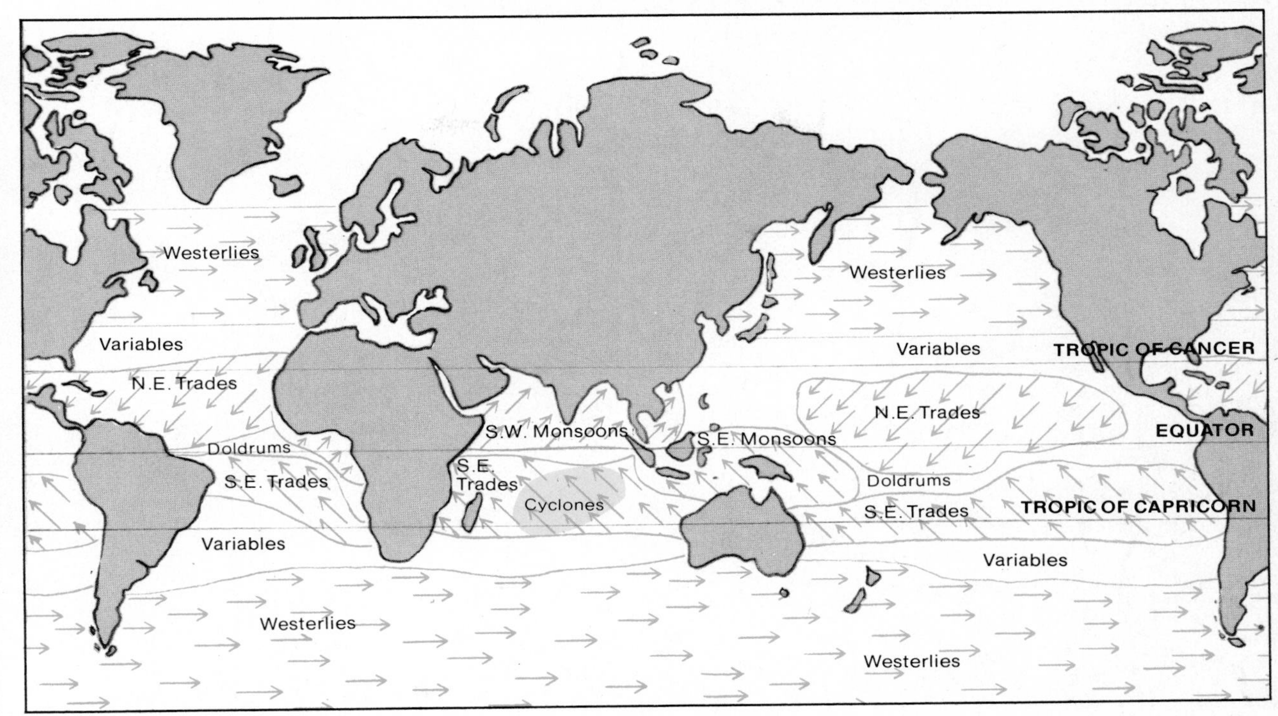


**April to June**

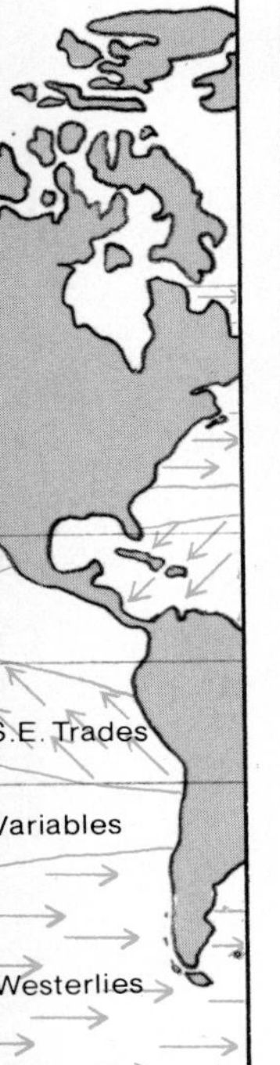


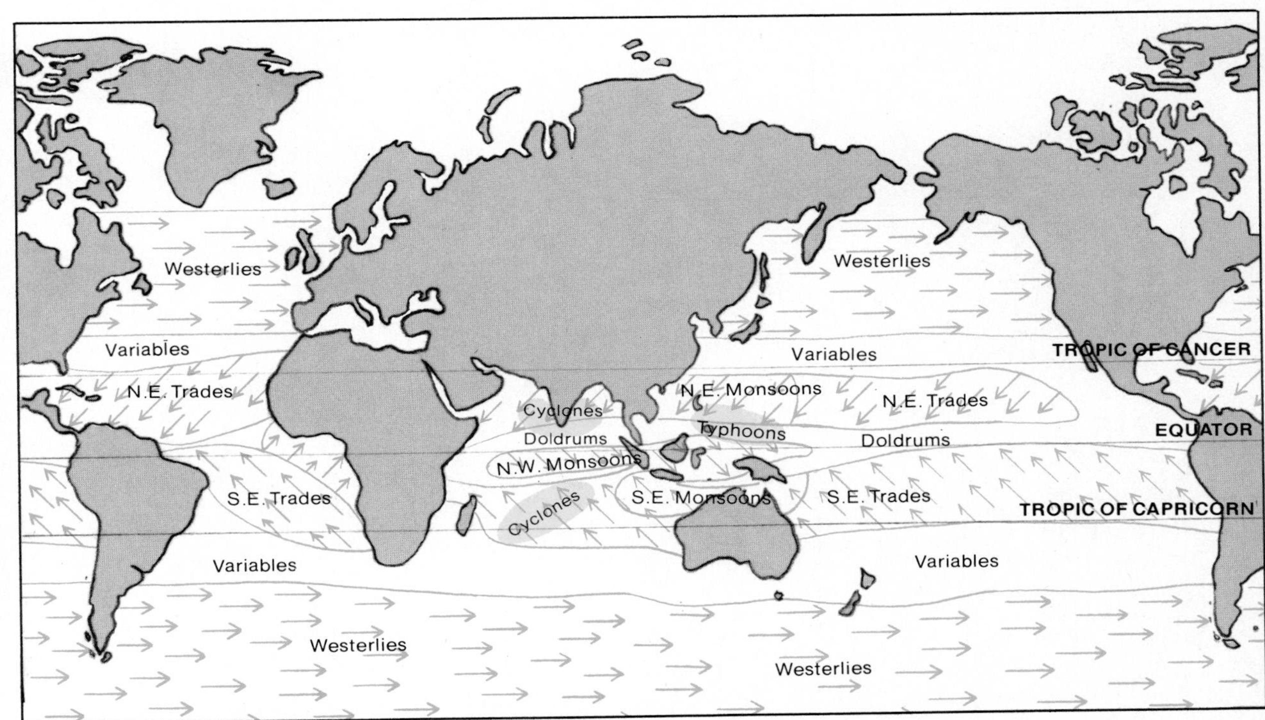


**October to December**

*The regular shifts of prevailing ocean winds and storm locales are shown on these seasonal maps. Blue-tinted areas identify dangerous storm centers. A mariner timing an offshore voyage so as to catch helpful prevailing winds should remember that from January to March cyclones, willy-willies and northerly monsoon winds lash the waters of the western Pacific and Indian oceans. By April, the Pacific is calmer as the remaining monsoon winds switch to southerly. The third quarter brings hurricanes to the Caribbean and typhoons to the western Pacific. By the end of the year, the cyclones have reappeared as the monsoon winds begin to blow from the north.*

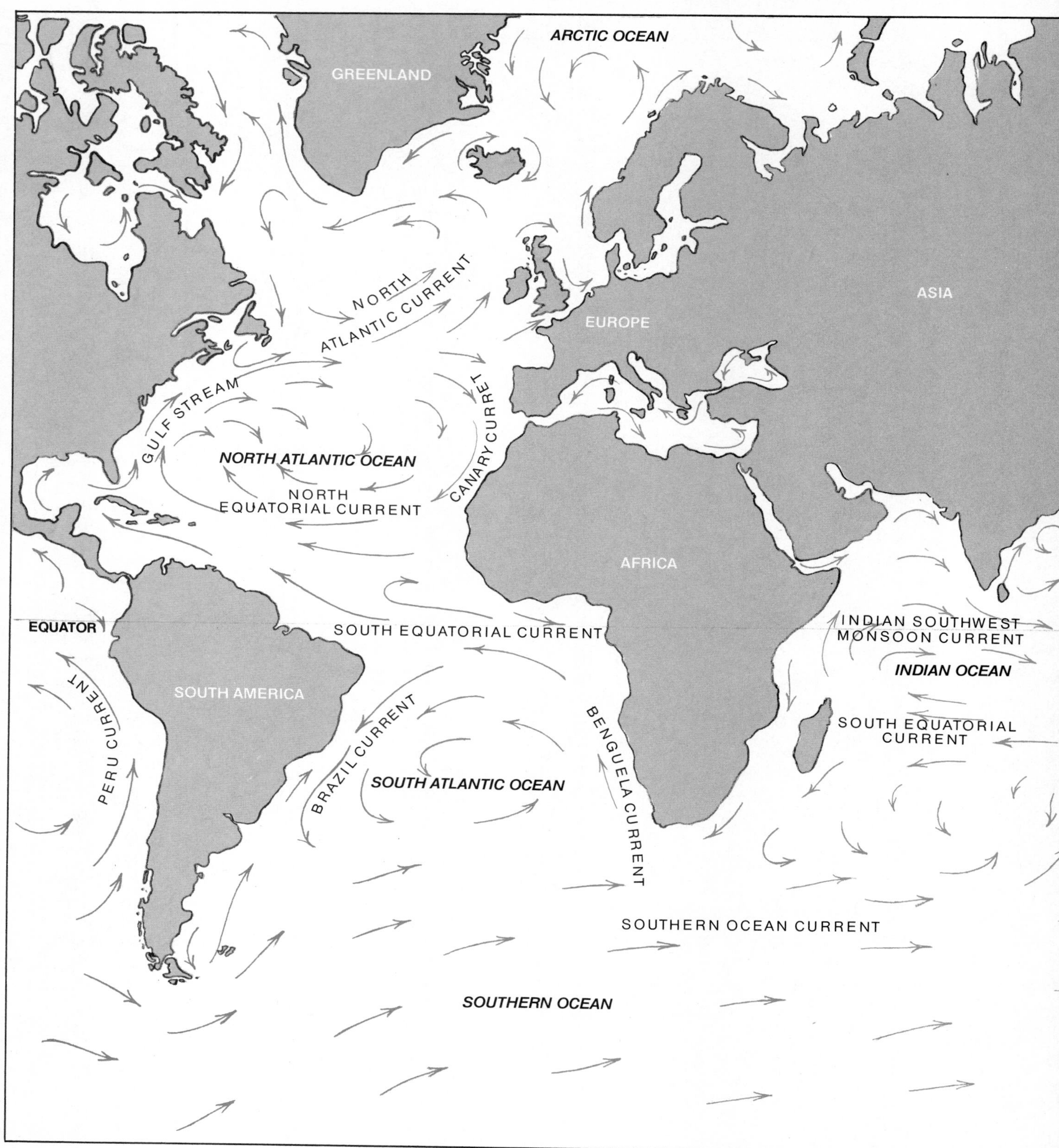
ARCTIC OCEAN
GREENLAND
ASIA
EUROPE
NORTH ATLANTIC CURRENT
GULF STREAM
CANARY CURRENT
NORTH ATLANTIC OCEAN
NORTH EQUATORIAL CURRENT
AFRICA
EQUATOR
SOUTH EQUATORIAL CURRENT
INDIAN SOUTHWEST MONSOON CURRENT
INDIAN OCEAN
SOUTH AMERICA
PERU CURRENT
BRAZIL CURRENT
SOUTH ATLANTIC OCEAN
BENGUELA CURRENT
SOUTH EQUATORIAL CURRENT
SOUTHERN OCEAN CURRENT
SOUTHERN OCEAN

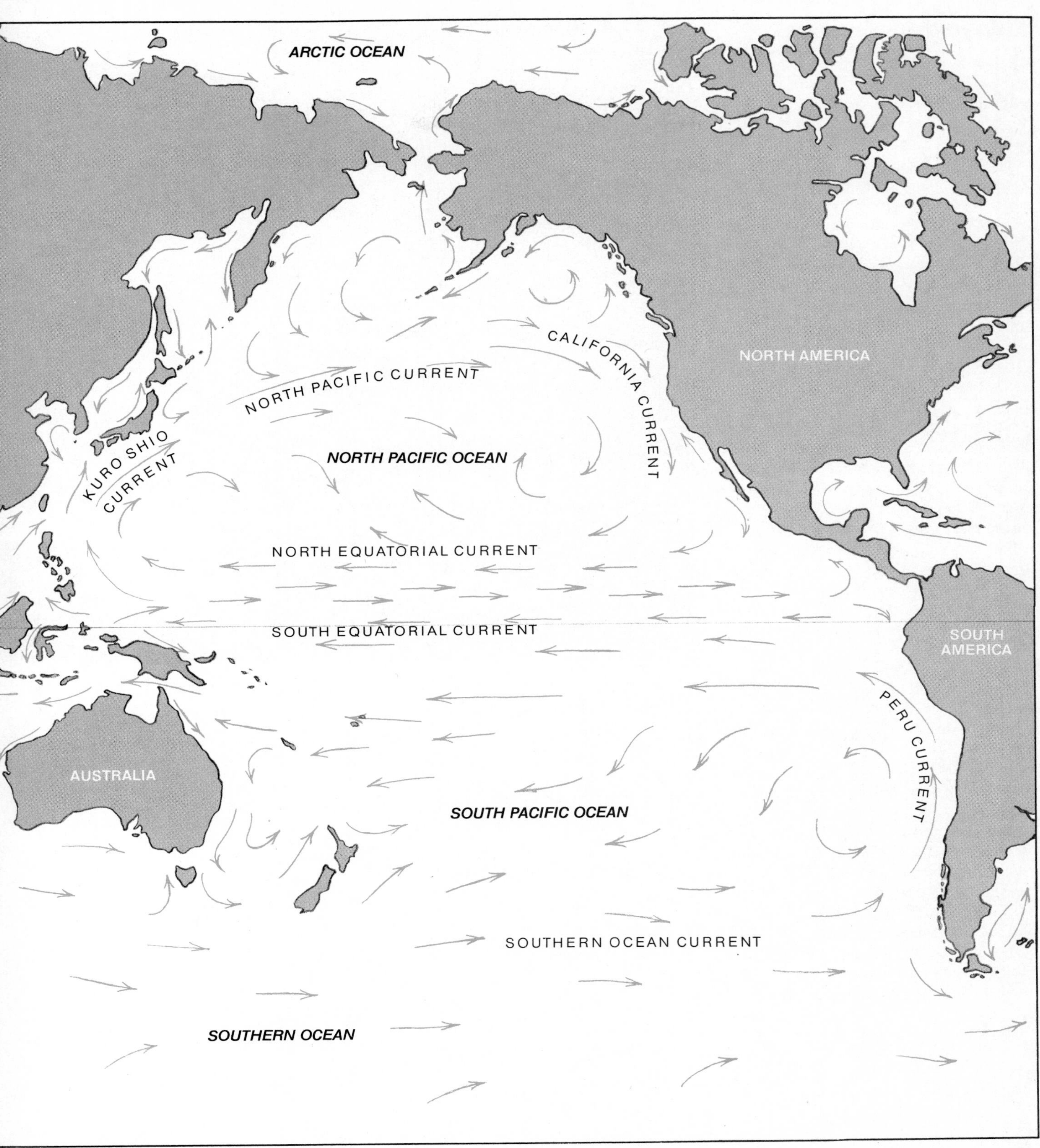


*The circling movements of major ocean currents, clockwise in the Northern Hemisphere and counterclockwise in the Southern—follow the general directions of the prevailing winds that push the surface waters along at 14 to 22 miles a day. Longer arrows indicate strong currents like the Gulf Stream, which flows up the U.S. Atlantic coast at a speed of up to 160 miles a day, as fast as a sailboat in a good breeze. Most of the great currents vary little from season to season; a major exception is in the Indian Ocean, where shifting monsoon winds propel the currents clockwise from May to October, as shown here, and counterclockwise the rest of the year.*

## A Voyager's Guides

While a basic knowledge of ocean winds and currents is essential to the planning and execution of a long offshore cruise, a skipper will also need to consult a number of books and charts for more detailed information.

A good starting point in this kind of detailed research, especially for a mariner uncertain of his route, is the British Admiralty's *Ocean Passages for the World,* which briefly and pungently describes all the world's major sailing routes, and many of its minor ones. A skipper bound for the South Seas, for example, will be advised that "the southeast trade winds are tolerably regular among the Samoan, Tonga, Fiji and New Caledonia islands, from April to October." But he will be warned to avoid too southerly a course across the Indian Ocean in summer, since "the islands in the higher latitudes are so frequently shrouded in fog that often the first sign of their vicinity is the sound of the surf beating against them."

Further aid in selecting a route is to be found in the wealth of recent information about regional weather, local sailing conditions and ports of call contained in the various volumes of two United States government publications.

*Sailing Directions* covers all foreign destinations, and the *Coast Pilot* is packed with data about American coastlines—including those of Hawaii, Puerto Rico and the Virgin Islands. Both, commonly known as pilots, are available in marine-supply stores—as the similar British pilots (these latter volumes of worldwide navigational guides are so noted for dire descriptions of potential hazards that they have been nicknamed "The Handbooks of Peril and Woe"). All such publications should be studied in conjunction with their corresponding pilot charts *(pages 46-47),* as well as with navigation charts that include information on water depths and land formations.

### Key Books and Charts

*The U.S. and British government publications listed below are the basic English-language sources of information for offshore sailing. They are all available in marine-supply stores. Since they are revised frequently, a prospective voyager should equip himself with the latest editions.*

### U.S. Government Publications

**Sailing Directions,** *published by the Defense Mapping Agency Hydrographic Center (DMAHC), consists of 62 loose-leaf volumes of detailed information about foreign coastlines, harbors, passages, perils and aids to navigation.*

**Pilot Charts,** *issued by the DMAHC, are made for each month of the year and cover the heavily traveled North Atlantic and North Pacific Oceans. Larger-scale sets containing all 12 months are available for the South Atlantic, South Pacific and Indian oceans and for Central American waters. All supply valuable information in visual form on winds, currents and weather prospects.*

**Coast Pilot,** *published by the National Ocean Survey (NOS) in eight paper-bound volumes, is a domestic version of the Sailing Directions and contains information about all U.S. coastlines, including the Great Lakes and the overseas possessions of the United States.*

**Great Circle Charts,** *provided by the DMAHC for all ocean areas, are based on a system of cartographic projection that allows a navigator quickly to determine the distance between any two points on the earth's curved surface by drawing a straight line (pages 48-49). Such a line appears as a curve when transferred to any chart based on a Mercator projection—such as navigation and pilot charts.*

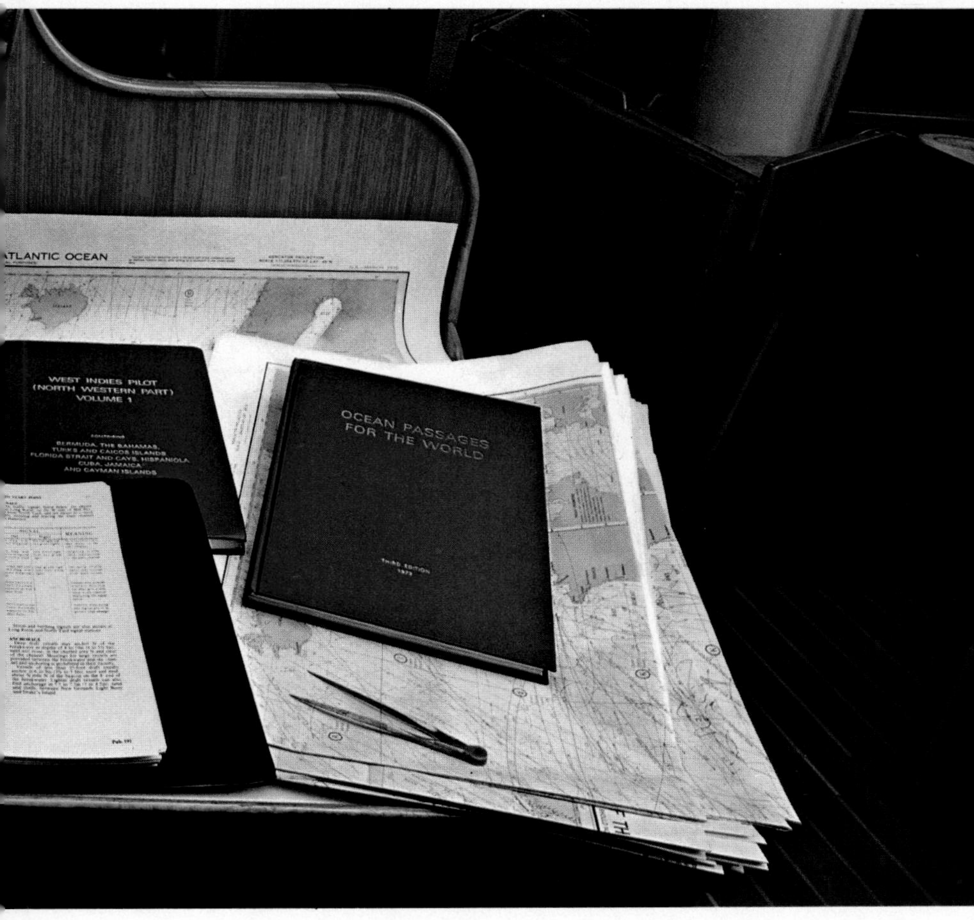


*Documents of prime importance for an offshore passage like the one described on pages 48-53 are arranged on a sailboat's chart table. From Ocean Passages for the World and the North Atlantic Pilot Charts, the skipper would select the best routes and times for Atlantic crossings. The pilots for England (shown opened), the West Indies and the west coast of Africa, including the Canary Islands, provide detailed guidance for sailing in those areas. Navigation charts like the one for Plymouth, England, would be helpful when entering or leaving ports.*

**Tracking Charts,** *available from the DMAHC, feature dotted grids that help a skipper plot the coordinates of a moving weather front.*

**Navigation Charts,** *used for planning and navigation, are issued by NOS and DMAHC in scales varying from 1:10,000—for detailed harbor charts—to 1:8,500,000 for ocean charts. A sailor needs enough of them to cover his entire route.*

**Worldwide Marine Weather Broadcasts,** *compiled by the National Weather Service, lists frequencies and schedules for U.S. and foreign radio weather reports.*

**Tide Tables,** *issued by NOS, predict times and heights of high and low tides in major harbors, and provide formulas for estimating tides in other places.*

**Light Lists,** *published by the Coast Guard for U.S. and by the DMAHC for foreign coasts, locate and describe navigation lights and other aids to navigation.*

## British Admiralty Publications

**Ocean Passages for the World** *is an excellent one-volume guide to ocean voyaging, with a special section on sailing-vessel routes and several separate charts.*

**Pilots,** *published in 74 hardbound volumes, contain descriptions, sailing directions, and an index of charts for virtually every coast ever visited by a sailing ship.*

**Charts,** *like those of U.S. agencies, vary in scale and function. Especially useful are the monthly pilot charts called routeing charts that, like U.S. pilot charts, include traditional shipping routes and data on winds and currents.*

## Seagoing Road Maps

Much valuable information required in planning an offshore voyage is packed into the monthly pilot charts, which are available in both American and British versions, covering all the world's oceans. Portions of three such charts for the month of December are shown here. Two of them are of the North Atlantic—an American and a British version—and the third is from an American chart of Central American waters. All three charts predict for December the winds, currents, temperatures and other conditions prevailing in Florida waters.

Most of this oceanographic lore, painstakingly assembled from reports filed over the span of a century or more by hundreds of vessels, is conveyed by colored lines and symbols. The most ingenious of the symbols are wind roses, printed in blue on American charts and in red on their British counterparts *(opposite, bottom)*. Radiating from each rose are arrows (or equivalent devices) that indicate the probable direction, force and consistency of winds in the vicinity.

The single figure in the center of an American rose indicates the percentage of time during the month when calms or light or variable winds can be expected. Of the three figures in the center of a British rose, the topmost is the number of observations from which the rose was drawn. The middle figure is the percentage of time during which a skipper can expect to encounter variable winds; the bottom figure represents the probable percentage of calms. Green arrows on all three of the charts show the directions of ocean currents. Numbers printed in green above the arrows show current speed in knots, given in half-knot increments on British charts and in tenths of knots on the American charts.

The dotted red lines on American charts are isotherms that connect points having the same mean monthly temperatures. Solid red lines mark the tracks of severe storms recorded over the years during that particular month. The number of such lines crossing any portion of the chart indicates to the navigator the probability of encountering bad weather in that area at that time of year.

Solid black lines on both British and American charts trace major shipping lanes, which are generally avoided by sailboats because of the danger of collision. Some American charts helpfully add broken black lines indicating alternate routes for "low-powered ships," a category that includes most pleasure craft.

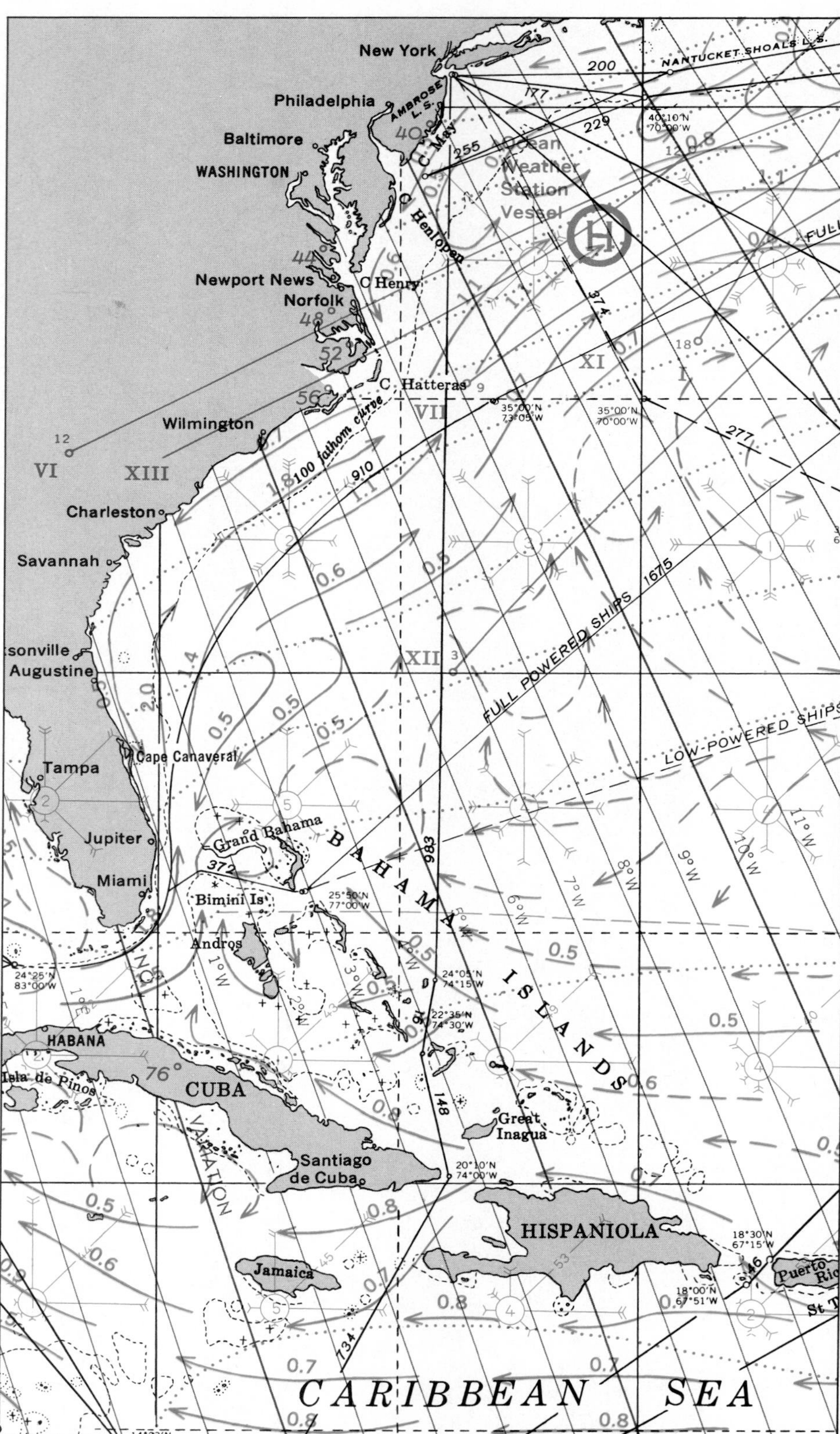


*Despite its relatively small scale—1:11,264,570—a segment of a December pilot chart of the North Atlantic contains a surprising quantity of information. The length and direction of the arrows radiating from the blue wind roses reveal that predominantly northerly winds off the east coast of Florida turn more westerly farther north. The number of "feathers" on each arrow indicates wind force as measured on the Beaufort scale. Solid green arrows show well-charted currents. Those with broken shafts indicate known currents for which few data are available. The dotted blue line running through the Bahamas marks the northern limit of the northeast trade winds.*

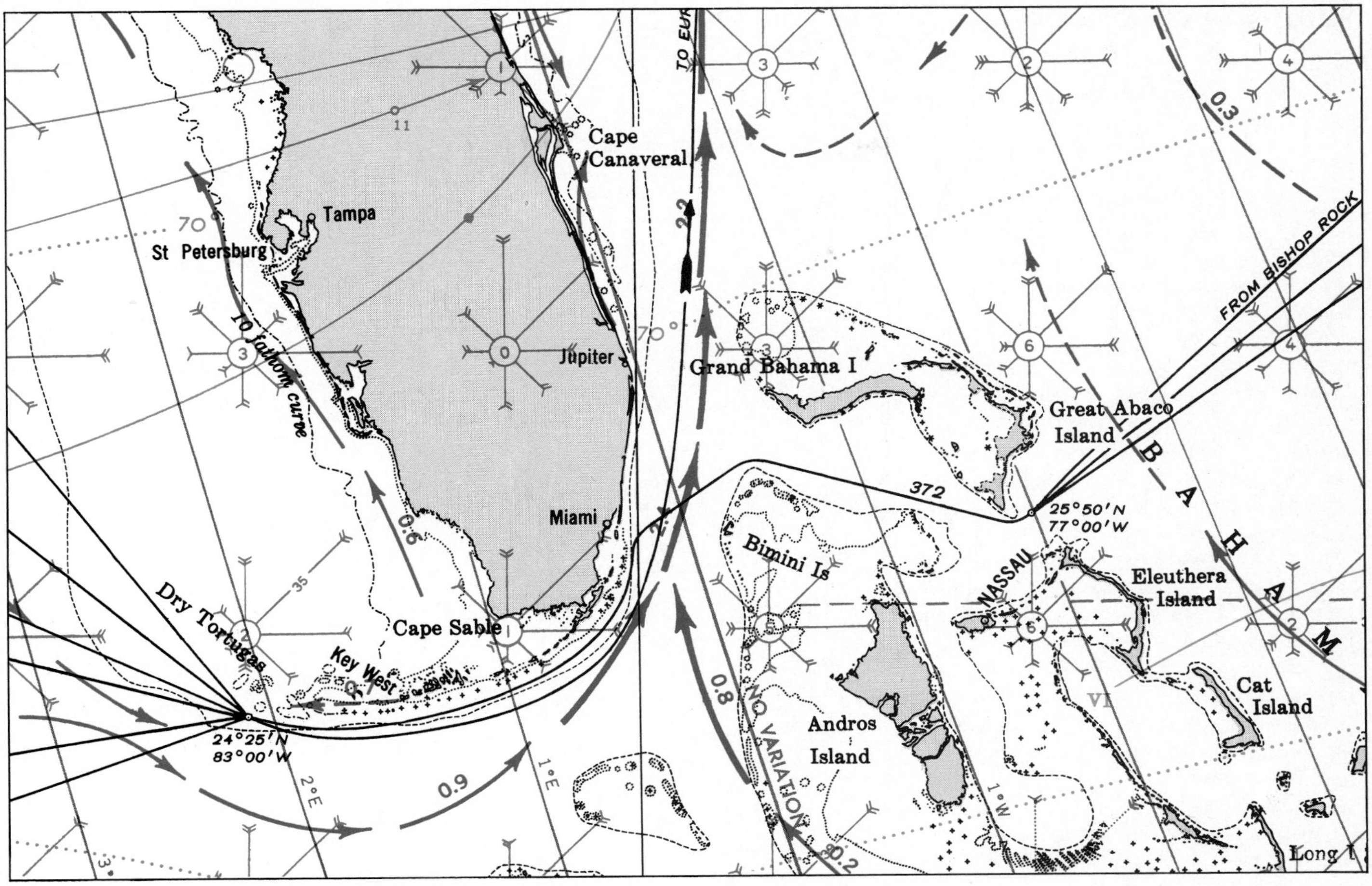

Cape Canaveral
Tampa
St Petersburg
10 fathom curve
Jupiter
Grand Bahama I
Great Abaco Island
FROM BISHOP ROCK
TO EUR
372
25°50′N
77°00′W
Miami
Bimini Is
NASSAU
Eleuthera Island
Cat Island
Andros Island
BAHAMA
Dry Tortugas
Cape Sable
Key West
24°25′N
83°00′W
NO VARIATION
0.9
0.8
0.6
2.2
0.3
0.2
Long I.

A more detailed guide to the Florida vicinity is provided by this larger-scale segment of a December pilot chart for Central American waters. The wind roses are only 120 nautical miles apart—versus 300 miles on the American chart for the entire North Atlantic. Various green arrows indicate currents that run with three different degrees of steadiness—less than 25 per cent of the time (broken lines), 25 to 50 per cent (solid), and more than 50 per cent (extra-thick arrows). The solid red line traces the only severe storm ever recorded in this area during December.

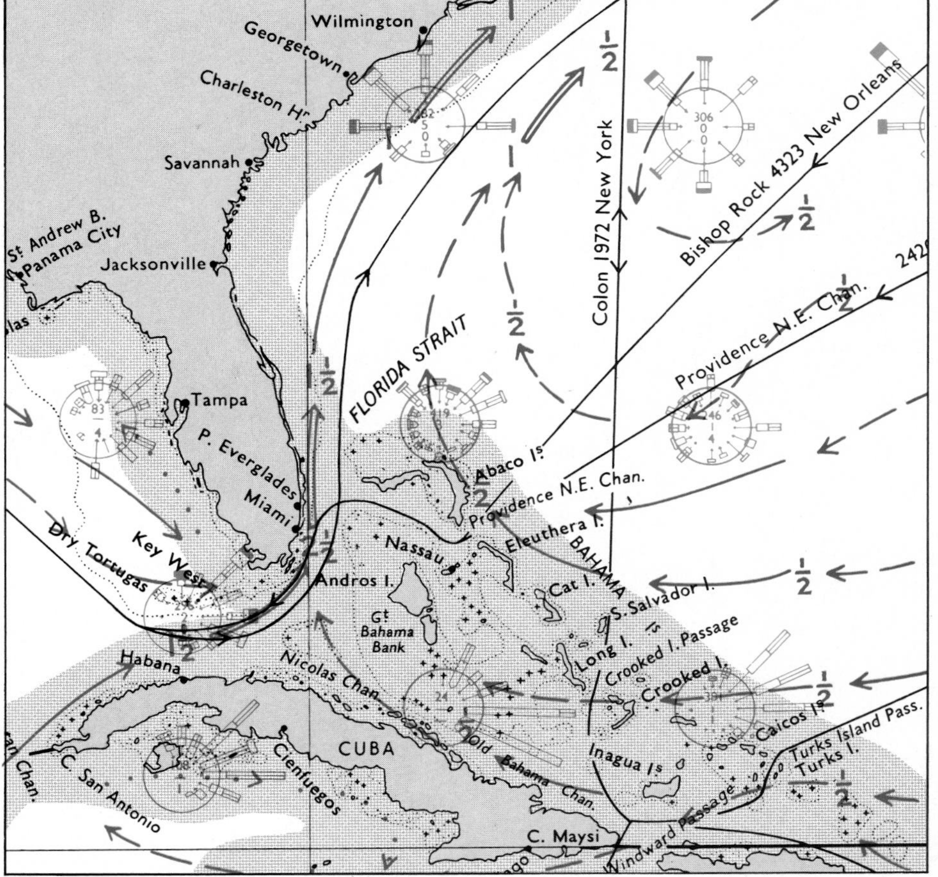


In this portion of a British pilot chart of the North Atlantic for December, the length of each wind-rose arrow indicates relative frequency; its thickness and density show relative wind force. The shafts of the green arrows indicate the steadiness of ocean currents—which are classified as those that flow 25 to 50 per cent of the time (broken lines), those of 51 to 74 per cent constancy (solid single lines) and those that are 75 to 100 per cent steady (double lines). Such data as probable air and sea temperatures, fog conditions and tracks of recorded storms appear on small inset maps not shown here.

## Charting a Voyage

A skipper contemplating an offshore sailing voyage will naturally attempt to arrange his itinerary so that he spends as much time as possible traveling in fair winds, favorable currents, smooth seas and sunshine—at the same time keeping clear of busy shipping lanes and iceberg areas. A powerboat voyager uses much the same criteria, except that he seeks out calms rather than avoiding them.

In either case, an essential step toward satisfying these requirements is to examine the pilot charts that cover all the possible time periods and routes for the proposed trip. If, for example, a mariner wishes to sail from Miami to England and back by stages of two or three weeks each, a study of pilot charts would show that he will probably encounter favorable conditions by sailing from Miami to Newport, R.I., in the latter part of July, crossing to England in August, sailing south to the Canary Islands late in October and recrossing the Atlantic late in November.

To avoid overlooking any potential problem, a careful skipper would actually plot his roughed-out route on the pilot charts so that he can see precisely where a passage between any two ports will take him. This is done by first plotting the various legs of the trip as straight lines on a great circle chart like the one at right.

The projection of a great circle chart allows for the earth's curvature in such a way that the straight lines measure the shortest distances to be sailed between two points. Using latitude and longitude readings as a guide, the mariner transfers these lines to the appropriate pilot charts, as shown on the pages that follow. The long straight lines on the great circle chart will appear on a pilot chart—or any other chart on the Mercator projections—as short, straight segments, each representing a slight change of course. Together, the segments approximate a curve that represents the sailor's most direct route.

Having laid out a general plan like the one at right, a skipper would then gather the latest and most detailed information about conditions on every leg of his proposed voyage. He would study the volumes of the *Sailing Directions* that apply to the areas he plans to traverse, read cruising guides and periodicals, talk with other yachtsmen who have made the trip —and, if necessary, alter and refine his plan. On learning, for example, that icebergs are particularly prevalent off Newfoundland that year, he might decide to swing a little farther south on his way to England than he had originally intended.

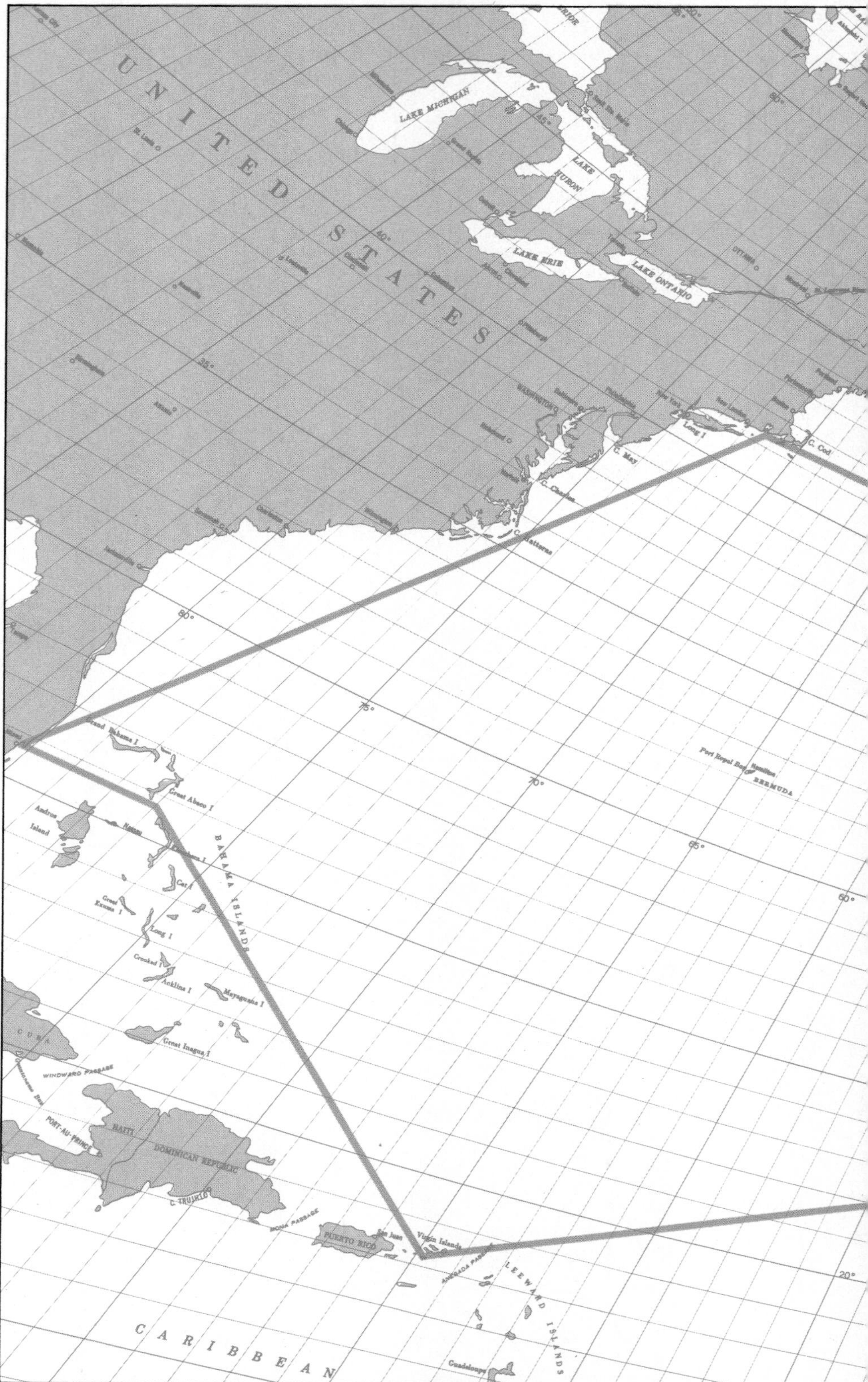

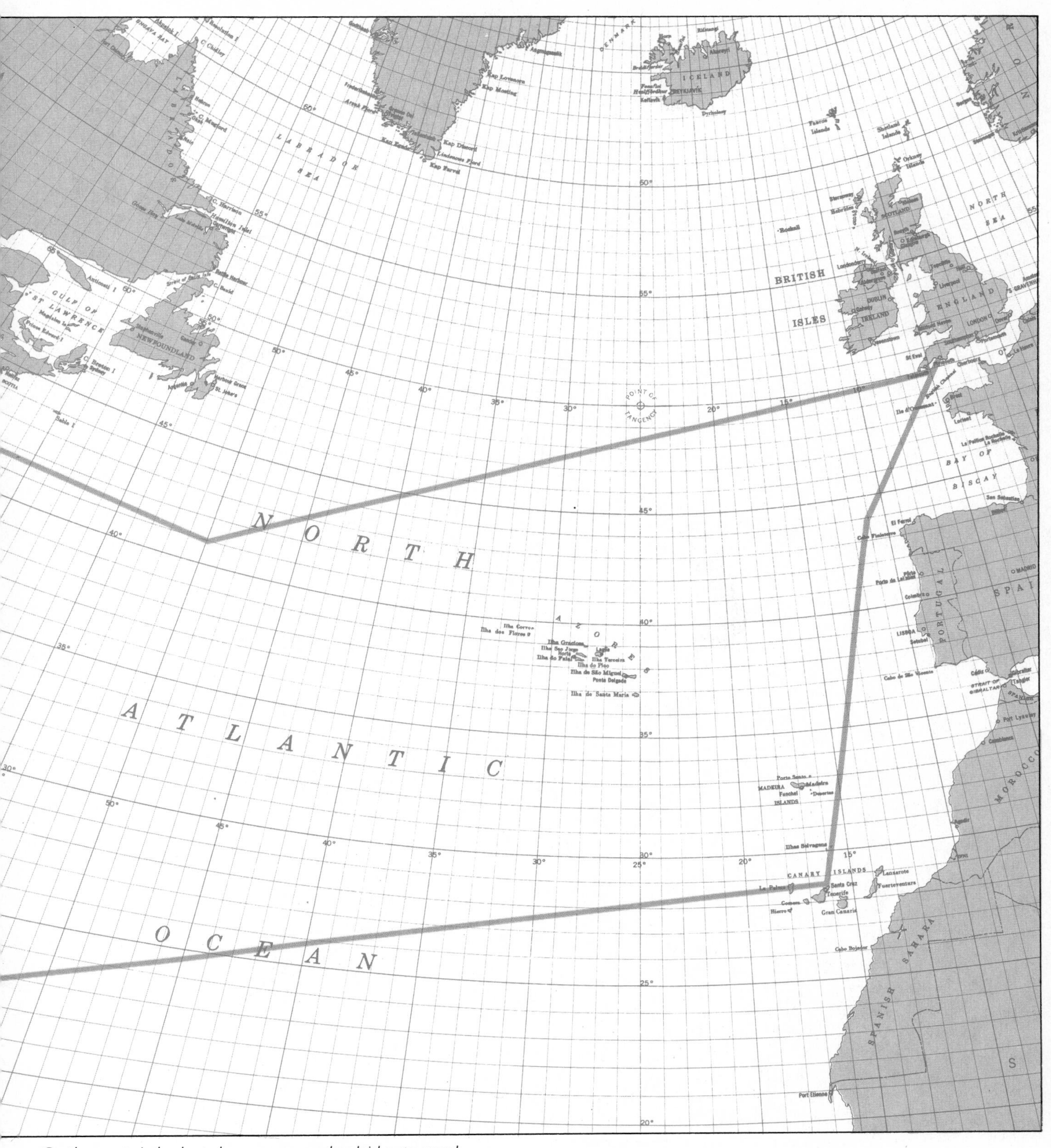


On the great circle chart above, a voyager has laid out a rough plan of his course for sailing from Miami to England and back. As shown in greater detail on the next four pages, he goes first to Newport, R.I., aided by the northbound Gulf Stream; on the transatlantic crossing, he can expect favorable winds and current all the way, although he must veer southward to avoid icebergs and to get well clear of the shipping lanes (overleaf). On the return voyage, by first sailing south to the Canaries before recrossing the Atlantic, he gains the assistance of the northeast trades and arrives in the Caribbean after the end of the hurricane season (pages 52-53).

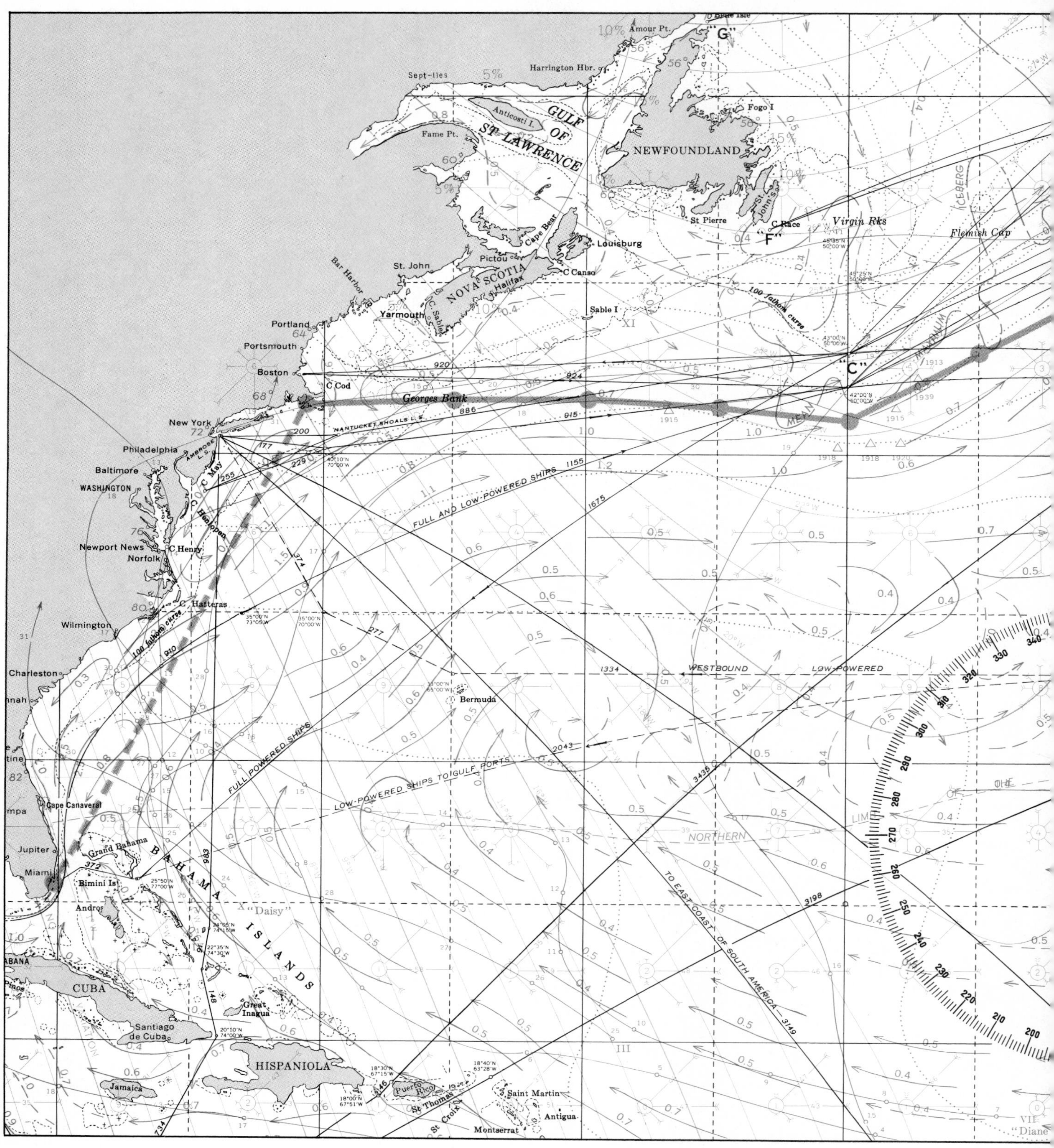
NEWFOUNDLAND
GULF OF ST LAWRENCE
NOVA SCOTIA
Sept-Iles
Harrington Hbr.
Amour Pt.
Anticosti I.
Fame Pt.
Fogo I
St Pierre
C Race
Virgin Rks
Flemish Cap
Cape Bear
Louisburg
Pictou
C Canso
Halifax
St. John
Bar Harbor
Yarmouth
C Sable
Sable I
100 fathom curve
Portland
Portsmouth
Boston
C Cod
Georges Bank
NANTUCKET SHOALS L.S.
New York
AMBROSE L.S.
Philadelphia
Baltimore
WASHINGTON
C May
C Henlopen
Newport News
Norfolk
C Henry
C Hatteras
Wilmington
Charleston
Cape Canaveral
Jupiter
Miami
Grand Bahama
Bimini Is
Andros
BAHAMA ISLANDS
"Daisy"
Bermuda
CUBA
Santiago de Cuba
Great Inagua
HISPANIOLA
Jamaica
Puerto Rico
St Thomas
St Croix
Saint Martin
Antigua
Montserrat
"Diane"
FULL AND LOW-POWERED SHIPS
FULL POWERED SHIPS
LOW-POWERED SHIPS TO GULF PORTS
WESTBOUND
LOW-POWERED
NORTHERN
TO EAST COAST OF SOUTH AMERICA
"C"
"F"
"G"
ICEBERG
MEAN

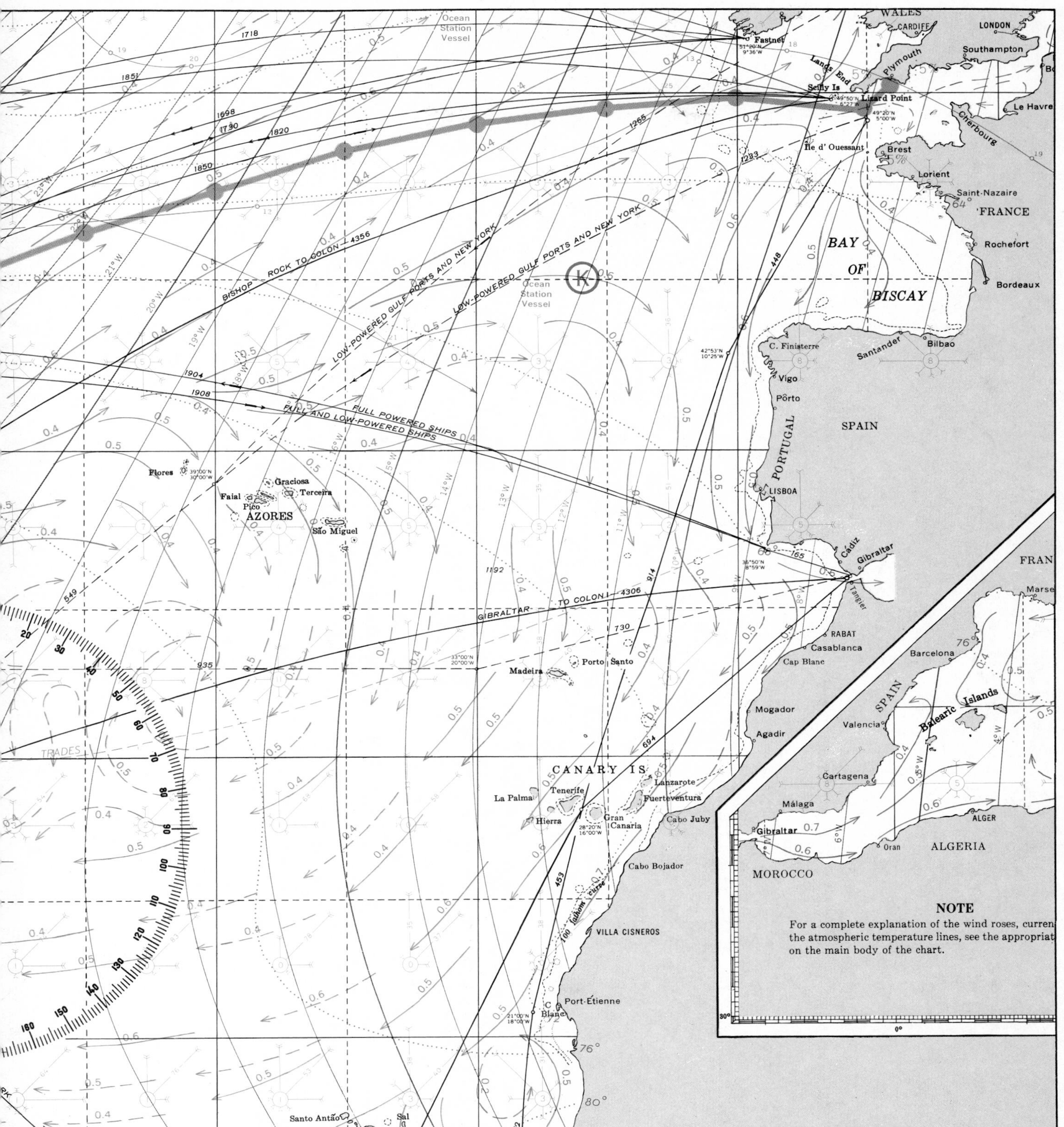


*Having arrived from Miami late in July (dashed line at left), the voyager leaves Newport, R.I., in August. The data on the portion of a North Atlantic pilot chart for August shown above indicate good sailing conditions. Wind roses, green arrows and dotted red lines respectively predict mostly northwest and southwest winds of from seven to 16 knots, favorable currents of from 0.4 to 1.2 knots, and temperatures of from 64° to 76°. The course line at first crosses the tracks of commercial craft—which habitually steer along the edge of the mean maximum iceberg limit—and thereafter, to minimize the danger of collision, keeps well south of these shipping lanes.*

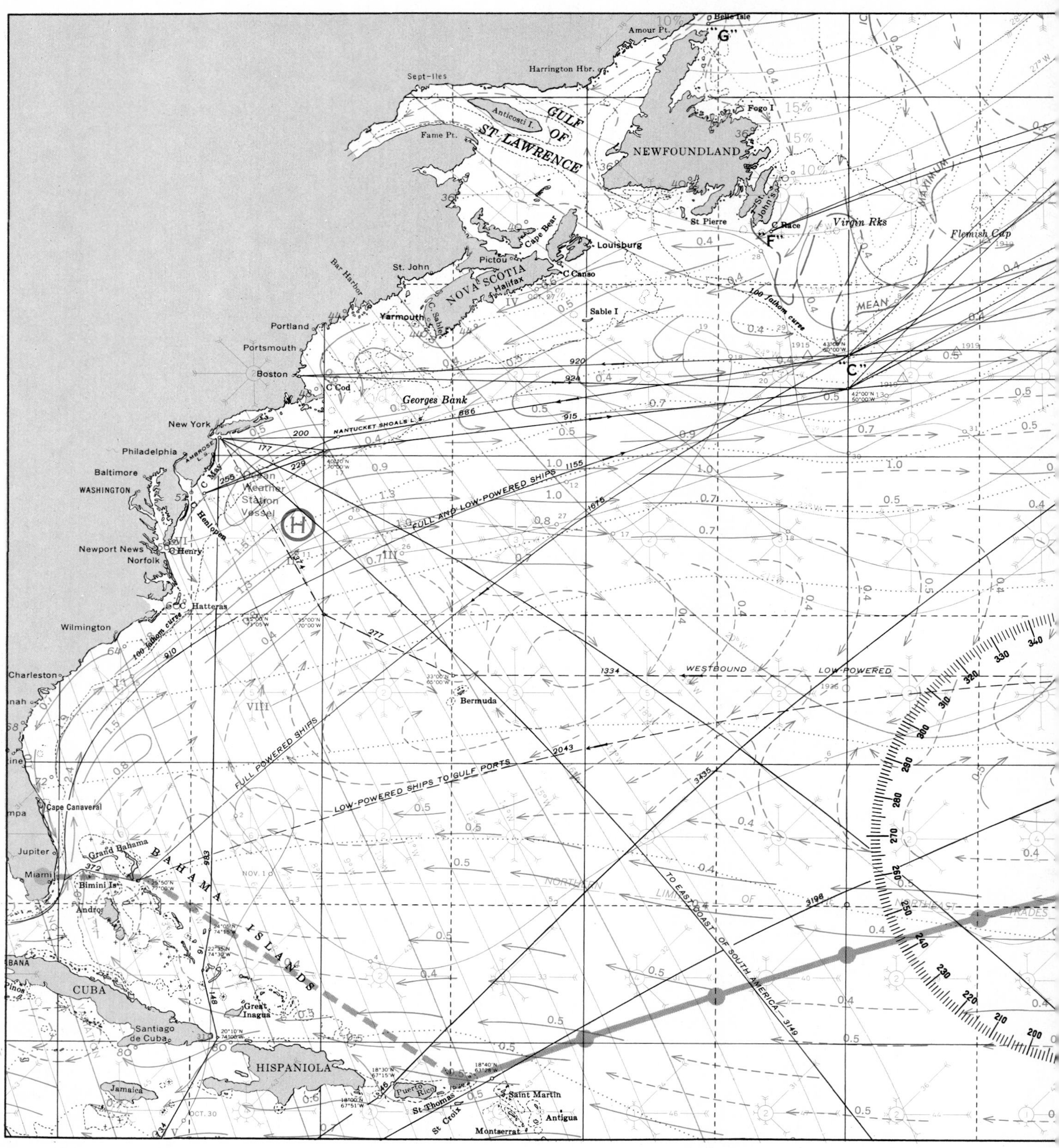

GULF OF ST. LAWRENCE
NEWFOUNDLAND
NOVA SCOTIA
Anticosti I.
Amour Pt.
Belle Isle
Harrington Hbr.
Sept-Iles
Fame Pt.
Fogo I
St Pierre
C Race
Virgin Rks
Flemish Cap
Louisburg
Cape Bear
Pictou
C Canso
Halifax
Sable I
St. John
Bar Harbor
Yarmouth
C. Sable
Portland
Portsmouth
Boston
C Cod
Georges Bank
New York
Philadelphia
Baltimore
WASHINGTON
C May
Henlopen
Ocean Weather Station Vessel
Newport News
Norfolk
C Henry
C Hatteras
Wilmington
Charleston
Cape Canaveral
Jupiter
Miami
Grand Bahama
BAHAMA ISLANDS
Bimini Is
Andros
CUBA
Great Inagua
Santiago de Cuba
HISPANIOLA
Jamaica
Puerto Rico
St Thomas
St Croix
Saint Martin
Antigua
Montserrat
Bermuda
100 fathom curve
NANTUCKET SHOALS L.S.
FULL AND LOW-POWERED SHIPS
FULL POWERED SHIPS
LOW-POWERED SHIPS TO GULF PORTS
WESTBOUND LOW-POWERED
TO EAST COAST OF SOUTH AMERICA—3149
NORTHERN LIMIT OF NORTHEAST TRADES
MAXIMUM
MEAN

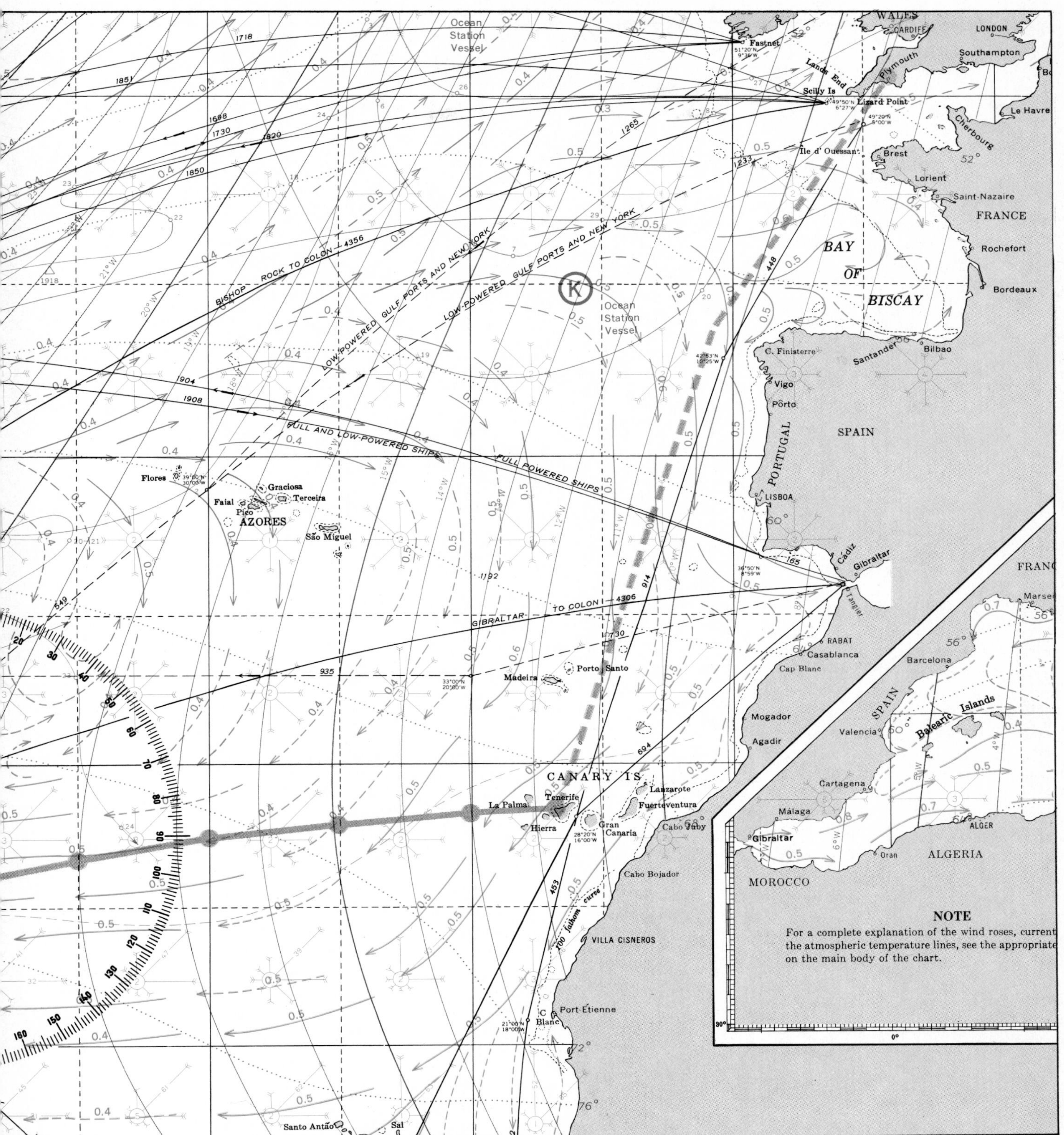


*After a late October passage from England to the Canaries (dashed line at right), the voyager picks mid-November to sail for St. Thomas in the U.S. Virgin Islands. In November both calms and storms are rare along his intended course, plotted here on a portion of a North Atlantic pilot chart for November. Chart symbols indicate that he can expect steady northeast trades of from 11 to 21 knots and easterly currents ranging from 0.4 to 0.5 knots. Temperatures should be in the balmy 70°-to-80° range. The same general conditions will prevail as he makes his way to Miami (dashed line at left) in early December.*

## Prudent Provisioning

The choice of provisions for an offshore voyage is mostly a matter of personal taste. One seasoned offshore sailor subsists on nothing but raisins, nuts, honey and dehydrated cabbage. Another stocks only rice, canned tomatoes, potatoes and plenty of rum—plus fishing tackle to supplement this spartan fare. Most voyagers, however, plan a more varied diet.

The amount of food taken aboard will depend on the storage space available, the probable rate of consumption, the possibilities of replenishment and the length of the voyage. By keeping track of supplies in a kitchen ashore for a month or two, prospective voyagers can compile useful data on their normal needs, such as the amount of sugar two people eat in a week or how many cups can be made from a jar of instant coffee.

Dividing the boat's food-storage space by the number and size of the appetites involved can aid in determining how quickly the crew will devour a full load of supplies. Naturally, a skipper must arrange his itinerary so that he reaches a port where his stores can be replenished well before they are used up.

Because schedules can be drastically disrupted in offshore sailing, one expert espouses a provisioning formula that provides a large margin for error. He lays in sufficient supplies to provide normal-sized meals for the expected length of the cruise, and then he adds enough to permit a minimal diet for half again the estimated journey time. As a further precaution, he always keeps an additional 30 days' emergency rations on board. Implicit in this formula is a warning: fish caught en route should be considered a bonus rather than a dependable food supply.

A boat's equipment will also influence its provisioning. The master of a small boat with no refrigerator and only modest-sized fresh-water tanks should stock few highly perishable fresh foods and should buy only small amounts of items that spoil quickly after opening. Since each person aboard will need at least a gallon of fresh water a day for washing, drinking and cooking, he should buy few of the freeze-dried foods whose preparation consumes significant amounts of water.

Whatever his craft's capabilities, a skipper will do well to look into the experiences of other offshore sailors. Of particular benefit are annotated supply lists like the one at right, which details the fare that supported two men on a trip across the Atlantic and—hardly less important—also notes their reactions to it.

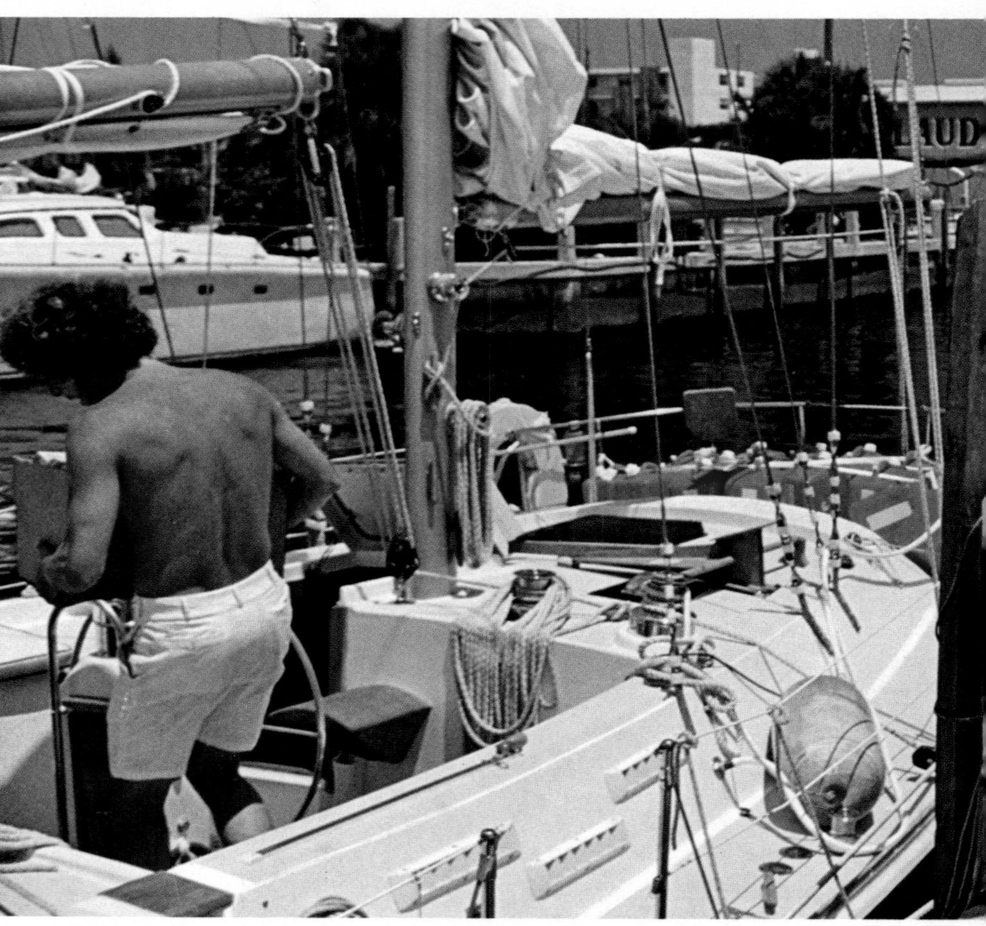

### "You can't have too much mustard"

*The list below is adapted from Cooking on Your Knees, a boating cookbook by Beverly Fuller. It shows approximate quantities of provisions carried by her husband, Dean (whose comments follow each category), and a friend on a seven-week trip from Connecticut to Ireland via Bermuda.*

**Fresh provisions**

| | | | |
|---|---|---|---|
| 3 lbs. onions | 2 melons | 4 green peppers | 2 French loaves |
| 5 lbs. potatoes | 3 lbs. apples | 12 tomatoes | 12 biscuits |
| 3 doz. oranges | 2 heads lettuce | 9 doz. eggs | 1 loaf rye |
| 2 doz. lemons | 5 cabbages | 1 loaf white bread | 1 loaf dark rye |

All fruit and vegetables were gone in three weeks and sorely missed thereafter. Lemons, melons and cabbage kept the longest. Of the bread, French and dark rye lasted best.

**Jams, syrups, sauces and soups**

| | | | |
|---|---|---|---|
| 8 ozs. maple syrup | 52 10¾-oz. cans assorted soups | 12 ozs. assorted powdered broths | 1 lb. hollandaise |
| 1 lb. marmalade | | | 1 lb. cranberry sauce |
| 1 lb. raspberry jam | | | 6 lbs. tomato sauce |

We saved sugar by using jam and syrup on cereal. Hot tea with jam and a little brandy saves sugar and warms the heart. Hollandaise enhanced the flavor of asparagus and steaks.

**Emergency rations**

| | | | |
|---|---|---|---|
| 6 C-type emergency rations | 18 1-oz. tropical chocolate bars | 7 3-oz. bacon bars | 12 1-oz. high-energy |
| | | 1 lb. beef jerky | |

Of those we sampled, the jerky was spicy and chewy, the chocolate good, the bacon bars ghastly.

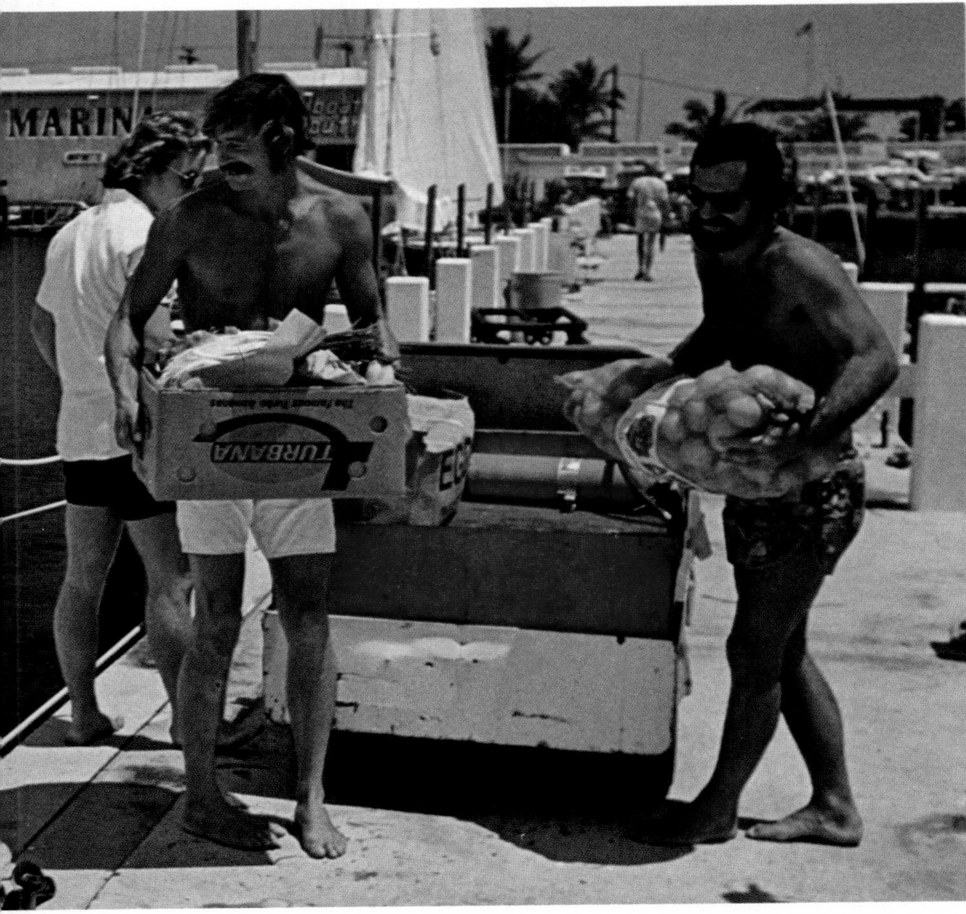

*In preparation for a transatlantic passage from Fort Lauderdale, Florida, a 51-foot freezer-equipped ketch receives the bulk of the supplies that will be used along the way, including 90 pounds of frozen meat, oranges and the canned food required for the trip. In Bermuda, the Azores and Gibraltar, the three-man crew replenished such perishables as cheese, bread and fresh vegetables.*

**Canned and dried vegetables and fruits**

61 1-lb. cans assorted vegetables
7 1-lb. cans assorted fruits
5 15-oz. boxes dried fruits

Canned fruit brightened breakfasts; dried fruit supplied quick energy.

**Staples**

9 lbs. mixes: biscuit, pancake, cornbread
12 lbs. flour
2 lbs. baking soda
32 ozs. olive oil
3½ lbs. oatmeal and Cream of Wheat
4 lbs. fresh butter
6 lbs. sugar
1 lb. table salt
19 lbs. starches: rice, mashed potatoes, grits and noodles
16 ozs. vinegar

Staples kept well in our (iceless) icebox, which was dry and had a lid. The butter, stored in the bilge, lasted the whole trip.

**Condiments and seasonings**

5 9-oz. jars mustard
15 assorted seasonings
6 lbs. mayonnaise
3 bottles catsup
1 bottle Tabasco
4 8-oz. bottles Parmesan cheese
50 garlic cloves

A ship's most important shelf; there's never enough Parmesan for spaghetti and you can't have too much mustard, mayonnaise or garlic.

**Desserts, candy, cookies**

1 24-oz. can cookies
12 ozs. hard candy
1 7-oz. can crêpes suzettes
1 1-oz. jar babas au rhum

The crêpes were fantastic; we wished we had had six tins of cookies.

**Lunch and snack ingredients**

2 lbs. canned sardines
6 lbs. pâté and chicken, cheese and ham spreads
1 6-oz. can Vienna sausage
2 lbs. canned crackers
2 10-oz. cans salami sticks
6 5-oz. cans cheeses
2 lbs. provolone
3 lbs. Danish salami
5 5-oz. cans olives
6 6½-oz. cans nuts
5 10-oz. boxes pretzels, potato chips

We liked lemon juice and onion on sardines, mayonnaise and Tabasco on ham and chicken. The superb salami lasted the whole trip.

**Canned and dried meat, fish and poultry**

20 ½-oz. freeze-dried pork chops
10 ¼-oz. freeze-dried steaks
4 lbs. Danish bacon
1 lb. each turkey and pork roasts
14 15-oz. cans meatballs and gravy
3 12-oz. cans ham
2½ lbs. each tuna and crab
2½ lbs. boned chicken
4 lbs. boned turkey

We had plenty of everything. The Danish bacon was superb though difficult to extract from the can. The meatballs and ham were the best of the other canned meats. The steaks were marvelous.

**Beverages**

18 fifths of Scotch
3 cases beer
1 bottle cooking vermouth
2 bottles brandy
36 bottles mixers
4 lbs. powdered fruit drinks
6 lbs. coffee
48 tea bags
3 lbs. powdered milk
14 ozs. instant chocolate
33 ozs. Coffee-mate

Plenty of everything except for tea bags, chocolate, Scotch and beer.

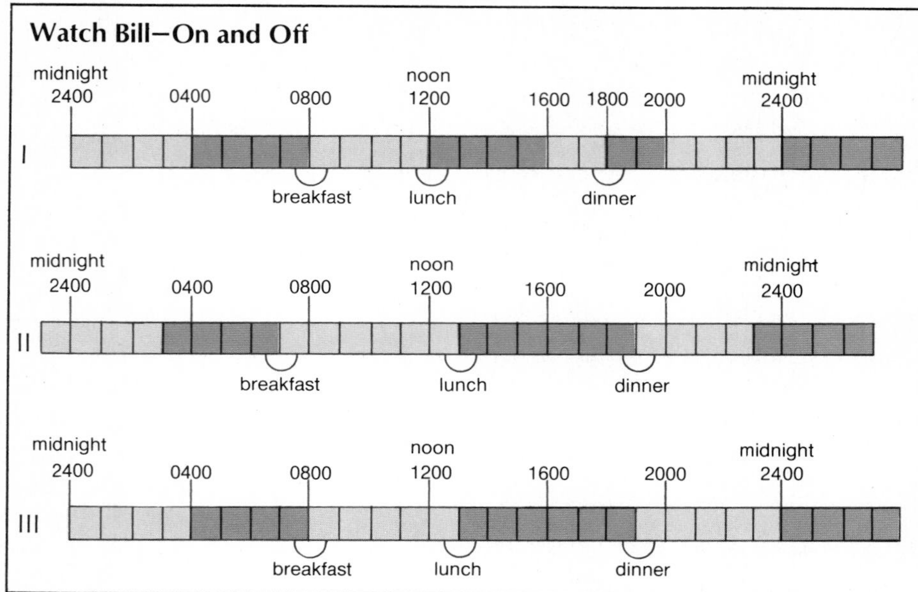


*The diagrams above show three ways of dividing 24 hours into watches. Each is arranged so that watches change conveniently at mealtimes, and in each case—whether the crew is divided into groups of two, three or four—the watches shift automatically so that each crewman's on-watch periods change daily. Example I provides for frequent watch changes such as might be necessary during a race or in rough weather. Examples II and III, with their longer on-watch and off-watch periods during the day, are more applicable to the crew of a cruising boat that is voyaging under fair-weather conditions.*

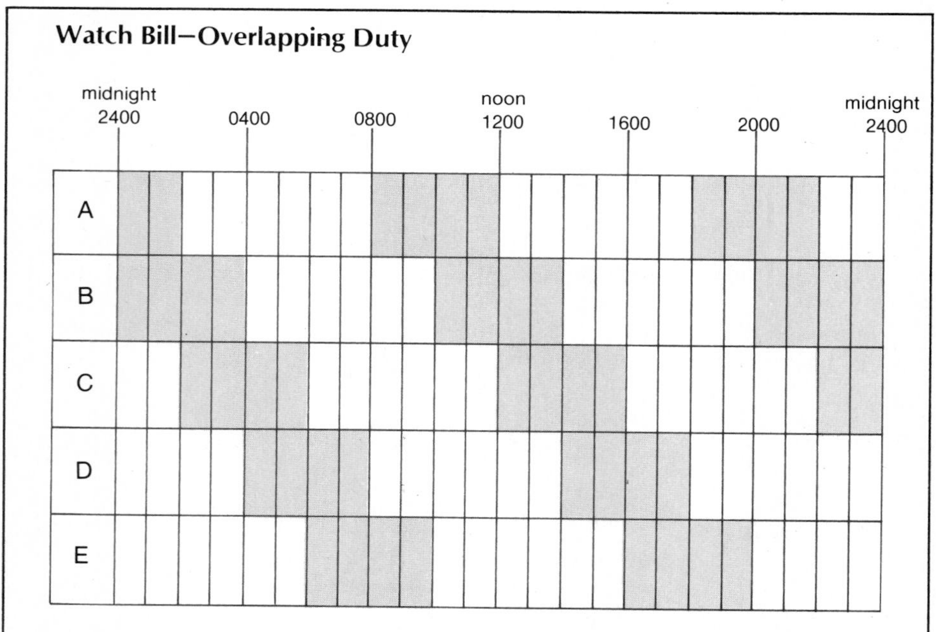


*A watch system like the one shown above, based on a crew divided into an odd number of groups, gives each group a regular succession of four hours on watch followed by six hours off. Every two hours, in this 24-hour example, one member of a five-man crew comes on watch and another goes off. Mealtimes may be inconvenient for some crew members, but nobody need steer for more than two hours at a stretch, and everyone gets regular six-hour rests. This system dogs the watch automatically and ensures that watches are always shared by the same crew members; the crew should therefore be divided into watches that share equally the skills of everyone aboard.*

## Watches and Logs

Amidst the cozy informality that usually attends offshore voyaging, meticulous attention to the logbook and the watch bill may seem as anachronistic as striking the ship's bell every half hour. Yet the log and the watches can be essential to the crew's morale, as well as its safety.

Even on boats with self-steering systems, somebody should be on watch, if only as a lookout, at all times in almost all waters; collision is a danger at sea second only to falling overboard. A watch system like one of those at left, well planned and strictly adhered to, ensures that some competent person is awake and in charge of the vessel whenever necessary and that both duties and leisure time are fairly shared by everyone.

The organization of watches may vary according to the nature and length of the voyage, the weather, the size of the crew, the number of people needed to handle the boat, and the nature and degree of possible dangers. Short watches are preferred for racing, when those on deck should be alert at all times. (Some racing skippers even designate captains of each watch.) The crew of a cruising boat can afford longer, more leisurely watches.

In either case, watches should be organized so that nobody is at the wheel for more than two or three hours at a time and so that everybody is off watch for at least four consecutive hours each day—the shortest time in which anyone can get much benefit from sleep. A good watch system should also shift, or "dog," every day to avoid having the same people eternally fixed in the same watches.

Systematical recording of happenings aboard ship is as important as standing watch. A ship's log can be kept in a single all-inclusive book or in separate volumes for deck, engine room and radio. But the log should include such details as sea and weather conditions, courses sailed, distances covered, speeds maintained and fuel consumed. This record of the boat's performance will be helpful in planning future voyages. Furthermore, a precise record of where the boat was and what it was doing at a particular time can be important evidence if there should be an accident and a subsequent insurance claim.

A good log should also note events of personal interest to the crew: spectacular sunsets, marine life observed, everyday triumphs and tragedies. Some logs even include drawings and photographs. A log full of concise but colorful entries makes good winter reading for years after the completion of the voyage.

| TIME | LOG | COURSE | SPEED | WEATHER | REMARKS |
|---|---|---|---|---|---|
| 0000 | 113.6 | 090 | 3.0 | LIGHT SW BREEZE CLEAR 1002 MB. | ON WATCH ALONE. BEAUTIFUL STARLIT NIGHT. NORTHERN LIGHTS SPECTACULAR. |
| 0200 | 118.4 | 090 | 5.5 | SW BREEZE 10 KNOTS CLOUDING UP. 997 MB | |
| 0300 | 124.6 | 090 | 7.5 | SW FRESH 22 KNOTS FOG 991 MB. | SHORTENED TO WORKING JIB |
| 0320 | 127.1 | 080 | 8.0 | WIND SW 25 KNOTS THICK FOG. | PUT IN MAINSAIL REEF. RIGGING FOR HEAVY WEATHER |
| 0400 | 132.5 | | 8.0 | WIND SAME. FOG CONTINUES. 986 MB. | FRITZ AND MARGE ON WATCH. HEARD A SHIP PASS 1 MILE AHEAD. |
| 0800 | 161.5 | 090 | 7.0 | WIND DIMINISHING. COLD BUT CLEARING 989 MB SW 15 KNOTS. | |
| 0840 | 165.9 | 120 | 6.5 | WIND WSW 12 KNOTS SEAS CHOPPY. | ICEBERG AHEAD TO STARBOARD. ALTERING COURSE TO ROUND WINDWARD OF IT. |
| 1200 | 184.9 | 090 | 5.0 | WIND WXS 10 KNOTS | ALCOHOL FIRE IN GALLEY. PUT OUT IMMEDIATELY WITH WATER. MARGE BURNED HAND. |
| 1400 | 194.3 | 105 | 4.5 | WIND W 5.0 KNOTS DRYING OUT IN BRIGHT SUN. 991 MB. | SET SPINNAKER. ADJUSTED COURSE FOR GOOD ANGLE TO BREEZE. |
| 1500 | 199.3 | 100 | 5.4 | WIND W 8.0 KNOTS CLEAR. | FINE AFTERNOON. CLOTHES AND FOUL WEATHER GEAR ARE DRYING OUT ON DECK. |
| 1525 | 201.2 | 090 | 3.0 | WIND WXW 5.0 KNOTS | BOYS FISHING. CAUGHT 12 LB. TUNA. GOOD FOR SUPPER TONIGHT. |
| 1800 | 212.4 | 090 | 5.4 | WIND WNW 10 KNOTS 1002 MBS | DINNER. TUNA STEAKS. EXCELLENT! SAW LARGE TANKER WESTBOUND, HULL DOWN ON HORIZON TO SOUTH. |

*A typical page from the logbook of a yacht cruising the North Atlantic might look like the one above: a series of brief but complete and reasonably accurate entries made whenever the boat's circumstances change significantly. Distances traveled, as noted in the "LOG" column, along with figures on course and speed, aid the skipper in reckoning his position. Weather data, including wind direction and barometric pressure, expressed in millibars (MB), complement radioed weather reports. Events of general interest—from a burned hand to a fresh-fish dinner—are also noted. Logbooks with printed page headings are available, but most skippers prefer to make their own.*

## A Weather Eye and Ear

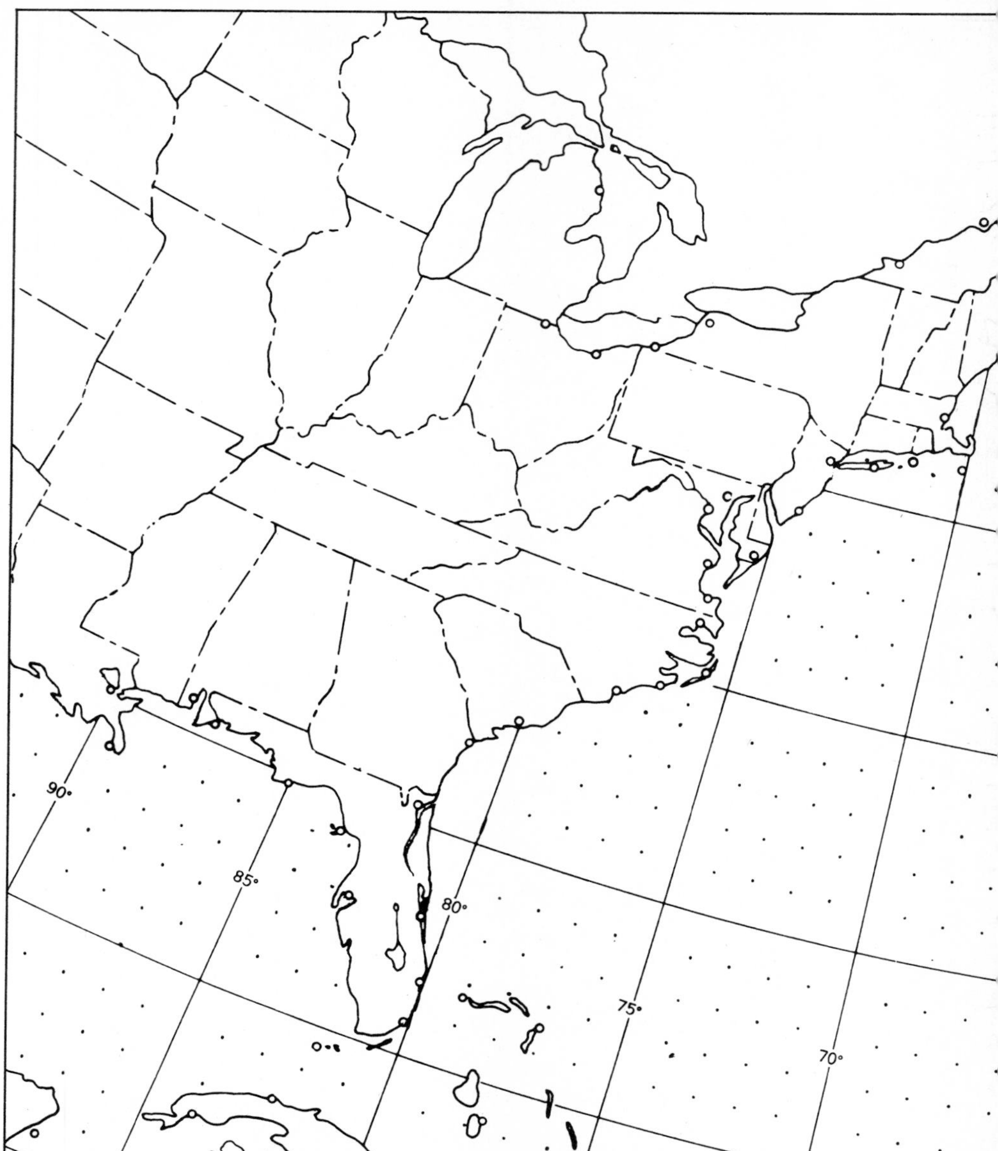


Nothing affects the safety and comfort of an offshore voyager more directly than the weather, and a skipper should constantly stay abreast of meteorological developments in his vicinity. While a knowledge of visual weather signs is important, radio reports like the one on the opposite page are an indispensable aid to preparedness. Thousands of such reports are broadcast several times a day from some 50 nations, both in Morse code and by voice. Most broadcasts are in English, and those given in other languages are usually repeated in English.

A comprehensive guide to these information resources is found in *Worldwide Marine Weather Broadcasts,* published annually by the National Weather Service. This book groups the stations by the areas that their reports cover; it also lists their frequencies, schedules, the mode of transmission and the kind of data offered—ranging from brief storm warnings to detailed forecasts and analyses.

To take advantage of this flow of information, a voyager will need, at a minimum, a good multiband shortwave receiver. The ultimate in weather-related electronic gear is a device that can turn the coded pulses sent by some stations into a graphic rendering, like the weather maps published in newspapers, of weather conditions over a large area.

In lieu of this professional weather map, many offshore sailors create a simpler record of evolving weather systems on a tracking chart, as shown at top. This is done by simply noting on the chart the boat's daily position and any pertinent weather conditions described in ordinary weather broadcasts. A voyager familiar with Morse, however, can produce a weather map every bit as thorough and exact as any facsimile version. The requisite information is regularly transmitted in a special Morse language composed of 45 different five-digit groups. With the help of a decoding key in the back of the Broadcasts book, the signals can be translated into a map of an area the size of the North Atlantic within a couple of hours.

Either sort of weather-depicting endeavor may be facilitated by a small cassette tape recorder, which allows a broadcast to be recorded and then transcribed whenever convenient. Portions that are hard to decipher—because of static, for instance—can be played back repeatedly until the meaning becomes clear; and on a machine with a speed control, Morse broadcasts can be replayed at slow speed for easier decoding.

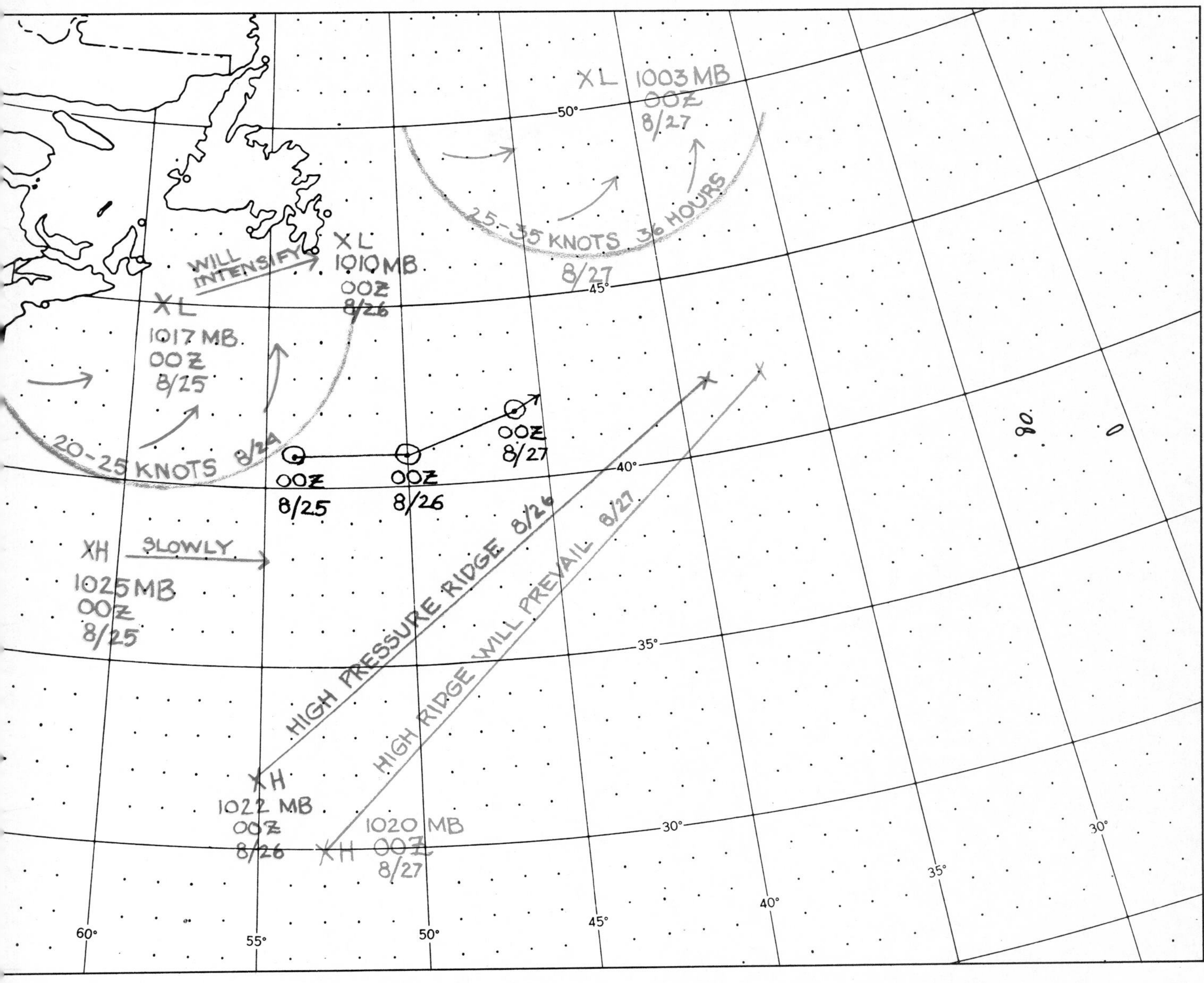


NATIONAL WEATHER SERVICE WASHINGTON DC MARINE FORECAST
FOR NORTH ATLANTIC WATERS NORTH OF 32N AND WEST OF 35W
BEGINNING 18Z AUG 26.

WARNING SYNOPSIS
NONE

PART ONE
NO WARNING

FPNT KWBC 151800Z
FORECAST X NORTH OF LATITUDE 32X

STATIONARY HIGH CENTER NEAR 30N 53W 1020 MB AT 00Z WITH
RIDGE EXTENDING NORTHEAST THROUGH 42N 37W WILL PREVAIL.
LOW CENTER NEAR 51N 42W 1003 MB AT 00Z WILL MOVE NORTH
EASTWARD 20 TO 25 KNOTS AND INTENSIFY IN 36 HOURS.
WINDS INCREASING TO 25 OCCASIONALLY 35 KNOTS WITHIN
300 MILE SOUTHWEST SEMICIRCLE IN 36 HOURS.

*On the tracking chart above, radio forecasts of weather likely to affect a boat heading for England have been recorded for August 25 (green), 26 (red) and 27 (blue). Notations include the boat's position (circled dots), dates, times (00Z means midnight Greenwich Mean Time), barometric pressures in millibars, the extent and trends of high- and low-pressure areas, and wind speeds and directions. Entries for the 27th, based on the radio-report excerpt at left, show that a stormy low-pressure area has moved away from the boat; a high-pressure ridge that could have becalmed it stays to the south.*

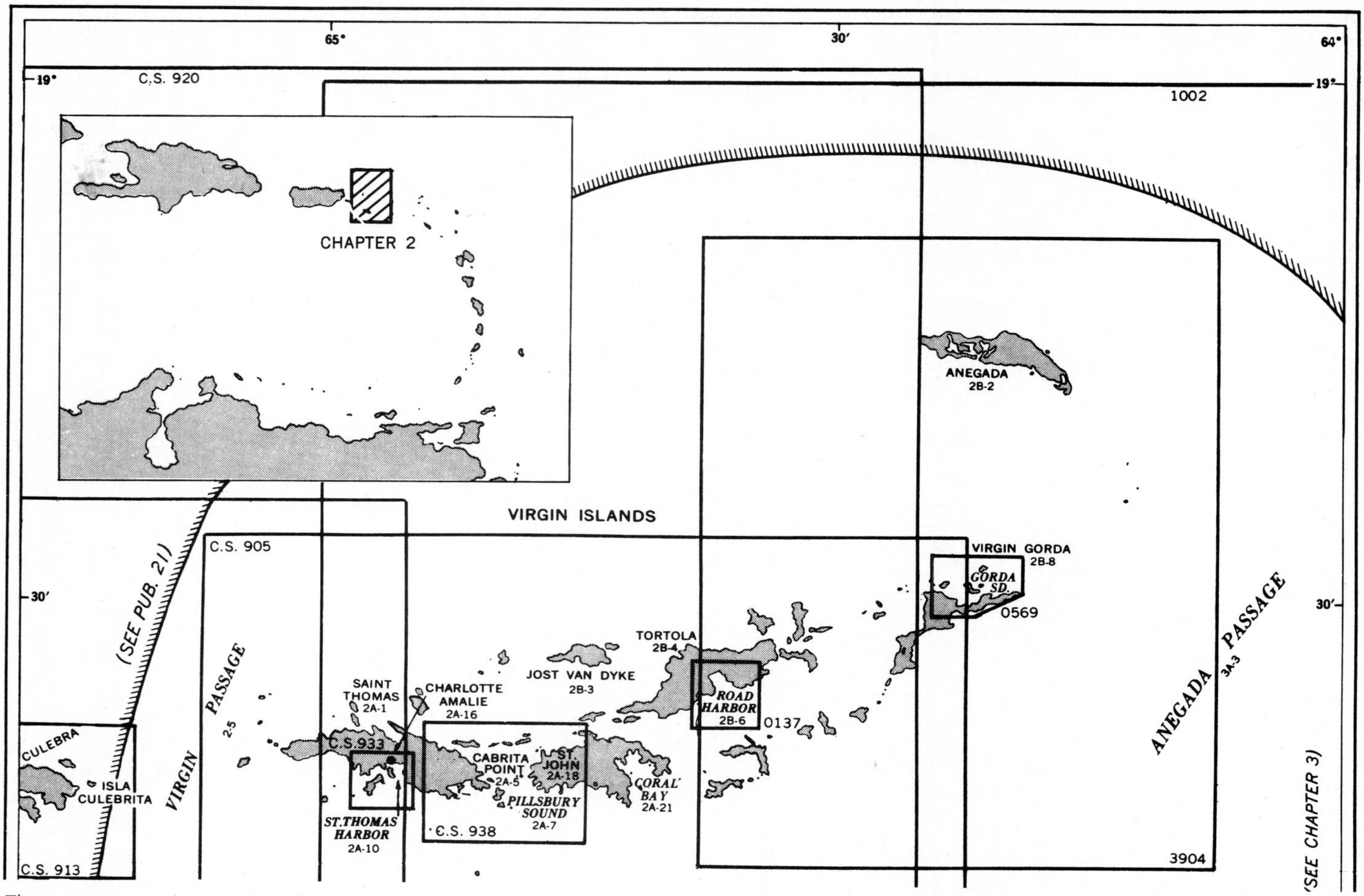

*The map excerpt above is part of a graphic index from chapter two of the Sailing Directions for the West Indies. The inset map locates the region covered; rectangles on the larger map denote charts of the enclosed areas. Letters and numbers identify these charts or relevant text passages. This index would direct a skipper headed for St. Thomas in the Virgin Islands to NOS chart 905 for navigating in the waters around the Virgins, to chart 933 for entering St. Thomas harbor and to section 2A-10 of the text for information on the harbor area.*

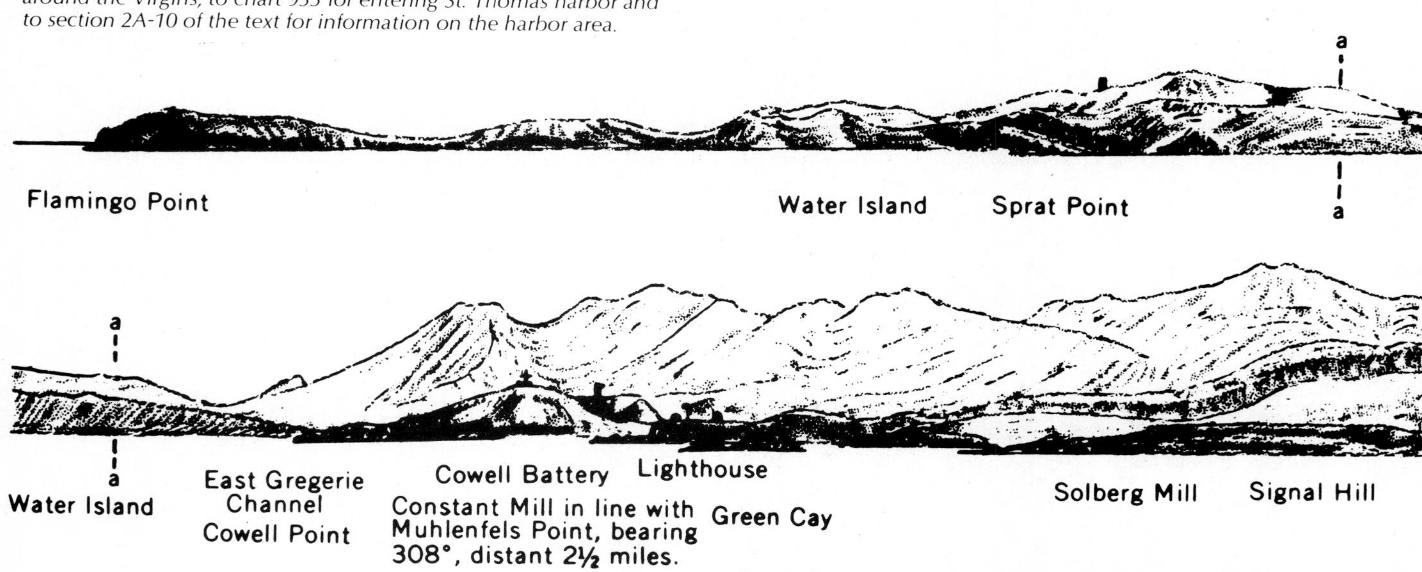


*As supplementary guidance for approaching and entering harbors, the text of the Sailing Directions offers detailed visual and text descriptions of landmarks, dangers to be avoided and aids to navigation. Sketches depict segments of coastline as they actually appear from a particular point at sea. The one above shows, in two overlapping sections, how the landscape around St. Thomas harbor appears to a skipper approaching it from the southeast.*

# Entering Foreign Ports

When setting out for a foreign port, a boatman should familiarize himself with any problems he may encounter either in making the harbor or in confronting local port regulations. For most of the world's ports, the 62 volumes of the *U.S. Sailing Directions* provide invaluable guidance in navigating through both these hazards. Other good sources of information are cruise guides, consuls in the countries concerned and yachtsmen who have been there before.

A number of precautions apply to planning for entry into almost every foreign port. Make sure that boat and crew have the necessary documentation. For example, an American yacht must be registered by a state or documented by the Coast Guard; if the boat has been purchased abroad, it must have a certificate of U.S. ownership. A list of the crew and their nationalities is generally obligatory. And every crewman needs a valid passport, an immunization record and, for some countries, a visa or other entry permit. Some ports demand such data as the boat's gross and net tonnages, and lists of any stores that might be considered cargo.

Choose an official port of entry as the first stop in any country, notifying the port captain of the impending arrival as far in advance as local laws require. Impromptu arrivals at harbors lacking port officials may lead to fines for illegal entry.

At some ports of entry, a pilot will be put on board to direct the boat to the correct anchorage. Otherwise, proceed to a quarantine area shown on the harbor chart; or, if such an anchorage seems too remote or unsafe, anchor in some conspicuous spot out of the way of other shipping. Hoist the boat's national flag at the stern and fly the host country's flag from a mast or staff forward, with the yellow "Q" international signal flag beneath it as an invitation to port authorities to inspect ship, crew and papers. Having crew and vessel neat and shipshape usually helps to speed the inspection.

If the authorities do not appear within two hours or so, the captain may go ashore with the ship's and crew's documents to request clearance for entry; no other crewman should set foot onshore until official permission is received.

Before leaving port, be sure to get some form of written clearance for departure; without it, entry into the next port may be difficult. If possible, time arrivals and departures to coincide with local working hours, thus avoiding extra charges for services rendered after hours or on holidays.

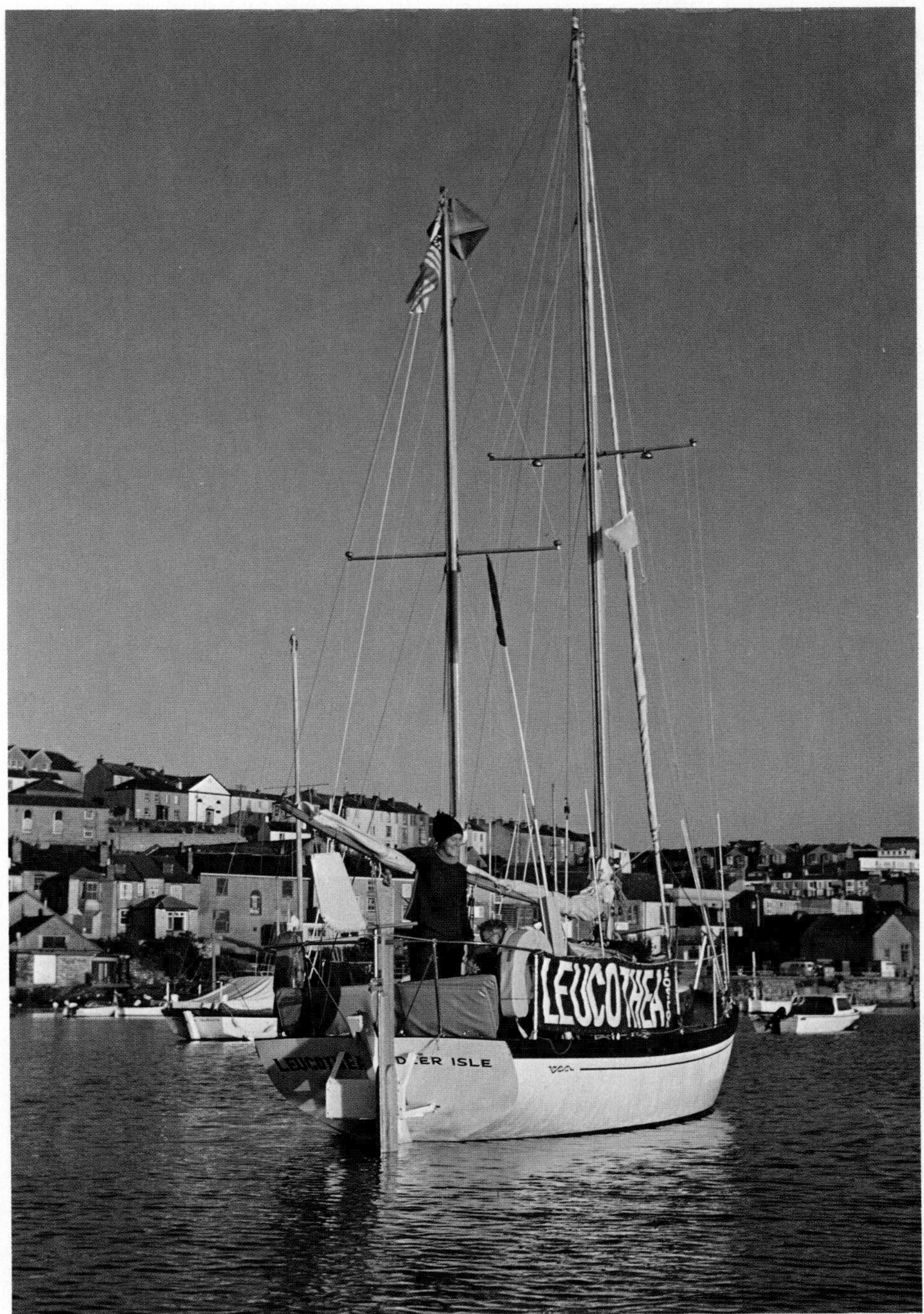


*An American boat newly arrived in Falmouth, England, displays two of the three flags required by port protocol. An American flag is flown from the mizzen, since the boat lacks a stern flagstaff. The yellow International Code "Q" flag just below the mainmast spreader shows that the skipper seeks official permission to enter the port. Before leaving the U.S., the skipper had searched in vain for a British flag to fly from the mainmast while in British ports—an omission he remedied once he was allowed ashore. The boat's name is painted on the cockpit dodger—a device often used by offshore voyagers who hope that other ships will note and report their positions.*

*Francis Chichester's Gypsy Moth IV braves the violent seas off Cape Horn in 1967; a storm jib steadies the boat and maintains steerageway. Six hours after this photograph was taken—by a plane sent out by London's Sunday Times to record Chichester's rounding of the Horn—the wind blew up to 85 knots. But the 65-year-old lone mariner and his vessel rode out the tempest without needing so much as a single adjustment of sail. In recognition of his valiant and successful circumnavigation, Queen Elizabeth knighted him with the sword of another great mariner, Sir Francis Drake.*

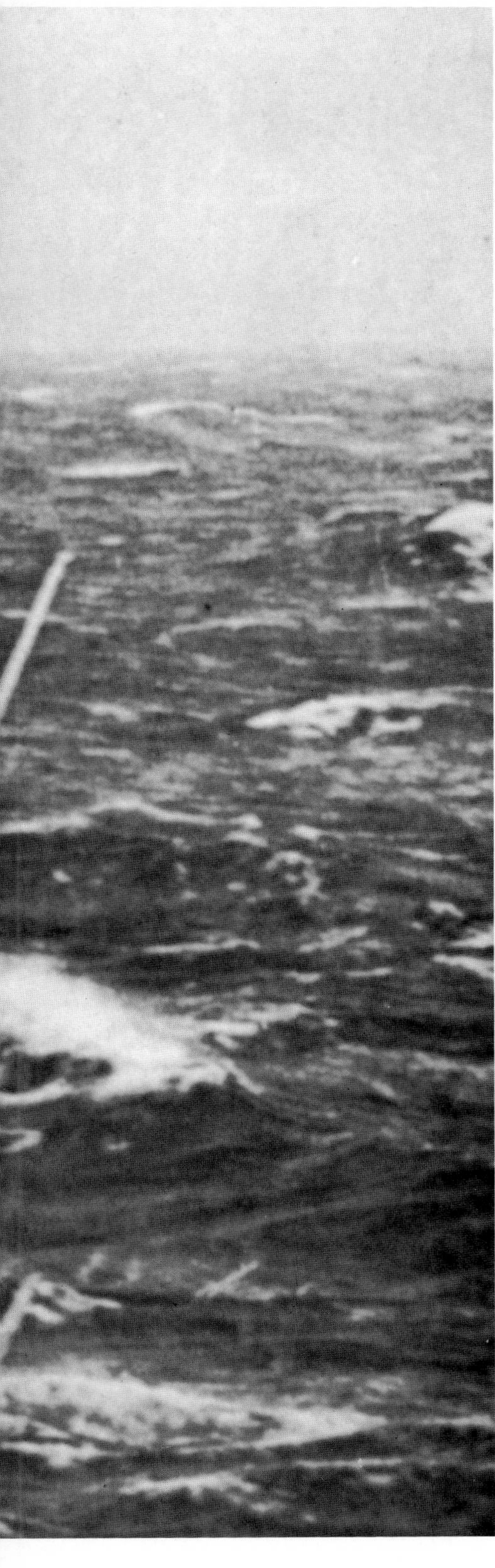

# WITHSTANDING THE SEA'S MALICE

Most of the sailors who go out onto the oceans of the world reach their destinations with no serious mishap and much satisfaction. Given a sturdy boat, properly equipped, an experienced mariner can ride out the most savage conditions of wind and sea, as demonstrated by the vessel at left, slogging along in gale-force winds off Cape Horn. Its skipper, the British mariner Sir Francis Chichester, was making his singlehanded circumnavigation of the globe, and had chosen the difficult route around the Horn for the very challenge it would provide. "I hate being frightened," he said later, "but, even more, I detest being prevented by fright."

But the sea can be an infinitely treacherous and unforgiving mistress, and on occasion it will lash out in such wildly unpredictable ways that neither the most careful planning nor the most skillful seamanship will serve to withstand it. Who would expect, for example, that a freak wave, tall as a seven-story building, would suddenly rise behind his boat and flip it transom over mast truck in a catastrophic somersault? Or that an enormous shark would mistake his boat for another fish and ram a hole through its bottom? Yet these astounding mishaps, and others like them, do in fact occur, as the stories on the following pages testify. Just as astounding, the victims have survived to tell about them.

Each of the survivors owed his life to a combination of remarkably good seamanship, ingenuity and coolness under fire. Though none of the particular disasters could have been foreseen, each person was, in a sense, prepared to meet it. For in every case, the victim possessed reserves of know-how and fortitude that allowed him to deal with the crisis at hand. And their stories hold lessons in survival for anyone—from a round-the-world voyager to a family on an offshore weekend—who may find himself in deep trouble at sea.

*Flung overboard by a wave during the 1960 Bermuda Race, Jack Weston brandishes a flashing strobe light to guide his rescuers to him. After he swam to the light, he failed to realize, in the dark and confusion, that it was attached to a life ring, and he treaded water until he was picked up. Strobe lights of this type, which are visible for a distance of many miles under normal conditions, have since been declared mandatory equipment for all boats on Bermuda Races.*

## Man Overboard

On the stormy sixth day of the 1960 Bermuda Race, the yawl *Scylla,* under a small jib, heavily reefed main and mizzen, drove south through the Gulf Stream against 50-knot head winds and 35-foot waves. At about midnight, crewman Jack Weston came off watch and, unhooking his safety harness from the railing, started down the companionway. At that moment, the boat swung violently into the trough of a wave. As the vessel lurched, Weston popped out of the hatch like a champagne cork. Sea water washing heavily over the deck swept him under the port life line and into the sea.

Despite the pitch black of mid-ocean storm conditions, another crewman, who was tending the mizzen, saw Weston go. Crying "Man overboard!", the mizzen-hand heaved over a life ring with a rescue light attached to it. At the same time, the helmsman checked *Scylla's* heading on the compass and called it out to the navigator, who noted it down. If Weston was to be found as quickly as possible, the boat would have to be put into a 180° turn and sailed back along a reciprocal course. To prepare for the turn, the crew began taking down sail and got ready to start up the engine.

So far, *Scylla's* rescue procedures were almost textbook perfect. But as often happens under stress and storm, everything started to go wrong. The rescue light had fouled in the mizzen; fortunately, the skipper had a backup, a powerful electronic strobe light. Quickly thrown overboard, it began pulsing brilliantly.

Then, with the sails already struck, the engine failed to start. The battery was dead; but again, forethought saved the situation. Before sailing, Weston himself had made *Scylla* a present of a 12-volt spare battery and a pair of jump cables. They were instantly hooked up, and the engine rumbled to life.

Weston, meanwhile, flailed about miserably in *Scylla's* wake. "I had no hope they could get back to me," he said later. "I wondered how long it would take to drown, and what it would feel like." Then he caught sight of the strobe light, flashing perhaps a hundred yards away. Unable to swim for it along the surface of the cresting seas, he set off in a series of underwater dives.

When he reached the light, Weston began treading water and waving the strobe overhead. Finally the boat hove into sight, and Weston was grappled aboard by two crewmen—exhausted and still thoroughly frightened, but safe.

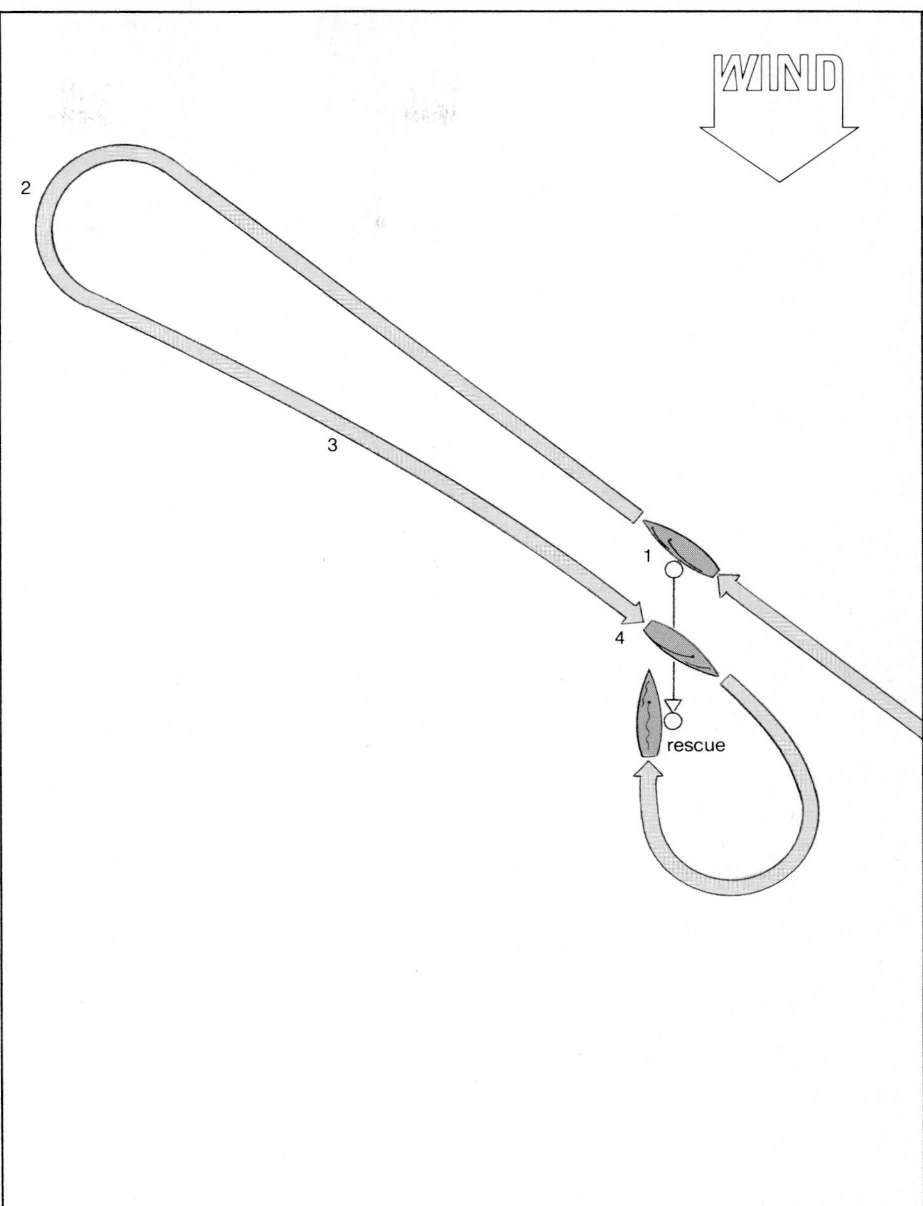


*The diagram above shows the path Scylla followed while rescuing Weston. After Weston was catapulted into the sea (1), the crew struck the sails and started the diesel to jibe the boat around. But heavy seas lifted the propeller out of water so often that the jib had to be raised to assist with the turn (2). Taking a return course (3) that allowed for Weston's being swept to leeward, Scylla approached downwind on a port tack, so that the crew could haul him aboard on the lee side (4). But the wind carried the boat by too fast for a pickup. Scylla had to jibe again and headed into the wind; Weston was lifted aboard by a swell after almost an hour in the water.*

*Holed by a huge white shark in the Indian Ocean, the junk-rigged yacht Galway Blazer II sails close-hauled on port tack. Only by heeling the boat well over and holding to this tack could skipper William King keep the damaged area above water. But the course took him ever farther out to sea. He was 400 miles from Australia when the incident occurred; by the time he had patched the hull and could turn back, he had gone another 200 miles. Believing that red antifouling paint had appeared to the shark as blood and had provoked the attack, King later painted the craft's underside green.*

## Stove by a Shark

In December the southern Indian Ocean is normally blessed with sparkling days, ample breezes and few cares for the sailor. It was on just such a morning, on December 15, 1971, that Commander William King, a former British submarine skipper in his mid-sixties, was heading west off the tip of Australia on his way to Cape Horn—"alone with my lovely boat in the ocean," he later wrote. Suddenly a horrifying impact rocked the boat, opening a splintered three-foot wound in its hull. Rushing on deck from the cabin King saw a green swirl astern—the trail of a huge shark that had just rammed him.

King's boat, the 42-foot *Galway Blazer II,* had been custom designed and fitted out to meet almost any challenge the sea might offer. Junk-rigged for easy handling, her cigar-shaped, laminated plywood hull was built to withstand any amount of battering by the sea—but not a chance-in-a-million shark attack.

The hull was stove in underwater on the lee side, but by some quick and deft seamanship *(left)* King managed to turn his boat so that the hole rose above the surface. Next he began the enormous task of bailing out the ton or so of water the boat had shipped before he changed tacks. Lacking an electric bilge pump, he had to hand-pump every 10 to 15 minutes for the next four days, breaking only to eat, catnap and perform major patchwork on the hull, both inside and out. Fortunately, the plywood at the point of impact had not completely ruptured; however, its glued laminations had sprung apart and it had many small rents.

By the fourth day most of the water had been pumped from the hull, and King could concentrate on adding more bracing and caulking to improve his repair. Five days later he felt confident enough to put the damaged area below water and turn back to Fremantle, Australia, 600 miles away. As he entered the harbor on December 30, after having ridden out 40-knot winds en route, a kindly Australian voice called out to him from the dock: "You look cut up. How about a nice strong cup of tea?"

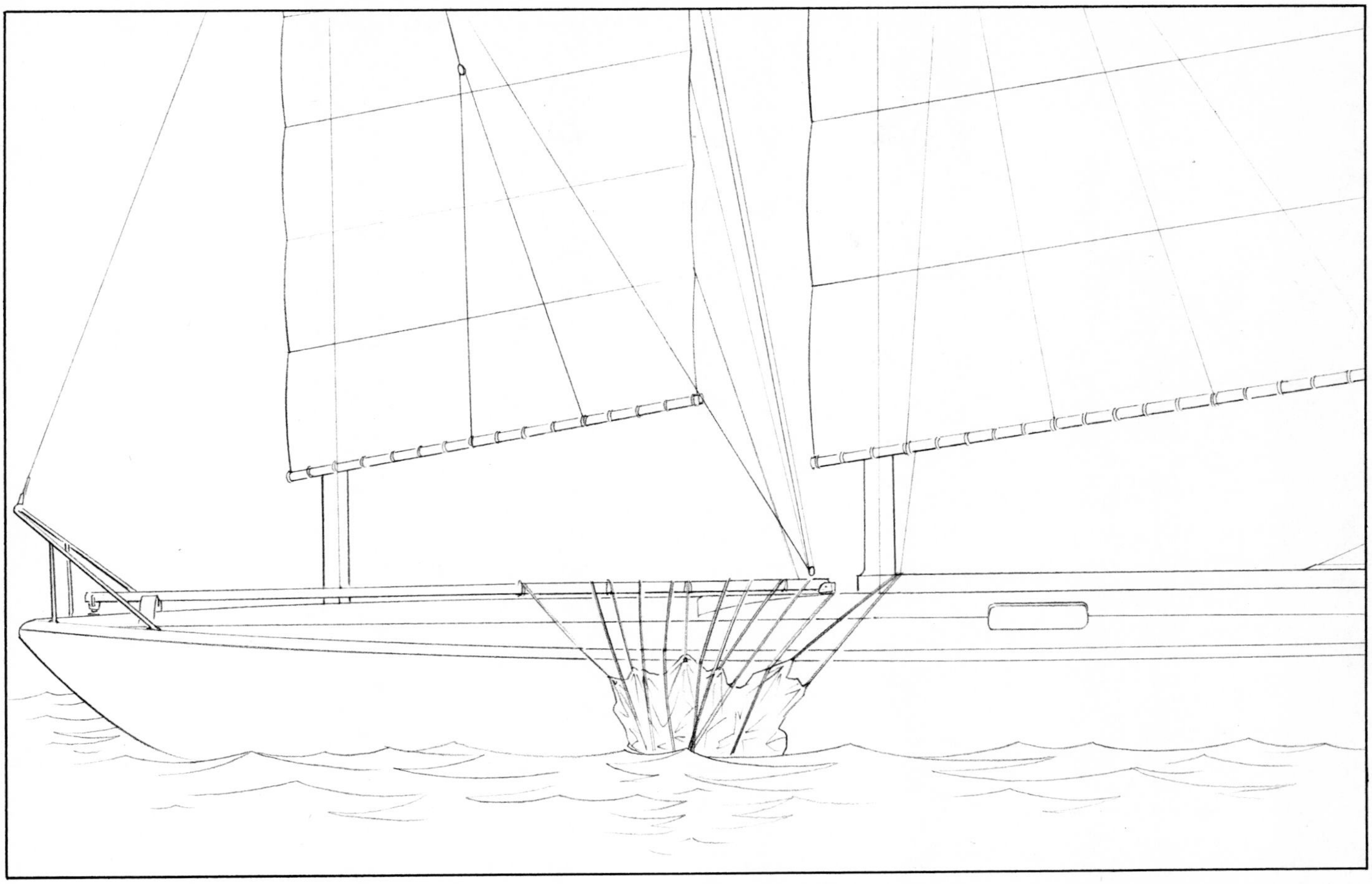

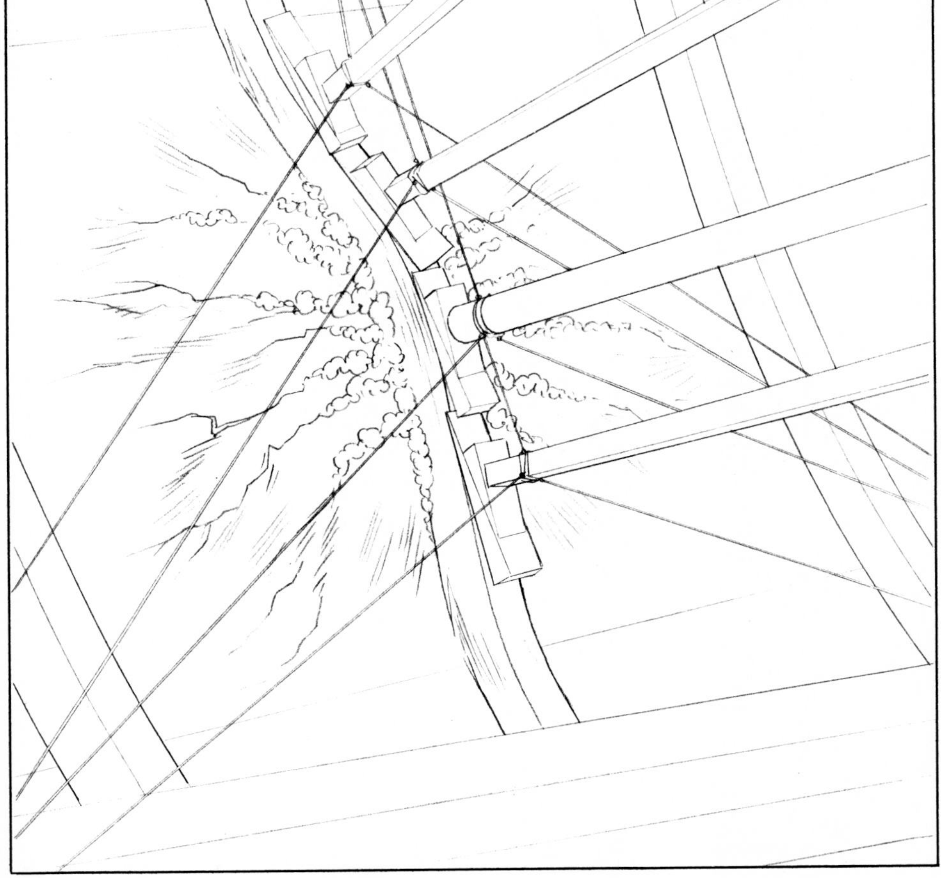

*Exterior patching consisted of multiple layers of foam rubber, sailcloth, a hatch cover and even King's waterproof rubber trousers, all bound securely by 13 separate lines wrapped around the hull and tied down like the ribbons on a Christmas package. The trussing temporarily kept water out but made the boat very sluggish; when King hit gale-force head winds a day from port, he had to bear off until the storm blew itself out.*

*Internal bracing shored up a vertical rib that lay across the center of the damaged area and held it together. Although the rib was sprung inward, King managed to keep it from breaking by wedging a spare boom, sawed down to the width of the cabin, from the rib's center to a structural member on the cabin's opposite side. For further support, King added struts cut from other pieces of wood on the boat, held in place by wedges and supported by a network of lashings.*

*Running under bare poles in winds of hurricane force and trailing 60 fathoms of three-inch hawser as a sea anchor, the ketch Tzu Hang is overtaken by a massive wave in the South Pacific. The sea lifted the stern vertically, then threw it over the bow, turning the boat belly up. The weight of the keel righted the boat immediately, but only after virtually all the vessel's abovedecks gear had been torn away.*

## A Ruinous Somersault

In the southern Pacific between Australia and Cape Horn, waves sweep 6,000 miles across an uninterrupted stretch of sea. During storms they can build to terrifying and destructive heights of 60 feet and more. Sailing with her husband, Miles, and a friend through these latitudes in February of 1957, Beryl Smeeton glanced aft from the helm of the 46-foot ketch *Tzu Hang* and saw just such a mountain of water rushing down on her. The wave caught the boat, turned it in a timber-shattering somersault called a pitchpole, and flung Beryl into the frigid ocean.

Her safety line had been broken, and so had a shoulder blade. Despite the injury, she swam 30 yards through stormy seas to reach the dismasted wreck, where her husband and the friend, John Guzzwell, were struggling to get out on deck.

The damage to the boat was appalling. Masts, tiller, rudder, compass binnacle and dinghies had all been torn away. The wave had ripped off the doghouse, leaving a six-by-six-foot hole through which water was cascading. John, a skilled ship's carpenter, roofed the hole with a door and floorboards—peaked so as to let water run off—and nailed folded sails over his work. Meanwhile Beryl, below in the cabin, bailed furiously. Knowing that the debris floating in the cabin would clog the two bilge pumps, she used her good arm to fill and refill a bucket, which Miles hauled up through an aperture in the deck. The mariners continued bailing by hand for 12 hours, until the water had been lowered to the level of the bilges.

When they were finally able to pause a moment and take stock of their situation, they found to their great relief that their sextants, chronometer and navigational books were intact; bits of charts could be pieced together; and the belowdecks jumble included enough unspoiled food and fresh water to last three months. They also had wood, tools, screws, wire and sails to rerig the crippled boat for a journey north to calmer waters.

John managed to fashion a mast and tiller of sorts *(pages 70-71)* to put them on course toward Chile, more than 1,000 miles away. But to make significant progress they found they needed more canvas and a stronger, taller rig to carry it. It took them almost a month to get these improvements in place. When the job was done they were finally able to relax. Indeed, they were so pleased and confident with their situation that, as land drew near, they triumphantly resolved to refuse a tow if one were offered.

*After the accident Tzu Hang was left with decks almost awash. The bowsprit had broken in two; shattered masts and spars lay strewn in the water—though still attached to the boat by the shrouds; the engine, totally submerged, was useless. Miles Smeeton is shown here standing on the engine housing, looking out the opening left by the sheared-off doghouse as his injured wife swims back to the boat.*

*Within six days of the accident, carpenter John Guzzwell had rigged a 14-foot mast made from two splintered spars: the spinnaker pole, which had sheared in two, was dovetailed to fit the surviving half of a spare staysail boom, and the joint was then bound by copper rivets and wire seizing. Held aloft by spare shrouds and stays, the jury mast could carry Tzu Hang's small square jib topsail, which tugged the vessel along at a bare one knot.*

*A full 28 days after the disaster, the three crew members completed a second jury-rig that allowed Tzu Hang to sail at a comfortable three to four knots. A new 20-foot mainmast—of hollow construction with inner bracing for added strength—was screwed together from spare planking and bunk boards. The working jib, cut down and fitted with a short boom, served as a mainsail; the storm jib was bent onto the new forestay. To balance the rig and increase overall sail area, the mariners set their original jury mast aft to act as a mizzen.*

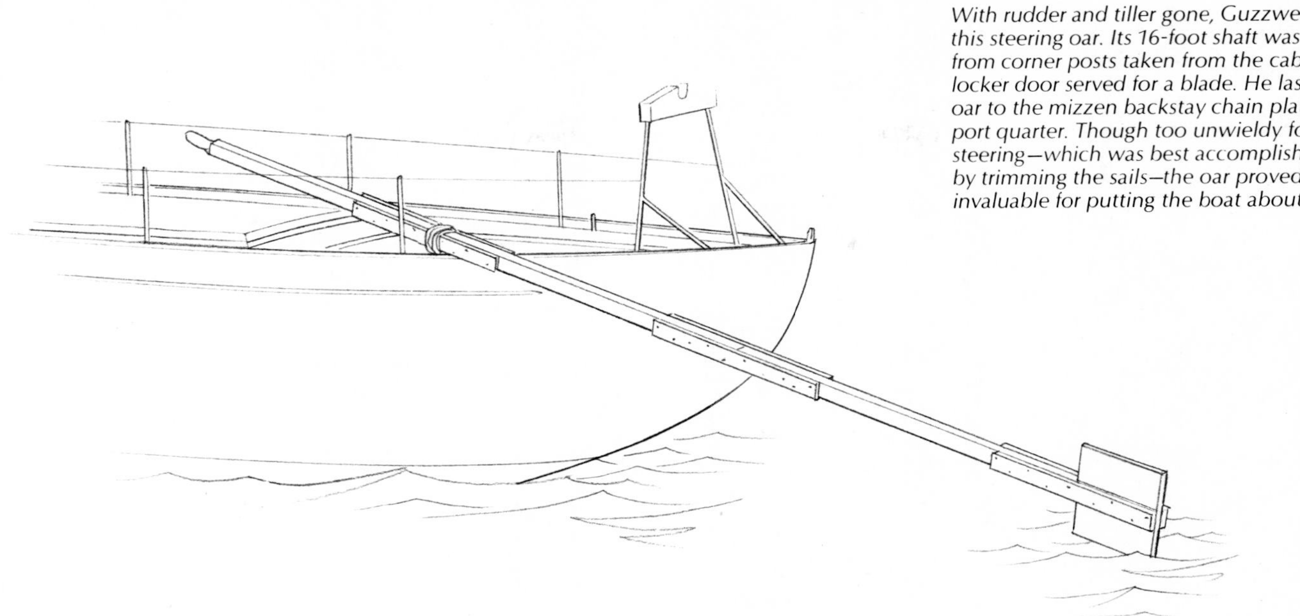

*With rudder and tiller gone, Guzzwell crafted this steering oar. Its 16-foot shaft was made from corner posts taken from the cabin, and a locker door served for a blade. He lashed the oar to the mizzen backstay chain plate on the port quarter. Though too unwieldy for normal steering—which was best accomplished by trimming the sails—the oar proved to be invaluable for putting the boat about.*

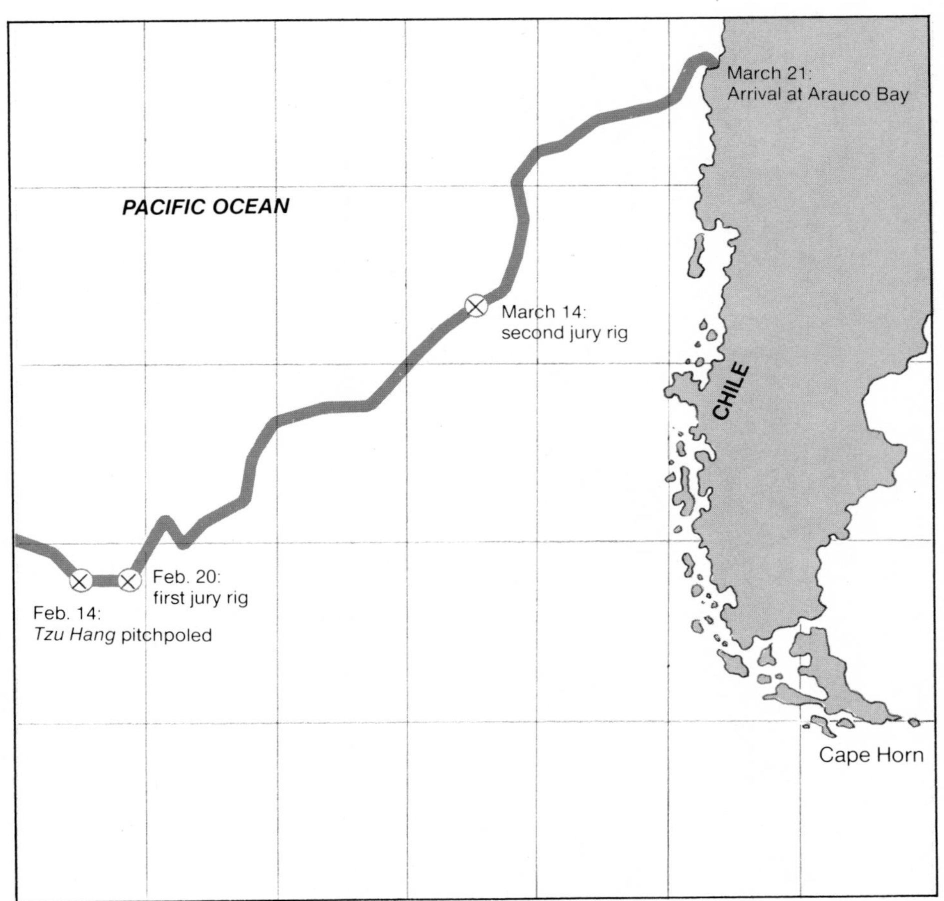


*Tzu Hang took this path to safe harbor after being pitchpoled some 1,100 miles west of Cape Horn. Instead of taking the direct course to land, the sea-wise Smeetons headed northeast toward calmer, more temperate waters. This course also freed the mariners from a strong easterly drift that might have swept them on around the Horn. On March 21, after sailing 1,350 miles, the battered vessel finally reached land at the small fishing town of Coronel in Arauco Bay, Chile.*

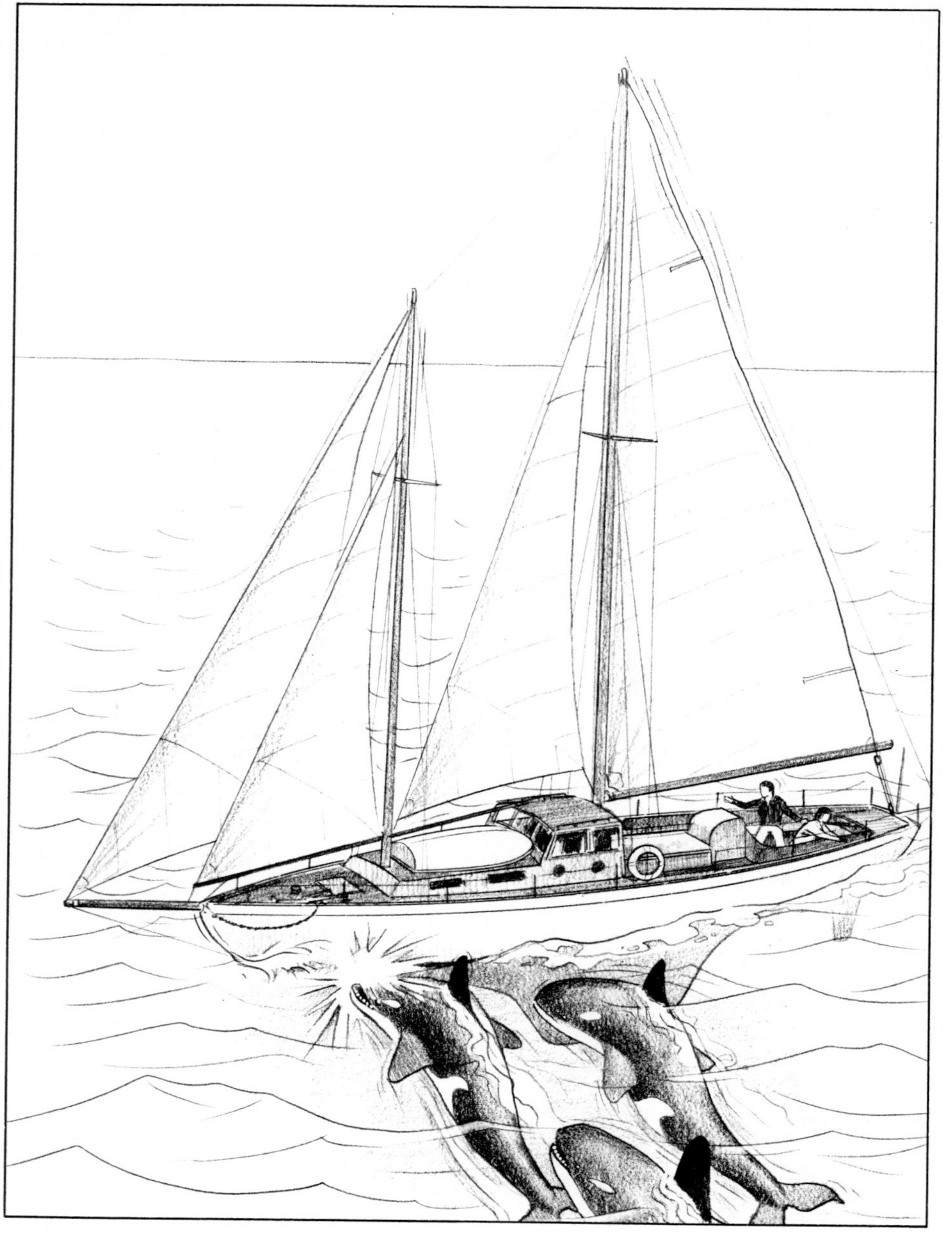

*The Robertsons' saga of survival began after three marauding killer whales inexplicably struck their schooner. Flooded through three gaping holes, the boat sank in just 60 seconds, allowing the voyagers barely time to launch both an inflatable rubber raft and a fiberglass dinghy. The dinghy had originally been rigged for sailing, but its mast and sail had gone down with the schooner; it held only two oars and 18 pints of fresh water. Aboard the raft was a paddle and an emergency survival kit containing a few dried provisions, some first-aid supplies, a repair kit and spare line. Before the schooner sank, the Robertsons were also able to salvage a genoa jib, a bag of Bermuda onions, a sewing kit and a vegetable knife from the galley.*

## Adrift for 1,000 Miles

"Rescue may come at any time but not necessarily when you expect it; and even if you give up hope you must never give up trying." Dougal Robertson, author of these words, should know. In June of 1972, two days' sail west of the Galápagos Islands, his schooner, *Lucette,* was stove in by whales and sunk. For the next 38 days, Robertson, his wife, three young sons and a 22-year-old passenger faced the Pacific in a life raft and dinghy. They stayed alive by a rare blend of grit, ingenuity and particularly fine seamanship on the part of the skipper, a veteran of 12 years in the British Merchant Navy.

When *Lucette* disappeared below the surface, the castaways' chances seemed anything but promising. They had salvaged a few simple tools, but food and water for only 10 days. Rowing back to the Galápagos was impossible because of a strong contrary current. The nearest shipping lanes were 400 miles north, in the area of equatorial calms called the doldrums. Only by reaching this region could the survivors hope to be picked up by a freighter or, failing that, to drift with the current (favorable in those more northerly latitudes) to Central America.

Robertson's primary concern was to keep the two small survival craft upright and moving in the South Pacific swell. His first solution was the unorthodox tandem rig at right. But soon an alarming new danger developed. As the raft worked in the seaway, a steady internal chafing began to wear holes in the rubber flotation compartments; by the 17th day the raft had sprung so many leaks it had to be abandoned, and the party continued north with the dinghy alone *(bottom right).*

For the first 17 days, the castaways lived in the 11-foot rubber life raft and were towed by the empty dinghy. The dinghy's sail was a cut-down section of the salvaged genoa, held aloft by an oar set in the mast step and held down by the raft paddle and the other dinghy oar. The genoa's wire luff line provided the tow rope. In a master stroke of seamanship, Robertson rigged the dinghy to proceed stern first, with its bow pointed into the following sea; otherwise it might have been swamped by waves breaking over the transom. A sea anchor prevented the raft from yawing. The canopy—standard for most life rafts—protected the passengers from overexposure to the sun.

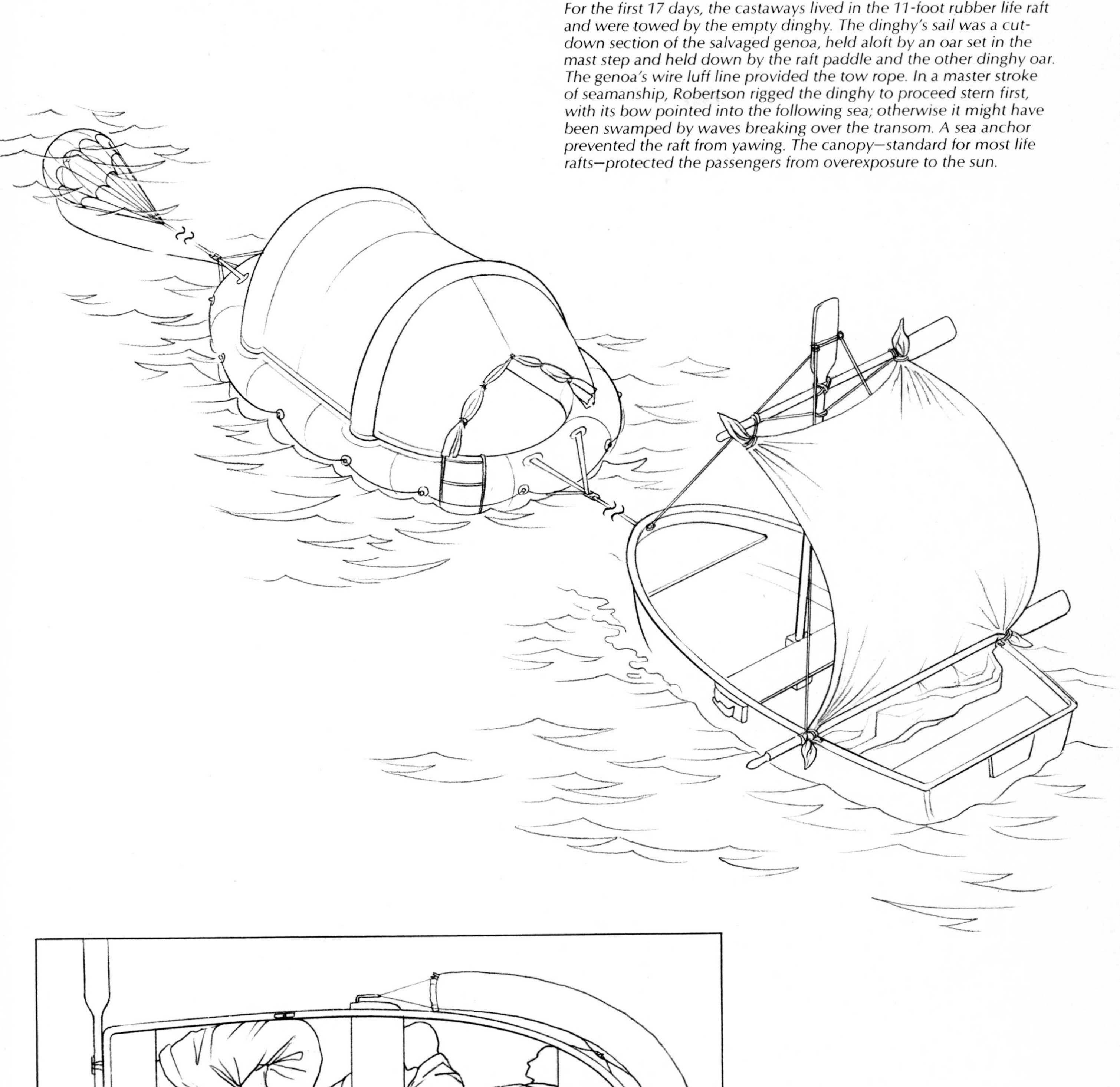

After the life raft began sinking and had to be jettisoned, all hands crowded into the dinghy for the next three weeks. The swell having subsided, the dinghy now moved head first, its bow buoyed up by a flotation collar fashioned from an inflatable support for the raft canopy. The boat's nine feet allowed cramped sleeping space for only five people: two curled up aft next to the water cans, two others next to the food supply in the bow, and one sprawled just forward of the center thwart. The other had to keep watch and bail out the water that constantly slopped in over the six-inch freeboard.

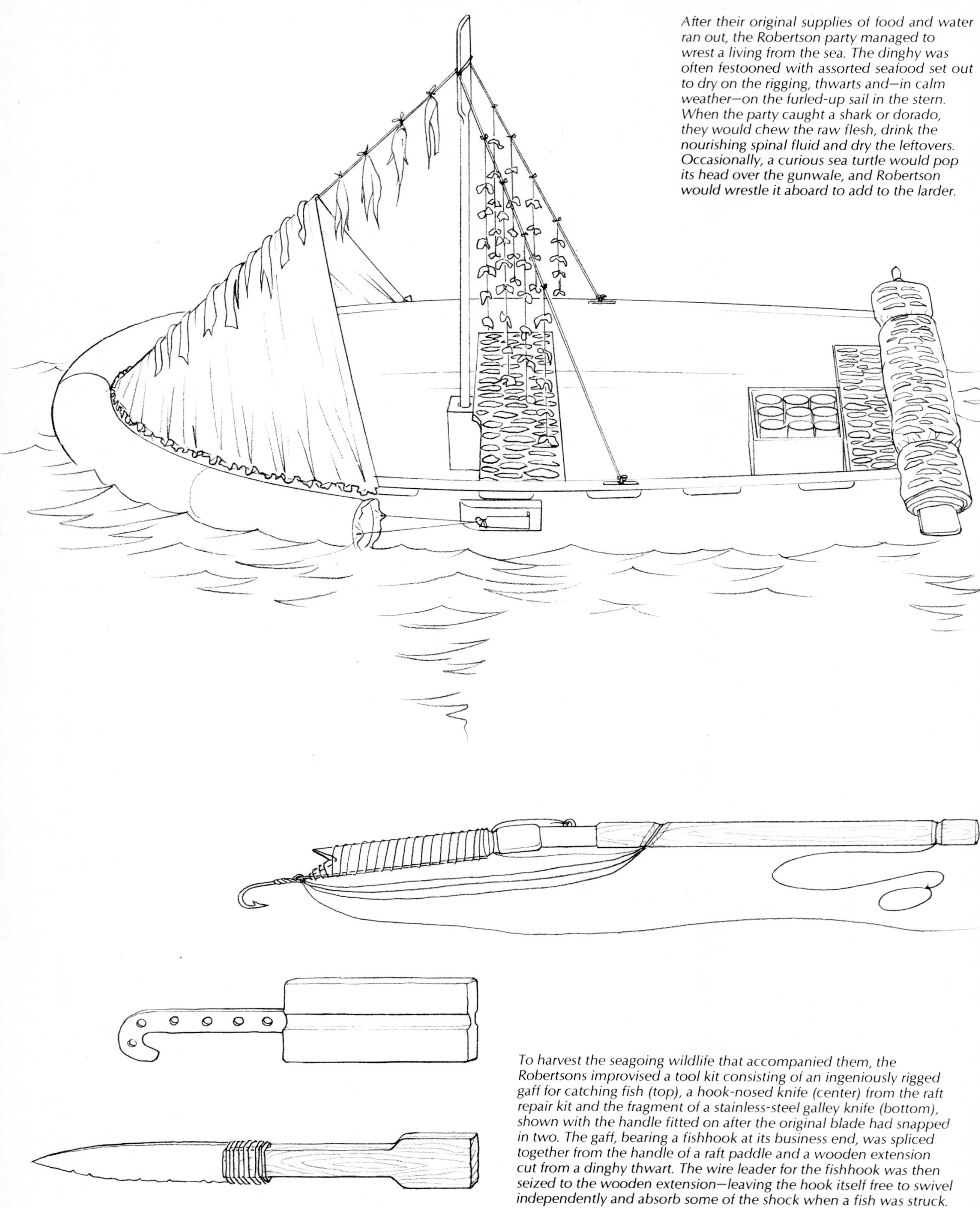

*After their original supplies of food and water ran out, the Robertson party managed to wrest a living from the sea. The dinghy was often festooned with assorted seafood set out to dry on the rigging, thwarts and—in calm weather—on the furled-up sail in the stern. When the party caught a shark or dorado, they would chew the raw flesh, drink the nourishing spinal fluid and dry the leftovers. Occasionally, a curious sea turtle would pop its head over the gunwale, and Robertson would wrestle it aboard to add to the larder.*

*To harvest the seagoing wildlife that accompanied them, the Robertsons improvised a tool kit consisting of an ingeniously rigged gaff for catching fish (top), a hook-nosed knife (center) from the raft repair kit and the fragment of a stainless-steel galley knife (bottom), shown with the handle fitted on after the original blade had snapped in two. The gaff, bearing a fishhook at its business end, was spliced together from the handle of a raft paddle and a wooden extension cut from a dinghy thwart. The wire leader for the fishhook was then seized to the wooden extension—leaving the hook itself free to swivel independently and absorb some of the shock when a fish was struck.*

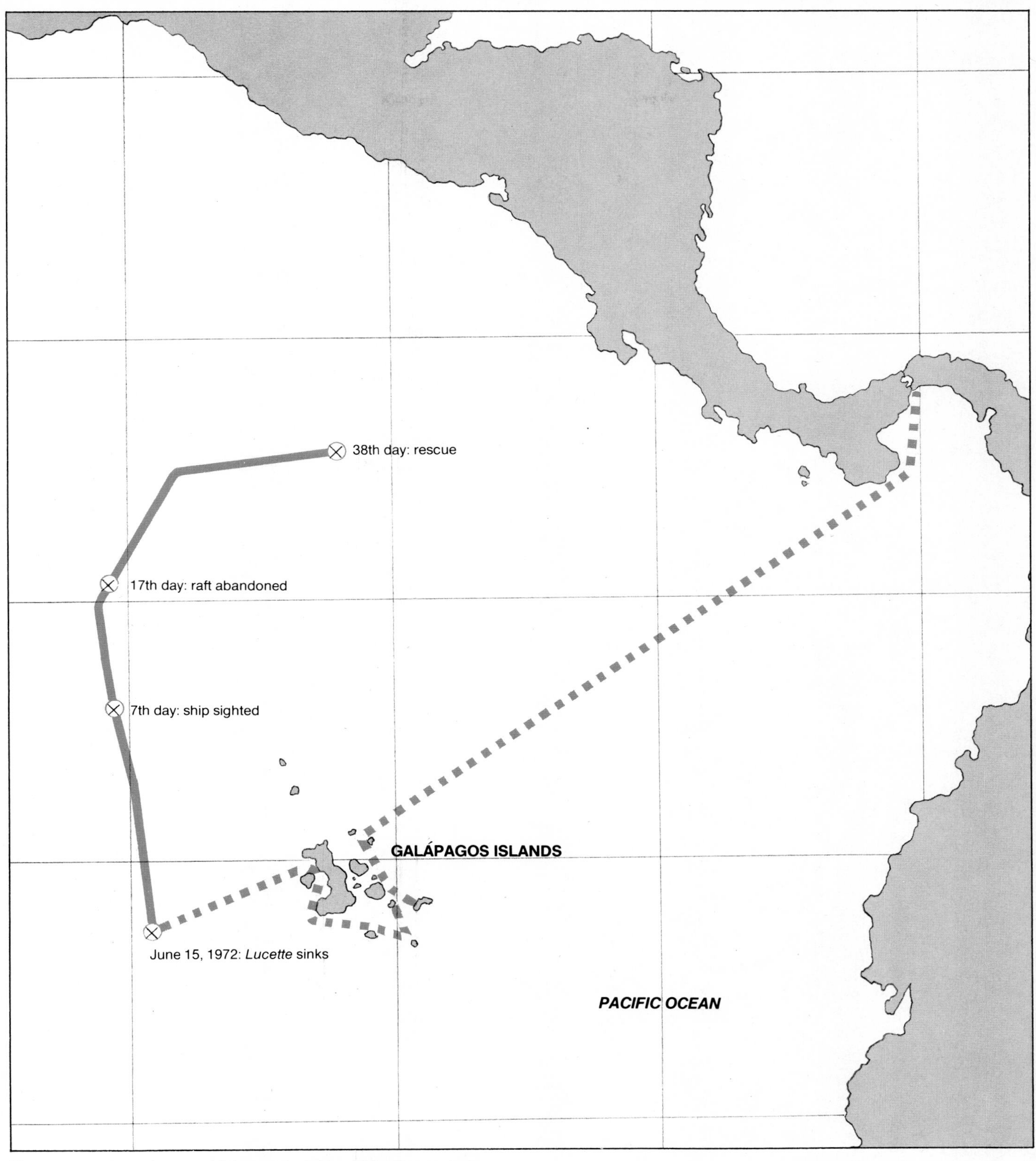


*The route to rescue began with Lucette's sinking 200 miles west of the Galápagos and proceeded first north and then east for 1,000 miles, assisted by the trade winds, the Humboldt Current and crosscurrents in the doldrums. Since he had no chart or compass, Robertson relied on the sun and stars to find direction, and on current speed and wind strength to determine boat speed. He noted each day's estimated position on a scrap of paper, along with major events: a heartbreaking moment on the seventh day when the castaways sighted a freighter steaming past; the sinking of the raft on the 17th day; and finally the rescue by the Japanese fishing boat Toka Maru II.*

2

Few things are more vital to the success of an offshore passage than knowledge of the boat's position at all times. Without this information the mariner cannot stay on course to his destination or plan his arrival to coincide with dwindling stores. Nor can he know whether he is sailing into a storm whose path has been predicted by weather reports, or stand clear of dangerous coasts and other nautical hazards. Though a few prosperous deepwater sailors rely on loran or other sophisticated radio systems to locate themselves, such automated plotting gear is beyond the pocketbooks of many boatmen. And, in any case, it is always vulnerable to breakdown or a failure of the boat's elec-

# SIGNPOSTS IN THE HEAVENS

trical system. For true self-sufficiency, an offshore voyager must know how to derive his position from the only natural signposts that exist far out on the open sea: the sun, the stars, the planets or the moon. These celestial bodies travel across the sky on consistent paths; hence they can serve as reference points just as effectively as any stationary object on earth.

In one way or another, sailors have been gleaning such guidance from the heavens for almost three millennia. The ancient Greeks, Phoenicians, Polynesians and Chinese utilized a crude form of celestial navigation in carrying out long-distance trade or oceanic migrations. From rough estimates of the height of celestial bodies above the horizon, they could gauge their progress north or south—but not east or west, a dimension at which they could only guess. During the Renaissance, European mariners improved the accuracy of their celestial fixes by devising such instruments as the astrolabe and the quadrant *(page 126)*—both of which were carried by Columbus to help him find his way to the New World.

The first real practitioner of modern-style celestial navigation was the Pacific explorer Captain James Cook of England, whose ships carried the basic complement of equipment used today. Included in his equipment were a sextant to make precision sights of heavenly bodies and a highly accurate clock whose readings, linked to the sightings and complemented by a series of calculations, allowed him to determine his longitude.

On the basis of a series of voyages between 1768 and 1779, Cook produced excellent charts of the Pacific. However, his charts and other feats of navigation were as much tributes to his enormous capacity for detail as to the excellence of his tools, for the mathematical calculations required for a precise fix in Cook's day could take a good hand as long as two hours. Happily, Yankee ingenuity alleviated this inconvenience only three decades after Cook's great voyages. Nathaniel Bowditch, a brilliant shipowner from Salem, Massachusetts, streamlined the mathematics so markedly that a navigator's calculating time was cut by at least half. His masterful book, *The New American Practical Navigator,* is still published in updated form by the Naval Oceanographic Office today and remains the most authoritative work in the field.

Despite the genius of Bowditch, today's navigator must still invest a fair degree of skill and energy in keeping track of his boat's whereabouts. His workday ordinarily includes at least seven different sessions with the sextant. Just before sunrise he takes sightings on three stars; this session is followed by two sun sights spaced a couple of hours apart during the morning; he then shoots the sun again exactly at noon, twice more in the afternoon, and ends the day with another round of star sights shortly after sunset. After each of these sessions, he must translate the sighting data into positions with the aid of special calculating and plotting work sheets. With all these labors, and often a share of watch duty as well, the navigator is likely to be the busiest man on the boat—and also the most indispensable.

*As seen through a sextant, the reflected image of the midmorning sun rests on the horizon—an illusion that makes possible an exact measurement of the sun's position in the sky.*

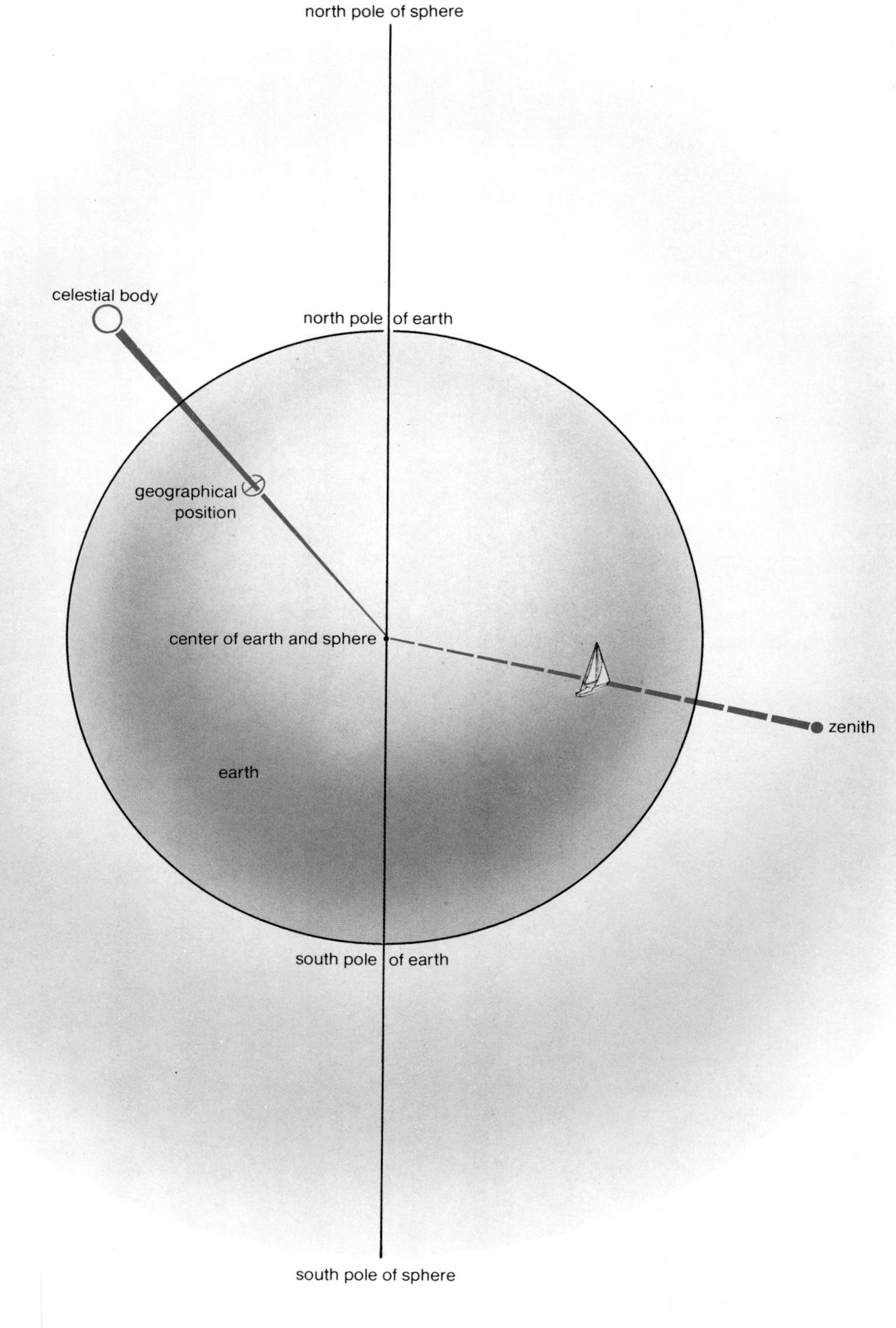


*This illustration shows the fundamental relationship between the earth and the shipboard navigator's theoretical celestial sphere. Note that the north and south poles of both are in direct alignment. A line drawn from the center of the earth to a given celestial body passes through a point on earth called the body's geographical position; another line, drawn from the center of the earth and through a boat, intersects the sphere at a point known as the zenith. These theoretical points are among the basic building blocks that a celestial navigator uses to determine his position at sea.*

## Companion Spheres

All of the calculations in celestial navigation are based on a highly simplified—and mathematically convenient—view of the universe. In this concept, the earth is surrounded not by limitless space but by an imaginary celestial sphere on which is placed every visible heavenly body. Furthermore, the earth does not rotate but remains stationary while the celestial sphere, concentric to the earth, revolves around it from east to west, carrying along the sun, stars and other planets.

The celestial sphere is considered by navigators to have directly corresponding poles and latitudes in common with the earth, and vice versa. Longitude lines cannot be matched up in this fashion, but earthly longitudes nonetheless are linked to celestial bodies by the system described below and overleaf.

Whenever a navigator makes celestial observations or calculations, he assumes the celestial sphere has halted. He thus deals with a situation in which the relative positions of his boat and the celestial bodies are frozen at one particular instant of time, allowing him to work out his position without having to deal with the prohibitively complex factors that movement of the sphere would introduce.

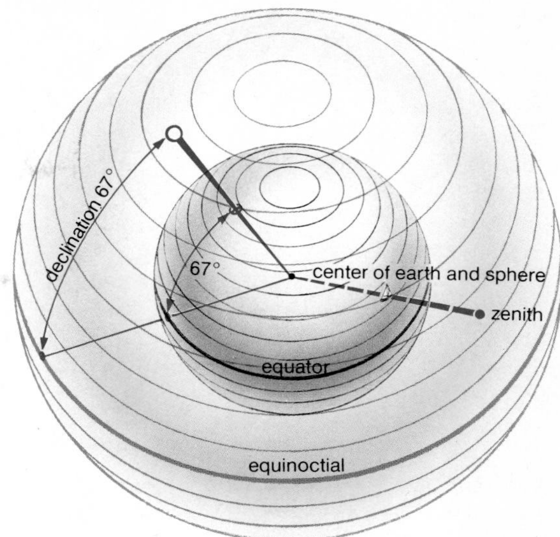


*On the celestial sphere, the counterparts to earth's parallel latitudes are called lines of declination. Like latitudes, the lines of declination start from a center line—the equinoctial, equivalent to the earth's equator—and are marked off in major divisions of 10° north and south until they reach 90° at each pole; between are smaller divisions of single degrees, minutes and seconds. A line drawn from the center of the earth to a celestial body will pass through the earth's surface at a latitude that matches the body's declination; here, the common figure is 67° N.*

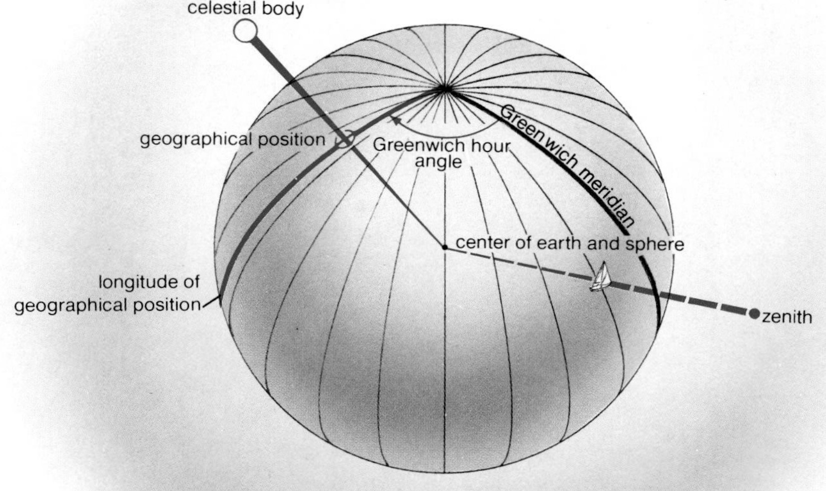


*Unlike latitudes, longitudes cannot be transferred from the earth to the sphere, since by navigational convention the earth and its longitudes stand still while the sphere rotates. However, when the imaginary sphere stops for a navigational problem, the geographical position of any celestial body is located along a particular earth longitude; this longitude is used in an important measurement called Greenwich hour angle. The body's Greenwich hour angle equals the number of degrees westward from a base longitude called the Greenwich meridian to the geographical-position longitude.*

## The Uses of Longitude

Longitude plays a special role for the celestial navigator because it is related to both distance and time. Longitude lines —denoted, like latitudes, in degrees, minutes and seconds—are drawn to the east and west of a base, or prime meridian, that passes through Greenwich, England, and is designated as zero degrees. They march around the world in ascending numerical designations until they meet on the opposite side from Greenwich at a longitude designated as 180°.

Degrees of both longitude and latitude can be translated into distance. However, while a degree of latitude encompasses a fixed distance—precisely 60 nautical miles—the number of miles to a degree of longitude varies according to the latitude, as shown at right.

Longitude's link with time is rooted in its relationship to the movement of the sun—and, in fact, the entire celestial sphere—around the stationary globe. Each degree of longitude represents the distance the sun travels across the earth in four minutes at an equinox, that is, when the sun is directly above the equator (which occurs at the end of the third weeks of March and September). Major longitude lines are customarily drawn on charts and maps of the world every 15°, the distance the sun covers in an hour.

In navigational calculations, elapsed time of the sun's movement—like the longitudinal scale to which that time relates —is measured from Greenwich. There, at the Royal Observatory, is a 24-hour atomic clock that precisely designates the only time of real importance in celestial navigation—Greenwich Mean Time (GMT). Every navigator has a clock that registers Greenwich Mean Time no matter where his boat is located on the earth, and he uses this base time as another building block in establishing his position.

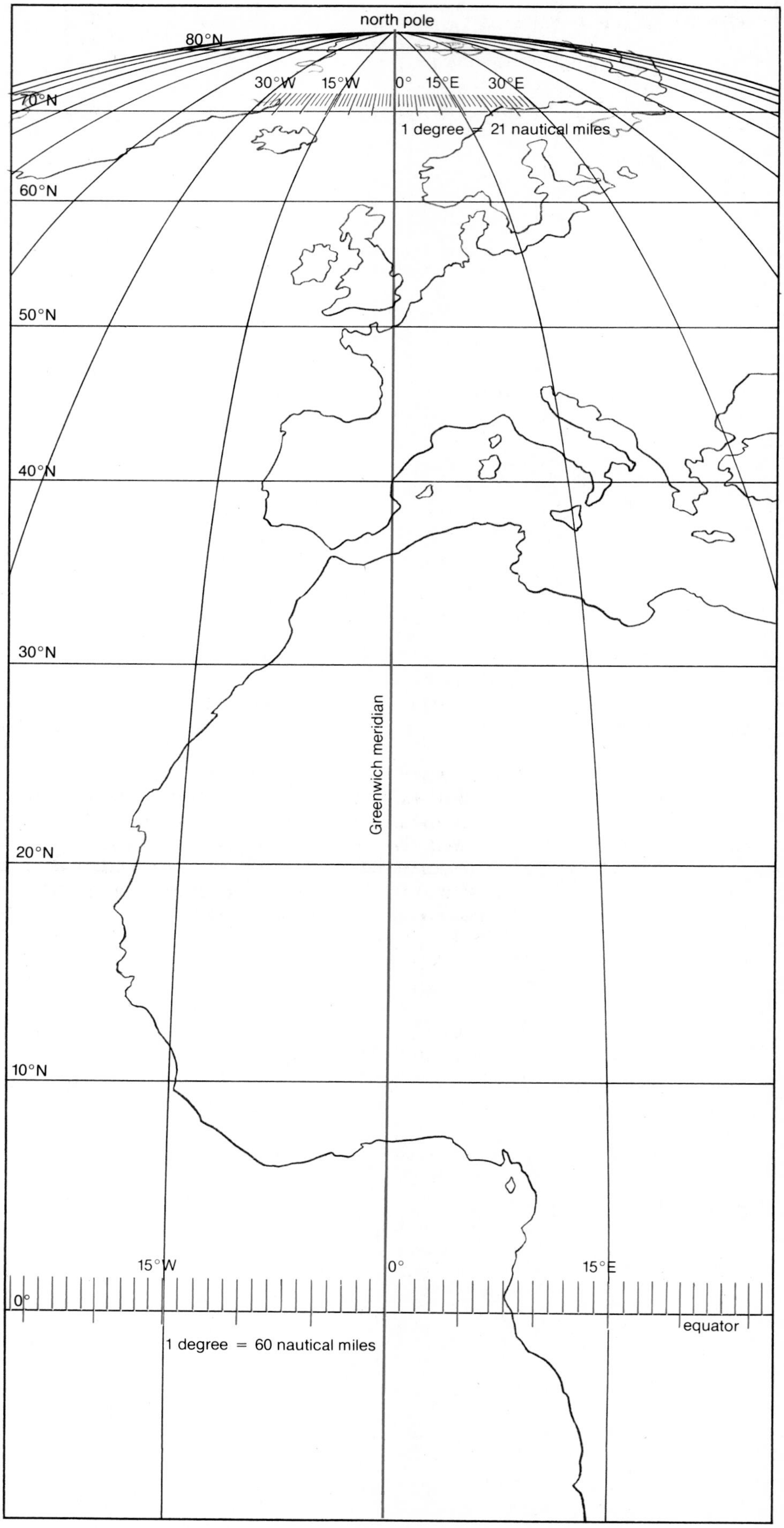

*All longitudinal lines and measurements are noted on charts as being east (E) or west (W) of the 0° meridian that goes through Greenwich in southeastern England. Since the earth is a sphere, the distance between these lines is far greater at the equator than near the poles, as shown by the scales on this chart. However, regardless of the latitude at which a navigator finds himself, degrees of longitude always have the same value in his calculations.*

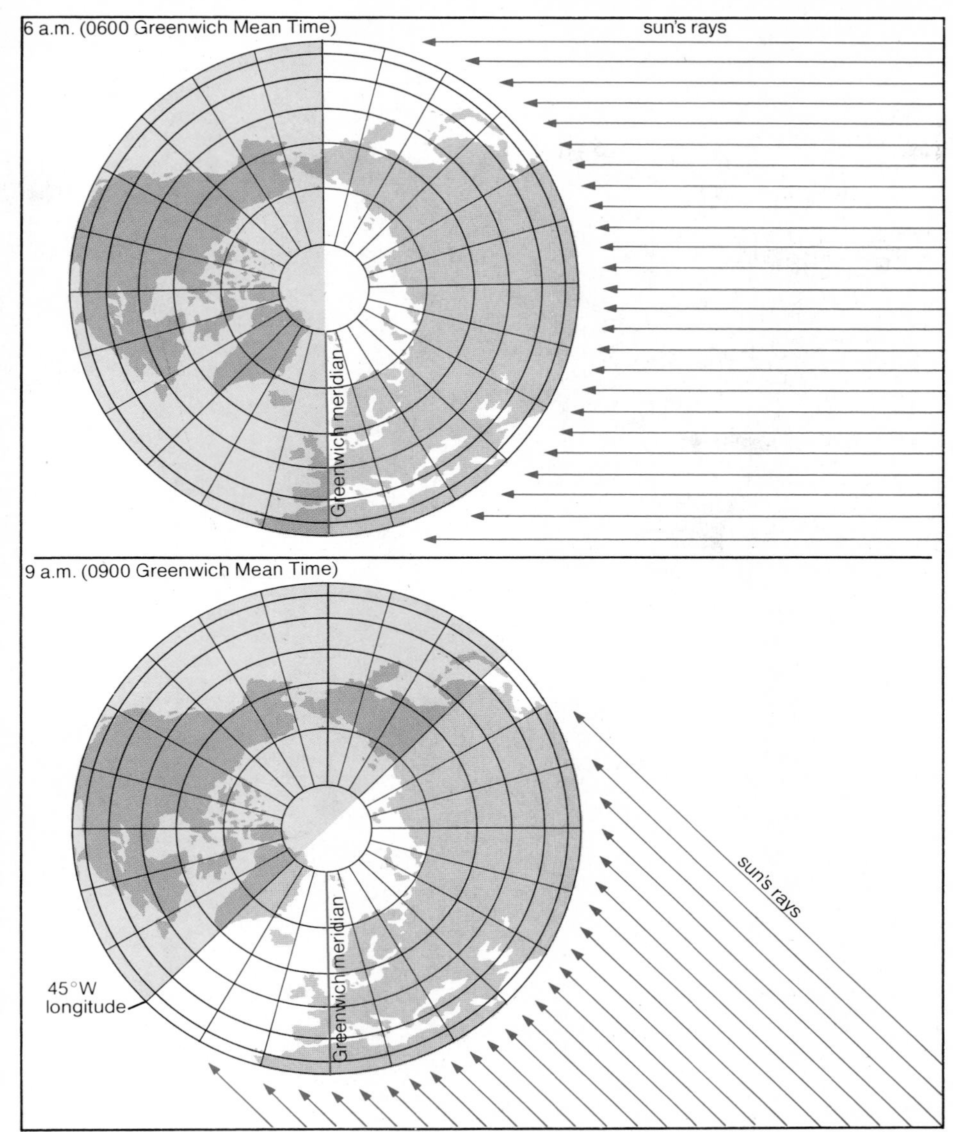


*The relationship of longitude and time is revealed in the two views of the earth at left, both looking down on the North Pole, with the sun above the equator. Dawn arrives all along the Greenwich meridian at 6 a.m. (top) —expressed as 0600 Greenwich Mean Time. Three hours later (below), the sun's rays have moved 45° west of Greenwich—though the distance traveled in miles varies with the latitude. Because the movement of the sun or any other celestial body is uniform, a navigator who knows the exact time also knows the celestial body's exact position as observed from any point on earth—another aid in computing a boat's position.*

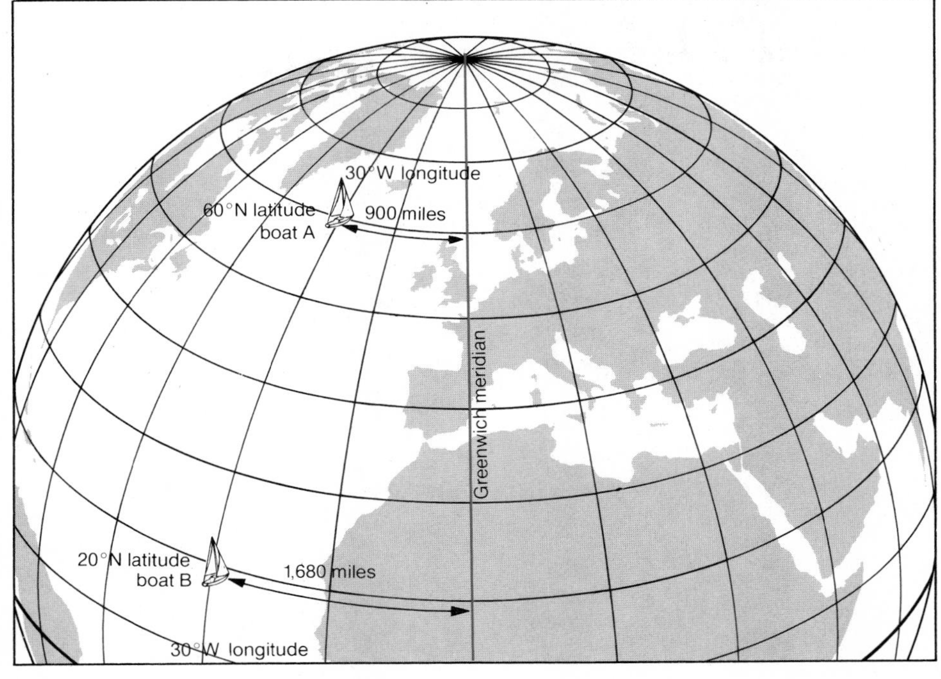


*As with the sun, at any given longitude the lateral distance of a boat from the Greenwich meridian depends on its latitude. Both boat A and boat B are at 30°W longitude. However, boat A, at 60°N latitude, is just 900 nautical miles from the prime meridian, while boat B, at 20°N latitude, is 1,680 nautical miles from the prime meridian.*

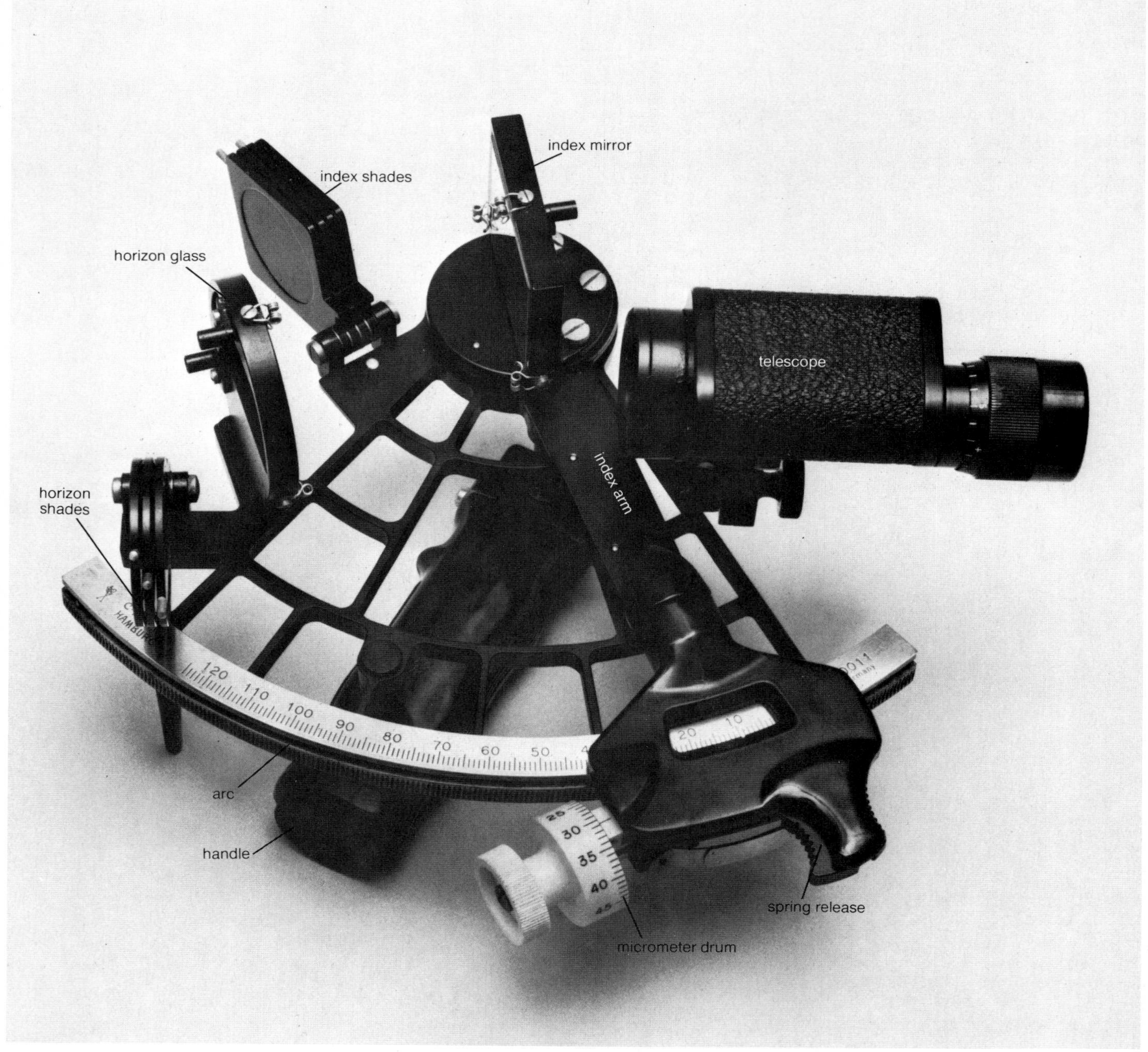


*The sextant is a hand-held optical device weighing about four pounds. A navigator peers through a telescope that magnifies the image of a celestial body reflected from the index mirror and horizon glass. A spring release allows the index arm and its mirror to be moved so as to bring the image to horizon level; when the body is positioned on the horizon, its altitude is indicated on an arc marked in degrees. A micrometer drum operates in conjunction with the spring-release mechanism (page 85) to supply a detailed reading of minutes of arc.*

# The Vital Sextant

An offshore navigator's most useful instrument is the sextant *(left)*. In essence, the sextant is a sophisticated optical protractor that determines a celestial body's angle of elevation above the horizon. This bit of geometric information, called an altitude, is essential in determining the exact location of a boat in the open sea.

In order to measure the altitude of the sun, a star, a planet or the moon, a navigator must manipulate the sextant so the body's reflected image appears to rest on the horizon. As shown at right, the sextant achieves this illusion by bouncing the light rays of the celestial body off two reflecting surfaces—a movable index mirror and a stationary horizon glass—before delivering the rays through a small telescope to the eye of the viewer.

The horizon glass is vertically divided into two portions—one clear glass, the other a mirror. When the navigator looks through the telescope at this two-part optical element, he sees a vertically split view. The clear glass provides a window through which the sea's horizon is visible. At the same time, the reflected image of the celestial body shows on the clear glass and even more plainly on the mirror portion (in effect, the mirror plays a backup role, helping the navigator to sight dimmer bodies whose reflections on the glass are faint).

Filters of varying densities, known as shades, are mounted on pivots near both the index mirror and the horizon glass to protect the eyes of the navigator from the reflected light of the sun—light whose harmful potential is compounded by the magnification of the viewing telescope. These shades can be swung out of the way for star, moon and planet sightings.

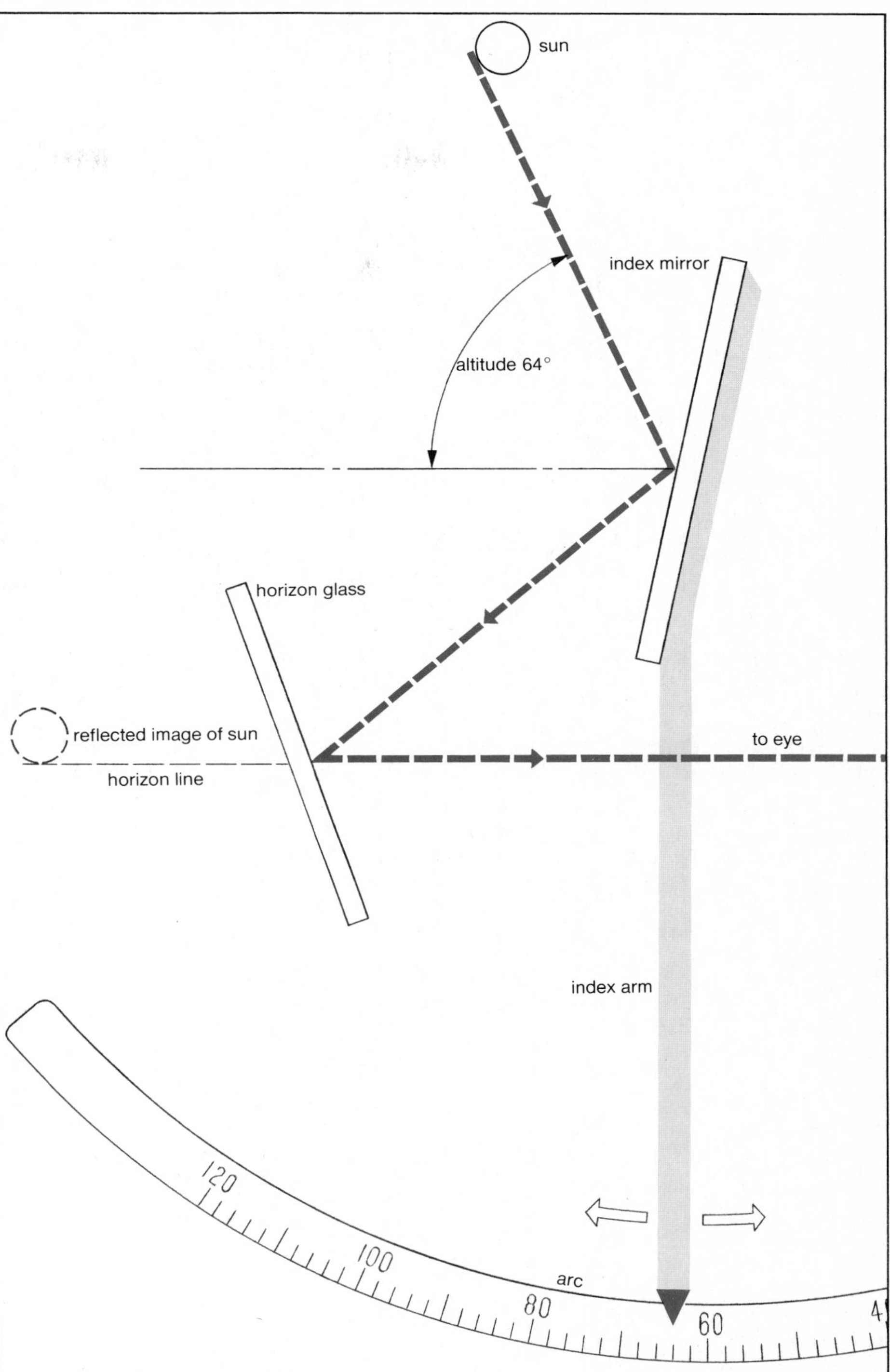


*A schematic view of the workings of a sextant shows how light rays from a celestial body are reflected first off the movable index mirror (top), then off a stationary horizon glass, to travel to the navigator's eye (blue line). The navigator adjusts the index mirror so that the reflected image of the celestial body (dotted circle) just appears to touch the horizon. In this case the angle of the incoming light rays above the horizontal (dotted blue line) is 64°, indicated on the arc at the bottom of the sextant.*

*Aiming his sextant at the horizon, a navigator takes a reading of the sun's elevation. The instrument is held perpendicular to the horizon with the right hand while the left closes around the spring-release grip that frees the index bar. Shades over the index mirror and in front of the horizon glass protect his eyes from the sun.*

## How to Work a Sextant

To learn how to sight and read a sextant, the navigator must invest some time in practice sessions, and since the sun is the most visible celestial body, it is the obvious choice for training purposes. Novices often familiarize themselves with the sextant by taking sightings from boats that are moored or docked, where conditions are more stable and more controllable than at sea.

Before undertaking a sun sighting, pivot at least two shades over the index mirror and one over the horizon glass. Squeeze the spring release firmly to slide the index bar backward along the arc until it is set at a low number. With the sextant held in the right hand, aim the telescope at a spot on the horizon directly under the sun. With the spring release still pressed tightly, move the index arm forward until the reflected image of the sun appears in the horizon glass. More shades may now have to be added for viewing safety and comfort.

Continue to work the index bar forward until the sun's reflection is close to the horizon. Then let go of the spring release and turn the micrometer drum with the left hand. This drum has a worm gear that meshes with teeth along the lower edge of the arc, and the rotation will gently adjust the sun's image into the desired position. The bottom curve of the sun should just make contact with the line of the horizon. Because the instrument must be vertical when the sun's image and horizon meet, a final check, called swinging the arc *(page 89)*, must be run.

As the sextant is lowered from eye level so that the altitude can be read, be careful not to turn the micrometer drum or jar the index arm. Note the degrees on the arc first, then the minutes of the micrometer drum *(top right)*. Then, either make an estimate of the reading in tenths of a minute—necessary for later calculations—or perform this refinement with the vernier scale that is provided on many sextants *(bottom right)*.

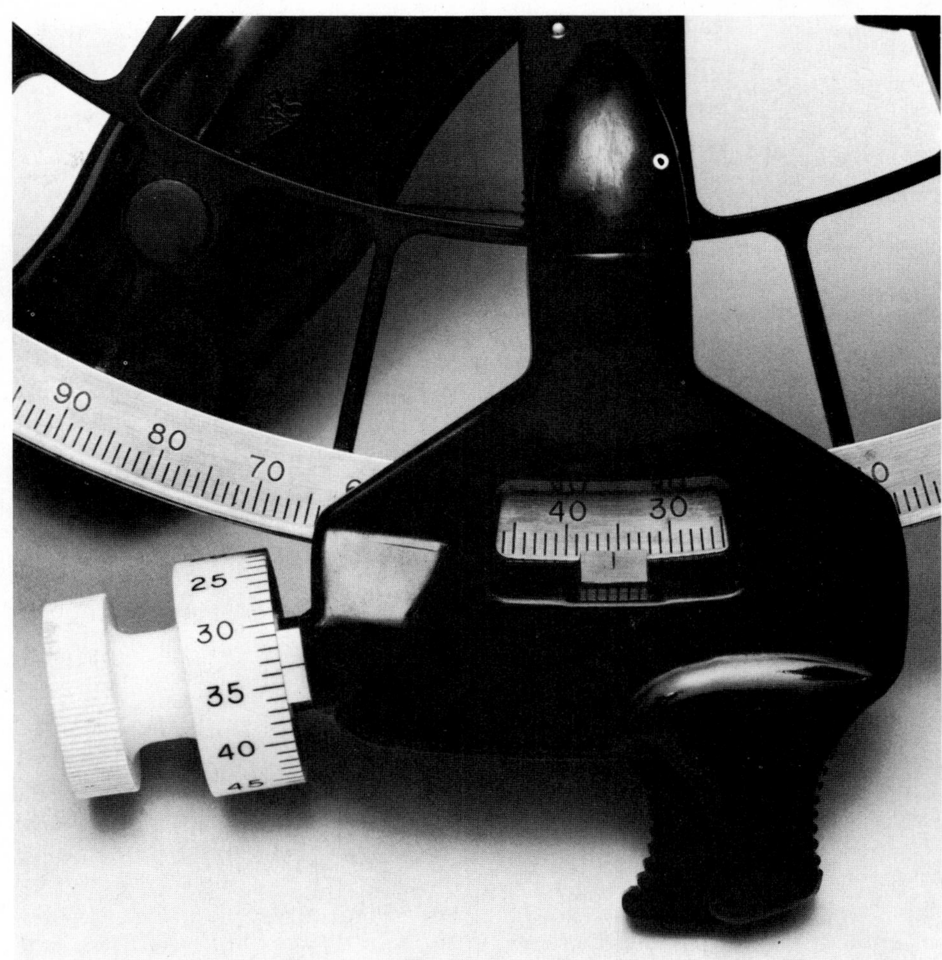


*To read the degree figure in the sextant, consult the indicator line on the window of the index bar; in this case, it points just past 35°. On the micrometer drum, the indicator line rests slightly more than halfway between 33 and 34 minutes, or 33.6 minutes. The altitude is thus 35°, 33.6 minutes.*

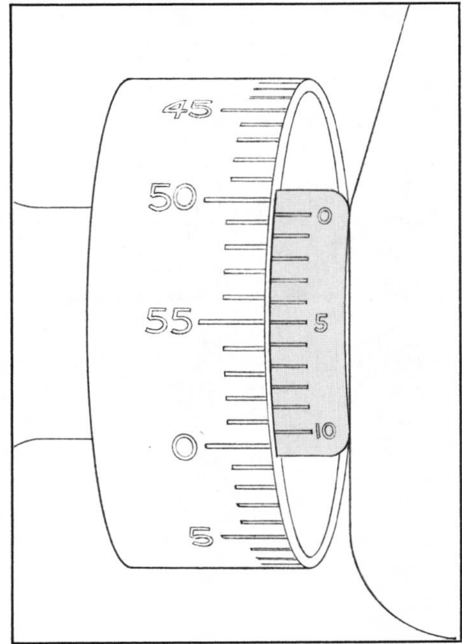


*Some sextants are fitted with a vernier scale (blue), adjacent to the micrometer drum, that reliably details an altitude reading to tenths of a minute. The zero mark on the scale indicates the number of minutes of altitude—in this case, 50—on the drum. To refine the reading further, find the vernier mark that lines up with a minute mark on the micrometer drum (only one pair of marks can be aligned at a time). This vernier mark is the decimal that should be added to the minute reading. Here, the 55-minute mark and the fifth mark on the vernier scale are aligned; thus the sextant reading is 50.5 minutes.*

*To test the alignment of the index mirror, set the index arm at about 60°, then place the sextant on its handle and legs so that the scale of the arc reflects in the mirror. If the scale and its reflection, viewed from the side, form a continuous image—as they do in the photograph above—the index mirror needs no adjustment.*

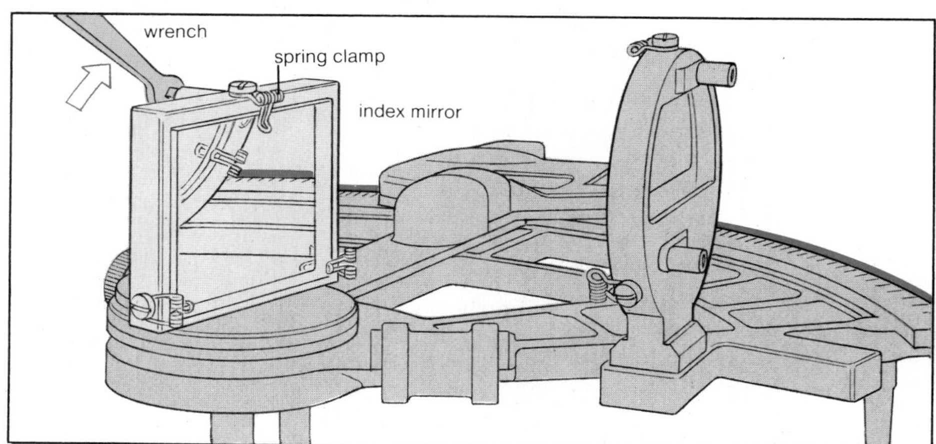


*Whenever the top of the index mirror is tilted forward, the reflection of the scale will appear to be higher than the actual scale, as at right (for clarity, the telescope is not shown). To bring the mirror back in line, loosen the screw behind the frame with the wrench; spring clamps pressing against the mirror's surface will force it backward.*

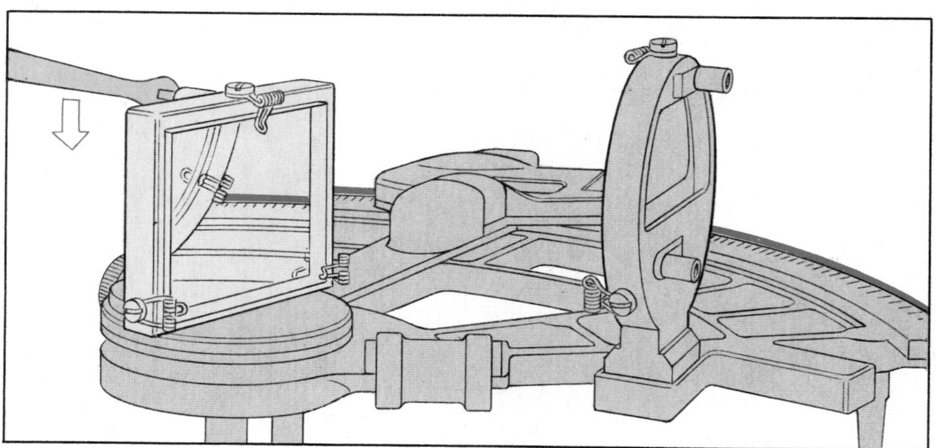

*If the reflection dips below the actual scale, the top of the index mirror is leaning backward from a plane that is perpendicular to the sextant. When this happens, tighten the adjustment screw with clockwise turns until the mirror is correctly aligned.*

## Lining Things Up

In order for a sextant to work properly, its two reflecting surfaces have to be in precise optical alignment. This means that both the index mirror and the horizon glass must be exactly perpendicular to the frame of the instrument; in addition, the horizon glass must be cocked at an angle that places it in a position parallel to the index mirror whenever the index arm is at 0°. Otherwise, the light rays from a celestial body will stray from their proper path through the instrument and will yield erroneous readings.

Correct alignment should never be taken for granted, since even the minor jolts of ordinary usage can cause the mirror and glass to slip out of position. Every few days at sea, a careful navigator readjusts the reflecting surfaces by means of screws fitted into their frames. The adjustments are performed with the aid of a miniature tool like the wrench shown here.

Corrections of the index mirror—always done first—are carried out simply by laying the sextant on its side and examining the reflection in the mirror, as explained at left. In order to make the horizon-glass adjustments, the navigator must look through the telescope at an object and manipulate two different screws until any hint of a double image is eliminated *(right)*.

Not every horizon-glass misalignment must be remedied by the adjustment screws. If a navigator knows that his altitude readings are awry by only three minutes of arc or less, he can make a so-called index correction—a mathematical compensation for a minor error. To determine if the error is within the manageable range, aim the sextant at the horizon, with the index arm set at 0°. If the horizon appears as an uninterrupted line, the instrument is properly aligned and has no index correction. If there is a double horizon image, turn the micrometer drum until the horizon again forms a single line. The reading on the drum is the amount of error due to misalignment and can easily be computed into final calculations.

For example, whenever the micrometer drum has been turned forward by one or two minutes, the index correction must be subtracted from the sextant reading to yield the correct altitude of a celestial body. When the micrometer drum has been turned backward and reads 59 or 58 minutes, the index correction must be added to the sextant reading. If the index correction exceeds three minutes, either plus or minus, the horizon glass should be manually readjusted.

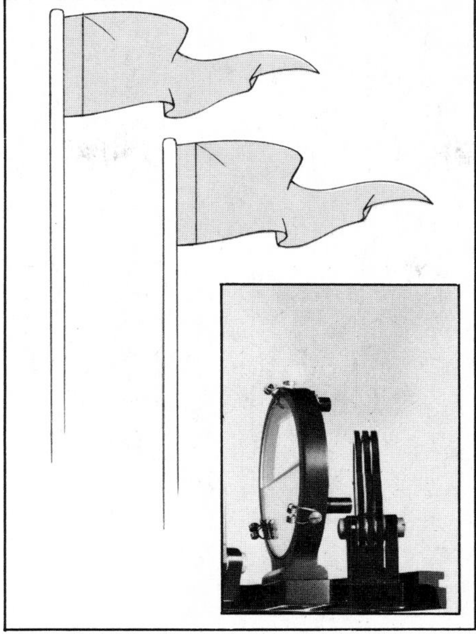

*To test for misalignment of a sextant's horizon glass (inset), set the index arm and micrometer drum at zero and aim the instrument either at a star or a nearby object, such as the pennant shown here. If the glass is not perpendicular to the frame of the sextant and also is incorrectly angled in relation to the index mirror, the view through the telescope will reveal a double image that is separated both vertically and horizontally —calling for both of the adjustments below.*

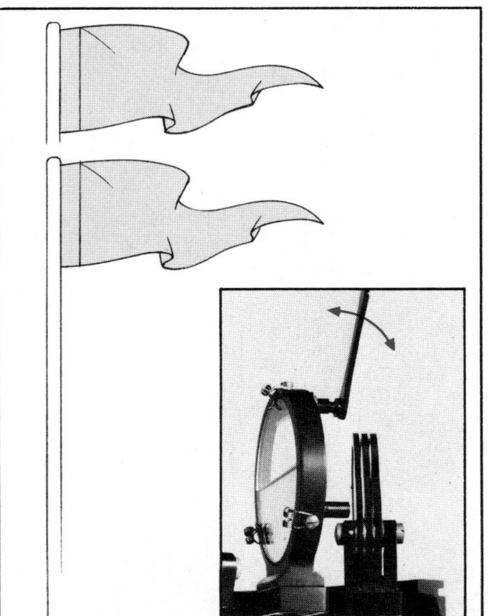

*In order to reset the horizon glass so that it is perpendicular to the instrument, insert the wrench into the screw farthest from the sextant's frame. While looking through the telescope, gently turn the wrench either clockwise or counterclockwise until the double image is vertically aligned.*

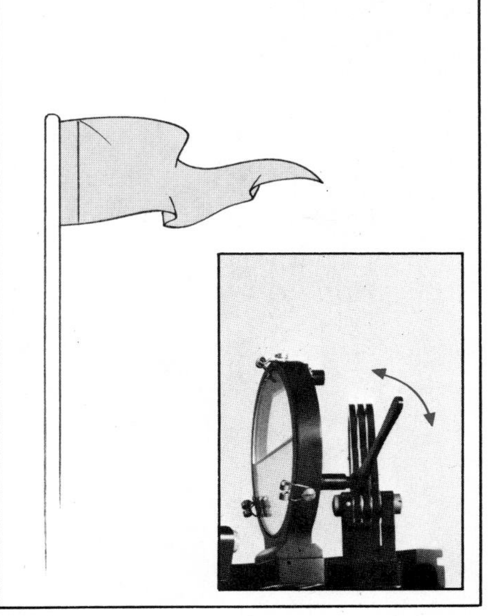

*Next, switch the wrench to the screw nearest the sextant frame and turn it either way until the two images merge. Because corrections made with the two screws may throw each other off, completion of the horizon-glass alignment may require an alternating series of fine adjustments with both screws.*

## Sighting Tricks

*To hold a sextant level as a boat pitches, rolls or yaws during a sighting, a navigator should brace his lower body while bending from the waist. In these two photographs, navigator Halsey Herreshoff straddles the backstay and life-preserver rack, planting himself firmly on the deck. When the boat heels sharply (above), he leans back against the tilt and steadies the sextant by locking his elbows against his body. On a relatively level deck (above, right), he widens his stance and leans forward at the waist to roll with the boat's motion.*

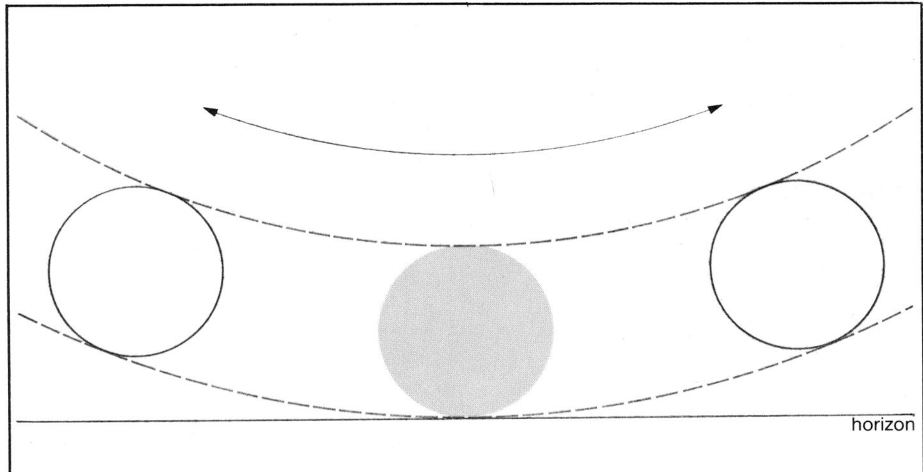


*For accurate measurement of an altitude, the sextant must be perpendicular at the moment it shows a celestial body's image touching the horizon. This crucial verticality is ensured by an exercise called swinging the arc. In the three pictures above, the navigator first tilts the sextant to the left, then swings it around until it ends up inclined to the right. As seen through the sextant telescope (left), the sun's image will describe an arc as though swung from a pendulum. The lowest point in this arc occurs when the sextant is perpendicular; since the sun just touches the horizon at that point, the altitude reading will be correct.*

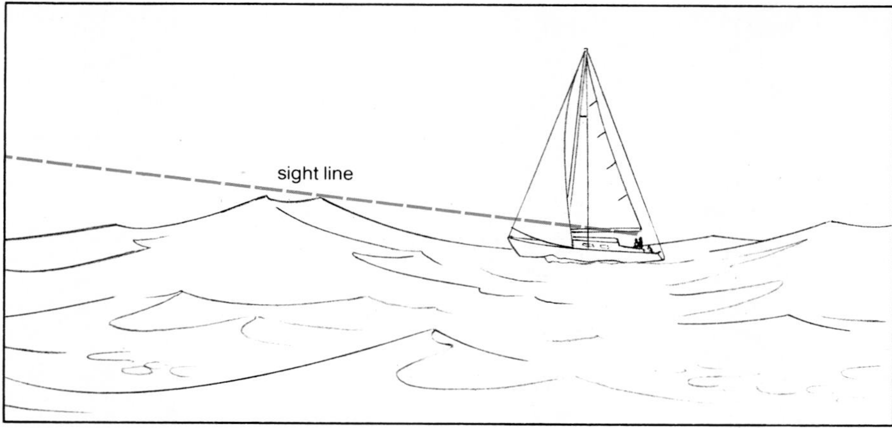


An inexperienced navigator attempting to take a sighting from the trough of a large ocean swell *(above)*, may mistake the crest of the wave for the horizon. The ragged profile of the image of the wave crest in the horizon glass *(right)* signals such an error; the actual horizon will always be a straight, sharply defined line.

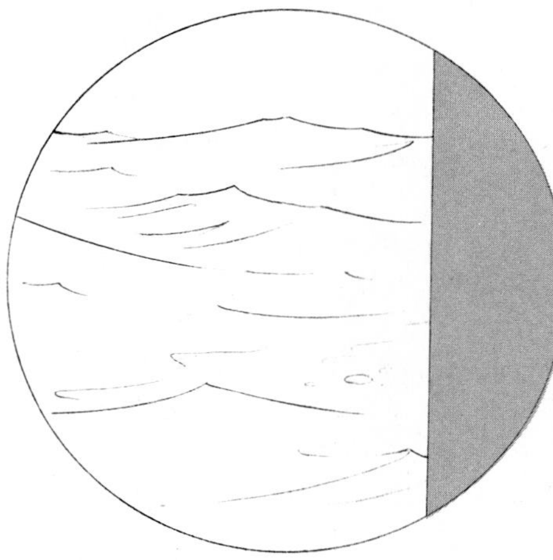

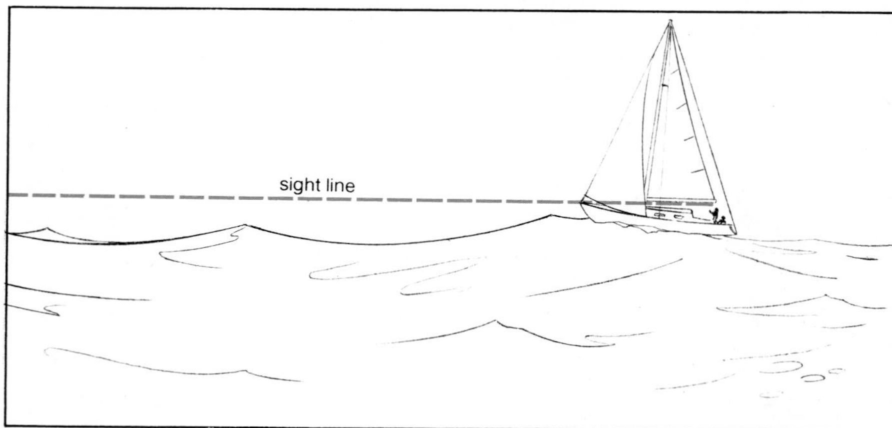


By sighting from the crest of a wave in rough seas *(above)*, the navigator can gain an unobstructed view of the horizon in the telescope *(right)*. Since this view lasts only a second or two, he may have to string together several wave-top sightings to position the celestial body on the horizon.

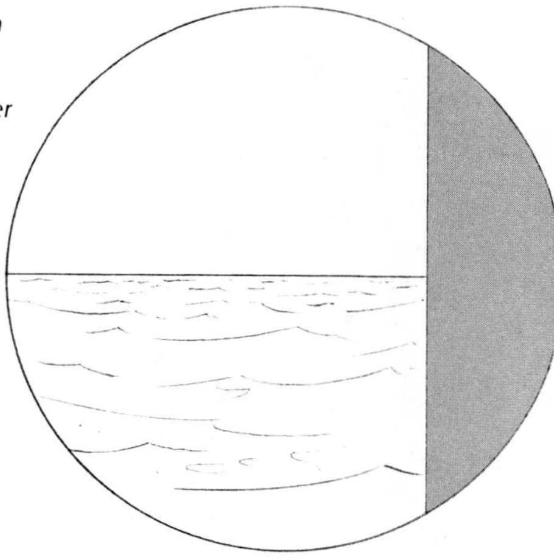

## The Tough Shots

When working with a sextant, a navigator frequently has to contend with high seas, which compound the basic problem of holding the instrument steady. They also may obscure the line of vision to the horizon, causing him to mistake large waves for the horizon line each time the boat slips into a trough. To minimize these difficulties, experienced navigators take rough-weather sightings only when the boat is on the crest of a wave.

Another set of sighting problems arises when an offshore navigator attempts to gauge his position by stars or planets rather than by the sun. Such sightings can be made only during a period of approximately 15 minutes at dawn or dusk, when the horizon is clearly defined yet the sky is dark enough for the celestial bodies to show up plainly. Not only is time short, but normal technique for a sighting—moving the index arm first to spot the celestial body and then placing the body on the horizon—is not sufficient for the smaller, fainter images of stars and planets. A navigator employing the normal daytime technique on a star would have trouble locating the desired speck of light amid a sprinkling of other stars, and he might well lose sight of it as he tries to lower it into position.

These hazards can be met by literally reversing the sextant. The navigator turns the instrument upside down *(right)*, locates the star by looking through the clear portion of the horizon glass, then slides the index arm to move the horizon up to the star—rather than the other way around. He then takes the sextant away from his eye and turns it right side up; the star can be quickly picked up when he again aims at the horizon. Then he fine-tunes his sighting by turning the micrometer knob until the horizon line cuts the star's image in half *(opposite, far right)*.

Remember, when making any kind of sighting, to handle the sextant gently. After every use, wipe the sextant dry with a soft cloth. If it has been exposed to sea spray, rinse it with fresh water and dry it off immediately to avoid corrosion. After every cruise, lubricate all moving parts with watchmaker's oil and polish the glasses, mirrors and shades with lens tissue. Whenever the instrument is not in use, store it in the box supplied by the manufacturer, where it will be protected from the inimical influences of dampness, heat and vibration.

*With his sextant inverted, the navigator shoots a star at twilight. The instrument's handle is grasped in the left hand and the index arm moved with the right hand; in this position, sliding the index arm forward brings the horizon up to the celestial image instead of moving the image downward.*

**Sextant Inverted**

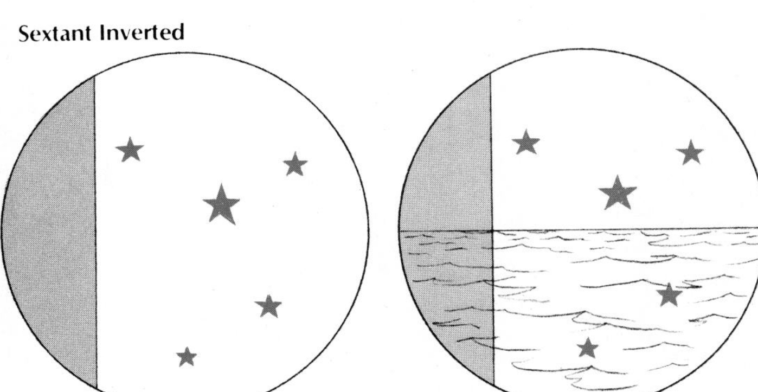

*When a navigator makes a star sighting, a sequence of four views will appear in his sextant's telescope. First, with the sextant upside down, the star to be sighted (the largest one) is positioned in the clear side of the horizon glass; the mirror side is opaque. As the index arm is moved, the horizon is raised into view and appears on both sides of the glass—while the star remains visible in the clear part (right).*

**Sextant Right Side Up**

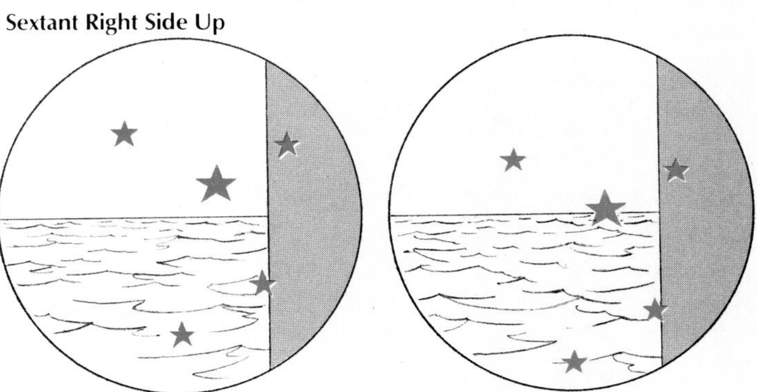

*After the sextant has been turned right side up, the horizon appears in the clear side of the horizon glass, while the star has become a reflected image (left). The navigator then turns the micrometer drum and lowers the star image until it is split by the horizon (right). At this point, he marks the time and reads the sextant.*

154
1975 AUGUST 5, 6, 7 (TUES.,
G.M.T.
ARIES
VENUS −4.1
MARS +0.5
JUPITER −2.2
G.H.A.
Dec.
H.O. PUB. NO. 249
VOL. II
SIGHT REDUCTION TABLES
FOR
THE
NAUTICAL ALMANAC
FOR THE YEAR
WASHINGTON:
United States
Naval Observatory
1973
LONDON:
Her Majesty's
Stationery Off
1973

## Supplementary Tools

To help translate his sextant readings into the boat's position, an offshore navigator needs an extremely accurate clock called a chronometer, which is always set to Greenwich Mean Time (GMT). The chronometer may be an electronic clock or a spring-driven nautical timepiece like the one at left, mounted on gimbals and housed in a box that shields it from shocks and sudden temperature changes.

Even the best-engineered chronometer may develop a slight deviation from GMT during a voyage. But as long as the exact amount of error is known, it can be incorporated mathematically in navigational calculations. To detect a chronometer's waywardness, a navigator should regularly tune in on the Greenwich Mean Time signals on government radio bands.

Chronometers are usually kept out of harm's way belowdecks. However, celestial navigation requires that GMT be recorded the instant a sighting is made. To this end, the navigator employs a second timepiece that is "compared" to the chronometer, i.e., set to its time and brought up on deck to be used with the sextant. Since the comparison watch is reset with each use and thus cannot develop serious inaccuracies, it can be any inexpensive portable timepiece, so long as it has an easily read face and a sweep second hand.

The correct GMT of a sighting, along with the date, enables a navigator to gain other vital information from yet another source, the Nautical Almanac, a volume of figures predicting the positions of celestial bodies throughout the year. Additional data on celestial movements can be found in sight reduction tables. These latter come in several versions, one of the simplest and most useful being a three-volume set known as H.O. 249 (H.O. is the abbreviation for Hydrographic Office, a government agency that publishes nautical information). The Almanac and the volumes of H.O. 249 are sold at marine-supply stores or through the Superintendent of Documents, Washington, D.C.

*Four crucial tools of the celestial navigator —a chronometer, a comparing watch, sight reduction tables and the Nautical Almanac —are set against an enlarged page from the latter volume. The page gives the Greenwich hour angle for a celestial bench mark called Aries (page 113), and four planets at various times and dates; it also supplies positional data for other commonly used stars—listed alphabetically in the right-hand column.*

## The Error Factor

The readings that a navigator gets from his sextant are always subject to certain uncontrollable errors. One of these errors results from the fact that the navigator's perch is above the level of the water, causing the horizon to seem lower. For example, a six-foot navigator standing on a deck two feet above the water takes his sighting from a height of about eight feet. This produces an altitude error of 2.8 minutes of arc—which would throw off the navigator's estimate of his position by 2.8 miles if left uncorrected.

The other unavoidable errors that a navigator encounters whenever he makes a sighting are diagramed on these pages. Happily, all of them can be overcome by adding in the mathematical compensations found in the altitude-correction tables printed on the inside of the Nautical Almanac's cover.

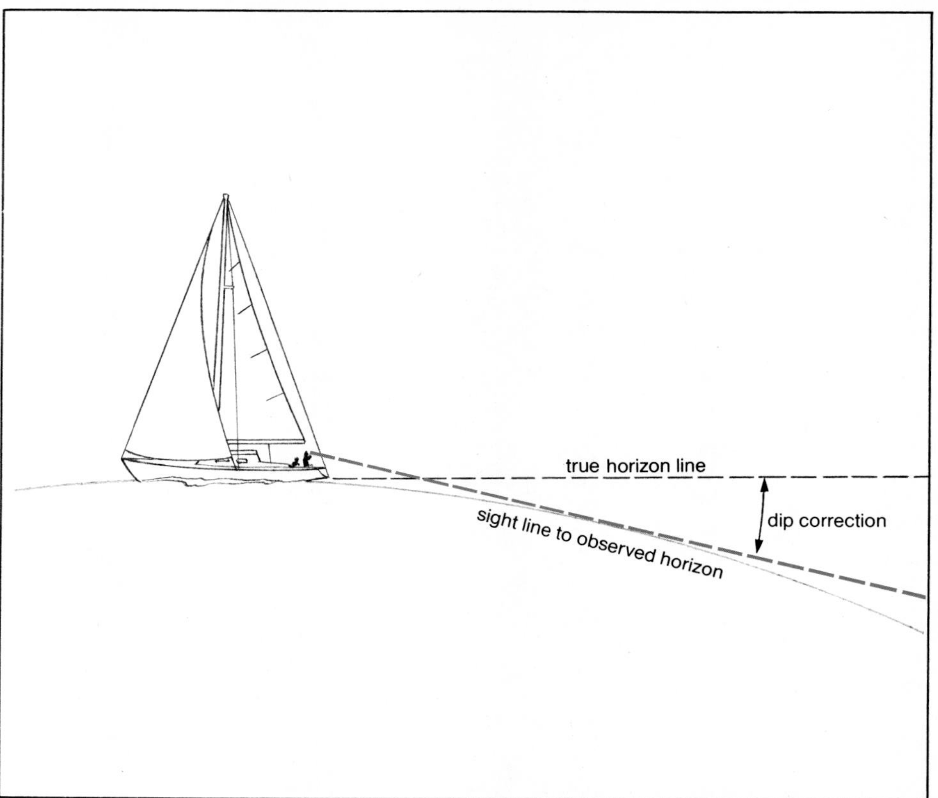


*Because of the earth's curvature, the higher a sextant is held above water level during a sighting, the farther the sight line of the observed horizon lies below the sight line of the true, sea-level horizon. The navigator remedies this error with a mathematical adjustment called dip correction, which is obtained by determining his eye-level height, then consulting a table in the Nautical Almanac that translates the height into minutes of arc. To arrive at a true reading, the dip correction is subtracted from the sextant reading.*

*A true altitude reading of the sun is computed from a point precisely halfway between the sun's upper and lower edges, called limbs. Because the exact center of the sun is difficult to sight, navigators customarily line up the lower limb with the horizon; if the lower limb is obscured by clouds, they use the upper. The distance between the center and edge of the sun is then taken into account by adding or subtracting Nautical Almanac adjustments called limb corrections; these are changed according to the time of year, since the sun's varying distance from the earth alters its apparent size.*

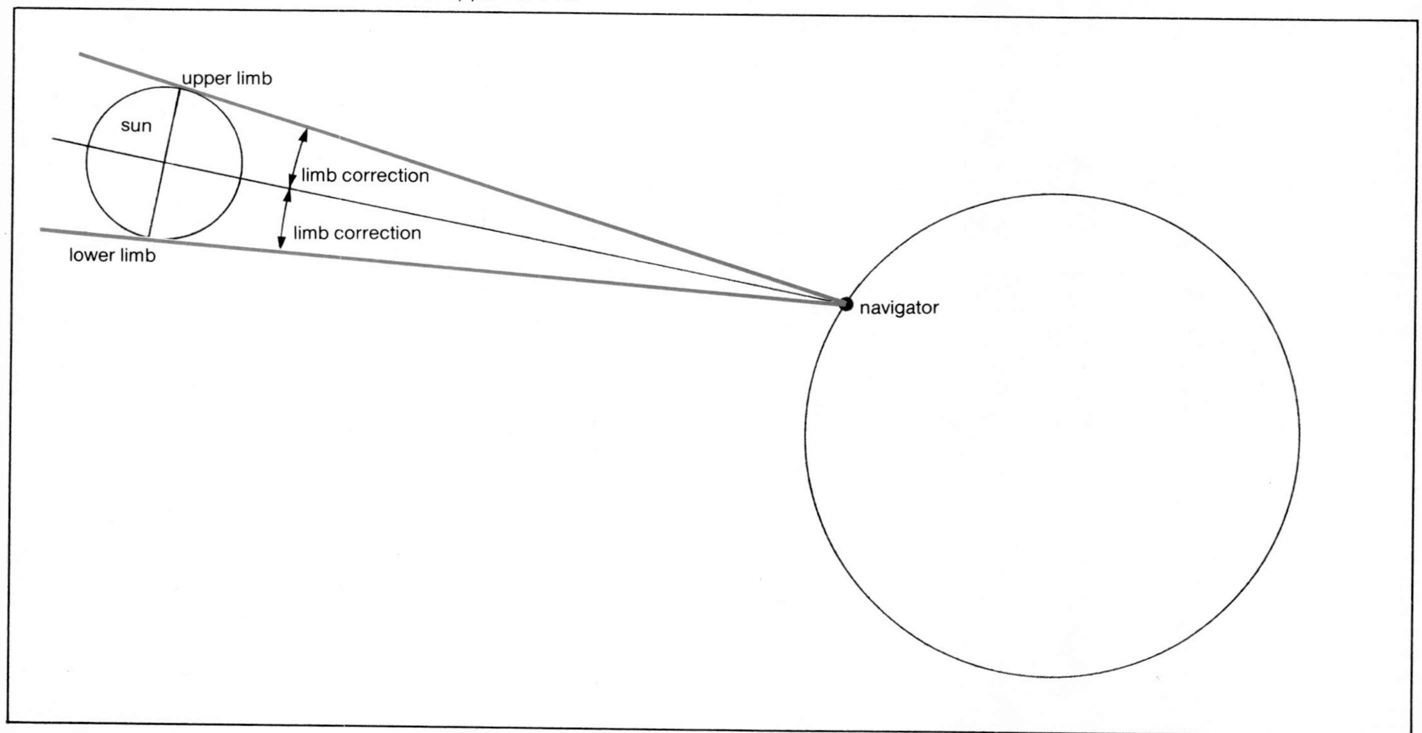

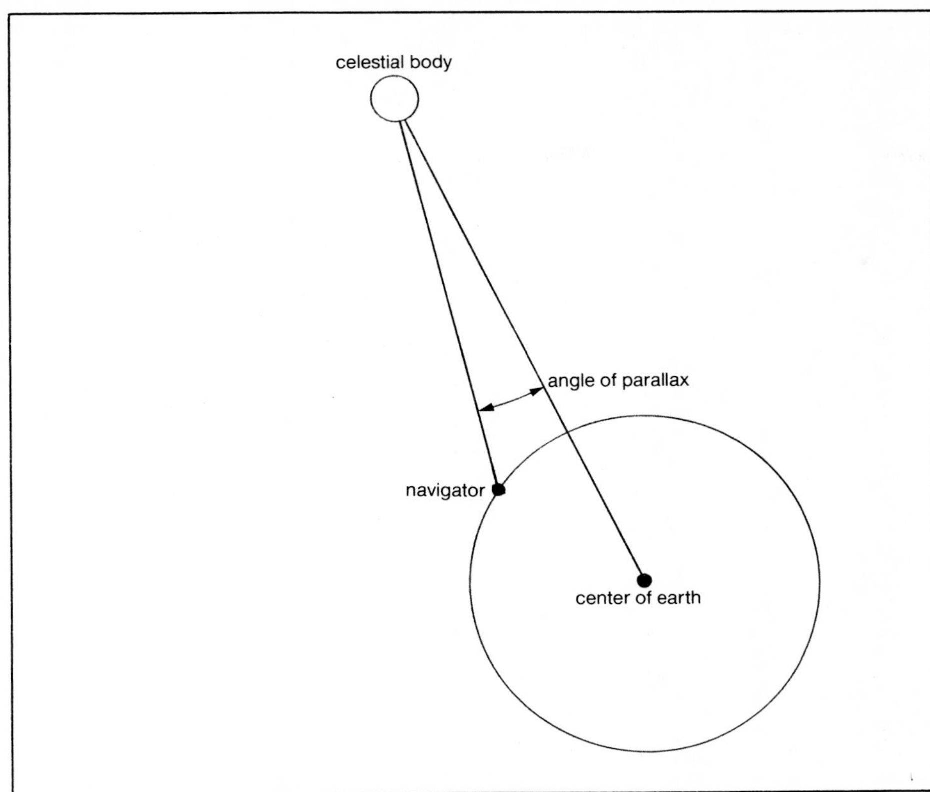


*All sextant readings are theoretically made from the center of the earth. However, in practice, the only time an imaginary straight line of altitude can be drawn from the earth's center and through the navigator's sextant occurs when the celestial body is directly overhead—a rare circumstance. When the navigator is not directly under the celestial body, a so-called angle of parallax is created between it, him and the center of the earth. This is a serious problem for sightings of the closest celestial bodies—the moon and certain planets—and the Nautical Almanac's tables include corrections for each.*

*If the earth had no atmosphere, a celestial body would always be sighted in the sextant just where it appears to be in the sky. But light rays from such an object bend, or refract, in the atmosphere (solid line) rather than traveling straight to the navigator (dotted blue line). This refraction causes the celestial body to have a greater apparent altitude (black arrow) than is actually the case (blue arrow). The lower its actual position in the sky, the more pronounced this type of sighting error becomes—and the greater the correction indication in the Nautical Almanac's correction tables.*

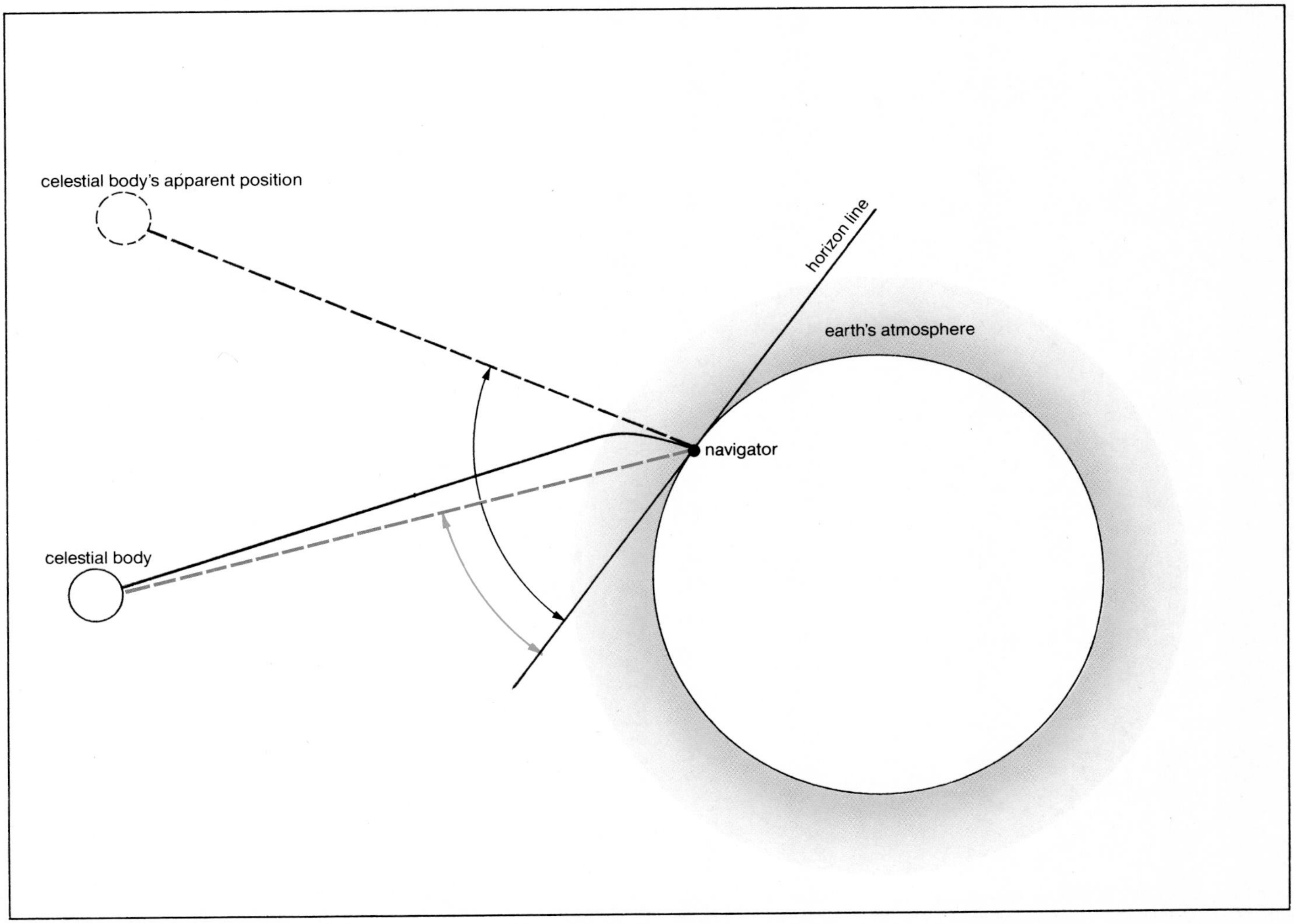

celestial body's apparent position
horizon line
earth's atmosphere
navigator
celestial body

## The Simple Noon Sight

Usually, a navigator performs an extended series of calculations to find his position. However, if he makes a sextant sighting at noon, he can arrive at half the positional solution—his latitude—with a minimum of arithmetic and only one supplementary tool, the Nautical Almanac. At noon the sun lies directly above the boat's longitude; therefore, sun, boat, the earth's center and both poles are on the same vertical plane, greatly simplifying the mathematics of the problem.

Start by taking a series of sightings as the sun climbs toward its peak, then begins to descend. The greatest reading is the one that occurs precisely at noon —when the sun is directly on the boat's meridian; correct this highest altitude reading for all errors *(pages 94-95)*.

The computations in a noon sight follow a two-step formula whose basis is the 90° angle created by the horizon line and the boat's zenith. First, subtract the sun's corrected altitude from 90°. Then, depending on the relative positions of the sun and boat *(right and opposite)*, either add or subtract the sun's declination—its angular position on either side of the equinoctial of the celestial sphere, found in the Almanac under the sighting date.

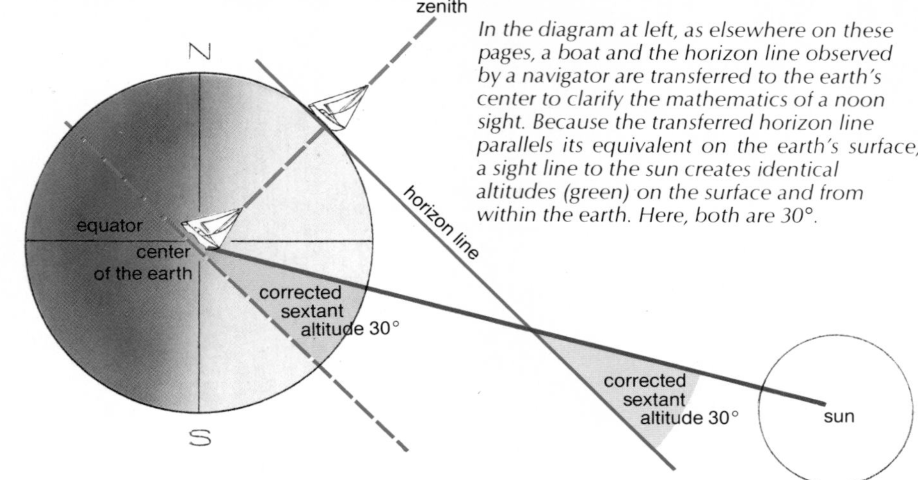


*In the diagram at left, as elsewhere on these pages, a boat and the horizon line observed by a navigator are transferred to the earth's center to clarify the mathematics of a noon sight. Because the transferred horizon line parallels its equivalent on the earth's surface, a sight line to the sun creates identical altitudes (green) on the surface and from within the earth. Here, both are 30°.*

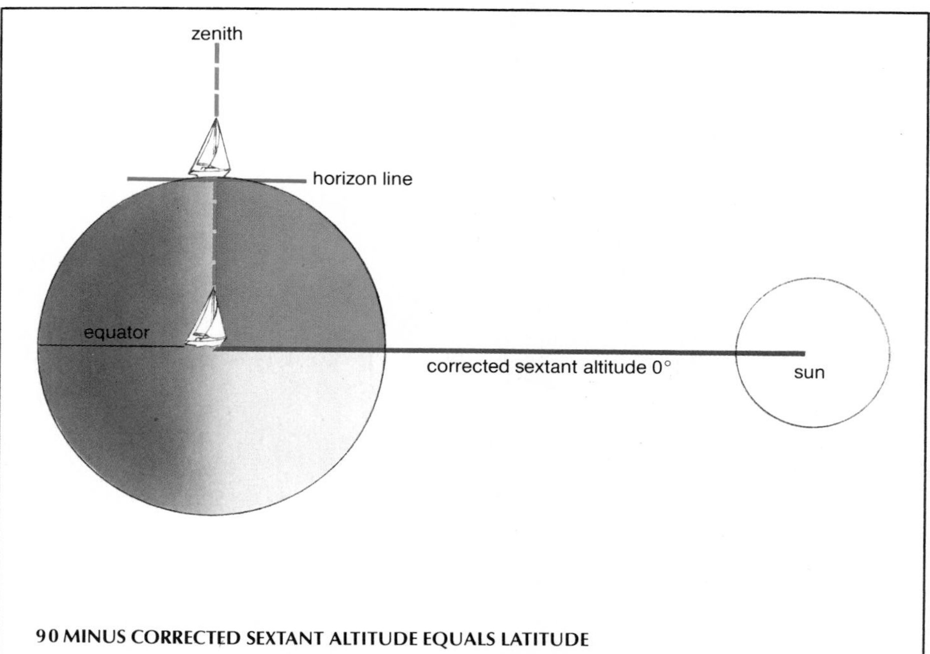


*The simplest noon sight would occur with a boat at the North Pole and the sun at its equinox, thus with no declination. Since the sun is exactly on the horizon, the sextant reads 0°. The latitude (red sector) is thus 90°, as there is no declination to subtract.*

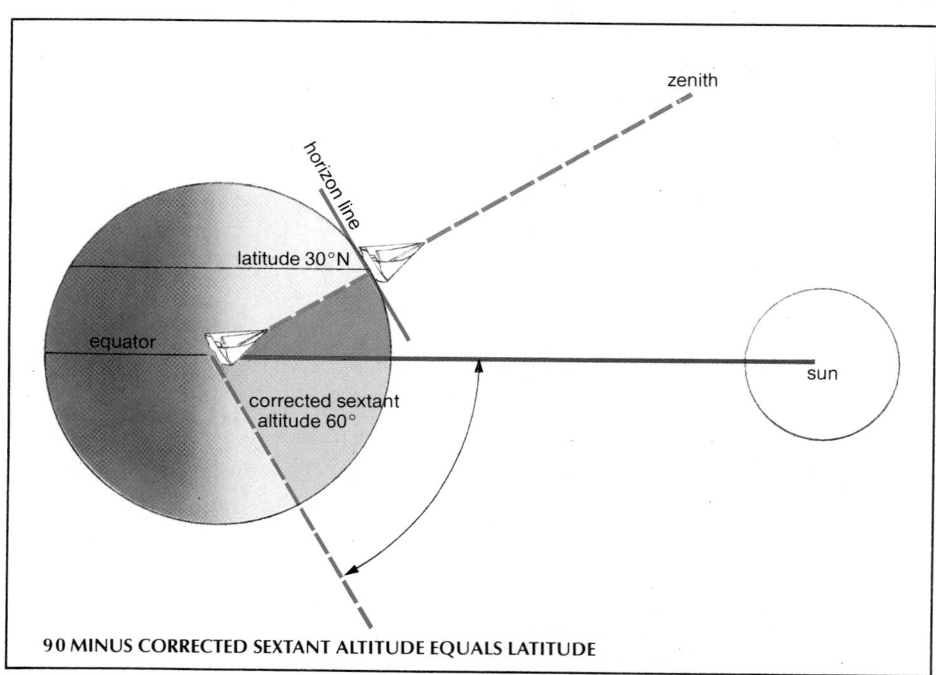


*A slightly more complicated sighting situation than the idealized one above occurs when the sun has an altitude of more than 0°—in this case, 60° (green)—but still is dead on the equator and thus lacks declination. The navigator merely subtracts 60° from 90°, yielding a latitude of 30°.*

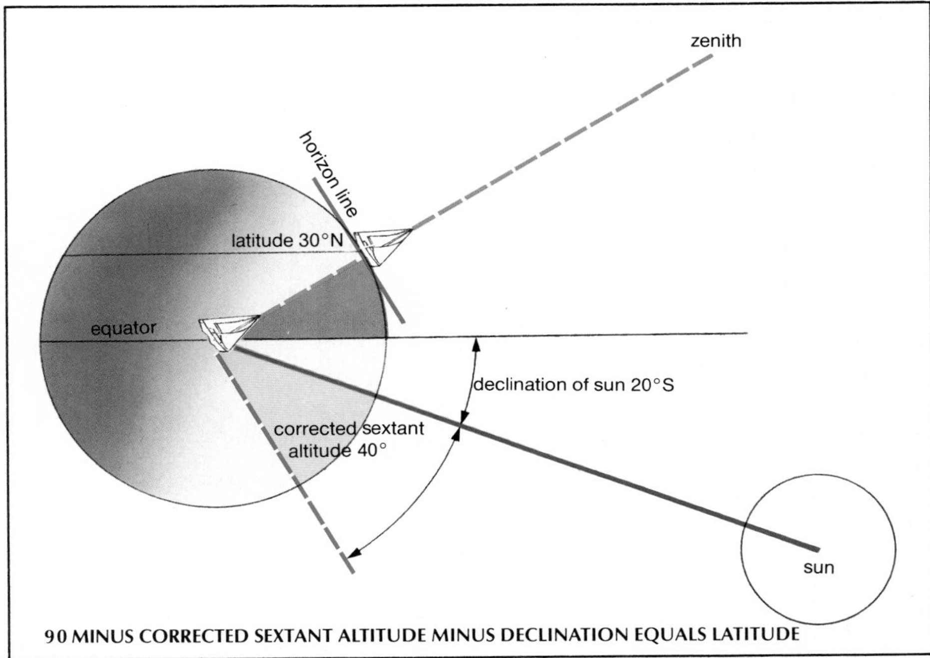


90 MINUS CORRECTED SEXTANT ALTITUDE MINUS DECLINATION EQUALS LATITUDE

*As soon as the sun moves off the equator, declination enters the navigator's equation. And whenever the boat and sun are on opposite sides of the equator, as here, the declination of the sun is a minus factor in noon-sight calculations. In the diagram at left, the noon altitude taken from a boat in the Northern Hemisphere is 40°, and the sun's declination is 20° south of the equator (blank sector). Thus, to determine his latitude the navigator first subtracts 40° from 90° —yielding 50°—then subtracts the 20° declination from 50°, giving a 30° latitude.*

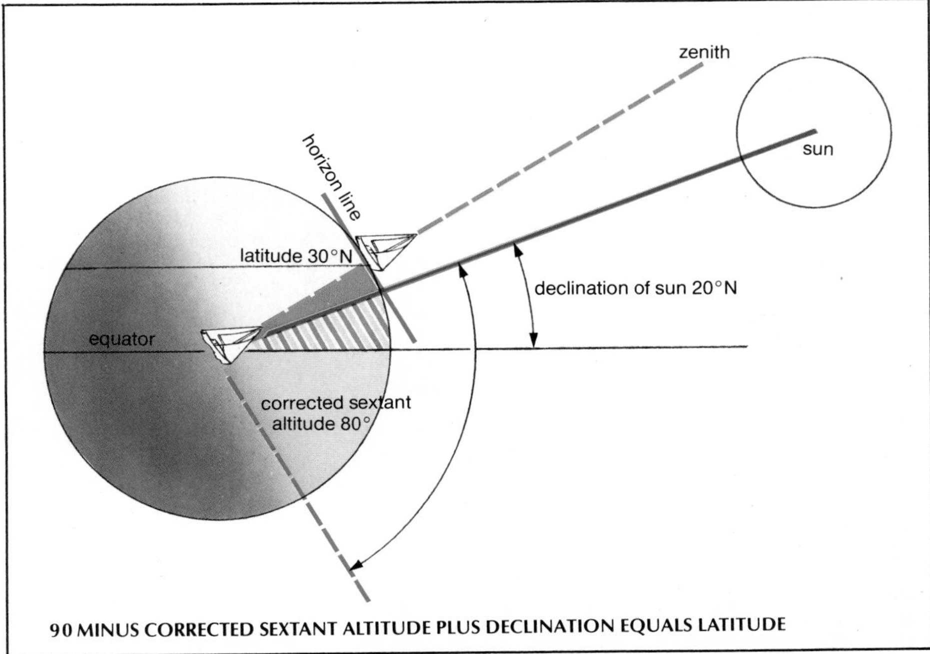


90 MINUS CORRECTED SEXTANT ALTITUDE PLUS DECLINATION EQUALS LATITUDE

*When both the sun and boat are in the same hemisphere, the declination is added to the noon-sight calculations. Here the sextant reading, taken from a boat in the Northern Hemisphere, is 80°; the declination is 20° north. The navigator first subtracts the altitude of 80° from 90°, leaving 10°; he then adds the 20° declination (red and green stripes), producing a latitude of 30°.*

## The Necessary Plane

Navigational situations usually lack the mathematical convenience provided by a noon sight of the sun *(page 96)*. Therefore, when sighting other celestial bodies—or the sun at other times of the day—the navigator must in effect create a special plane on which lie certain key ingredients in his navigational equation. This critical plane, shown at right, is oriented according to an element called true azimuth—the true compass direction, stated in degrees, from the boat to the celestial body's geographical position. The coordinates of that position are determined by the body's declination and its Greenwich hour angle, which are found in the Nautical Almanac.

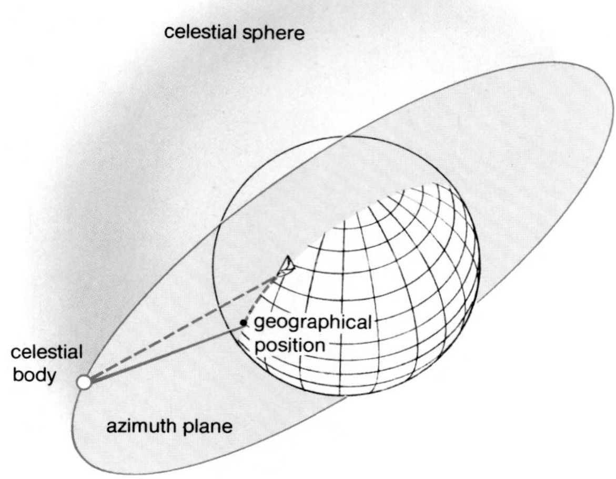


*The azimuth plane splits the celestial sphere—and the earth—in half to provide a geometrical framework for many crucial elements of celestial navigation. In this plane are the boat, the celestial body the navigator has selected to sight, the body's geographical position, the line from boat to body and the direction line of the true azimuth.*

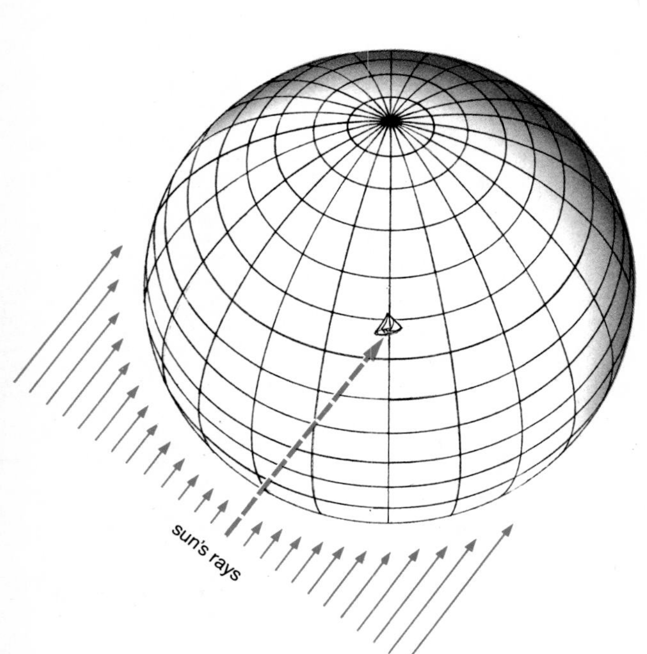


*Although the true azimuth is ordinarily determined by assuming a position for the boat, then consulting the Nautical Almanac and H.O. 249 for the geographical position of the celestial body, it can also be roughly estimated by sighting along a compass to a point on the horizon directly beneath the celestial body. In the drawing at left, the sun's rays are coming at the boat from a southwesterly direction, as emphasized by the dashed blue arrow. When lined up along the compass (below), the sun, then, has an azimuth reading of 220° (dashed red line). Since the compass direction is based on magnetic north rather than true, this reading must be adjusted according to the compass deviation and to the variation noted on navigational charts.*

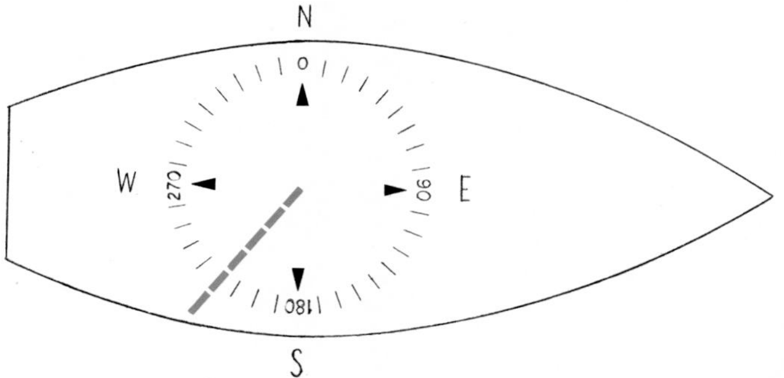

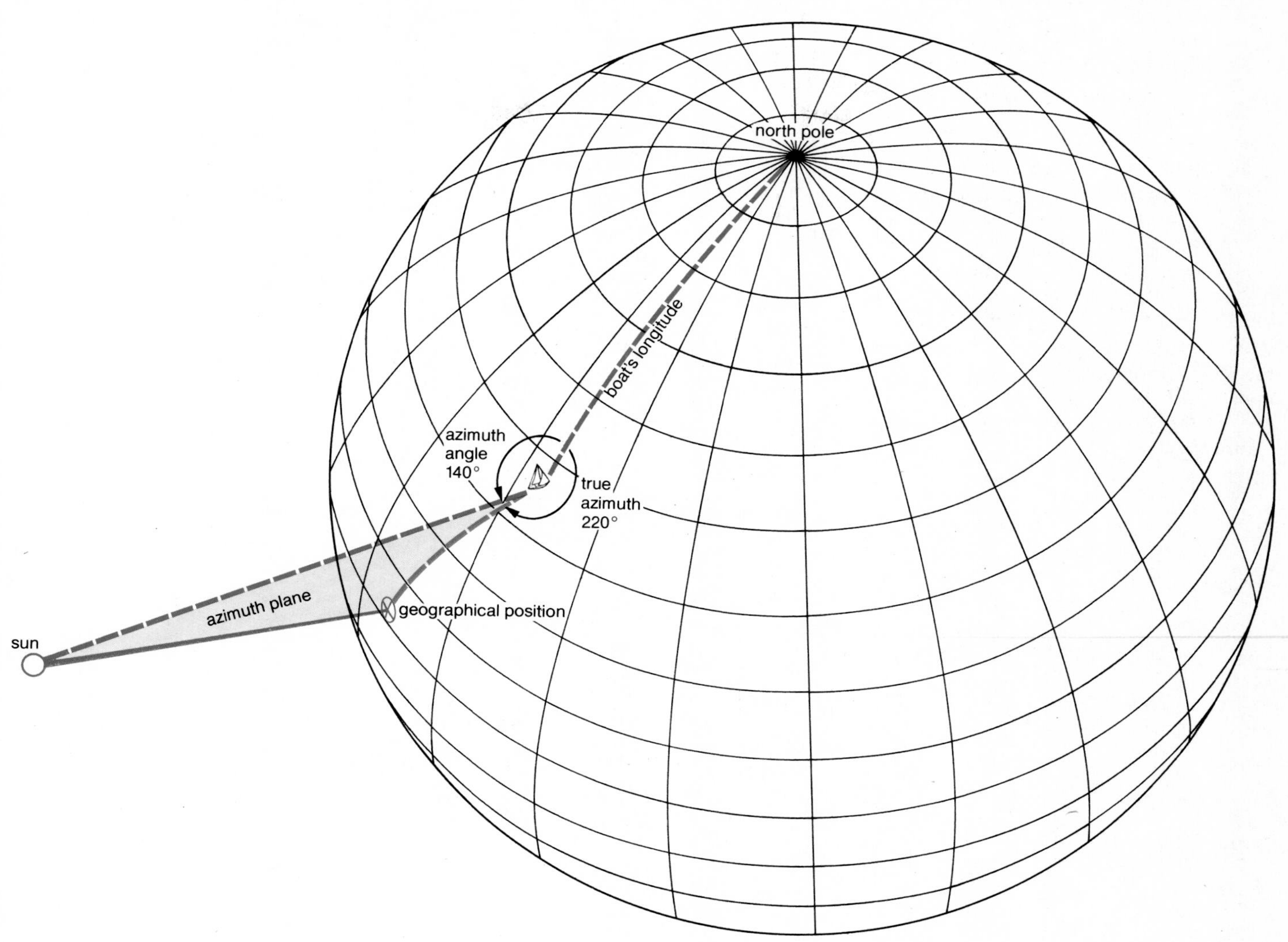


*Due to mathematical complications, H.O. 249 does not always directly list the true azimuth of a celestial body. With the planets, moon and sun, for example, the tables work through an element called azimuth angle that is formed by lines running from the boat to the pole and the boat to the body's geographical position. In the example here, with a boat in the Northern Hemisphere and the sun in the west, the azimuth angle is subtracted from a so-called reference figure of 360° to determine the true azimuth—the result is 220°. With the sun in the east, the azimuth angle is identical to the true azimuth and no calculation is needed. In the Southern Hemisphere the process is essentially the same, but the reference figure is 180°.*

## Theoretical Triangle

The embracing device by which all offshore way-finding data, except the simple noon sight, are utilized is a geometric figure called the navigational triangle, which is directly linked to the azimuth plane *(opposite)*. Built on the earth's surface from a combination of facts and logical assumptions, such triangles enable the navigator to determine a boat's true latitude and longitude. The diagrams on these and the following two pages explain in theory how a navigational triangle works; in practice, a navigator translates this theory into mathematical and graphic shorthand *(pages 104-119)*.

A navigational triangle is formed by joining two known points and a third point that is estimated. The known points are the geographical position of the celestial body and the pole nearest the boat; the estimated point is the boat's assumed position—a modified latitude and longitude close to where the navigator believes the boat to be. The triangle that emerges from these points is then adjusted according to a new piece of information: a sextant reading *(pages 102-103)*.

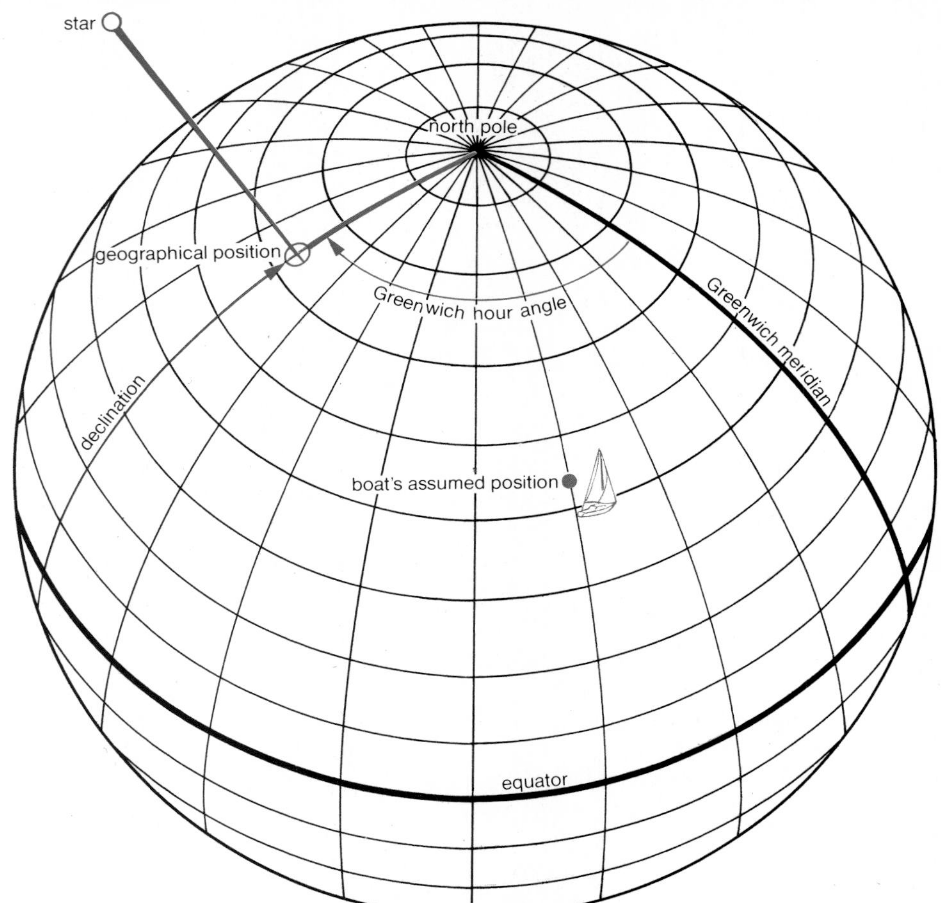


*The starting point for the navigational triangle is the geographical position of a celestial body—in this case, a star. The two components of the position are the celestial body's declination and its Greenwich hour angle. With this point established one side of the triangle can be formed by linking the geographical position with a second known point, the North Pole (solid blue line).*

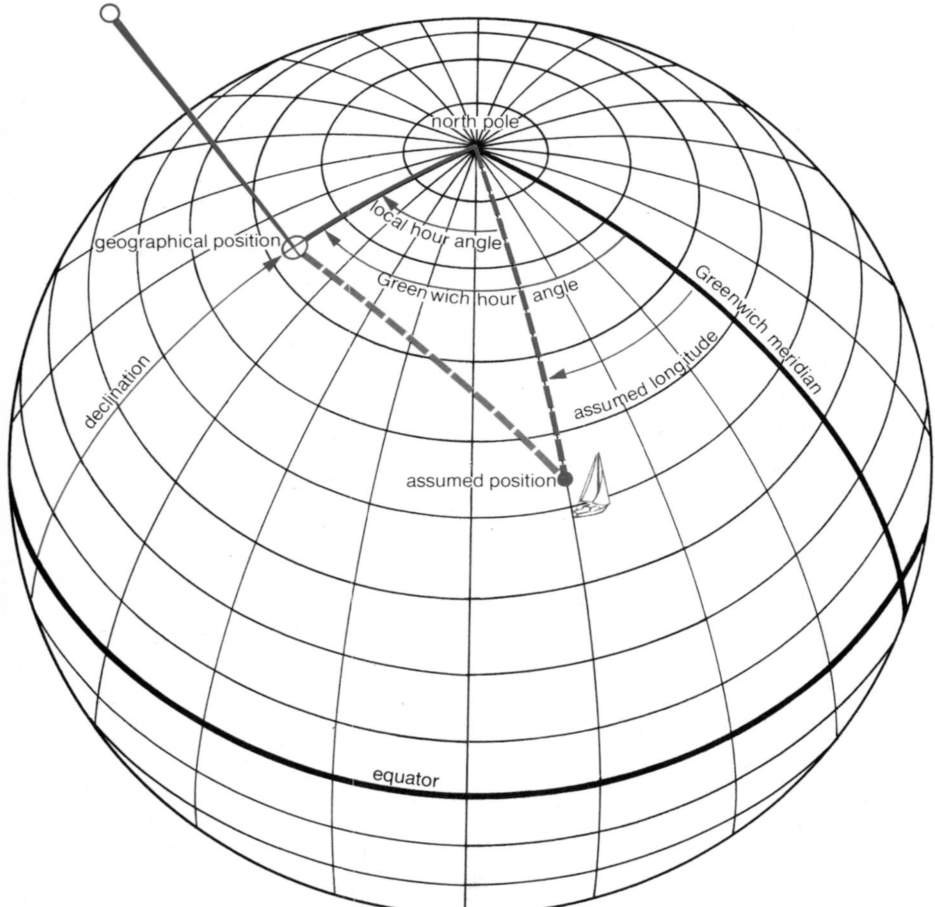


*The triangle is completed by lines drawn from the assumed position of the boat to the North Pole (blue dashed line) and from the boat to the star's geographical position (red dashes). The latter line represents the direction of the true azimuth. Both lines are dashed because they are based on the navigator's guess as to his whereabouts rather than on certain knowledge. Another vital figure—the local hour angle—can now be derived from the navigational triangle by subtracting the boat's assumed longitude from the star's Greenwich hour angle.*

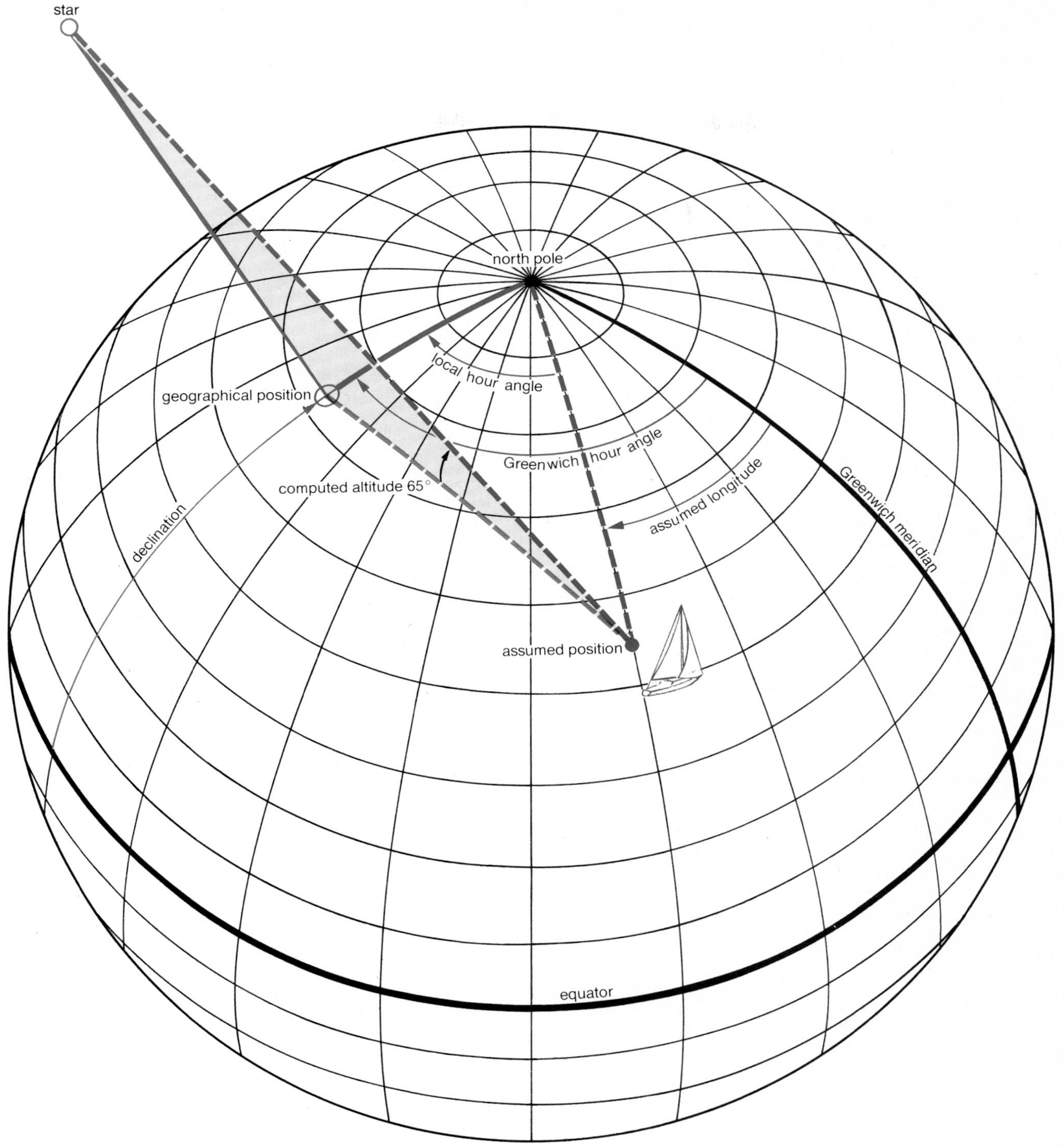


*With the navigational triangle formed, the next step is to compute the altitude of the celestial body—basing this computation on the assumed position of the boat. The altitude is a function of the assumed latitude of the boat, the star's declination and the local hour angle. Fortunately, the tables of H.O. 249 offer a precalculated solution—in this case, a computed altitude of 65°. The elongated green triangle formed by the star, its geographical position and the boat lies in the azimuth plane, within which the hypothetical altitude also falls. The solution to any celestial navigational problem is derived directly from the length of that elongated triangle's base (red dashed line)—which also serves as one leg of the navigational triangle.*

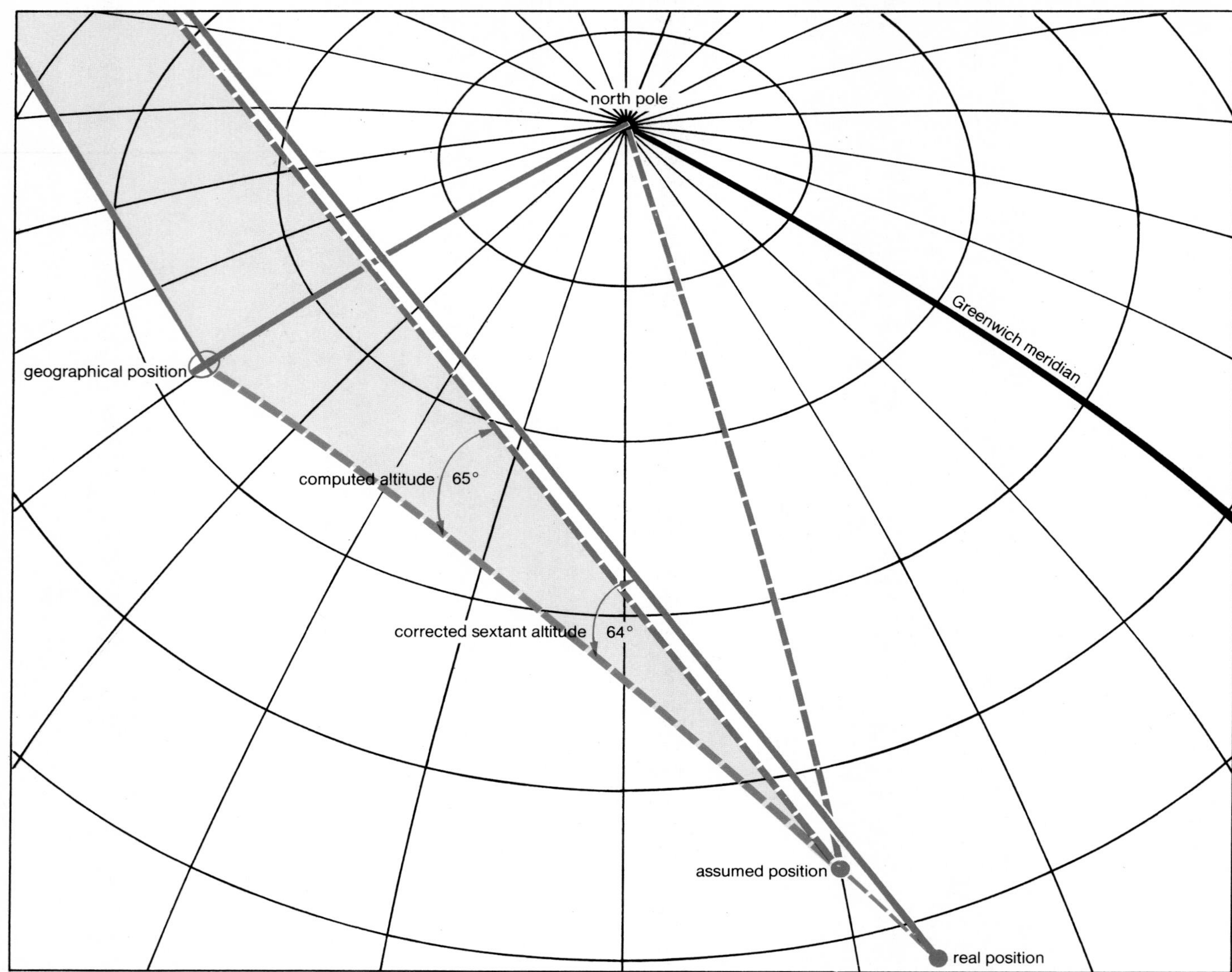


*After a navigator has computed the altitude of a celestial body on the basis of a boat's assumed position, the sextant altitude of the celestial body is taken (solid blue line). This altitude, incorporating necessary corrections, will be matched against the computed one to establish the boat's real position. If the computed altitude is smaller, the boat is closer to the star's geographical position than was assumed. If the computed altitude is greater, as here, the boat is farther away (navigators memorize this relationship with the maxim "Computed greater away"). In this diagram, the computed altitude of 65° is 1° greater than the sextant altitude of 64°. The boat's real position is therefore farther away from the star's geographical position—as indicated by the thin extension of the red dashed line. Since the difference is an even degree, the distance between the assumed and real positions is 60 nautical miles.*

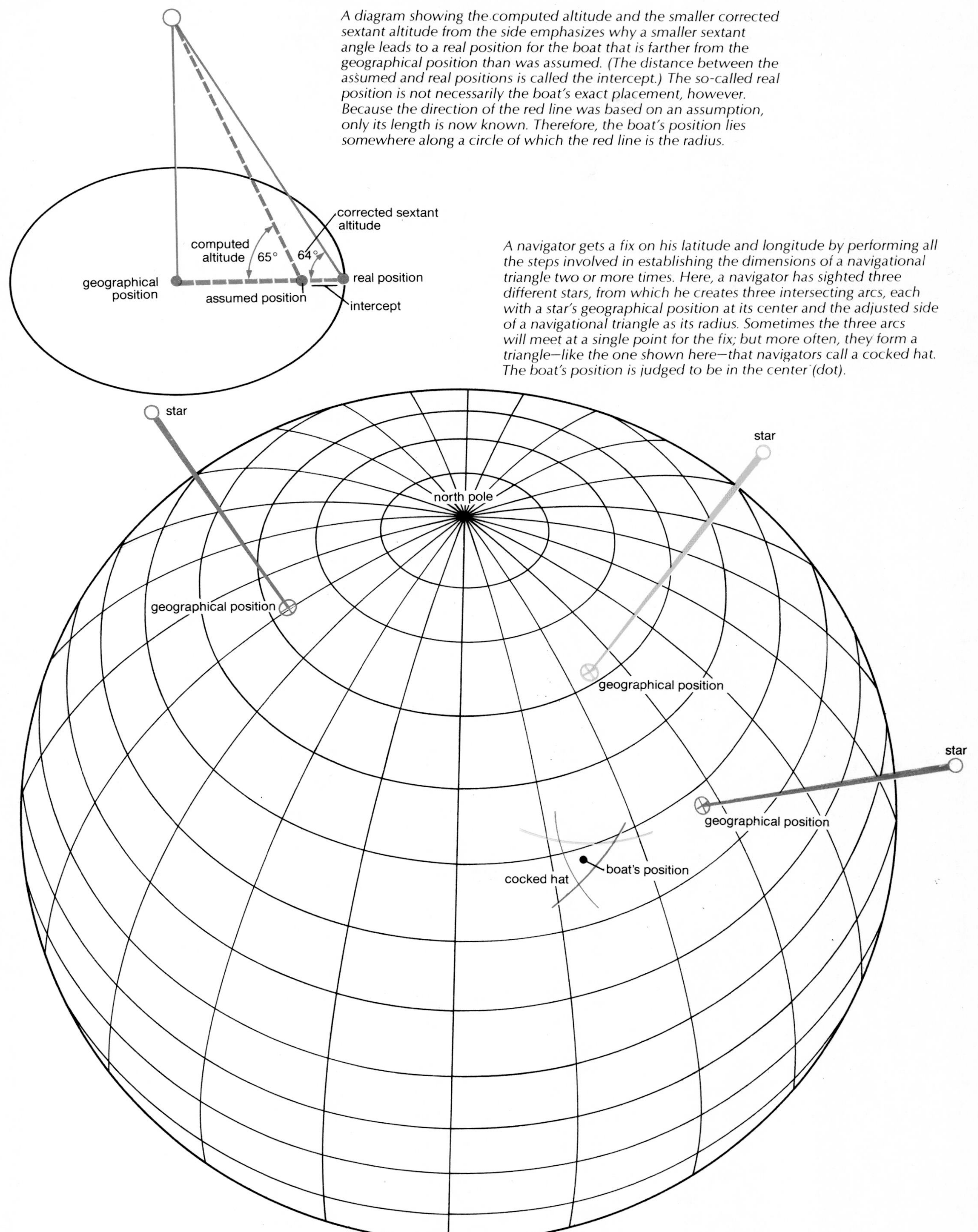


*A diagram showing the computed altitude and the smaller corrected sextant altitude from the side emphasizes why a smaller sextant angle leads to a real position for the boat that is farther from the geographical position than was assumed. (The distance between the assumed and real positions is called the intercept.) The so-called real position is not necessarily the boat's exact placement, however. Because the direction of the red line was based on an assumption, only its length is now known. Therefore, the boat's position lies somewhere along a circle of which the red line is the radius.*

*A navigator gets a fix on his latitude and longitude by performing all the steps involved in establishing the dimensions of a navigational triangle two or more times. Here, a navigator has sighted three different stars, from which he creates three intersecting arcs, each with a star's geographical position at its center and the adjusted side of a navigational triangle as its radius. Sometimes the three arcs will meet at a single point for the fix; but more often, they form a triangle—like the one shown here—that navigators call a cocked hat. The boat's position is judged to be in the center (dot).*

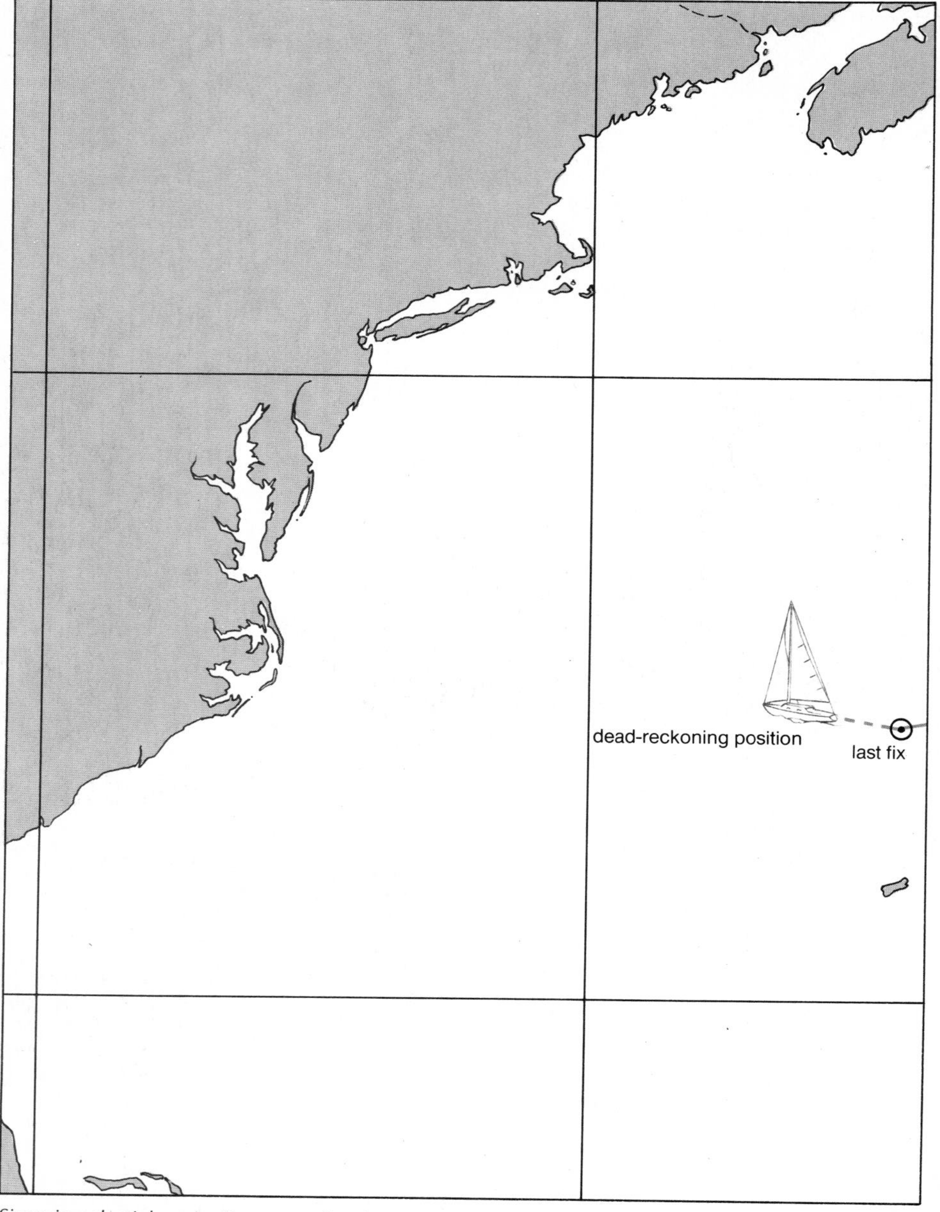


Since in celestial navigation every fix of longitude and latitude is based on a previously established position, before beginning his calculations the navigator estimates his present position by dead reckoning—i.e., by estimating his heading, speed and the elapsed time since the last fix (circled dot). The dead-reckoning position, in turn, will be used to devise a so-called assumed position, required by the navigational-triangle theory; the assumed position is simply a nearby point whose latitude and longitude coordinates are mathematically convenient.

# A Fix from the Sun—I

When putting into practice the navigational theories introduced on the preceding pages, a navigator performs three basic tasks: he obtains altitudes with the aid of a sextant; he incorporates the sextant data into a series of calculations on a special form *(page 106);* and he extracts his boat's position from the resulting figures by plotting lines on another special sheet *(pages 110-111).*

Certain steps in the calculating and plotting phases of this process differ when a navigational problem is solved by means of the sun (following seven pages) as compared to a problem solved by stars or planets *(pages 112-119).* And even the initial step of gathering altitude readings differs in one fundamental respect. With the sun, a navigator must space his altitude readings several hours apart to create the intersecting lines that will reveal his position. With stars or planets he can obtain the altitudes from several celestial bodies during one sighting session.

In most other respects, however, the procedures used for sun and star sights are identical. For example, the navigator must never shoot any celestial body that is less than 20° above the horizon; at lesser angles, the earth's atmosphere bends light rays so drastically that an altitude reading would be unreliable. For each of the sextant altitudes that a navigator needs to determine his position, he will actually make a series of three to six sightings at intervals of less than a minute; from this group he selects an average figure. Finally, no matter what celestial body he is sighting, he achieves more accurate results by enlisting an assistant to write down the crucial information *(right).*

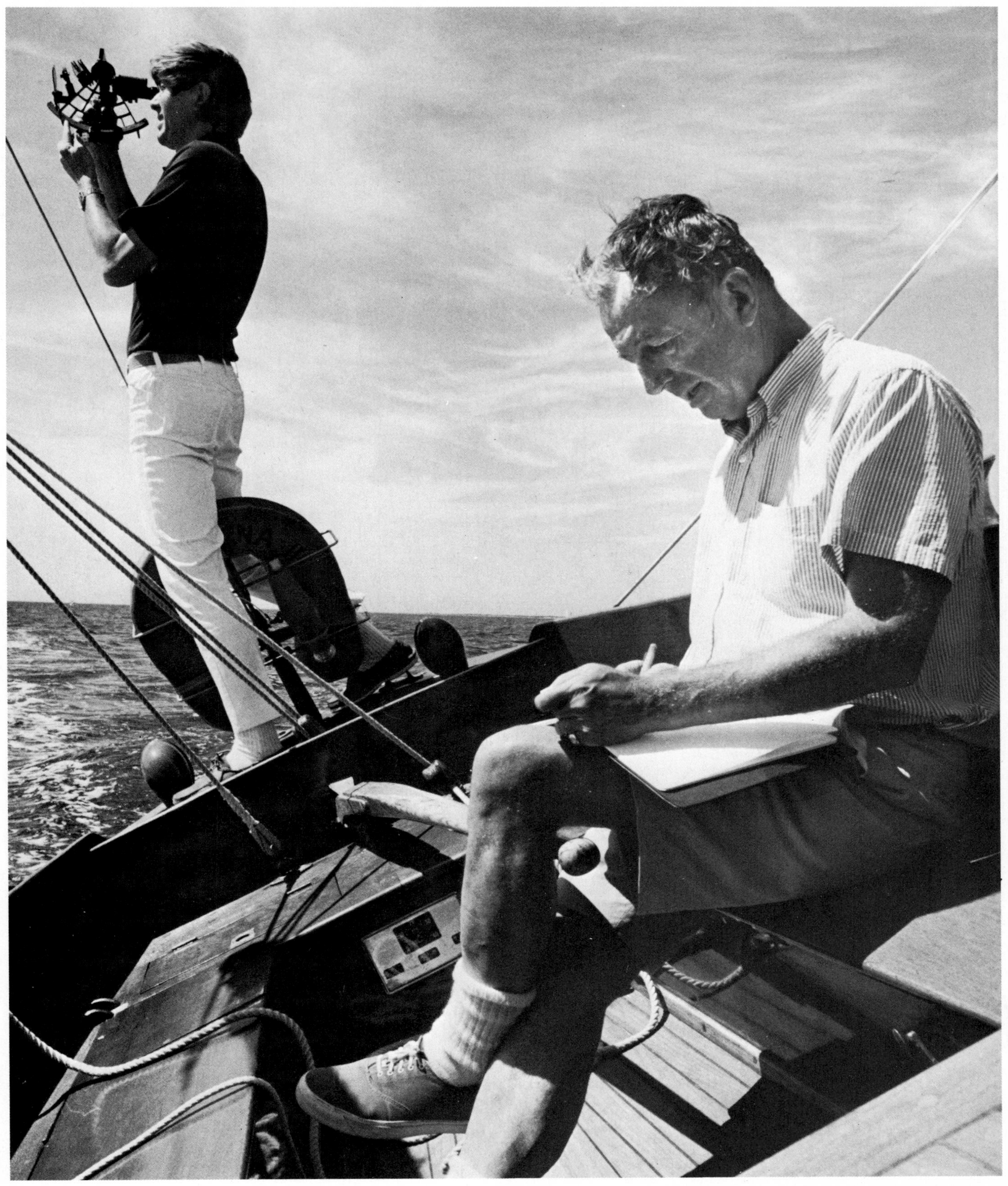

*During a series of sightings, the navigator adjusts his sextant to bring the reflected image of the sun down to the horizon. At that point he will shout "Mark!"—the traditional signal that is used to instruct an assistant to read Greenwich Mean Time off his comparing watch and to make a note of it, along with the altitude.*

## A Fix from the Sun—II

After making his sun sights, the navigator works out his position on two special forms: a sight form *(right and page 108)* and a plotting sheet *(pages 110-111)*. Though sight forms are commercially available in several versions, some navigators make up their own, such as the one at right, devised by master navigator Halsey Herreshoff. The unshaded portions are explained on these pages.

Begin work on the form by plotting on the graph at the top of the form all sextant readings from a sighting session according to their times and altitudes. Draw a straight line roughly connecting the staggered points; for calculation purposes, pick the sight the line runs through or is nearest to *(arrow)*. Record this sight's date and Greenwich Mean Time (GMT), along with the dead-reckoning (DR) position during the sights.

Write the chosen reading—73°35.2′—on the form as the actual sextant altitude. Then enter the sextant's index correction, taken from its micrometer drum, along with the altitude and dip corrections. The latter two are from the Nautical Almanac, excerpted opposite. (For clarity, the figures entered on the form and the source figures in the Almanac have been coded with matching colors.) Next, total the figures and add the result to the actual sextant altitude to get a corrected sextant altitude—73°49.1′.

Enter the time of the selected sight and subtract or add the clock error—here established arbitrarily as minus 13 seconds—to arrive at a corrected time: 17 hours 12 minutes and 33 seconds. The Greenwich hour angle (GHA) of the sun can now be calculated by looking in two places in the Nautical Almanac. First open the Almanac to the correctly dated daily page—Tuesday, July 15. Opposite the 17 (for 1700 hours) is the hour portion of the GHA, 73°31.8′ *(orange)*. Now turn to a yellow-tinted page headed by the proper GMT minute figure—12m. Opposite the correct number of GMT seconds—33—is the figure 3°08.3′ *(red)*. Add the two angle portions for a total GHA of 76°40.1′.

Next, as a mathematical convenience, change the dead-reckoning longitude's minutes to match the GHA minutes; this yields an assumed longitude of 65°40.1′. Circle this assumed longitude in red, since it is one of the critical figures that will be used in establishing the boat's position on the plotting sheet. The next step is to subtract this figure from the Greenwich hour angle. The result is a local hour angle (LHA) that is without minutes—11°.

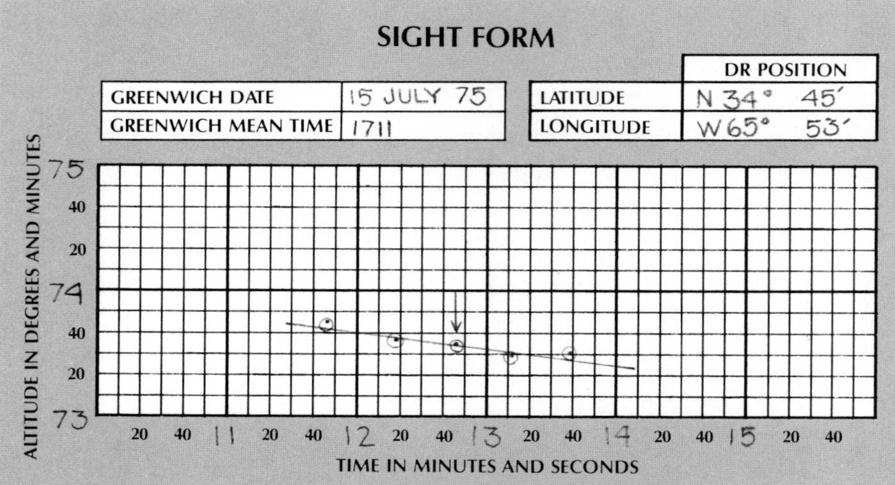


| | | | |
|---|---|---|---|
| CELESTIAL BODY | | | SUN |
| CORRECTED SEXTANT ALTITUDE (Ho) | Actual Sextant Altitude | | 73° 35.2′ |
| | Corrections — Index | + 1.2′ | |
| | Altitude | + 15.7′ | |
| | Dip | − 3.0′ | |
| | Total | +13.9′ | +13.9′ |
| | Corrected Sextant Altitude | | 73° 49.1′ |
| GREENWICH MEAN TIME (GMT) | Chronometer | | 17h 12m 46s |
| | Chronometer Correction | | −0 13s |
| | Greenwich Mean Time | | 17h 12m 33s |
| GREENWICH HOUR ANGLE (GHA) | GMT hour listing | | 73° 31.8′ |
| | GMT min./sec. listing | | 3° 08.3′ |
| | Total Greenwich Hour Angle | | 76° 40.1′ |
| EAST-WEST MEASUREMENTS | Assumed Longitude | | 65 40.1′ |
| | Local Hour Angle (GHA minus assumed longitude) | | 11° |
| NORTH-SOUTH MEASUREMENTS | Assumed Latitude | | |
| | Declination | | |
| COMPUTED ALTITUDE (Hc) | Hc (using latitude, declination and LHA) | | |
| | Addition for minutes of declination | | |
| | Computed Altitude (Corrected) | | |
| Ho | | | |
| INTERCEPT | Difference between Hc and Ho | | |
| TRUE AZIMUTH (Zn) | Reference | | |
| | Azimuth Angle (using latitude, declination and LHA) | | |
| | True Azimuth | | |

## FROM NAUTICAL ALMANAC

### FRONT COVER

**SUN**

| OCT.—MAR. App. Alt. | Lower Limb | Upper Limb | APR.—SEPT. App. Alt. | Lower Limb | Upper Limb |
|---|---|---|---|---|---|
| ° ′ | ′ | ′ | ° ′ | ′ | ′ |
| 9 34 | +10.8 | −21.5 | 9 39 | +10.6 | −21.2 |
| 9 45 | +10.9 | −21.4 | 9 51 | +10.7 | −21.1 |
| 9 56 | +11.0 | −21.3 | 10 03 | +10.8 | −21.0 |
| 10 08 | +11.1 | −21.2 | 10 15 | +10.9 | −20.9 |
| 10 21 | +11.2 | −21.1 | 10 27 | +11.0 | −20.8 |
| 10 34 | +11.3 | −21.0 | 10 40 | +11.1 | −20.7 |
| 10 47 | +11.4 | −20.9 | 10 54 | +11.2 | −20.6 |
| 11 01 | +11.5 | −20.8 | 11 08 | +11.3 | −20.5 |
| 11 15 | +11.6 | −20.7 | 11 23 | +11.4 | −20.4 |
| 11 30 | +11.7 | −20.6 | 11 38 | +11.5 | −20.3 |
| 11 46 | +11.8 | −20.5 | 11 54 | +11.6 | −20.2 |
| 12 02 | +11.9 | −20.4 | 12 10 | +11.7 | −20.1 |
| 12 19 | +12.0 | −20.3 | 12 28 | +11.8 | −20.0 |
| 12 37 | +12.1 | −20.2 | 12 46 | +11.9 | −19.9 |
| 12 55 | +12.2 | −20.1 | 13 05 | +12.0 | −19.8 |
| 13 14 | +12.3 | −20.0 | 13 24 | +12.1 | −19.7 |
| 13 35 | +12.4 | −19.9 | 13 45 | +12.2 | −19.6 |
| 13 56 | +12.5 | −19.8 | 14 07 | +12.3 | −19.5 |
| 14 18 | +12.6 | −19.7 | 14 30 | +12.4 | −19.4 |
| 14 42 | +12.7 | −19.6 | 14 54 | +12.5 | −19.3 |
| 15 06 | +12.8 | −19.5 | 15 19 | +12.6 | −19.2 |
| 15 32 | +12.9 | −19.4 | 15 46 | +12.7 | −19.1 |
| 15 59 | +13.0 | −19.3 | 16 14 | +12.8 | −19.0 |
| 16 28 | +13.1 | −19.2 | 16 44 | +12.9 | −18.9 |
| 16 59 | +13.2 | −19.1 | 17 15 | +13.0 | −18.8 |
| 17 32 | +13.3 | −19.0 | 17 48 | +13.1 | −18.7 |
| 18 06 | +13.4 | −18.9 | 18 24 | +13.2 | −18.6 |
| 18 42 | +13.5 | −18.8 | 19 01 | +13.3 | −18.5 |
| 19 21 | +13.6 | −18.7 | 19 42 | +13.4 | −18.4 |
| 20 03 | +13.7 | −18.6 | 20 25 | +13.5 | −18.3 |
| 20 48 | +13.8 | −18.5 | 21 11 | +13.6 | −18.2 |
| 21 35 | +13.9 | −18.4 | 22 00 | +13.7 | −18.1 |
| 22 26 | +14.0 | −18.3 | 22 54 | +13.8 | −18.0 |
| 23 22 | +14.1 | −18.2 | 23 51 | +13.9 | −17.9 |
| 24 21 | +14.2 | −18.1 | 24 53 | +14.0 | −17.8 |
| 25 26 | +14.3 | −18.0 | 26 00 | +14.1 | −17.7 |
| 26 36 | +14.4 | −17.9 | 27 13 | +14.2 | −17.6 |
| 27 52 | +14.5 | −17.8 | 28 33 | +14.3 | −17.5 |
| 29 15 | +14.6 | −17.7 | 30 00 | +14.4 | −17.4 |
| 30 46 | +14.7 | −17.6 | 31 35 | +14.5 | −17.3 |
| 32 26 | +14.8 | −17.5 | 33 20 | +14.6 | −17.2 |
| 34 17 | +14.9 | −17.4 | 35 17 | +14.7 | −17.1 |
| 36 20 | +15.0 | −17.3 | 37 26 | +14.8 | −17.0 |
| 38 36 | +15.1 | −17.2 | 39 50 | +14.9 | −16.9 |
| 41 08 | +15.2 | −17.1 | 42 31 | +15.0 | −16.8 |
| 43 59 | +15.3 | −17.0 | 45 31 | +15.1 | −16.7 |
| 47 10 | +15.4 | −16.9 | 48 55 | +15.2 | −16.6 |
| 50 46 | +15.5 | −16.8 | 52 44 | +15.3 | −16.5 |
| 54 49 | +15.6 | −16.7 | 57 02 | +15.4 | −16.4 |
| 59 23 | +15.7 | −16.6 | 61 51 | +15.5 | −16.3 |
| 64 30 | +15.8 | −16.5 | 67 17 | +15.6 | −16.2 |
| 70 12 | +15.9 | −16.4 | 73 16 | +15.7 | −16.1 |
| 76 26 | +16.0 | −16.3 | 79 43 | +15.8 | −16.0 |
| 83 05 | +16.1 | −16.2 | 86 32 | +15.9 | −15.9 |
| 90 00 | | | 90 00 | | |

### FRONT COVER

**DIP**

| Ht. of Eye | Corr^n | Ht. of Eye |
|---|---|---|
| m | ′ | ft. |
| 2.4 | −2.8 | 8.0 |
| 2.6 | −2.9 | 8.6 |
| 2.8 | −3.0 | 9.2 |
| 3.0 | −3.1 | 9.8 |
| 3.2 | −3.2 | 10.5 |
| 3.4 | −3.3 | 11.2 |
| 3.6 | −3.4 | 11.9 |
| 3.8 | −3.5 | 12.6 |
| 4.0 | −3.6 | 13.3 |
| 4.3 | −3.7 | 14.1 |
| 4.5 | −3.8 | 14.9 |
| 4.7 | −3.9 | 15.7 |
| 5.0 | −4.0 | 16.5 |
| 5.2 | −4.1 | 17.4 |
| 5.5 | −4.2 | 18.3 |
| 5.8 | −4.3 | 19.1 |
| 6.1 | −4.4 | 20.1 |
| 6.3 | −4.5 | 21.0 |
| 6.6 | −4.6 | 22.0 |
| 6.9 | −4.7 | 22.9 |
| 7.2 | −4.8 | 23.9 |
| 7.5 | −4.9 | 24.9 |
| 7.9 | −5.0 | 26.0 |
| 8.2 | −5.1 | 27.1 |
| 8.5 | −5.2 | 28.1 |
| 8.8 | −5.3 | 29.2 |
| 9.2 | −5.4 | 30.4 |
| 9.5 | −5.5 | 31.5 |
| 9.9 | −5.6 | 32.7 |
| 10.3 | −5.7 | 33.9 |
| 10.6 | −5.8 | 35.1 |
| 11.0 | −5.9 | 36.3 |
| 11.4 | −6.0 | 37.6 |
| 11.8 | −6.1 | 38.9 |
| 12.2 | −6.2 | 40.1 |
| 12.6 | −6.3 | 41.5 |
| 13.0 | −6.4 | 42.8 |
| 13.4 | −6.5 | 44.2 |
| 13.8 | −6.6 | 45.5 |
| 14.2 | −6.7 | 46.9 |
| 14.7 | −6.8 | 48.4 |
| 15.1 | −6.9 | 49.8 |
| 15.5 | −7.0 | 51.3 |
| 16.0 | −7.1 | 52.8 |
| 16.5 | −7.2 | 54.3 |
| 16.9 | −7.3 | 55.8 |
| 17.4 | −7.4 | 57.4 |
| 17.9 | −7.5 | 58.9 |
| 18.4 | −7.6 | 60.5 |
| 18.8 | −7.7 | 62.1 |
| 19.3 | −7.8 | 63.8 |
| 19.8 | −7.9 | 65.4 |
| 20.4 | −8.0 | 67.1 |
| 20.9 | −8.1 | 68.8 |
| 21.4 | | 70.5 |

| Ht. of Eye | Corr^n |
|---|---|
| m | ′ |
| 1.0 | −1.8 |
| 1.5 | −2.2 |
| 2.0 | −2.5 |
| 2.5 | −2.8 |
| 3.0 | −3.0 |
| See table ← | |
| m | ′ |
| 20 | −7.9 |
| 22 | −8.3 |
| 24 | −8.6 |
| 26 | −9.0 |
| 28 | −9.3 |
| 30 | −9.6 |
| 32 | −10.0 |
| 34 | −10.3 |
| 36 | −10.6 |
| 38 | −10.8 |
| 40 | −11.1 |
| 42 | −11.4 |
| 44 | −11.7 |
| 46 | −11.9 |
| 48 | −12.2 |
| ft. | ′ |
| 2 | −1.4 |
| 4 | −1.9 |
| 6 | −2.4 |
| 8 | −2.7 |
| 10 | −3.1 |
| See table ← | |
| ft. | ′ |
| 70 | −8.1 |
| 75 | −8.4 |
| 80 | −8.7 |
| 85 | −8.9 |
| 90 | −9.2 |
| 95 | −9.5 |
| 100 | −9.7 |
| 105 | −9.9 |
| 110 | −10.2 |
| 115 | −10.4 |
| 120 | −10.6 |
| 125 | −10.8 |
| 130 | −11.1 |
| 135 | −11.3 |
| 140 | −11.5 |
| 145 | −11.7 |
| 150 | −11.9 |
| 155 | −12.1 |

### DAILY PAGE—JULY

**SUN**

| G.M.T. d h | G.H.A. | Dec. |
|---|---|---|
| | ° ′ | ° ′ |
| 15 00 | 178 32.9 | N21 39.4 |
| 01 | 193 32.8 | 39.1 |
| 02 | 208 32.8 | 38.7 |
| 03 | 223 32.7 | · · 38.3 |
| 04 | 238 32.6 | 37.9 |
| 05 | 253 32.6 | 37.5 |
| 06 | 268 32.5 | N21 37.2 |
| 07 | 283 32.4 | 36.8 |
| T 08 | 298 32.4 | 36.4 |
| U 09 | 313 32.3 | · · 36.0 |
| E 10 | 328 32.2 | 35.6 |
| S 11 | 343 32.2 | 35.2 |
| D 12 | 358 32.1 | N21 34.8 |
| A 13 | 13 32.0 | 34.4 |
| Y 14 | 28 32.0 | 34.1 |
| 15 | 43 31.9 | · · 33.7 |
| 16 | 58 31.8 | 33.3 |
| 17 | 73 31.8 | 32.9 |
| 18 | 88 31.7 | N21 32.5 |
| 19 | 103 31.6 | 32.1 |
| 20 | 118 31.6 | 31.7 |
| 21 | 133 31.5 | · · 31.3 |
| 22 | 148 31.4 | 30.9 |
| 23 | 163 31.4 | 30.5 |
| 16 00 | 178 31.3 | N21 30.1 |
| 01 | 193 31.3 | 29.7 |
| 02 | 208 31.2 | 29.3 |
| 03 | 223 31.1 | · · 28.9 |
| 04 | 238 31.1 | 28.5 |
| 05 | 253 31.0 | 28.1 |
| 06 | 268 30.9 | N21 27.7 |
| W 07 | 283 30.9 | 27.3 |
| E 08 | 298 30.8 | 26.9 |
| D 09 | 313 30.8 | · · 26.5 |
| N 10 | 328 30.7 | 26.1 |
| E 11 | 343 30.6 | 25.7 |
| S 12 | 358 30.6 | N21 25.3 |
| D 13 | 13 30.5 | 24.9 |
| A 14 | 28 30.5 | 24.5 |
| Y 15 | 43 30.4 | · · 24.1 |
| 16 | 58 30.3 | 23.7 |
| 17 | 73 30.3 | 23.3 |
| 18 | 88 30.2 | N21 22.9 |
| 19 | 103 30.2 | 22.5 |
| 20 | 118 30.1 | 22.1 |
| 21 | 133 30.0 | · · 21.7 |
| 22 | 148 30.0 | 21.3 |
| 23 | 163 29.9 | 20.8 |
| 17 00 | 178 29.9 | N21 20.4 |
| 01 | 193 29.8 | 20.0 |
| 02 | 208 29.8 | 19.6 |
| 03 | 223 29.7 | · · 19.2 |
| 04 | 238 29.6 | 18.8 |
| 05 | 253 29.6 | 18.4 |
| 06 | 268 29.5 | N21 18.0 |
| 07 | 283 29.5 | 17.5 |
| T 08 | 298 29.4 | 17.1 |
| H 09 | 313 29.4 | · · 16.7 |
| U 10 | 328 29.3 | 16.3 |
| R 11 | 343 29.2 | 15.9 |
| S 12 | 358 29.2 | N21 15.5 |
| D 13 | 13 29.1 | 15.0 |
| A 14 | 28 29.1 | 14.6 |
| Y 15 | 43 29.0 | · · 14.2 |
| 16 | 58 29.0 | 13.8 |
| 17 | 73 28.9 | 13.3 |
| 18 | 88 28.9 | N21 12.9 |
| 19 | 103 28.8 | 12.5 |
| 20 | 118 28.8 | 12.1 |
| 21 | 133 28.7 | · · 11.7 |
| 22 | 148 28.7 | 11.2 |
| 23 | 163 28.6 | 10.8 |
| | S.D. 15.8 | *d* 0.4 |

### YELLOW PAGE

| 12^m | SUN PLANETS |
|---|---|
| s | ° ′ |
| 00 | 3 00.0 |
| 01 | 3 00.3 |
| 02 | 3 00.5 |
| 03 | 3 00.8 |
| 04 | 3 01.0 |
| 05 | 3 01.3 |
| 06 | 3 01.5 |
| 07 | 3 01.8 |
| 08 | 3 02.0 |
| 09 | 3 02.3 |
| 10 | 3 02.5 |
| 11 | 3 02.8 |
| 12 | 3 03.0 |
| 13 | 3 03.3 |
| 14 | 3 03.5 |
| 15 | 3 03.8 |
| 16 | 3 04.0 |
| 17 | 3 04.3 |
| 18 | 3 04.5 |
| 19 | 3 04.8 |
| 20 | 3 05.0 |
| 21 | 3 05.3 |
| 22 | 3 05.5 |
| 23 | 3 05.8 |
| 24 | 3 06.0 |
| 25 | 3 06.3 |
| 26 | 3 06.5 |
| 27 | 3 06.8 |
| 28 | 3 07.0 |
| 29 | 3 07.3 |
| 30 | 3 07.5 |
| 31 | 3 07.8 |
| 32 | 3 08.0 |
| 33 | 3 08.3 |
| 34 | 3 08.5 |
| 35 | 3 08.8 |
| 36 | 3 09.0 |
| 37 | 3 09.3 |
| 38 | 3 09.5 |
| 39 | 3 09.8 |
| 40 | 3 10.0 |
| 41 | 3 10.3 |
| 42 | 3 10.5 |
| 43 | 3 10.8 |
| 44 | 3 11.0 |
| 45 | 3 11.3 |
| 46 | 3 11.5 |
| 47 | 3 11.8 |
| 48 | 3 12.0 |
| 49 | 3 12.3 |
| 50 | 3 12.5 |
| 51 | 3 12.8 |
| 52 | 3 13.0 |
| 53 | 3 13.3 |
| 54 | 3 13.5 |
| 55 | 3 13.8 |
| 56 | 3 14.0 |
| 57 | 3 14.3 |
| 58 | 3 14.5 |
| 59 | 3 14.8 |
| 60 | 3 15.0 |

*The source tables above, needed to complete the first portion of the sight form (left), are labeled according to the pages in the Nautical Almanac on which they appear. In two of these tables, the requisite figures are found through a process called bracketing. For example, to determine the altitude correction for a sun sighting, look down a column titled "App. Alt." (Apparent Altitude) for two numbers that bracket the actual sextant altitude. If the bottom edge of the sun is sighted, the figure under "Lower Limb" gives the correction (green). Bracketing is also used to find the dip correction (blue).*

## A Fix from the Sun—III

Begin work on the second half of the sight form (unshaded here) by rounding off the dead-reckoning latitude of 34°45′N to the nearest whole degree. This produces an assumed latitude of 35°; circle it—and all succeeding numbers that will be needed for work on the plotting sheet. Then go back to the Almanac's daily page for Tuesday, July 15, to the proper hour listing —1700—and note the sun's declination: 21°32.9′N *(orange)*. Because the actual time of the sight—1712:33—falls about a fifth of an hour between 1700 and 1800, lower the declination proportionately toward the 1800 value *(dotted orange line)* and round off to the nearest decimal: 21°32.8′N.

Open H.O. 249 to a page headed by the boat's assumed latitude—35°. The proper declination and LHA listings—21° and 11° respectively—lead to three figures *(purple)* under the headings "Hc" (for computed altitude), "d" (for differential) and "Z" (for azimuth angle). Enter the computed altitude—72°59′. Since the declination is actually 21°32.8′ rather than 21°, the altitude must be adjusted upward, using as a guide the full differential between altitudes for 21° and 22°—51′. Turn to another table in H.O. 249 that corrects for minutes of declination. Since there are nearly 33 minutes, move down the "33" column to the row designated at left as 51; this leads to 28′ *(yellow)*. Add 28′ to the computed altitude for a corrected figure of 73°27′.

Beneath this figure, put the corrected sextant altitude (from the first half of the form). Subtract the smaller figure, in this case the corrected computed altitude, from the larger one. Their difference—22.1′, or 22.1 nautical miles—represents the intercept *(pages 102-103)*. Since the computed altitude was the lesser figure, the intercept is labeled "toward"—meaning that the boat is nearer to the sun's geographical position than was assumed.

Returning to the first H.O. 249 table, look under the "Z" heading for the azimuth angle: 143° *(purple)*. Because the sun's declination is roughly halfway between 21° and 22°, change the azimuth angle to 142°, splitting the difference between the "Z" readings of 143° for 21° and 141° for 22° *(dotted purple line)*. And since the sun is west of the boat, subtract 142° from a reference figure of 360 *(pages 98-99)*; this yields a true azimuth of 218°. With this last bit of information in hand, you are ready to turn to your plotting sheet *(pages 110-111)* and establish the position of your vessel.

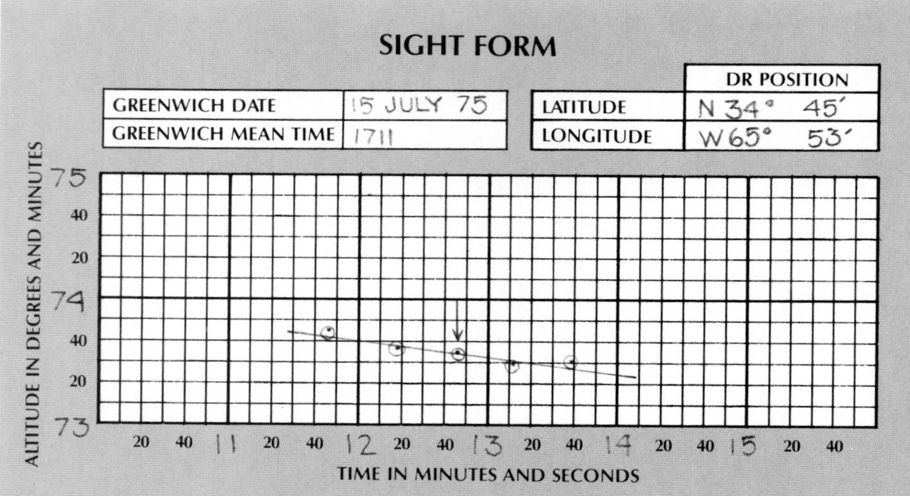

**SIGHT FORM**

| | |
|---|---|
| GREENWICH DATE | 15 JULY 75 |
| GREENWICH MEAN TIME | 1711 |

| DR POSITION | |
|---|---|
| LATITUDE | N 34° 45′ |
| LONGITUDE | W 65° 53′ |



| CELESTIAL BODY | | | SUN |
|---|---|---|---|
| CORRECTED SEXTANT ALTITUDE (Ho) | Actual Sextant Altitude | | 73° 35.2′ |
| | Corrections: Index | + 1.2′ | |
| | Altitude | + 15.7′ | |
| | Dip | − 3.0′ | |
| | Total | +13.9′ | + 13.9′ |
| | Corrected Sextant Altitude | | 73° 49.1′ |
| GREENWICH MEAN TIME (GMT) | Chronometer | | 17h 12m 46s |
| | Chronometer Correction | | −0 13s |
| | Greenwich Mean Time | | 17h 12m 33s |
| GREENWICH HOUR ANGLE (GHA) | GMT hour listing | | 73° 31.8′ |
| | GMT min./sec. listing | | 3° 08.3′ |
| | Total Greenwich Hour Angle | | 76° 40.1′ |
| EAST-WEST MEASUREMENTS | Assumed Longitude | | 65 40.1′ |
| | Local Hour Angle (GHA minus assumed longitude) | | 11° |
| NORTH-SOUTH MEASUREMENTS | Assumed Latitude | | N 35° |
| | Declination | | N 21° 32.8′ |
| COMPUTED ALTITUDE (Hc) | Hc (using latitude, declination and LHA) | | 72° 59′ |
| | Addition for minutes of declination | | 28′ |
| | Computed Altitude (Corrected) | | 73° 27′ |
| Ho | | | 73° 49.1′ |
| INTERCEPT | Difference between Hc and Ho | | TOWARD 22.1 |
| TRUE AZIMUTH (Zn) | Reference | | 360° |
| | Azimuth Angle (using latitude, declination and LHA) | | 142° |
| | True Azimuth | | 218° |

## NAUTICAL ALMANAC

### DAILY PAGE—JULY

| G.M.T. | | SUN | |
|---|---|---|---|
| d | h | G.H.A. | Dec. |
| | | ° ′ | ° ′ |
| 15 | 00 | 178 32.9 | N21 39.4 |
| | 01 | 193 32.8 | 39.1 |
| | 02 | 208 32.8 | 38.7 |
| | 03 | 223 32.7 | · · 38.3 |
| | 04 | 238 32.6 | 37.9 |
| | 05 | 253 32.6 | 37.5 |
| | 06 | 268 32.5 | N21 37.2 |
| | 07 | 283 32.4 | 36.8 |
| | 08 | 298 32.4 | 36.4 |
| T | 09 | 313 32.3 | · · 36.0 |
| U | 10 | 328 32.2 | 35.6 |
| E | 11 | 343 32.2 | 35.2 |
| S | 12 | 358 32.1 | N21 34.8 |
| D | 13 | 13 32.0 | 34.4 |
| A | 14 | 28 32.0 | 34.1 |
| Y | 15 | 43 31.9 | · · 33.7 |
| | 16 | 58 31.8 | 33.3 |
| | 17 | 73 31.8 | 32.9 |
| | 18 | 88 31.7 | N21 32.5 |
| | 19 | 103 31.6 | 32.1 |
| | 20 | 118 31.6 | 31.7 |
| | 21 | 133 31.5 | · · 31.3 |
| | 22 | 148 31.4 | 30.9 |
| | 23 | 163 31.4 | 30.5 |
| 16 | 00 | 178 31.3 | N21 30.1 |
| | 01 | 193 31.3 | 29.7 |

## FROM H.O. 249

### LAT 35° DECLINATION (15°-29°) SAME NAME AS LATITUDE

| LHA | 15° Hc | d | Z | 16° Hc | d | Z | 17° Hc | d | Z | 18° Hc | d | Z | 19° Hc | d | Z | 20° Hc | d | Z | 21° Hc | d | Z | 22° Hc | d | Z | 23° Hc | d | Z | 24° Hc | d | Z | 25° Hc | d | Z |
|---|---|---|---|---|---|---|---|---|---|---|---|---|---|---|---|---|---|---|---|---|---|---|---|---|---|---|---|---|---|---|---|---|---|
| | ° ′ | ′ | ° | ° ′ | ′ | ° | ° ′ | ′ | ° | ° ′ | ′ | ° | ° ′ | ′ | ° | ° ′ | ′ | ° | ° ′ | ′ | ° | ° ′ | ′ | ° | ° ′ | ′ | ° | ° ′ | ′ | ° | ° ′ | ′ | ° |
| 0 | 70 00 | +60 | 180 | 71 00 | +60 | 180 | 72 00 | +60 | 180 | 73 00 | +60 | 180 | 74 00 | +60 | 180 | 75 00 | +60 | 180 | 76 00 | +60 | 180 | 77 00 | +60 | 180 | 78 00 | +60 | 180 | 79 00 | +60 | 180 | 80 00 | +60 | 180 |
| 1 | 69 59 | 60 | 177 | 70 59 | 60 | 177 | 71 59 | 60 | 177 | 72 59 | 60 | 177 | 73 59 | 59 | 177 | 74 58 | 60 | 176 | 75 58 | 60 | 176 | 76 58 | 60 | 176 | 77 58 | 60 | 176 | 78 58 | 60 | 175 | 79 58 | 60 | 175 |
| 2 | 69 55 | 60 | 174 | 70 55 | 60 | 174 | 71 55 | 59 | 174 | 72 54 | 60 | 174 | 73 54 | 60 | 173 | 74 54 | 59 | 173 | 75 53 | 60 | 172 | 76 53 | 59 | 172 | 77 52 | 60 | 171 | 78 52 | 59 | 171 | 79 51 | 59 | 170 |
| 3 | 69 49 | 60 | 172 | 70 49 | 59 | 171 | 71 48 | 60 | 171 | 72 48 | 59 | 170 | 73 47 | 59 | 170 | 74 46 | 59 | 169 | 75 45 | 59 | 169 | 76 44 | 59 | 168 | 77 43 | 59 | 167 | 78 42 | 58 | 166 | 79 40 | 58 | 165 |
| 4 | 69 41 | 59 | 169 | 70 40 | 59 | 168 | 71 39 | 59 | 168 | 72 38 | 59 | 167 | 73 37 | 58 | 167 | 74 35 | 59 | 166 | 75 34 | 58 | 165 | 76 32 | 58 | 164 | 77 30 | 58 | 163 | 78 28 | 57 | 161 | 79 25 | 57 | 160 |
| 5 | 69 30 | +59 | 166 | 70 29 | +58 | 166 | 71 27 | +59 | 165 | 72 26 | +58 | 164 | 73 24 | +58 | 163 | 74 22 | +58 | 162 | 75 20 | +57 | 161 | 76 17 | +57 | 160 | 77 14 | +57 | 159 | 78 11 | +55 | 157 | 79 06 | +56 | 155 |
| 6 | 69 17 | 58 | 163 | 70 15 | 58 | 163 | 71 13 | 58 | 162 | 72 11 | 57 | 161 | 73 08 | 58 | 160 | 74 06 | 56 | 159 | 75 02 | 57 | 158 | 75 59 | 56 | 156 | 76 55 | 55 | 155 | 77 50 | 54 | 153 | 78 44 | 54 | 151 |
| 7 | 69 02 | 58 | 161 | 70 00 | 57 | 160 | 70 57 | 57 | 159 | 71 54 | 56 | 158 | 72 50 | 57 | 157 | 73 47 | 56 | 156 | 74 43 | 55 | 154 | 75 38 | 54 | 153 | 76 32 | 54 | 151 | 77 26 | 53 | 149 | 78 19 | 51 | 147 |
| 8 | 68 45 | 57 | 158 | 69 42 | 56 | 157 | 70 38 | 56 | 156 | 71 34 | 56 | 155 | 72 30 | 55 | 154 | 73 25 | 55 | 153 | 74 20 | 54 | 151 | 75 14 | 53 | 150 | 76 07 | 53 | 148 | 77 00 | 51 | 146 | 77 51 | 49 | 143 |
| 9 | 68 26 | 56 | 156 | 69 22 | 55 | 155 | 70 17 | 56 | 154 | 71 13 | 55 | 153 | 72 08 | 54 | 151 | 73 02 | 53 | 150 | 73 55 | 53 | 148 | 74 48 | 52 | 146 | 75 40 | 51 | 144 | 76 31 | 49 | 142 | 77 20 | 48 | 140 |
| 10 | 68 05 | +55 | 153 | 69 00 | +55 | 152 | 69 55 | +54 | 151 | 70 49 | +54 | 150 | 71 43 | +53 | 148 | 72 36 | +52 | 147 | 73 28 | +52 | 145 | 74 20 | +50 | 143 | 75 10 | +50 | 141 | 76 00 | +47 | 139 | 76 47 | +46 | 137 |
| 11 | 67 42 | 54 | 151 | 68 36 | 54 | 150 | 69 30 | 53 | 149 | 70 23 | 53 | 147 | 71 16 | 52 | 146 | 72 08 | 51 | 144 | 72 59 | 51 | 143 | 73 50 | 49 | 141 | 74 39 | 47 | 139 | 75 26 | 47 | 136 | 76 13 | 44 | 134 |
| 12 | 67 17 | 53 | 149 | 68 10 | 53 | 148 | 69 03 | 53 | 146 | 69 56 | 52 | 145 | 70 48 | 51 | 143 | 71 39 | 50 | 142 | 72 29 | 48 | 140 | 73 17 | 48 | 138 | 74 05 | 46 | 136 | 74 51 | 45 | 133 | 75 36 | 43 | 131 |
| 13 | 66 50 | 53 | 147 | 67 43 | 52 | 145 | 68 35 | 52 | 144 | 69 27 | 50 | 143 | 70 17 | 50 | 141 | 71 07 | 49 | 139 | 71 56 | 48 | 137 | 72 44 | 46 | 135 | 73 30 | 45 | 133 | 74 15 | 43 | 131 | 74 58 | 41 | 128 |
| 14 | 66 23 | 51 | 144 | 67 14 | 52 | 143 | 68 06 | 50 | 142 | 68 56 | 50 | 140 | 69 46 | 48 | 139 | 70 34 | 48 | 137 | 71 22 | 46 | 135 | 72 08 | 46 | 133 | 72 54 | 43 | 131 | 73 37 | 42 | 128 | 74 19 | 40 | 126 |

### Correction to Tabulated Altitude for Minutes of Declination

| d / ′ | 1 | 2 | 3 | 4 | 5 | 6 | 7 | 8 | 9 | 10 | 11 | 12 | 13 | 14 | 15 | 16 | 17 | 18 | 19 | 20 | 21 | 22 | 23 | 24 | 25 | 26 | 27 | 28 | 29 | 30 | 31 | 32 | 33 | 34 | 35 | 36 | 37 | 38 | 39 | 40 | 41 | 42 | 43 | 44 | 45 |
|---|---|---|---|---|---|---|---|---|---|---|---|---|---|---|---|---|---|---|---|---|---|---|---|---|---|---|---|---|---|---|---|---|---|---|---|---|---|---|---|---|---|---|---|---|---|
| 0 | 0 | 0 | 0 | 0 | 0 | 0 | 0 | 0 | 0 | 0 | 0 | 0 | 0 | 0 | 0 | 0 | 0 | 0 | 0 | 0 | 0 | 0 | 0 | 0 | 0 | 0 | 0 | 0 | 0 | 0 | 0 | 0 | 0 | 0 | 0 | 0 | 0 | 0 | 0 | 0 | 0 | 0 | 0 | 0 | 0 |
| 1 | 0 | 0 | 0 | 0 | 0 | 0 | 0 | 0 | 0 | 0 | 0 | 0 | 0 | 0 | 0 | 0 | 0 | 0 | 0 | 0 | 0 | 0 | 0 | 0 | 0 | 0 | 0 | 0 | 0 | 0 | 1 | 1 | 1 | 1 | 1 | 1 | 1 | 1 | 1 | 1 | 1 | 1 | 1 | 1 | 1 |
| 2 | 0 | 0 | 0 | 0 | 0 | 0 | 0 | 0 | 0 | 0 | 0 | 0 | 0 | 0 | 0 | 1 | 1 | 1 | 1 | 1 | 1 | 1 | 1 | 1 | 1 | 1 | 1 | 1 | 1 | 1 | 1 | 1 | 1 | 1 | 1 | 1 | 1 | 1 | 1 | 1 | 1 | 1 | 1 | 1 | 2 |
| 3 | 0 | 0 | 0 | 0 | 0 | 0 | 0 | 0 | 0 | 0 | 1 | 1 | 1 | 1 | 1 | 1 | 1 | 1 | 1 | 1 | 1 | 1 | 1 | 1 | 1 | 1 | 1 | 1 | 1 | 2 | 2 | 2 | 2 | 2 | 2 | 2 | 2 | 2 | 2 | 2 | 2 | 2 | 2 | 2 | 2 |
| 47 | 1 | 2 | 2 | 3 | 4 | 5 | 5 | 6 | 7 | 8 | 9 | 9 | 10 | 11 | 12 | 13 | 13 | 14 | 15 | 16 | 16 | 17 | 18 | 19 | 20 | 20 | 21 | 22 | 23 | 24 | 24 | 25 | 26 | 27 | 27 | 28 | 29 | 30 | 31 | 31 | 32 | 33 | 34 | 34 | 35 |
| 48 | 1 | 2 | 2 | 3 | 4 | 5 | 6 | 6 | 7 | 8 | 9 | 10 | 10 | 11 | 12 | 13 | 14 | 14 | 15 | 16 | 17 | 18 | 18 | 19 | 20 | 21 | 22 | 22 | 23 | 24 | 25 | 26 | 26 | 27 | 28 | 29 | 30 | 30 | 31 | 32 | 33 | 34 | 34 | 35 | 36 |
| 49 | 1 | 2 | 2 | 3 | 4 | 5 | 6 | 7 | 7 | 8 | 9 | 10 | 11 | 11 | 12 | 13 | 14 | 15 | 16 | 16 | 17 | 18 | 19 | 20 | 20 | 21 | 22 | 23 | 24 | 24 | 25 | 26 | 27 | 28 | 29 | 29 | 30 | 31 | 32 | 33 | 33 | 34 | 35 | 36 | 37 |
| 50 | 1 | 2 | 2 | 3 | 4 | 5 | 6 | 7 | 8 | 8 | 9 | 10 | 11 | 12 | 12 | 13 | 14 | 15 | 16 | 17 | 18 | 18 | 19 | 20 | 21 | 22 | 22 | 23 | 24 | 25 | 26 | 27 | 28 | 28 | 29 | 30 | 31 | 32 | 32 | 33 | 34 | 35 | 36 | 37 | 38 |
| 51 | 1 | 2 | 3 | 3 | 4 | 5 | 6 | 7 | 8 | 8 | 9 | 10 | 11 | 12 | 13 | 14 | 14 | 15 | 16 | 17 | 18 | 19 | 20 | 20 | 21 | 22 | 23 | 24 | 25 | 26 | 26 | 27 | 28 | 29 | 30 | 31 | 31 | 32 | 33 | 34 | 35 | 36 | 37 | 37 | 38 |
| 52 | 1 | 2 | 3 | 3 | 4 | 5 | 6 | 7 | 8 | 9 | 10 | 10 | 11 | 12 | 13 | 14 | 15 | 16 | 16 | 17 | 18 | 19 | 20 | 21 | 22 | 23 | 23 | 24 | 25 | 26 | 27 | 28 | 29 | 29 | 30 | 31 | 32 | 33 | 34 | 35 | 36 | 36 | 37 | 38 | 39 |
| 53 | 1 | 2 | 3 | 4 | 4 | 5 | 6 | 7 | 8 | 9 | 10 | 11 | 11 | 12 | 13 | 14 | 15 | 16 | 17 | 18 | 19 | 19 | 20 | 21 | 22 | 23 | 24 | 25 | 26 | 26 | 27 | 28 | 29 | 30 | 31 | 32 | 33 | 34 | 34 | 35 | 36 | 37 | 38 | 39 | 40 |
| 54 | 1 | 2 | 3 | 4 | 4 | 5 | 6 | 7 | 8 | 9 | 10 | 11 | 12 | 13 | 14 | 14 | 15 | 16 | 17 | 18 | 19 | 20 | 21 | 22 | 22 | 23 | 24 | 25 | 26 | 27 | 28 | 29 | 30 | 31 | 32 | 32 | 33 | 34 | 35 | 36 | 37 | 38 | 39 | 40 | 40 |
| 55 | 1 | 2 | 3 | 4 | 5 | 6 | 6 | 7 | 8 | 9 | 10 | 11 | 12 | 13 | 14 | 15 | 16 | 16 | 17 | 18 | 19 | 20 | 21 | 22 | 23 | 24 | 25 | 26 | 27 | 28 | 28 | 29 | 30 | 31 | 32 | 33 | 34 | 35 | 36 | 37 | 38 | 38 | 39 | 40 | 41 |
| 56 | 1 | 2 | 3 | 4 | 5 | 6 | 7 | 7 | 8 | 9 | 10 | 11 | 12 | 13 | 14 | 15 | 16 | 17 | 18 | 19 | 20 | 21 | 21 | 22 | 23 | 24 | 25 | 26 | 27 | 28 | 29 | 30 | 31 | 32 | 33 | 34 | 35 | 35 | 36 | 37 | 38 | 39 | 40 | 41 | 42 |
| 57 | 1 | 2 | 3 | 4 | 5 | 6 | 7 | 8 | 9 | 10 | 10 | 11 | 12 | 13 | 14 | 15 | 16 | 17 | 18 | 19 | 20 | 21 | 22 | 23 | 24 | 25 | 26 | 27 | 28 | 28 | 29 | 30 | 31 | 32 | 33 | 34 | 35 | 36 | 37 | 38 | 39 | 40 | 41 | 42 | 43 |
| 58 | 1 | 2 | 3 | 4 | 5 | 6 | 7 | 8 | 9 | 10 | 11 | 12 | 13 | 14 | 14 | 15 | 16 | 17 | 18 | 19 | 20 | 21 | 22 | 23 | 24 | 25 | 26 | 27 | 28 | 29 | 30 | 31 | 32 | 33 | 34 | 35 | 36 | 37 | 38 | 39 | 40 | 41 | 42 | 43 | 44 |
| 59 | 1 | 2 | 3 | 4 | 5 | 6 | 7 | 8 | 9 | 10 | 11 | 12 | 13 | 14 | 15 | 16 | 17 | 18 | 19 | 20 | 21 | 22 | 23 | 24 | 25 | 26 | 27 | 28 | 29 | 30 | 30 | 31 | 32 | 33 | 34 | 35 | 36 | 37 | 38 | 39 | 40 | 41 | 42 | 43 | 44 |

*Completion of the sight form (left) requires one Almanac table used earlier (top) and two new tables from H.O. 249. The middle table above is labeled "same name as latitude." This means that the table applies only to situations in which the boat and the sun are in the same hemisphere; if they were in opposite hemispheres, the navigator would use a table labeled "contrary name to latitude." In using the top two tables, a navigator must generally calculate values lying between those indicated by solid colors and those by dotted lines.*

## A Fix from the Sun—IV

As his final step, the navigator applies sight-form data to a plotting sheet *(opposite)*—a rudimentary large-scale chart inscribed with latitude and longitude lines and a compass rose. He utilizes two sets of sight-form figures, which are noted in the upper left corner of the sheet, along with the dead-reckoning coordinates: one set *(blue notations)* comes from the form worked out on the preceding pages, the other set is from a second sight made several hours later *(red)*.

Start by marking the dead-reckoning position (DR), using dividers to measure off minutes of latitude and longitude according to the scales printed on the chart's edges. Next, mark the assumed position for the first sun sight at latitude 35°N and longitude 65°40.1′W.

With parallel rules, line up the true azimuth (Zn) of 218° on the compass rose; then shift the rules to draw the true azimuth from the assumed position *(dashed blue)*. Along this line, measure off the intercept of 22.1′. At the end of the intercept, draw a line *(solid blue)* perpendicular to the dashed blue line. This "sun line" is the straight-line equivalent of an arc of position on the earth's curved surface, as represented in the theoretical triangle explained on pages 102-103.

To roughly determine the boat's location on the line of position, draw a line *(dashed black)* from the DR position perpendicular to the sun line. At the juncture, inscribe a small square labeled EP—the best estimate of the boat's position at the time of the sight. For a more precise position, the sun line must be made to intersect with a second sun line. Following the steps detailed above, plot a sun line *(solid red)* for the second sight, made at 2042.

The solid blue line will now be moved, or advanced, to the solid red line. To accomplish this, estimate the boat's average course steered and miles traveled since the first sight; in this case the advance is 18 miles at a course of 260°. With parallel rules, line up 260° on the rose and shift it to the EP. Then set the dividers to 18 minutes of latitude and draw a line of that length along the rules from the EP. At the tip of this line, draw another line *(dashed black)* parallel to the solid blue line; it represents the first sun line advanced to the second. Its intersection with the solid red line is a running fix, so-called because the first sun line has been run forward. Read this fix off the chart with dividers; it indicates the position of the boat at the time of the second sight to be: latitude 34°48′N, longitude 66°30′W.

*Making his final plot, the navigator measures off the intercept with dividers set to the proper number of minutes on the plotting sheet's latitude scale—each minute of latitude being equal to one nautical mile.*

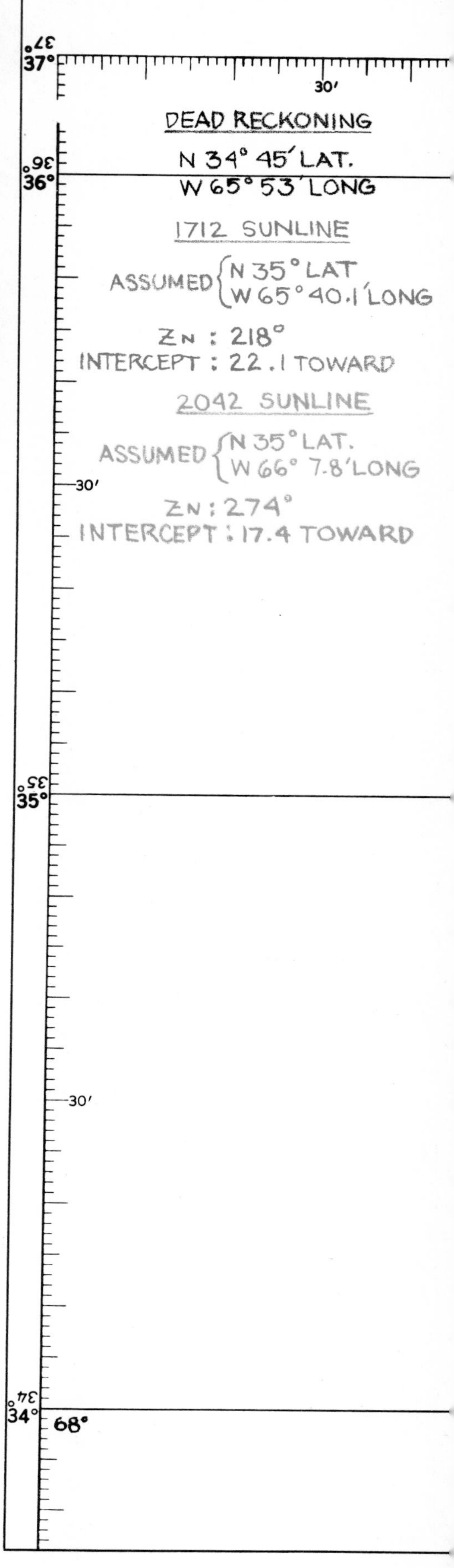

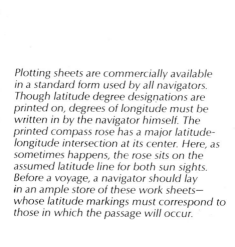

*Plotting sheets are commercially available in a standard form used by all navigators. Though latitude degree designations are printed on, degrees of longitude must be written in by the navigator himself. The printed compass rose has a major latitude-longitude intersection at its center. Here, as sometimes happens, the rose sits on the assumed latitude line for both sun sights. Before a voyage, a navigator should lay in an ample store of these work sheets—whose latitude markings must correspond to those in which the passage will occur.*

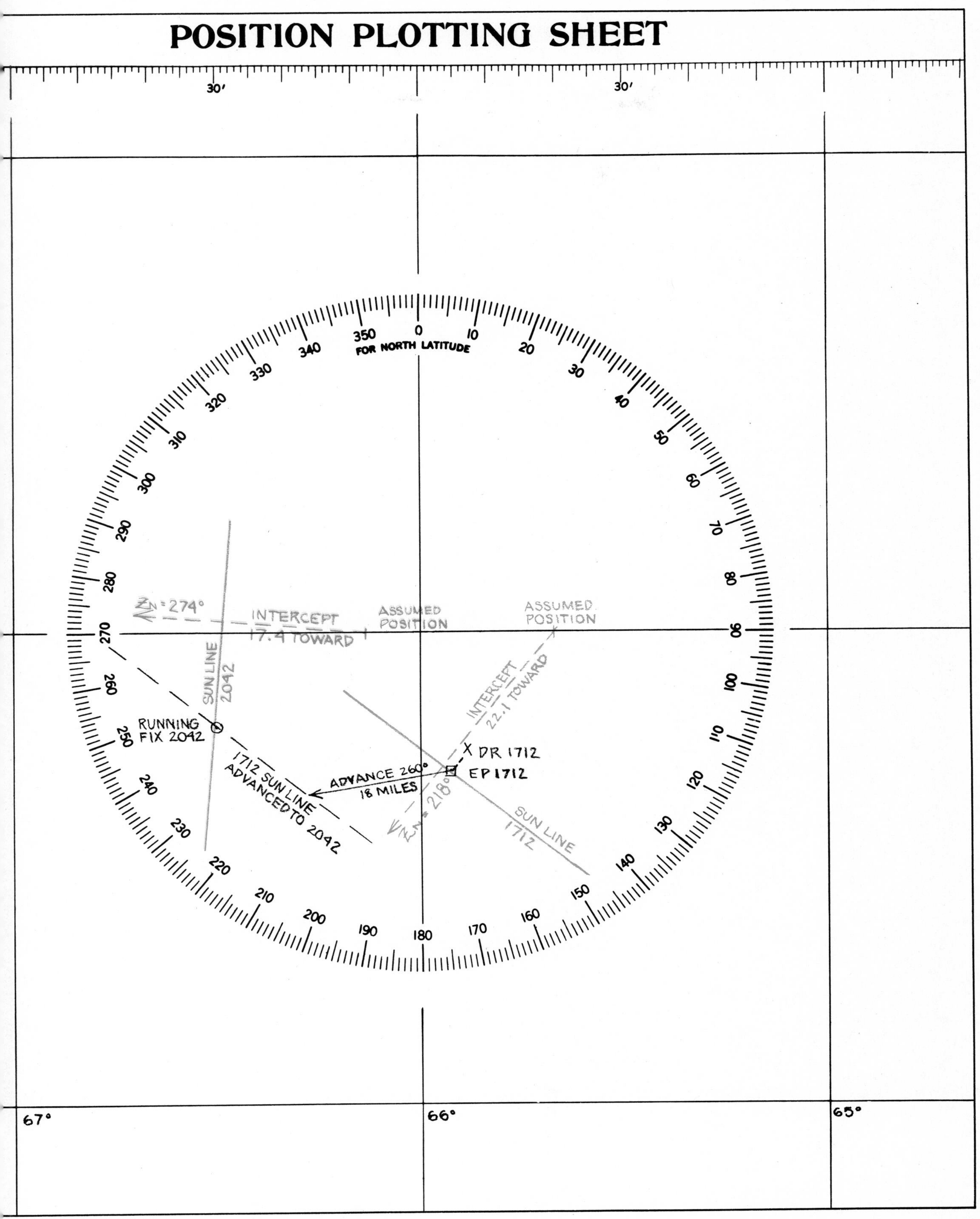
POSITION PLOTTING SHEET
30′
30′
FOR NORTH LATITUDE
ZN = 274°
INTERCEPT
17.4 TOWARD
ASSUMED POSITION
ASSUMED POSITION
SUN LINE 2042
INTERCEPT 22.1 TOWARD
RUNNING FIX 2042
X DR 1712
EP 1712
ADVANCE 260°
18 MILES
1712 SUN LINE ADVANCED TO 2042
ZN = 218°
SUN LINE 1712
67°
66°
65°

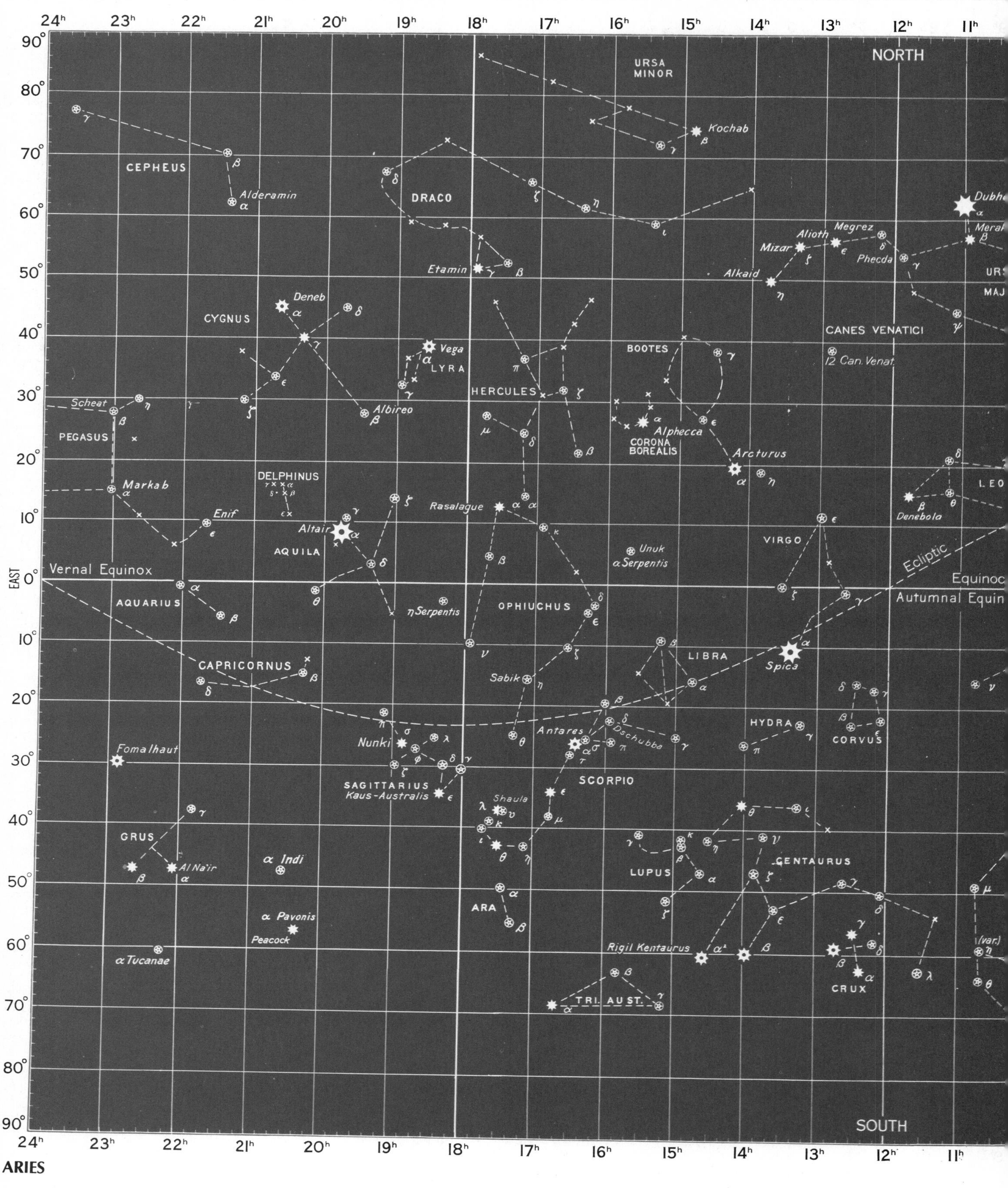
NORTH
SOUTH
EAST
Vernal Equinox
Autumnal Equinox
Ecliptic
ARIES
URSA MINOR
CEPHEUS
DRACO
CYGNUS
LYRA
HERCULES
BOOTES
CORONA BOREALIS
CANES VENATICI
PEGASUS
DELPHINUS
AQUILA
AQUARIUS
OPHIUCHUS
VIRGO
LEO
CAPRICORNUS
LIBRA
HYDRA
CORVUS
SAGITTARIUS
SCORPIO
GRUS
LUPUS
CENTAURUS
ARA
CRUX
TRI. AUST.
Kochab
Alderamin
Etamin
Deneb
Vega
Albireo
Scheat
Markab
Enif
Altair
Rasalague
Alphecca
Arcturus
Unuk
α Serpentis
η Serpentis
Sabik
Antares
Dschubba
Spica
Nunki
Kaus-Australis
Shaula
Fomalhaut
Al Na'ir
α Indi
α Pavonis
Peacock
α Tucanae
Rigil Kentaurus
Mizar
Alioth
Megrez
Phecda
Alkaid
Dubhe
Merak
12 Can. Venat.
Denebola

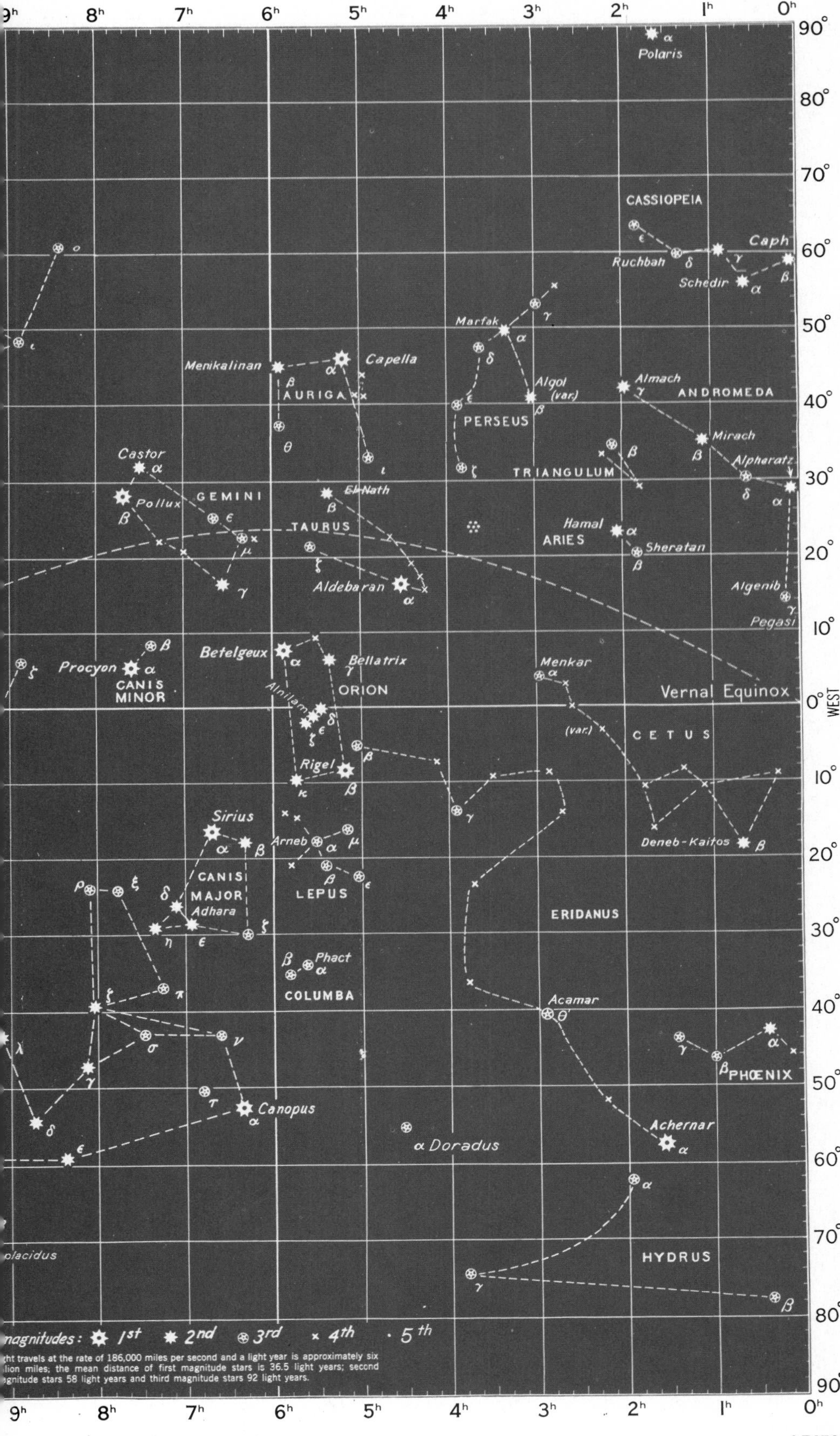


# A Star Fix—I

When a navigator gets ready to take dawn or dusk sights, he has a choice of three sorts of celestial reference points: stars, planets or the moon. Of the three, the stars are the easiest to use. Both the moon and the planets, due to their closeness to the earth, require extra calculations to account for their complex movements through the celestial sphere over the course of a year. The stars, by contrast, are so distant from the earth that they hold a nearly constant position within the sphere. Moreover, stars are especially useful because there are so many of them that they present an almost unlimited number of sighting options.

A novice navigator can familiarize himself with the stars by buying a chart like the one at left—a Mercator projection of the celestial sphere. On this map appear all of the stars favored by mariners for brightness and convenient distribution across the heavens. Many of them are parts of constellations—star configurations that are of value to the navigator as quick, offhand guides to the location of particular stars in them.

As with the sun, the position of each star can be expressed by the coordinates of declination (listed along the sides of the chart in degrees) and hour angles (listed at top and bottom). However, the navigator never has to worry about the Greenwich hour angle of a star in the twilight sky. Instead, he need know only the Greenwich hour angle of an ingenious celestial bench mark called Aries. This is an arbitrary meridian drawn across the celestial sphere; it is located at both the 0-hour and 24-hour meridians on the chart. Because all stars maintain a constant position relative to this base line, the angular distance between Aries and individual stars has been precomputed in H.O. 249, greatly simplifying the calculations a navigator must perform.

*This star chart, available at any map store, flattens out the celestial sphere into a Mercator projection. Constellations are in capital letters, and individual stars in both capital and lower-case letters. All stars are represented by symbols of their magnitude, or brightness, as noted at the bottom of the chart. Here, three first-magnitude symbols have been given extra size in order to locate the stars that will be sighted in the navigational problem on pages 114-119.*

## A Star Fix—II

While sun sights can be as unhurried as a navigator desires, star-sighting sessions call for swift, efficient execution, since the stars and the horizon are simultaneously visible for only a quarter of an hour or so after sunset or before sunrise. Careful advance planning is crucial.

To begin with, a navigator needs to know when twilight (applied here to both the periods before sunrise and after sunset) will occur at his longitude so he and his equipment will be ready. He obtains this information by consulting the Nautical Almanac and doing a bit of arithmetic *(right)*. In making these predictions, he must deal with two closely allied concepts of twilight—nautical and civil. Nautical twilight is the span of time between sunrise or sunset and the moment when the sun lies 12° below the horizon. Civil twilight is a half portion of the nautical twilight span—the lighter half, between sunrise or sunset and the moment the sun is 6° below the horizon. The optimal period for sighting lies roughly midway through nautical twilight, or around the beginning of civil twilight in the morning and its conclusion in the evening.

The next planning task is to choose three suitable stars as celestial reference points. They should lie in widely separated directions so that they produce widely angled lines of position on a plotting sheet; and their altitudes should be less than 80° or so, since stars almost directly overhead are difficult to sight. Although stars can be picked out freehand at the time of the sighting session, many navigators employ an inexpensive device called a star finder *(opposite)* to make the selection in advance. This is advisable because the navigator must check H.O. 249 to be sure it contains figures for the chosen stars: not all stars are precalculated in the tables for all boat positions.

The star finder predicts the true azimuths and approximate altitudes of major stars as observed from any point on earth, allowing the navigator to select stars that meet the sighting criteria of wide separation and manageable elevation. To operate the device, the navigator must first work out the local hour angle of Aries. This is done by looking up the Greenwich hour angle of Aries on the daily page of the Nautical Almanac under the anticipated time of the sight, then subtracting the boat's estimated longitude from the figure. When the navigator has made his choices and goes on deck for the sightings, the star-finder data will help him to spot his chosen celestial bodies quickly.

LOCAL DATE: JULY 15, 1975
DEAD RECKONING POSITION: LATITUDE, 35°W
LONGITUDE, 67°W

TIME OF SUNSET AT THE GREENWICH MERIDIAN: 1914

CONCLUDING TIMES OF TWILIGHT AT THE GREENWICH MERIDIAN: CIVIL, 1943; NAUTICAL, 2019

TIME DIFFERENTIAL BETWEEN THE GREENWICH MERIDIAN AND THE BOAT'S LONGITUDE:

67° ÷ 15° = 4 HRS. WITH 7° REMAINING
7° x 4 MINS. = 28 MINS.
TOTAL 4 HRS. 28 MINS.

TIME (GMT) OF SUNSET AND TWILIGHT AT BOAT'S LONGITUDE:

| | SUNSET | | | TWILIGHT | | | | |
|---|---|---|---|---|---|---|---|---|
| | | | | CIVIL | | | NAUTICAL | |
| | HRS. | MINS. | | HRS. | MINS. | | HRS. | MINS. |
| ALMANAC | 19 | 14 | | 19 | 43 | | 20 | 19 |
| DIFFERENCE FOR 67°W LONGITUDE | +4 | 28 | + | 4 | 28 | + | 4 | 28 |
| TIME (GMT) AT BOAT'S LONGITUDE | 23 | 42 | | 23 OR 24 OR 00 | 71 OR 11 OR 11 (JULY 16) | | 24 OR 00 | 47 OR 47 (JULY 16) |

*This work sheet shows how a navigator predicts the optimum star-sighting time—in this case, after sunset—at his longitude. First, he jots down the local date and the dead-reckoning coordinates. On the correct daily page of the Nautical Almanac, in the columns dealing with sunset and twilight (opposite), he finds the row for the boat's latitude—35°. That gives him the times when sunset occurs and civil and nautical twilight conclude at the Greenwich meridian (blue). To adjust the times to the boat's longitude—67°W—the navigator divides 67° by 15, since there are 15° of longitude to an hour. This yields 4 hours with 7° left over. Since a degree equals 4 minutes of time, 4 hours and 28 minutes must be added to the Almanac times (if the boat were east of Greenwich it would be subtracted).*

| Lat. | Sunset | Twilight Civil | Twilight Naut. |
|---|---|---|---|
| ° | h m | h m | h m |
| N 72 | ▭ | ▭ | ▭ |
| N 70 | ▭ | ▭ | ▭ |
| 68 | ▭ | ▭ | ▭ |
| 66 | 22 32 | //// | //// |
| 64 | 21 54 | //// | //// |
| 62 | 21 27 | 23 14 | //// |
| 60 | 21 07 | 22 24 | //// |
| N 58 | 20 50 | 21 54 | //// |
| 56 | 20 36 | 21 31 | 23 19 |
| 54 | 20 24 | 21 13 | 22 33 |
| 52 | 20 13 | 20 58 | 22 05 |
| 50 | 20 04 | 20 45 | 21 44 |
| 45 | 19 44 | 20 20 | 21 06 |
| N 40 | 19 28 | 19 59 | 20 39 |
| 35 | 19 14 | 19 43 | 20 19 |
| 30 | 19 02 | 19 29 | 20 02 |
| 20 | 18 43 | 19 07 | 19 35 |
| N 10 | 18 26 | 18 48 | 19 15 |
| 0 | 18 10 | 18 32 | 18 58 |
| S 10 | 17 54 | 18 16 | 18 42 |
| 20 | 17 37 | 18 01 | 18 28 |
| 30 | 17 18 | 17 44 | 18 13 |
| 35 | 17 07 | 17 34 | 18 06 |
| 40 | 16 54 | 17 24 | 17 57 |
| 45 | 16 39 | 17 12 | 17 48 |
| S 50 | 16 21 | 16 58 | 17 38 |
| 52 | 16 12 | 16 51 | 17 34 |
| 54 | 16 02 | 16 44 | 17 29 |
| 56 | 15 51 | 16 36 | 17 24 |
| 58 | 15 39 | 16 28 | 17 18 |
| S 60 | 15 24 | 16 18 | 17 12 |

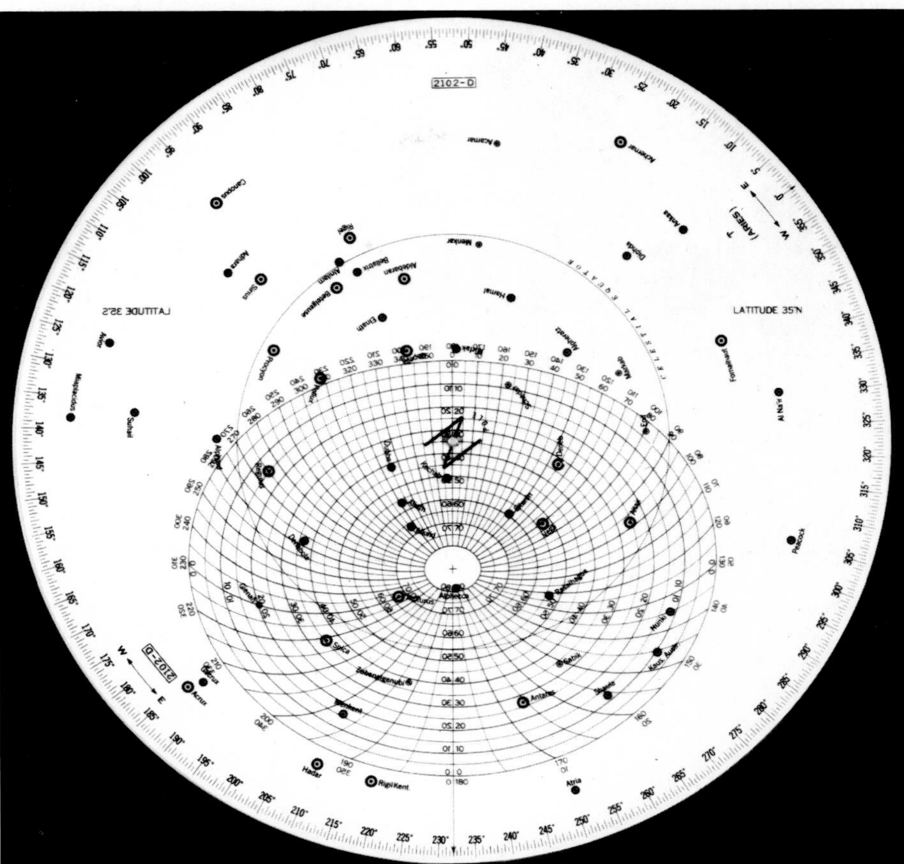


*The star finder consists of a white plastic disc on which major stars and a local-hour-angle index are inscribed, together with a set of nine transparent overlays exactly the size of the disc. On each overlay is an oval-shaped network of lines that represents the sky as seen from anywhere within a span of 10° of latitude. The numbered concentric lines of the oval predict the altitude of stars; the numbers on the oval's perimeter supply true azimuth. The device is operated by fitting the appropriate overlay on the disc and orienting the overlay so that its elongated arrow points to the local hour angle of Aries. The disc and the overlays are inscribed on both sides so they can be used in the Southern as well as the Northern Hemisphere.*

## A Star Fix—III

The same kind of calculating form used for navigating by the sun serves for a star sight. However, the simpler mathematics of star sights allows several spaces on the form to be ignored, as indicated at right and explained opposite. The figures on this particular form are based on a sighting of the star Dubhe.

As with the sun sight, begin the star exercise by using the graph to take an average altitude for Dubhe. Enter this actual sextant altitude on the form, then add up the corrections for index, altitude *(green)* and dip *(blue)*. Because the total correction is negative, subtract it from the actual sextant altitude to get the corrected sextant altitude.

After entering the chronometer time for the chosen sight and correcting it for known clock error, turn to the Nautical Almanac to determine the Greenwich hour angle (GHA) of Aries. Add the hourly portion found opposite the date and hour listing on the daily page *(orange)* to the minutes-and-seconds portion from a yellow-tinted page in the Almanac *(red)*. The total GHA is 298°57.9′.

Establish an assumed longitude by altering the minutes of the dead-reckoning longitude to match those of the total GHA of Aries. Circle it, since this figure will be needed on the plotting sheet. Subtract the assumed longitude from the GHA to obtain a local hour angle (LHA) of Aries that has no minutes—232°. Round off the dead-reckoning latitude to the nearest whole degree for an assumed latitude of 35°N. Circle it. Since this is a star sight, declination is not entered. Open H.O. 249 to the page for the assumed latitude; locate the column for Dubhe, and go down to the row for the correct LHA of Aries. Opposite this figure is the computed altitude (Hc)—41°19′ *(purple)*. Enter it (no correction is required). Copy the corrected sextant altitude below and compare it with the computed altitude. Here, the computed altitude is greater by 13.2′—representing the length of the intercept. Following the maxim "Computed greater away," label the intercept "away," and circle it. Consult H.O. 249 again for the true azimuth (Zn); here, it is 325° *(purple)*. Circle this, too.

The sight form for Dubhe is now complete. Fill out two identical forms for the other star sights to obtain all the data needed to solve the navigational problem on the plotting sheet *(pages 118-119)*.

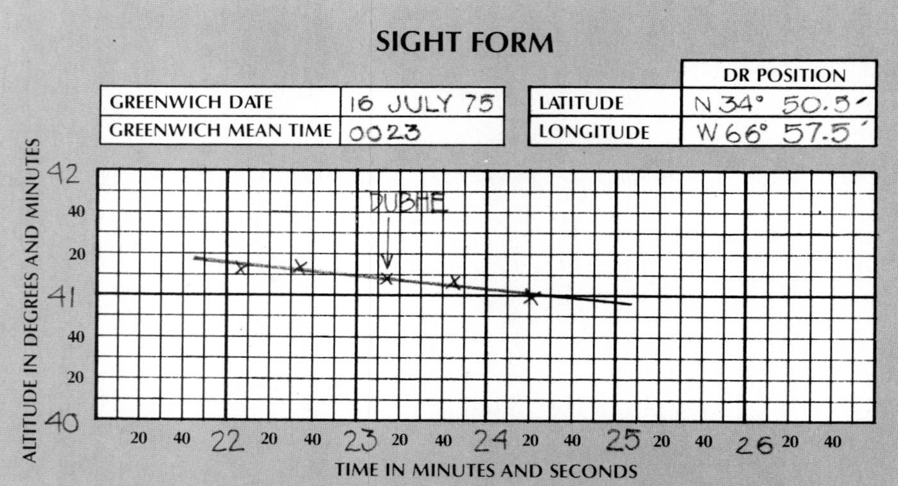

SIGHT FORM

| GREENWICH DATE | 16 JULY 75 |
|---|---|
| GREENWICH MEAN TIME | 0023 |

| DR POSITION | |
|---|---|
| LATITUDE | N 34° 50.5′ |
| LONGITUDE | W 66° 57.5′ |



| CELESTIAL BODY | | | DUBHE |
|---|---|---|---|
| CORRECTED SEXTANT ALTITUDE (Ho) | Actual Sextant Altitude | | 41° 08.7′ |
| | Corrections: Index | + 1.2′ | |
| | Altitude | − 1.1′ | |
| | Dip | − 3.0′ | |
| | Total | − 2.9′ | −2.9′ |
| | Corrected Sextant Altitude | | 41° 05.8′ |
| GREENWICH MEAN TIME (GMT) | Chronometer | | ooh 23m 11s |
| | Chronometer Correction | | −14s |
| | Greenwich Mean Time | | ooh 22m 57s |
| GREENWICH HOUR ANGLE (GHA) | GMT hour listing | | 293° 12.7′ |
| | GMT min./sec. listing | | 5° 45.2′ |
| | Total Greenwich Hour Angle ARIES | | 298° 57.9′ |
| EAST-WEST MEASUREMENTS | Assumed Longitude | | 66° 57.9′ |
| | Local Hour Angle (GHA minus assumed longitude) ARIES | | 232° |
| NORTH-SOUTH MEASUREMENTS | Assumed Latitude | | N 35° |
| | Declination | | — |
| COMPUTED ALTITUDE (Hc) | Hc (using latitude, declination and LHA) | | 41° 19′ |
| | Addition for minutes of declination | | — |
| | Computed Altitude (Corrected) | | 41° 19′ |
| Ho | | | 41° 05.8′ |
| INTERCEPT | Difference between Hc and Ho | | AWAY 13.2 |
| TRUE AZIMUTH (Zn) | Reference | | — |
| | Azimuth Angle (using latitude, declination and LHA) | | — |
| | True Azimuth | | 325° |

## FROM NAUTICAL ALMANAC

### FRONT COVER

**STARS AND PLANETS**

| App. Alt. | Corr$^n$ |
|---|---|
| 9 56 | |
| | −5·3 |
| 10 08 | |
| | −5·2 |
| 10 20 | |
| | −5·1 |
| 10 33 | |
| | −5·0 |
| 10 46 | |
| | −4·9 |
| 11 00 | |
| | −4·8 |
| 11 14 | |
| | −4·7 |
| 11 29 | |
| | −4·6 |
| 11 45 | |
| | −4·5 |
| 12 01 | |
| | −4·4 |
| 12 18 | |
| | −4·3 |
| 12 35 | |
| | −4·2 |
| 12 54 | |
| | −4·1 |
| 13 13 | |
| | −4·0 |
| 13 33 | |
| | −3·9 |
| 13 54 | |
| | −3·8 |
| 14 16 | |
| | −3·7 |
| 14 40 | |
| | −3·6 |
| 15 04 | |
| | −3·5 |
| 15 30 | |
| | −3·4 |
| 15 57 | |
| | −3·3 |
| 16 26 | |
| | −3·2 |
| 16 56 | |
| | −3·1 |
| 17 28 | |
| | −3·0 |
| 18 02 | |
| | −2·9 |
| 18 38 | |
| | −2·8 |
| 19 17 | |
| | −2·7 |
| 19 58 | |
| | −2·6 |
| 20 42 | |
| | −2·5 |
| 21 28 | |
| | −2·4 |
| 22 19 | |
| | −2·3 |
| 23 13 | |
| | −2·2 |
| 24 11 | |
| | −2·1 |
| 25 14 | |
| | −2·0 |
| 26 22 | |
| | −1·9 |
| 27 36 | |
| | −1·8 |
| 28 56 | |
| | −1·7 |
| 30 24 | |
| | −1·6 |
| 32 00 | |
| | −1·5 |
| 33 45 | |
| | −1·4 |
| 35 40 | |
| | −1·3 |
| 37 48 | |
| | −1·2 |
| 40 08 | |
| | −1·1 |
| 42 44 | |
| | −1·0 |
| 45 36 | |
| | −0·9 |
| 48 47 | |
| | −0·8 |
| 52 18 | |
| | −0·7 |
| 56 11 | |
| | −0·6 |
| 60 28 | |
| | −0·5 |
| 65 08 | |
| | −0·4 |
| 70 11 | |
| | −0·3 |
| 75 34 | |
| | −0·2 |
| 81 13 | |
| | −0·1 |
| 87 03 | |
| | 0·0 |
| 90 00 | |

| App. Alt. | Additional Corr$^n$ |
|---|---|
| **1975** | |
| **VENUS** | |
| Jan. 1 – June 7 | |
| 0° | |
| 42° | + 0·1 |
| June 8 – July 21 | |
| 0° | |
| 46° | + 0·3 |
| July 22 – Aug. 6 | |
| 0° | |
| 11° | + 0·4 |
| 41° | + 0·5 |
| Aug. 7 – Aug. 15 | |
| 0° | |
| 6° | + 0·5 |
| 20° | + 0·6 |
| 31° | + 0·7 |
| Aug. 16 – Sept. 10 | |
| 0° | |
| 4° | + 0·6 |
| 12° | + 0·7 |
| 22° | + 0·8 |
| Sept. 11 – Sept. 19 | |
| 0° | |
| 6° | + 0·5 |
| 20° | + 0·6 |
| 31° | + 0·7 |
| Sept. 20 – Oct. 5 | |
| 0° | |
| 11° | + 0·4 |
| 41° | + 0·5 |
| Oct. 6 – Nov. 22 | |
| 0° | |
| 46° | + 0·3 |
| Nov. 23 – Dec. 31 | |
| 0° | |
| 42° | + 0·1 |
| **MARS** | |
| Jan. 1 – Sept. 8 | |
| 0° | |
| 60° | + 0·1 |
| Sept. 9 – Nov. 22 | |
| 0° | |
| 41° | + 0·2 |
| 75° | + 0·1 |
| Nov. 23 – Dec. 31 | |
| 0° | |
| 34° | + 0·3 |
| 60° | + 0·2 |
| 80° | + 0·1 |

**DIP**

| Ht. of Eye (m) | Corr$^n$ | Ht. of Eye (ft.) |
|---|---|---|
| 2·4 | | 8·0 |
| | −2·8 | |
| 2·6 | | 8·6 |
| | −2·9 | |
| 2·8 | | 9·2 |
| | −3·0 | |
| 3·0 | | 9·8 |
| | −3·1 | |
| 3·2 | | 10·5 |
| | −3·2 | |
| 3·4 | | 11·2 |
| | −3·3 | |
| 3·6 | | 11·9 |
| | −3·4 | |
| 3·8 | | 12·6 |
| | −3·5 | |
| 4·0 | | 13·3 |
| | −3·6 | |
| 4·3 | | 14·1 |
| | −3·7 | |
| 4·5 | | 14·9 |
| | −3·8 | |
| 4·7 | | 15·7 |
| | −3·9 | |
| 5·0 | | 16·5 |
| | −4·0 | |
| 5·2 | | 17·4 |
| | −4·1 | |
| 5·5 | | 18·3 |
| | −4·2 | |
| 5·8 | | 19·1 |
| | −4·3 | |
| 6·1 | | 20·1 |
| | −4·4 | |
| 6·3 | | 21·0 |
| | −4·5 | |
| 6·6 | | 22·0 |
| | −4·6 | |
| 6·9 | | 22·9 |
| | −4·7 | |
| 7·2 | | 23·9 |
| | −4·8 | |
| 7·5 | | 24·9 |
| | −4·9 | |
| 7·9 | | 26·0 |
| | −5·0 | |
| 8·2 | | 27·1 |
| | −5·1 | |
| 8·5 | | 28·1 |
| | −5·2 | |
| 8·8 | | 29·2 |
| | −5·3 | |
| 9·2 | | 30·4 |
| | −5·4 | |
| 9·5 | | 31·5 |
| | −5·5 | |
| 9·9 | | 32·7 |
| | −5·6 | |
| 10·3 | | 33·9 |
| | −5·7 | |
| 10·6 | | 35·1 |
| | −5·8 | |
| 11·0 | | 36·3 |
| | −5·9 | |
| 11·4 | | 37·6 |
| | −6·0 | |
| 11·8 | | 38·9 |
| | −6·1 | |
| 12·2 | | 40·1 |
| | −6·2 | |
| 12·6 | | 41·5 |
| | −6·3 | |
| 13·0 | | 42·8 |
| | −6·4 | |
| 13·4 | | 44·2 |
| | −6·5 | |
| 13·8 | | 45·5 |
| | −6·6 | |
| 14·2 | | 46·9 |
| | −6·7 | |
| 14·7 | | 48·4 |
| | −6·8 | |
| 15·1 | | 49·8 |
| | −6·9 | |
| 15·5 | | 51·3 |
| | −7·0 | |
| 16·0 | | 52·8 |
| | −7·1 | |
| 16·5 | | 54·3 |
| | −7·2 | |
| 16·9 | | 55·8 |
| | −7·3 | |
| 17·4 | | 57·4 |
| | −7·4 | |
| 17·9 | | 58·9 |
| | −7·5 | |
| 18·4 | | 60·5 |
| | −7·6 | |
| 18·8 | | 62·1 |
| | −7·7 | |
| 19·3 | | 63·8 |
| | −7·8 | |
| 19·8 | | 65·4 |
| | −7·9 | |
| 20·4 | | 67·1 |
| | −8·0 | |
| 20·9 | | 68·8 |
| | −8·1 | |
| 21·4 | | 70·5 |

### DAILY PAGE JULY

| Day | G.M.T. d h | ARIES G.H.A. ° ′ |
|---|---|---|
| | 15 00 | 292 13.6 |
| | 01 | 307 16.1 |
| | 02 | 322 18.5 |
| | 03 | 337 21.0 |
| | 04 | 352 23.5 |
| | 05 | 7 25.9 |
| | 06 | 22 28.4 |
| | 07 | 37 30.9 |
| | 08 | 52 33.3 |
| TUESDAY | 09 | 67 35.8 |
| | 10 | 82 38.2 |
| | 11 | 97 40.7 |
| | 12 | 112 43.2 |
| | 13 | 127 45.6 |
| | 14 | 142 48.1 |
| | 15 | 157 50.6 |
| | 16 | 172 53.0 |
| | 17 | 187 55.5 |
| | 18 | 202 58.0 |
| | 19 | 218 00.4 |
| | 20 | 233 02.9 |
| | 21 | 248 05.3 |
| | 22 | 263 07.8 |
| | 23 | 278 10.3 |
| | 16 00 | 293 12.7 |
| | 01 | 308 15.2 |
| | 02 | 323 17.7 |
| | 03 | 338 20.1 |
| | 04 | 353 22.6 |
| | 05 | 8 25.1 |
| | 06 | 23 27.5 |
| | 07 | 38 30.0 |
| | 08 | 53 32.5 |
| WEDNESDAY | 09 | 68 34.9 |
| | 10 | 83 37.4 |
| | 11 | 98 39.8 |
| | 12 | 113 42.3 |
| | 13 | 128 44.8 |
| | 14 | 143 47.2 |
| | 15 | 158 49.7 |
| | 16 | 173 52.2 |
| | 17 | 188 54.6 |
| | 18 | 203 57.1 |
| | 19 | 218 59.6 |
| | 20 | 234 02.0 |
| | 21 | 249 04.5 |
| | 22 | 264 07.0 |
| | 23 | 279 09.4 |
| | 17 00 | 294 11.9 |
| | 01 | 309 14.3 |
| | 02 | 324 16.8 |
| | 03 | 339 19.3 |
| | 04 | 354 21.7 |
| | 05 | 9 24.2 |
| | 06 | 24 26.7 |
| | 07 | 39 29.1 |
| | 08 | 54 31.6 |
| THURSDAY | 09 | 69 34.1 |
| | 10 | 84 36.5 |
| | 11 | 99 39.0 |
| | 12 | 114 41.4 |
| | 13 | 129 43.9 |
| | 14 | 144 46.4 |
| | 15 | 159 48.8 |
| | 16 | 174 51.3 |
| | 17 | 189 53.8 |
| | 18 | 204 56.2 |
| | 19 | 219 58.7 |
| | 20 | 235 01.2 |
| | 21 | 250 03.6 |
| | 22 | 265 06.1 |
| | 23 | 280 08.6 |
| Mer. Pass. | h m | 4 26.4 |

### YELLOW PAGE

**22m**

| 22m s | SUN PLANETS ° ′ | ARIES ° ′ |
|---|---|---|
| 00 | 5 30·0 | 5 30·9 |
| 01 | 5 30·3 | 5 31·2 |
| 02 | 5 30·5 | 5 31·4 |
| 03 | 5 30·8 | 5 31·7 |
| 04 | 5 31·0 | 5 31·9 |
| 05 | 5 31·3 | 5 32·2 |
| 06 | 5 31·5 | 5 32·4 |
| 07 | 5 31·8 | 5 32·7 |
| 08 | 5 32·0 | 5 32·9 |
| 09 | 5 32·3 | 5 33·2 |
| 10 | 5 32·5 | 5 33·4 |
| 11 | 5 32·8 | 5 33·7 |
| 12 | 5 33·0 | 5 33·9 |
| 13 | 5 33·3 | 5 34·2 |
| 14 | 5 33·5 | 5 34·4 |
| 15 | 5 33·8 | 5 34·7 |
| 16 | 5 34·0 | 5 34·9 |
| 17 | 5 34·3 | 5 35·2 |
| 18 | 5 34·5 | 5 35·4 |
| 19 | 5 34·8 | 5 35·7 |
| 20 | 5 35·0 | 5 35·9 |
| 21 | 5 35·3 | 5 36·2 |
| 22 | 5 35·5 | 5 36·4 |
| 23 | 5 35·8 | 5 36·7 |
| 24 | 5 36·0 | 5 36·9 |
| 25 | 5 36·3 | 5 37·2 |
| 26 | 5 36·5 | 5 37·4 |
| 27 | 5 36·8 | 5 37·7 |
| 28 | 5 37·0 | 5 37·9 |
| 29 | 5 37·3 | 5 38·2 |
| 30 | 5 37·5 | 5 38·4 |
| 31 | 5 37·8 | 5 38·7 |
| 32 | 5 38·0 | 5 38·9 |
| 33 | 5 38·3 | 5 39·2 |
| 34 | 5 38·5 | 5 39·4 |
| 35 | 5 38·8 | 5 39·7 |
| 36 | 5 39·0 | 5 39·9 |
| 37 | 5 39·3 | 5 40·2 |
| 38 | 5 39·5 | 5 40·4 |
| 39 | 5 39·8 | 5 40·7 |
| 40 | 5 40·0 | 5 40·9 |
| 41 | 5 40·3 | 5 41·2 |
| 42 | 5 40·5 | 5 41·4 |
| 43 | 5 40·8 | 5 41·7 |
| 44 | 5 41·0 | 5 41·9 |
| 45 | 5 41·3 | 5 42·2 |
| 46 | 5 41·5 | 5 42·4 |
| 47 | 5 41·8 | 5 42·7 |
| 48 | 5 42·0 | 5 42·9 |
| 49 | 5 42·3 | 5 43·2 |
| 50 | 5 42·5 | 5 43·4 |
| 51 | 5 42·8 | 5 43·7 |
| 52 | 5 43·0 | 5 43·9 |
| 53 | 5 43·3 | 5 44·2 |
| 54 | 5 43·5 | 5 44·4 |
| 55 | 5 43·8 | 5 44·7 |
| 56 | 5 44·0 | 5 44·9 |
| 57 | 5 44·3 | 5 45·2 |
| 58 | 5 44·5 | 5 45·4 |
| 59 | 5 44·8 | 5 45·7 |
| 60 | 5 45·0 | 5 45·9 |

## FROM H.O. 249

**LAT 35°N**

| LHA ♈ | Hc | Zn |
|---|---|---|
| | Dubhe | |
| 180 | 61 36 | 346 |
| 181 | 61 24 | 345 |
| 182 | 61 11 | 344 |
| 183 | 60 57 | 343 |
| 184 | 60 42 | 342 |
| 185 | 60 27 | 341 |
| 186 | 60 11 | 341 |
| 187 | 59 54 | 340 |
| 188 | 59 37 | 339 |
| 189 | 59 19 | 338 |
| 190 | 59 01 | 338 |
| 191 | 58 42 | 337 |
| 192 | 58 23 | 336 |
| 193 | 58 03 | 336 |
| 194 | 57 42 | 335 |
| | Dubhe | |
| 195 | 57 21 | 335 |
| 196 | 57 00 | 334 |
| 197 | 56 38 | 333 |
| 198 | 56 16 | 333 |
| 199 | 55 53 | 332 |
| 200 | 55 30 | 332 |
| 201 | 55 07 | 331 |
| 202 | 54 44 | 331 |
| 203 | 54 20 | 331 |
| 204 | 53 55 | 330 |
| 205 | 53 31 | 330 |
| 206 | 53 06 | 329 |
| 207 | 52 41 | 329 |
| 208 | 52 15 | 329 |
| 209 | 51 50 | 328 |
| | Dubhe | |
| 210 | 51 24 | 328 |
| 211 | 50 58 | 328 |
| 212 | 50 31 | 328 |
| 213 | 50 05 | 327 |
| 214 | 49 38 | 327 |
| 215 | 49 11 | 327 |
| 216 | 48 44 | 327 |
| 217 | 48 17 | 326 |
| 218 | 47 50 | 326 |
| 219 | 47 22 | 326 |
| 220 | 46 55 | 326 |
| 221 | 46 27 | 326 |
| 222 | 45 59 | 326 |
| 223 | 45 32 | 325 |
| 224 | 45 04 | 325 |
| | ♦Dubhe | |
| 225 | 44 36 | 325 |
| 226 | 44 08 | 325 |
| 227 | 43 40 | 325 |
| 228 | 43 11 | 325 |
| 229 | 42 43 | 325 |
| 230 | 42 15 | 325 |
| 231 | 41 47 | 325 |
| 232 | 41 19 | 325 |
| 233 | 40 50 | 325 |
| 234 | 40 22 | 325 |
| 235 | 39 54 | 325 |
| 236 | 39 25 | 325 |
| 237 | 38 57 | 325 |
| 238 | 38 29 | 325 |
| 239 | 38 01 | 325 |
| | ♦Alkaid | |
| 240 | 61 43 | 311 |
| 241 | 61 06 | 311 |
| 242 | 60 29 | 310 |
| 243 | 59 51 | 310 |
| 244 | 59 13 | 310 |
| 245 | 58 35 | 309 |
| 246 | 57 57 | 309 |
| 247 | 57 19 | 309 |
| 248 | 56 40 | 309 |
| 249 | 56 02 | 308 |
| 250 | 55 23 | 308 |
| 251 | 54 45 | 308 |
| 252 | 54 06 | 308 |
| 253 | 53 27 | 308 |
| 254 | 52 48 | 308 |
| | Kochab | |
| 255 | 47 43 | 348 |
| 256 | 47 33 | 347 |
| 257 | 47 22 | 347 |
| 258 | 47 10 | 347 |
| 259 | 46 59 | 346 |
| 260 | 46 47 | 346 |
| 261 | 46 35 | 346 |
| 262 | 46 23 | 346 |
| 263 | 46 11 | 345 |
| 264 | 45 58 | 345 |
| 265 | 45 46 | 345 |
| 266 | 45 33 | 345 |
| 267 | 45 19 | 344 |
| 268 | 45 06 | 344 |
| 269 | 44 53 | 344 |

*Star-sight calculations require the array of tables above—three from the Nautical Almanac and one from H.O. 249. The Almanac tables on the daily page and the yellow page differ from those used for sights in that they supply a Greenwich hour angle for Aries, rather than for the celestial body. The H.O. 249 table is also compiled somewhat differently from its sun-sight counterpart. Because the declination of a star remains constant, it is not a factor in the figures for the computed altitude (Hc); also, the star's true azimuth can be given directly, eliminating the need for azimuth angle and the related reference figure, both used to work out true azimuth for sun sights.*

## A Star Fix—IV

As with the sight form, the same kind of plotting sheet used for establishing a sun-sight position also serves for the stars. And just as the sight calculations were simpler for the stars, so, too, are plotting procedures: since all lines of position derive from a single sighting session, none of them have to be advanced to account for the passage of time.

Start work on the sheet by marking the assumed position for the first star sight —in this case, Dubhe *(blue notations);* use dividers to gauge minutes of latitude and longitude according to the scales on the sheet's edges. Label the position by the star's initial. Next, with parallel rules, line up Dubhe's true azimuth (Zn) of 325° on the compass rose. Then shift the rules to draw a line of corresponding direction *(dashed blue)* through the assumed position. Mark the line with an arrowhead to denote the direction from the observer to the star.

Again, place the dividers on the plotting sheet's latitude scale and adjust them to match the intercept—13.2 miles. Then, beginning at the assumed position, mark the intercept along the true-azimuth line *away* from the direction indicated by the arrowhead, in accordance with the sight-form notations. At the end of the intercept measurement, draw a line of position perpendicular to the line of true azimuth.

Repeat the plotting procedure for the other two stars, producing two additional lines of position. The intersection of the three lines of position forms the triangular cocked hat. A point in the middle of the triangle represents the boat's position at the time of the sighting session: latitude 34°45.8′N, longitude 66°53.4′W.



*In the plotting exercise for star sights, the sheet is annotated in much the same way as for sun problems. Note, however, that the dead-reckoning position (DR) and the fix are labeled with the time of the second of three star sights—to provide a rough time for all three. Another distinctive feature of star-sight plots is that the three lines of position offer the navigator a means of detecting a possible error in his calculations. If the cocked hat formed by the lines seems unusually large, he should recheck his figures—starting with those for any line of position that is particularly distant from the DR position.*

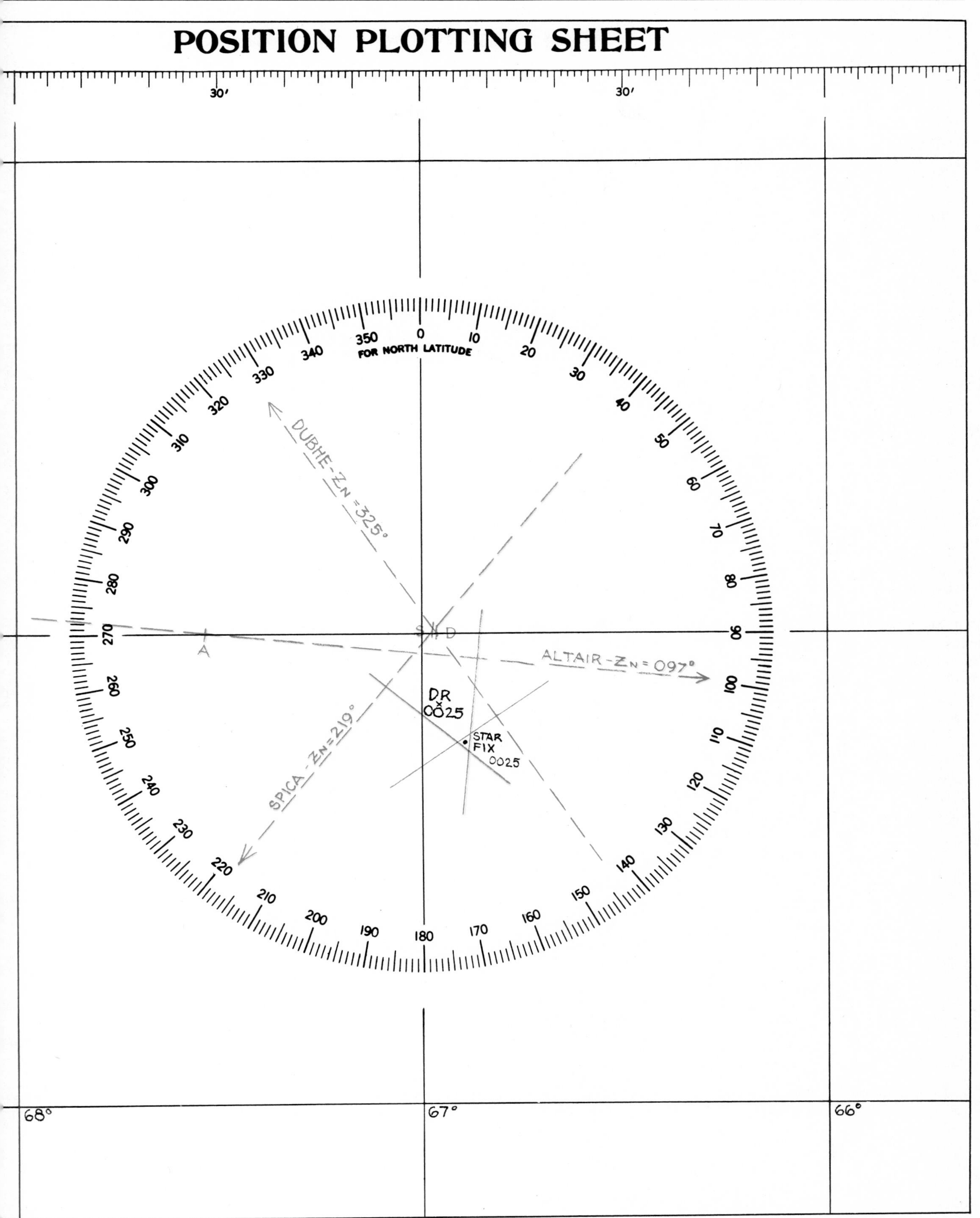
POSITION PLOTTING SHEET
30′
30′
FOR NORTH LATITUDE
DUBHE-ZN=325°
ALTAIR-ZN=097°
SPICA-ZN=219°
DR
0025
STAR
FIX
0025
A
S
D
68°
67°
66°

## A Navigator's Shortcut

In the early 1970s, the electronics industry presented offshore sailors with an expensive but almost miraculous alternative to traditional navigational techniques: compact electronic calculators that can liberate the navigator from sight reduction tables, the Nautical Almanac, the sight form and even the plotting sheet. These miniature computers can not only establish a boat's position but are also able to perform a multitude of related tasks, such as dead reckoning or making predictions of the time of twilight.

The core of a navigational calculator's genius is a set of magnetic strips, each one encoded with an astounding portion of the information in the printed volumes. On the single strip at far right, for example, is an equation that enables the calculator to generate all the figures in Volume II of H.O. 249.

To use the calculator, the navigator must still make sextant sightings and note their Greenwich Mean Times. Then, by inserting selected strips and punching data through the instrument's various keys, he works out his position. As each strip goes into the slot just below the display panel, the calculator stores the coded information in its memory bank and ejects the strip so that others can be passed through the machine.

The number and sequence of strips fed into the machine depend on the type of problem being solved—but the calculator always supplies answers much faster than could any novice navigator. When used to work out a fix, for instance, the device flashes a digital read-out of the boat's latitude and longitude about five minutes after the start of the problem. In addition to requiring little effort, this automated device carries what many navigators regard as the ultimate bonus: it never makes a mistake in arithmetic.

*After a sight has been taken with the sextant (top left) the navigator can extract all of the information needed for a fix from magnetic programing strips like those arrayed at right. The strips beneath the Nautical Almanac —plus the one that has been inserted in the calculator—contain all the data that is in the Almanac, including altitude corrections, declinations, Greenwich hour angles and local hour angles at the boat's assumed position. The remaining strip underneath H.O. 249 programs the calculator to work out computed altitudes and true-azimuth figures that would ordinarily come from that volume.*

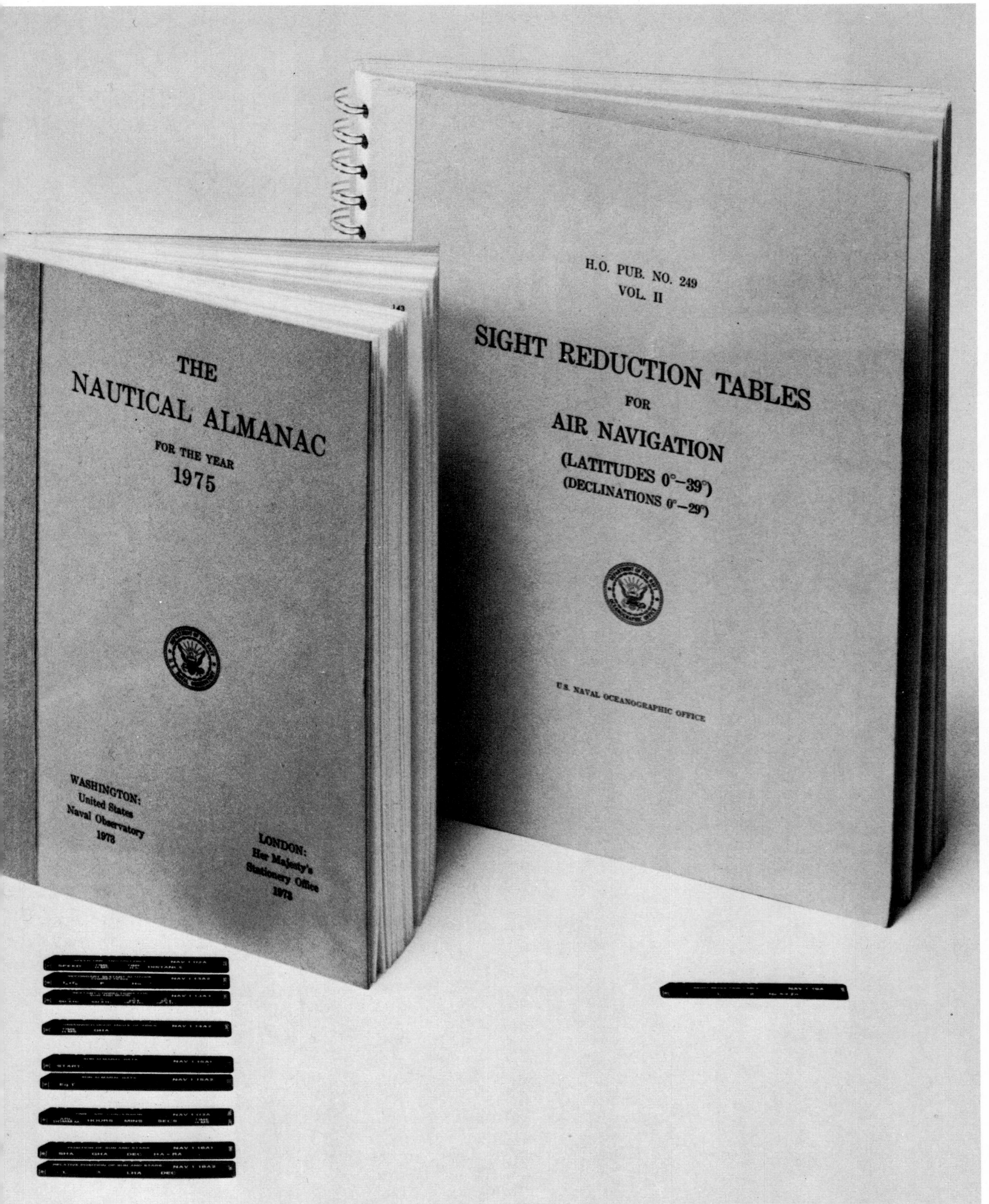
THE
NAUTICAL ALMANAC
FOR THE YEAR
1975
WASHINGTON:
United States
Naval Observatory
1973
LONDON:
Her Majesty's
Stationery Office
1973
H.O. PUB. NO. 249
VOL. II
SIGHT REDUCTION TABLES
FOR
AIR NAVIGATION
(LATITUDES 0°–39°)
(DECLINATIONS 0°–29°)
U.S. NAVAL OCEANOGRAPHIC OFFICE

# TOOLS OF THE ANCIENT WAYFINDERS

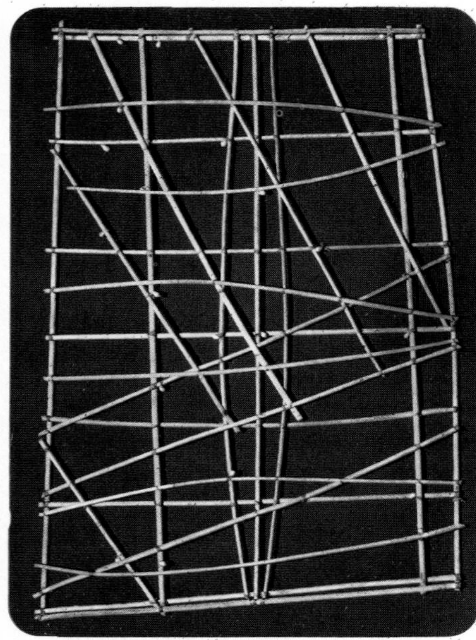

*A complex interweaving of wave patterns and two chains of islands are represented in this rebbelib, or stick chart, of the Marshall Islands. The chart was probably made by a navigator for teaching purposes. Its precise interpretation is not known, but it is believed that the straight lines are the map's framework, the small shells represent islands, the diagonals indicate ocean swells driven by the northeast trade winds, and the curved sticks show where patterns are deflected by islands. Where two wave sticks cross, the navigator can expect distinctive chop —a good chance to pinpoint his location.*

Celestial navigation was centuries in the making, and a series of scientific leaps had to occur before its fundamental tools were in hand. Mariners of many different cultures contributed to the development of instruments that could measure celestial positions and monitor such intangibles as the passage of time or the earth's magnetic field.

No early seafarers were more audacious than the Polynesians who, some two millennia ago, headed eastward to explore their Pacific Ocean world, navigating 2,100 miles until they came upon the Marquesas Islands. In the next few centuries their kin, using large double canoes resembling the vessel at right, sailed 2,200 miles to reach Hawaii and more than 3,000 miles to New Zealand.

The success of such ventures—and other feats of seafaring by their neighbors, the Micronesians—was no accident. The early mariners of the South Pacific were superb navigators. Young men admitted to the select fraternity of master pilots had to know dozens of stars by name and could recite fore-and-aft star bearings for every island their people visited. They observed flight patterns of birds and studied cloud formations to locate land masses beyond the horizon. These pilots studied the mysterious sea itself—to recognize prevailing ocean swells and read in the sea's chop the interaction of waves rebounding from an atoll 30 miles away. Various devices were used to teach such lore: among Marshall Islanders the relationship of waves and islands was taught on stick charts like the one at left.

Consistent winds and a benign climate helped nurture the remarkable skills of these Pacific peoples. Still, their exploits were not to be surpassed until the invention of quantitative measuring instruments—a process initiated about a thousand years after the Polynesians had first begun to enlarge their horizons.

*A 60-foot-long Tongan double canoe, portrayed by an artist in Captain James Cook's expedition in the 1770s, is a direct descendant of the large ocean-voyaging canoes used by the Polynesians in their migrations 20 centuries earlier. Unable to sail closer than 75° to the wind, such a vessel could nevertheless travel fast and far on the Pacific trade winds, to the east in winter and to the west in summer.*

# Breakthrough in China

The first great technological revolution in the art of navigation must be credited to the venturesome Chinese, who sometime before the 11th Century A.D. began to carry magnetic compasses to sea. Up to that time, their pilots had relied upon the same knowledge of stars, sun and sea as the Polynesians—although probably never to the same degree of refinement.

The compass had been used ashore for hundreds of years before its significance became apparent to sailors. Geomancers, in the business of siting buildings according to the yin (northward, female) direction and the yang (southward, male) direction, had performed their magical divinations with a device consisting of an iron needle that was magnetized by a chunk of lodestone and floated by surface tension in a saucer of water. When Chinese mariners struck out for the distant shores of Japan, Malaya, Indonesia and Africa in search of trade and tribute, they employed a more sophisticated version of this instrument *(far right)*, although an air of magic was still attached to it.

To these ancient mariners the oceanic unknown was a frightening place—"a vast expanse without a shore, strong and very dangerous, the abode of mysterious dragons and marvelous serpents," as one chronicler put it in 1275. He added with wonder that by night or in storms ships would travel "trusting to the compass alone, and the pilot steering dares not make the smallest error since the lives of all in this ship depend upon him."

As more and more voyages were successfully completed, knowledge of distant shores and seas grew. Simple celestial navigation continued to play a major role, as shown by the chart at bottom right.

However, the evolution of Chinese nautical charts is somewhat misty. The oldest surviving group, of which the map at top right is a sample, was created several centuries after the first sea maps appeared. But it is probable that the early cartographers never intended to match natural shorelines or draw to scale: distances were given in terms of the numbers of watches to be sailed. Lacking shipboard timepieces, the Chinese may have burned a measured incense stick to mark the passage of a watch. It would take the determination of a few Europeans to solve the problem of telling time accurately—and thus conquer the mysteries of longitude.

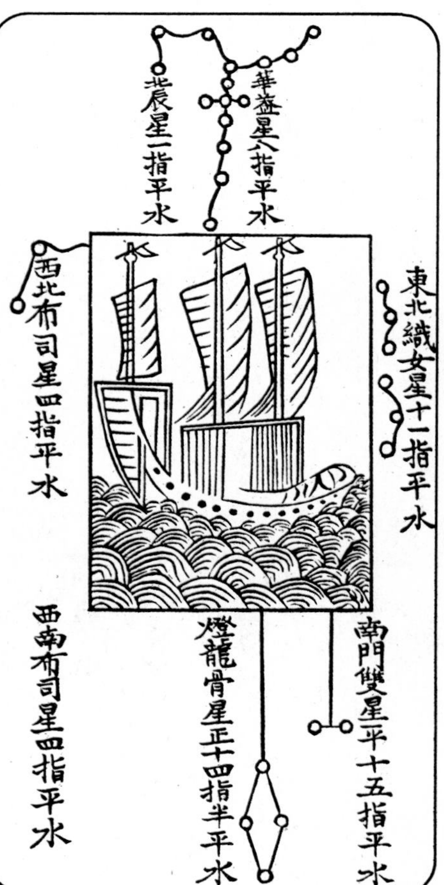


*Early Chinese navigators devised star charts for some heavily traveled trade routes. This one guided pilots between Ceylon and Sumatra, offering as celestial reference points such constellations as the "Lantern" (Southern Cross), the diamond-shaped grouping at the bottom. According to the accompanying text, a pilot on the correct latitude would find the Lantern 14½ fingerbreadths above the horizon at nightfall. To measure the angle, the pilot probably held his hand horizontally at arm's length so the lowest finger touched the horizon, then counted the digits between it and the star.*

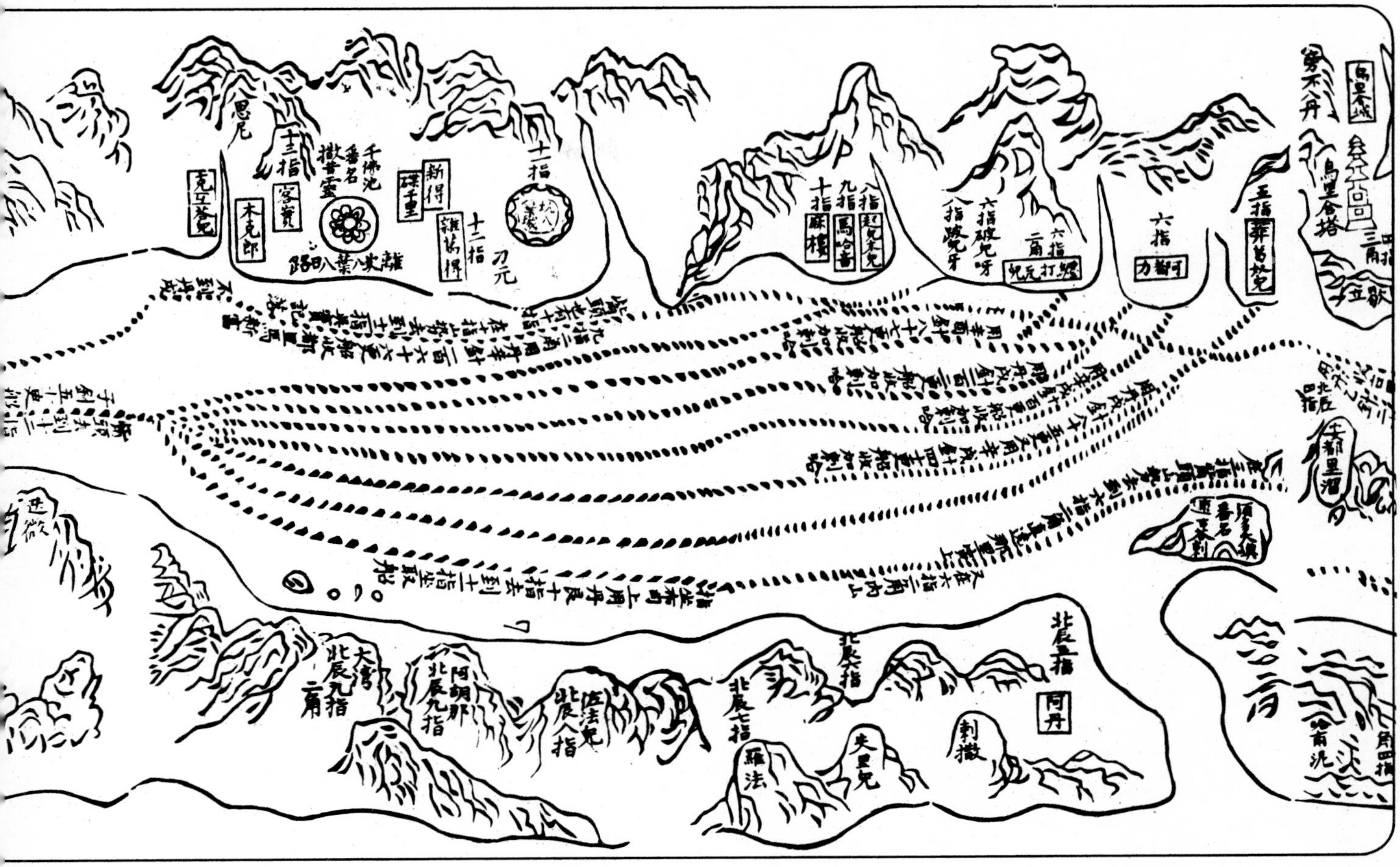

This mariner's chart, showing a section of the Arabian Sea, is based on information brought back to China by Admiral Cheng Ho, following seven voyages to the west in the 15th Century. A kind of pilot guide, it is not intended to convey an actual picture of land and sea areas; rather, it offers sailing instructions for a number of courses (dotted lines). Data written on the chart include distances to be sailed, coastal descriptions, names of port cities and their star bearings, locations of rocks and shoals, and occasional advice on the most favorable passages.

This bronze compass dates from the 16th Century. Its central well was filled with water; a magnetized needle that floated on the water would freely seek a north-south axis. By turning the compass to align the needle and the groove at the bottom of the well, the mariner could determine 24 compass points around the outer ring. The inner ring symbolizes the workings of the universe as told in the ancient Book of Changes.

*This brass instrument, made circa 1600, is a late variant on the first European altitude-measuring device that went to sea—the quadrant. To obtain a reading, the quadrant was held in a vertical plane and the sun or Pole Star lined up in its two raised sights. The pilot then noted the position of the plumb bob along the degree-calibrated arc and thereby calculated his latitude.*

## Advances in the West

Pious European map makers of the Middle Ages depicted a world that made eminent cosmologic sense. A flat circle with the Holy City of Jerusalem at its spiritual and geographical center, it offered few physical mysteries that could not be explained by theologians. Maritime exploration, which would have put these precepts to the test, had all but ceased to engage men's energies. Sailors whose ancient predecessors had sailed around Africa now coasted within range of shorelines they knew, using dead reckoning, the transit of the sun and a few stars to find their way.

A great breakthrough for Western navigators occurred in the 15th Century, when cartographers in Europe revived and adopted the latitude and longitude system of the Greek astronomer Ptolemy to project the first comprehensive view of the known world. Owing to the distortion produced in any flat depiction of the spherical earth, no single system would ever satisfy all sailors at every latitude. But projections like the one shown at right did enable mariners to relate a course direction to longitude and latitude more accurately than ever before.

The advances in map making were complemented by the development of a series of tools for celestial navigation. The Portuguese were in the van, under the leadership of a 15th Century prince, Henry the Navigator, who sponsored both research at home and exploration abroad. Among the resulting Portuguese innovations were the quadrant *(top left)* and the mariner's astrolabe *(bottom left)*, both used to find the rough altitude of the sun or a star and thus determine the latitude of a ship.

By Elizabethan times the English had become dominant in this field; among their many contributions was an ingenious sighting instrument called a backstaff *(page 128)*—a forerunner of the modern sextant. And in the mid-18th Century, England's John Harrison took a giant step in the march toward modern navigation when he produced the marine chronometer *(page 129)*, a precision timing instrument that afforded mariners a means of calculating longitude and thus measuring their progress east or west.

*This mariner's astrolabe, made circa 1585, was suspended by its ring to keep it perpendicular. The vane was rotated until the rays of the sun or a star passed through a pair of holes; then the altitude of the celestial body was read off the graduated rim.*

*The chart above, created around 1600 by Edward Wright of England, was one of the first practical adaptations of a new system for projecting the spherical world onto a flat surface, imperfectly worked out 30 years before by Flemish map maker Gerhard Mercator. Though the scale of this particular map was too small to have been very useful on board ship, its projection made it possible to draw point-to-point courses and lay them off against the chart's compass rose with a far smaller margin of error than earlier.*

*The traverse board, devised in the 16th Century, enabled pilots to keep track of the ship's course and speed during a watch. After the passage of each half hour (measured by a sandglass), a peg was placed in a hole in the compass rose, indicating the ship's most recent heading; a second peg was punched into the horizontal rows of holes to register hourly estimates of the ship's speed. At the end of a four-hour watch the account was transferred to a written logbook and the pegging begun all over again.*

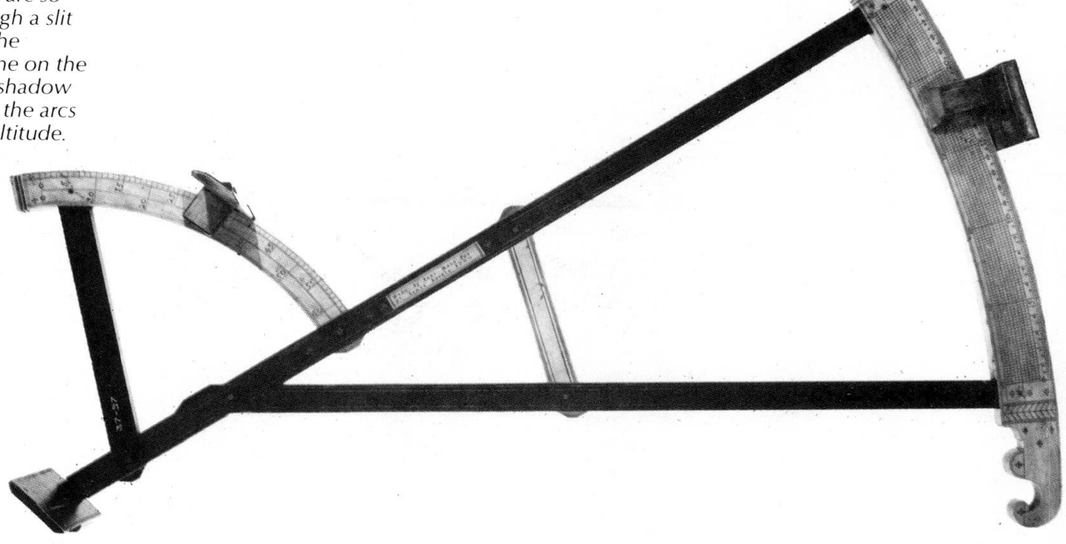

*This backstaff, a 17th Century improvement on a device invented by John Davis of England in the 1590s, permitted a navigator to measure the altitude of the sun without looking directly at its rays. Standing with his back to the celestial body and holding the instrument in a vertical plane, the navigator adjusted the sight vane on the large arc so that he could see the horizon through a slit in the vane at the opposite end of the instrument—while an adjustable vane on the smaller arc simultaneously threw a shadow across the horizon slit. Readings on the arcs were then added to find the sun's altitude.*

*The problem of finding longitude at sea remained insoluble until 1735, when London clockmaker John Harrison completed this chronometer. The 72-pound brass-and-wooden timepiece included a pair of double-ended balances (whose spherical upper ends show at the back of the machine) that compensated for temperature changes and the motion of a ship. Navigators set the clock at the time of any chosen meridian (Greenwich Time would not be adopted until 1884) and calculated east-west progress by comparing the clock's time to the local time indicated by the position of a celestial body.*

3

To many boatmen, ocean racing represents the ultimate in sailing. Some fleets number 500 boats and more, with the grandest vessels measuring over 70 feet and costing half a million dollars. Courses may be thousands of miles long, and the contestants must slug along day and night, often in winds that would produce a sure postponement of any inshore contest. Good foredeck men are expected to set a spinnaker in 30 seconds or less; and a navigator may have to establish fixes of position every few minutes—as opposed to every few hours on a cruising boat—so that the skipper can tack for a mark at exactly the proper time. Inevitably, the sport attracts the best helmsmen in

# RACING: THE CUTTING EDGE

the world. Among the top finishers in the 1974 race pictured at left, for instance, were Ted Hood and Ted Turner—both former national champions in small boats and both skippers of 12-meters during America's Cup campaigns later that year. At the height of his spectacular ocean-racing career aboard the classic yawl *Finisterre,* skipper Carleton Mitchell routinely carried along as crewmen two former World Star champions and one former International Lightning champion.

Ocean racing as a sport began little more than a century ago with informal contests between cruising boats of all sizes, shapes and rigs. The participants quickly developed handicapping systems to give every boat a chance—the approach still followed in most contests today. The ultimate key to any handicapping or rating system is a boat's waterline length, which determines its maximum speed. Some early rating rules used this dimension as the sole yardstick of potential performance. However, most subsequent rating systems, including the International Offshore Rule now dominant *(pages 143-145),* have been less simplistic. They have employed complex mathematical formulas to penalize every conceivable design feature that allows a boat to go fast—even the length of the battens—while providing a bonus for features, such as displacement and beam, that tend to slow a boat down. In a nod to tradition, a boat's final rating is expressed in feet: the lower the rated length, the higher the time allowance the boat receives.

Entrants in an ocean race are generally grouped into classes according to their rated lengths—from the 70-plus footers in Class A to small boats of 25 to 30 feet, usually ranking in Class F. Prizes are awarded both to the boats that place high on corrected time in the overall fleet and to those that do well in their class. Among knowledgeable yachtsmen, the class prizes tend to be regarded as the real measure of skill; though the fleet prizes are more publicized, in point of fact the winner may ultimately be picked by the weather. For example, if the wind dies out just after the big boats in a race have finished, the small boats are at a hopeless disadvantage. On the other hand, races sailed in very light winds throughout favor the small boats, since the larger ones never reach the potential speed computed into their rating.

Even within a given class, however, no handicapping rule can achieve a perfect balancing act with all the factors that determine boat speed. Loopholes exist in the rules. Yet the very existence of these loopholes has been a positive force in boat design. Before a naval architect sets down a single line for a prospective racer, he studies the rating formula closely, seeking a way to create a boat that is faster than its rated length implies. On occasion, this approach has produced some ridiculous boats. But, as demonstrated by the evolutionary vessels on the following pages, today's racers owe much of their superb performance qualities to the view of designers that, no matter how cleverly a handicapping rule contrives to make all boats equal, some can be designed more equal than others.

*Mainsails reefed for blustery weather, Class A yachts start the 1974 Miami-Nassau Race. Winds of up to 35 knots drove one boat around the 176-mile course in just 17 hours.*

## Niña

In the modern history of ocean-racing yacht design, the staysail schooner *Niña* stands out as a momentous breakthrough. When she appeared in 1928, the yachting scene was dominated by big, beamy boats that had evolved from the shapes of fishing schooners and were designed primarily for cruising. *Niña,* the visionary creation of marine architect Starling Burgess, changed all that.

Burgess designed *Niña* expressly to win the 1928 Transatlantic Race for owner Paul Hammond. At 59 feet, she was small by the day's standards and received a week's head start as a handicap. But she was first to finish, eliciting a cheer from spectators that "jibed the *Niña's* mainsail," according to one hyperbolic report.

*Niña's* rig was a radical departure from tradition. Most schooners of the era were gaff-headed—fast with the wind aft of the beam but unable to sail close to the wind. *Niña* achieved superior upwind performance with a pair of staysails and a radical Marconi main set on a mast so tall that many were convinced it would break in an ocean race. This rig towered over a moderately deep hull *(diagrams)* with a cutaway forefoot—a notable contrast to the shape of cruising yachts of the day.

Indeed, after *Niña* went on to win England's prestigious Fastnet Race that same year, some boatmen protested that, because she was a racing machine not suited for cruising, she and yachts of her type should be banned from the race in the future. But as time passed, *Niña's* critics were forced to accept the fact that henceforth ocean racers would—and should—be designed for racing. Before long she had many more admirers than detractors, and when *Niña* captured the Newport-to-Bermuda race in 1962 at the vintage age of 34, the victory ranked as one of the most popular in the history of the sport.

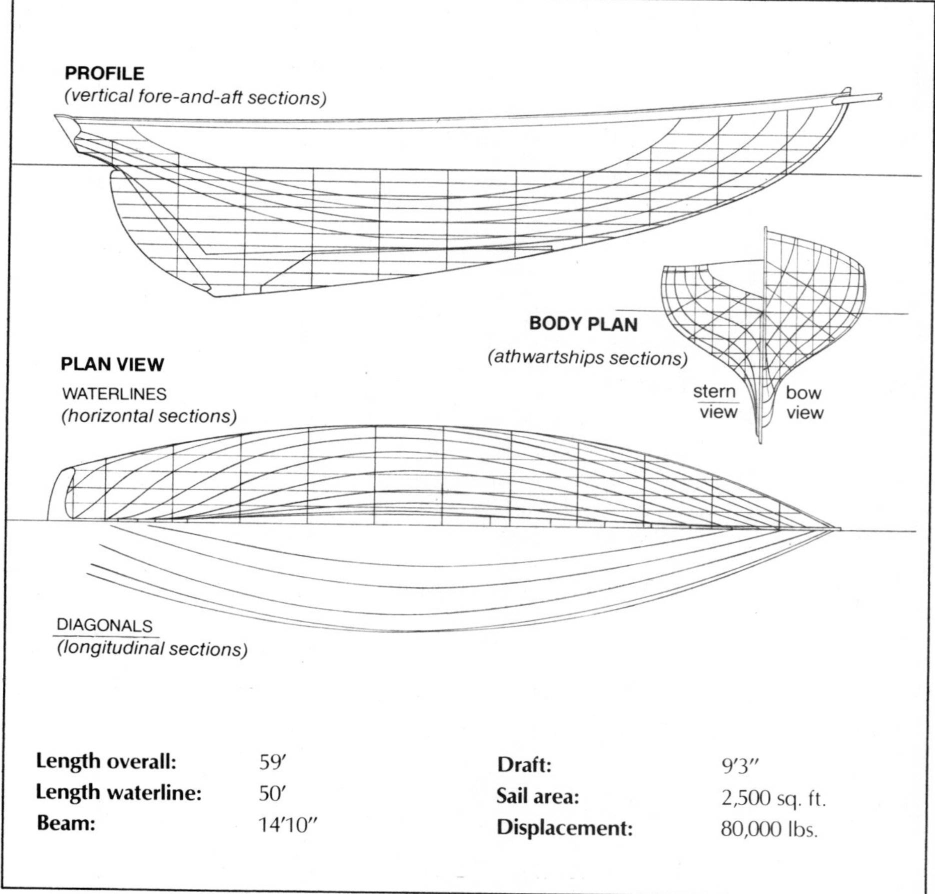


| | | | |
|---|---|---|---|
| **Length overall:** | 59′ | **Draft:** | 9′3″ |
| **Length waterline:** | 50′ | **Sail area:** | 2,500 sq. ft. |
| **Beam:** | 14′10″ | **Displacement:** | 80,000 lbs. |

*With her mainmast stepped unusually far forward for a schooner and her mainsail cut in a slim triangle (above, right), Niña's rig fit none of the handicap rules of the '20s. Niña's lines, as laid down by her designer, are shown at right. The lines or sections defined by the profile, body plan and waterlines (designers' parlance for lines parallel to the water) determine the boat's shape. The diagonals are check lines to confirm the hull's smooth curvature. (The designs on the following pages are drawn to the same scale.)*

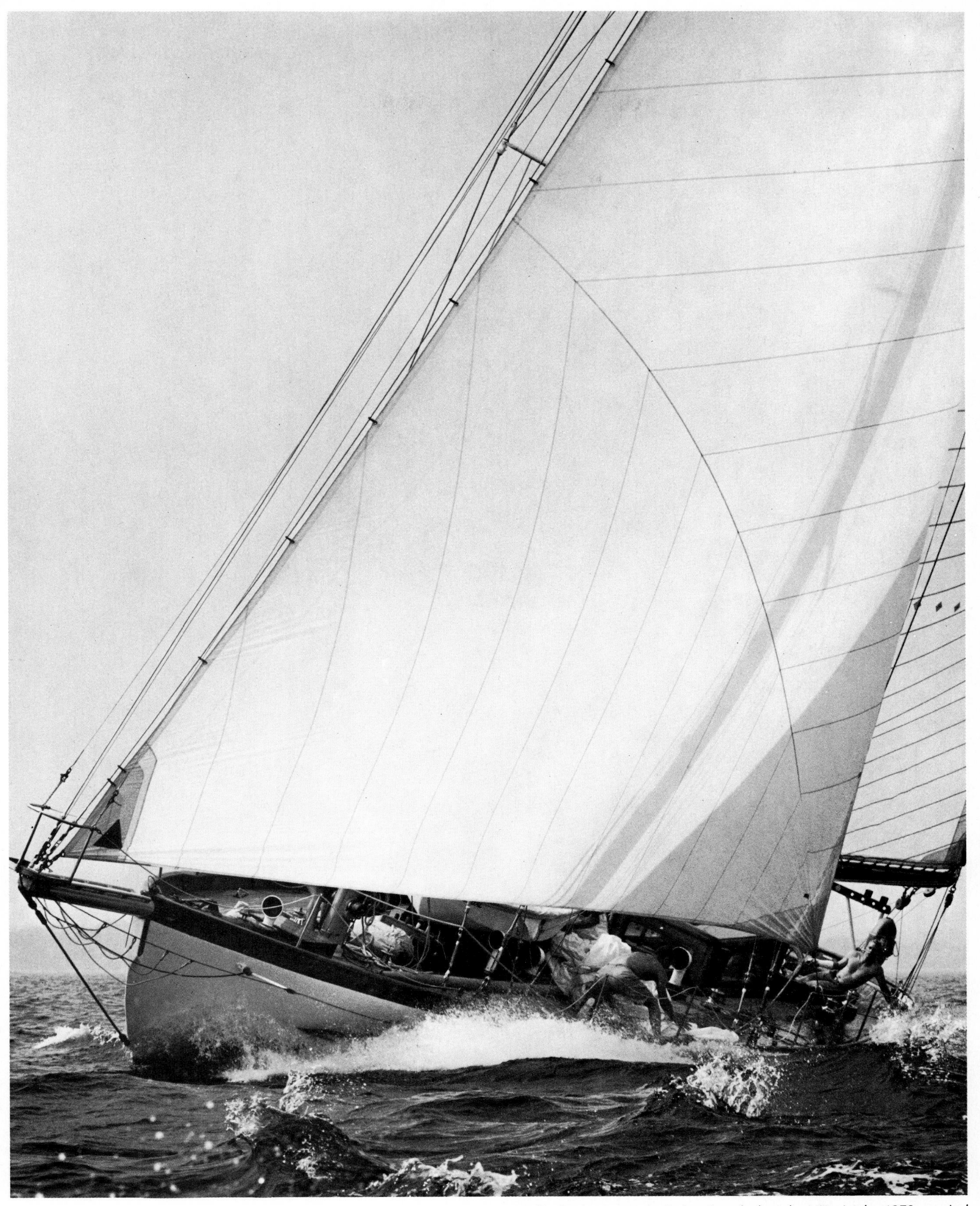

*Still a lively contender in her fourth decade, Niña in the 1970s carried a shortened bowsprit and a huge genoa. Her victory in the Bermuda Race in 1962 had an ironic twist: having begun a trend toward small size, she found herself a big boat in a fleet dominated by 40-footers.*

## Dorade

Two years after *Niña* first rocked the racing establishment, a brilliant 21-year-old designer and racer named Olin Stephens created *Dorade,* a second giant step away from the workboat tradition. *Dorade's* narrow beam gave her more in common with boats used for inshore day racing, and she was yawl-rigged to take advantage of a rating rule that allowed a mizzen and mizzen staysail to be set as unpenalized sail area.

In her first major outing, the 1930 running of the prestigious Bermuda Race, the graceful oddity took third over all, with her youthful designer at the helm. Unsatisfied, Stephens shortened her rig slightly for the Transatlantic Race the next year. In that contest Stephens reached the finish two days ahead of his nearest rival. A month later, *Dorade* won the Fastnet Race in a demonstration of pure speed that prompted the London *Times* to dub her "the most wonderful little ocean racing yacht ever built."

Thirteen feet shorter on the waterline than *Niña, Dorade* weighed half as much and had less than half the sail area. Her yawl rig made for easy handling, a quality that made her successful not only as a racer but also as a weekend cruiser.

Not long after designing *Dorade,* Stephens produced 53-foot *Stormy Weather (opposite),* plainly inspired by his first effort—and just as successful. Together the two craft became the prototypes for the swift, yawl-rigged racer-cruiser that dominated offshore yachting in America well into the 1960s.

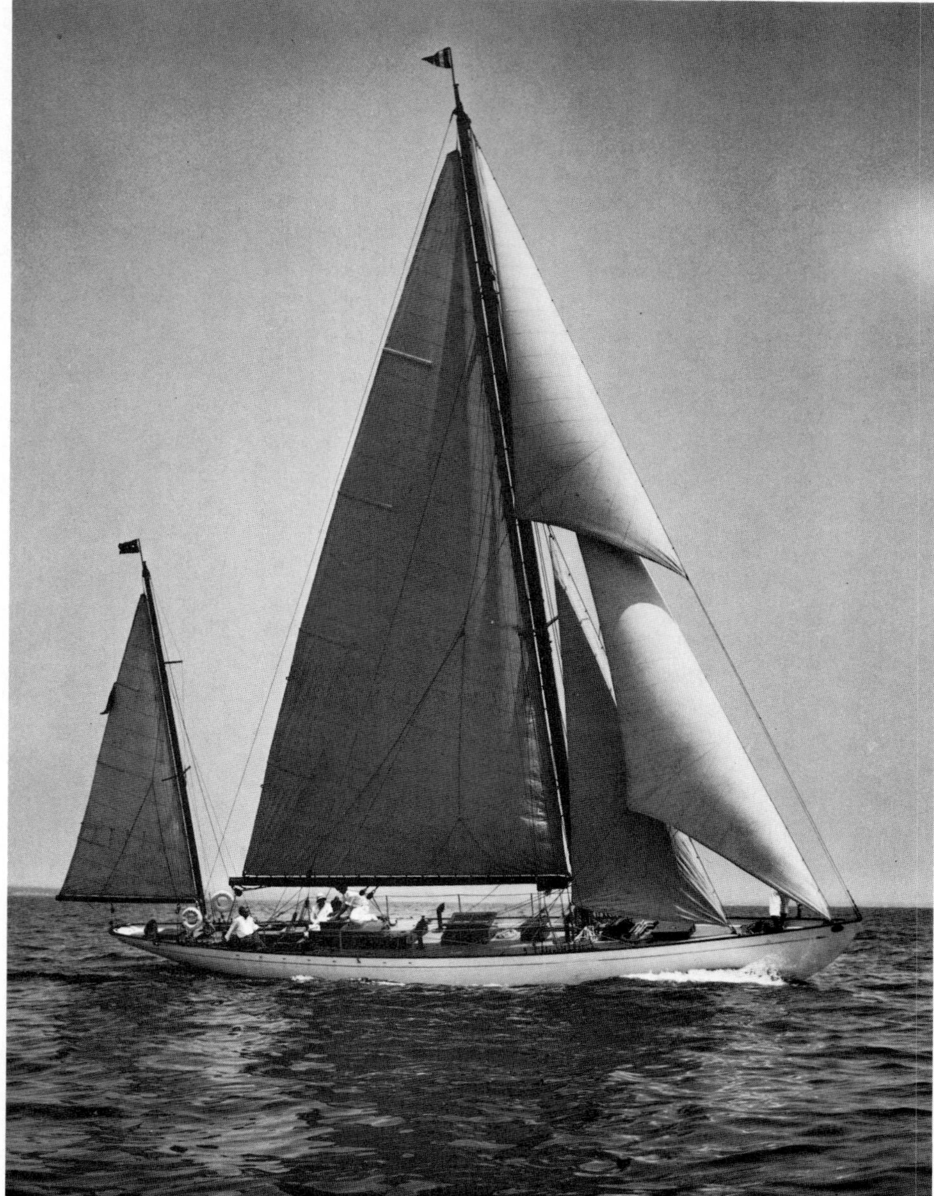

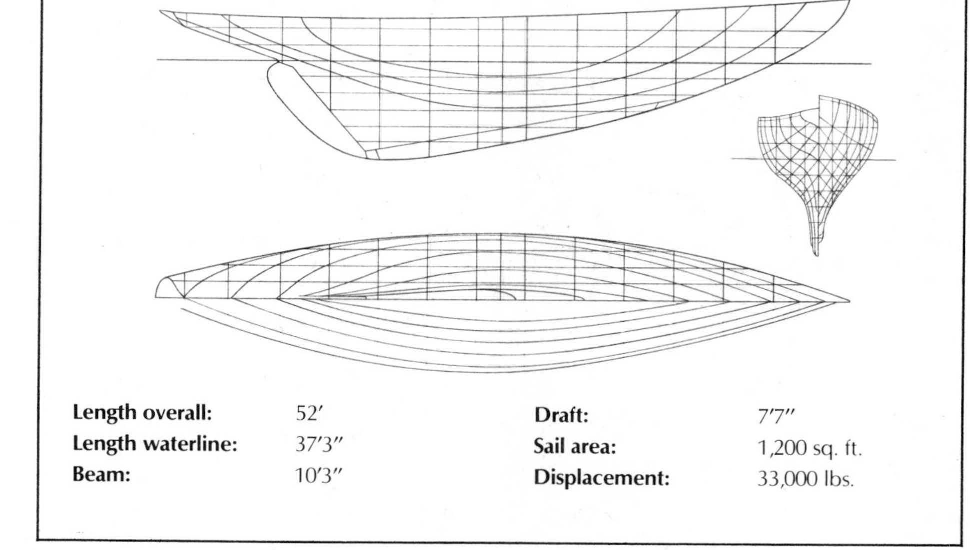

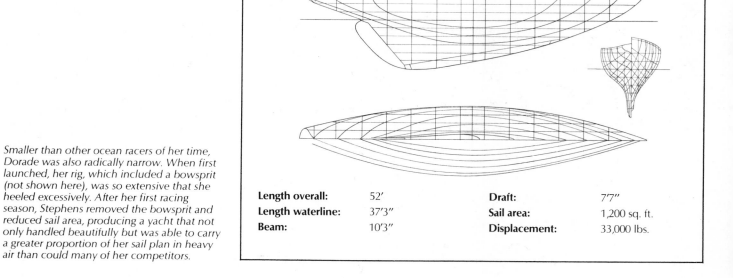

| | | | |
|---|---|---|---|
| **Length overall:** | 52′ | **Draft:** | 7′7″ |
| **Length waterline:** | 37′3″ | **Sail area:** | 1,200 sq. ft. |
| **Beam:** | 10′3″ | **Displacement:** | 33,000 lbs. |

*Smaller than other ocean racers of her time, Dorade was also radically narrow. When first launched, her rig, which included a bowsprit (not shown here), was so extensive that she heeled excessively. After her first racing season, Stephens removed the bowsprit and reduced sail area, producing a yacht that not only handled beautifully but was able to carry a greater proportion of her sail plan in heavy air than could many of her competitors.*

*Rail down during the 1948 Miami-Nassau Race, Dorade's successor, Stormy Weather, reveals a beam (12'6") almost as narrow as that of the earlier vessel. The boomkin at the stern carried a sheet block for the mizzen, allowing the sail to be trimmed efficiently even though the boom extended over the transom. Stormy Weather won the 1935 Fastnet and Transatlantic races, several Miami-Nassau races, and was overall winner of the Southern Ocean Racing Conference in 1948.*

## Myth of Malham

One of the most radically shaped yachts to have a lasting effect on ocean-racing design was the mellifluously named British boat *Myth of Malham*. She was drawn up in 1946 by Jack Laurent Giles of Lymington to the specifications of her owner, John Illingworth, a sometime marine architect himself. Illingworth's demands were so unconventional that Giles, concerned for his own reputation, insisted that Illingworth take full responsibility for the boat's performance.

His caution was understandable. Illingworth had ordered a chopped-off little duckling of a boat with a plumb transom and a bow that almost matched. But *Myth* turned out to be a cannily conceived evasion of existing handicap rules—and a brilliantly innovative ocean racer that Giles might have been forgiven for claiming as his own creation.

The transom and bow concept gave *Myth* an advantageously short measured length under the Royal Ocean Racing Club's rule. Another rating advantage derived from her high freeboard, normally associated with heavy displacement and slow speed. In point of fact, Illingworth had done everything possible to make *Myth* light. Planks, bulkheads and decking were all pared in weight. Illingworth even put holes in her winch handles to save a few ounces of metal.

*Myth* won the Channel and Fastnet races in 1947; a year later she placed first in two Long Island Sound races that were sailed under the less favorable Cruising Club of America rule. She took the Fastnet a second time in 1949, and eight years later won her class in the same event. The handicap rule that produced her was soon changed, but *Myth of Malham* by that time had launched a trend toward light displacement that established the mainstream of yacht design for years.

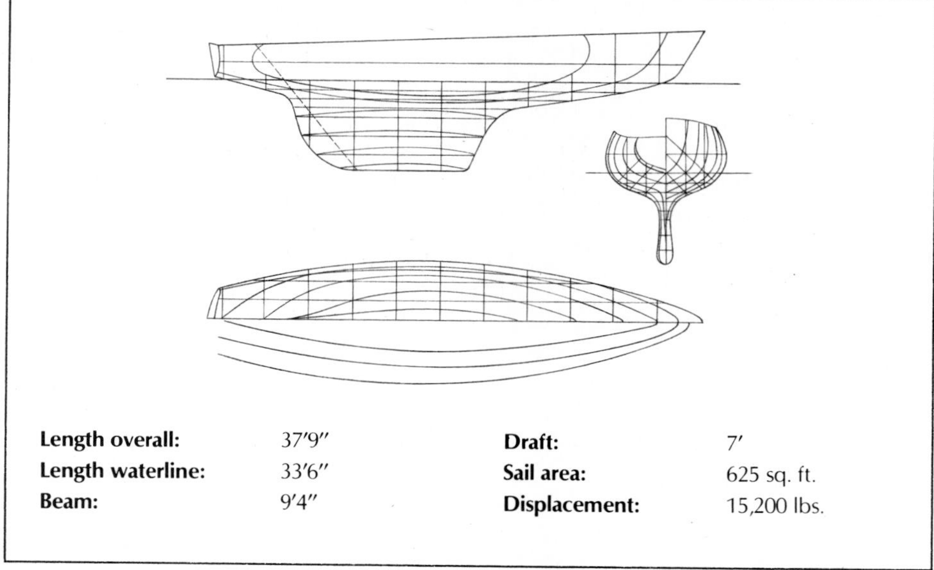

| | | | |
|---|---|---|---|
| **Length overall:** | 37′9″ | **Draft:** | 7′ |
| **Length waterline:** | 33′6″ | **Sail area:** | 625 sq. ft. |
| **Beam:** | 9′4″ | **Displacement:** | 15,200 lbs. |

*With her mast stepped almost amidships, the cutter-rigged Myth could accommodate a great variety of headsail arrangements, including a genoa that overlapped almost to her quarter. Her snubbed ends and straight sheer line were considered ugly innovations, but Myth was extremely fast, especially when hard on the wind in heavy weather.*

# Finisterre

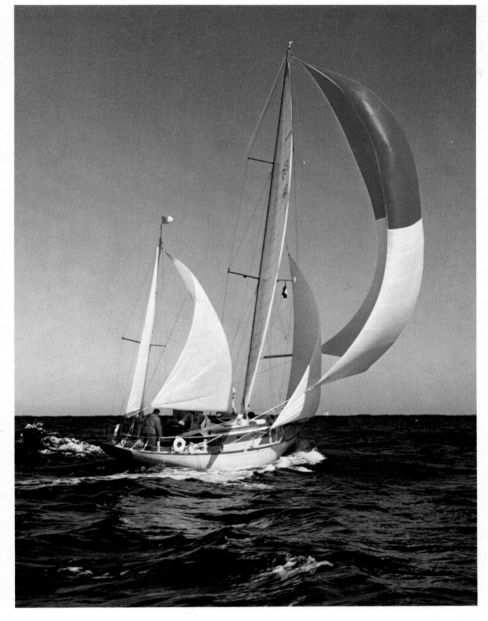

In the 1950s while the rule makers were busy seeing that narrow or light boats like *Dorade* and *Myth* were sufficiently penalized, a fat, heavy anomaly named *Finisterre* glided out of Annapolis, Maryland, and won every race in sight. She was another product of a collaboration between gifted architect and expert skipper—Olin Stephens and Carleton Mitchell, respectively. A devotee of cruising as well as racing, Mitchell wanted a boat with a seemingly impossible combination of traits, a boat "small enough to be taken for an afternoon sail by one person, yet comfortable enough to live aboard for weeks at a time; draft shoal enough to poke into the byways of the Chesapeake, yet possessing the ability to cross an ocean."

Stephens took care of the shallow draft requirement by making *Finisterre* a centerboarder, and he answered the call for small size plus comfort by giving her extraordinary beam for the length. Mitchell then fitted her out with equipment usually found only on larger boats, including a wheel instead of a tiller, an automatic pilot, a record player and an ice maker.

Many yachtsmen attributed *Finisterre's* first Bermuda victory to her very favorable handicap rating under the existing rule. When she won the race again two years later, after the rule had been revised, her critics had to admit something besides her rating was involved. And when she took the Bermuda Race for an unprecedented third time in 1960, credit went where it belonged—to Mitchell's great sailing skill and a truly inspired set of lines.

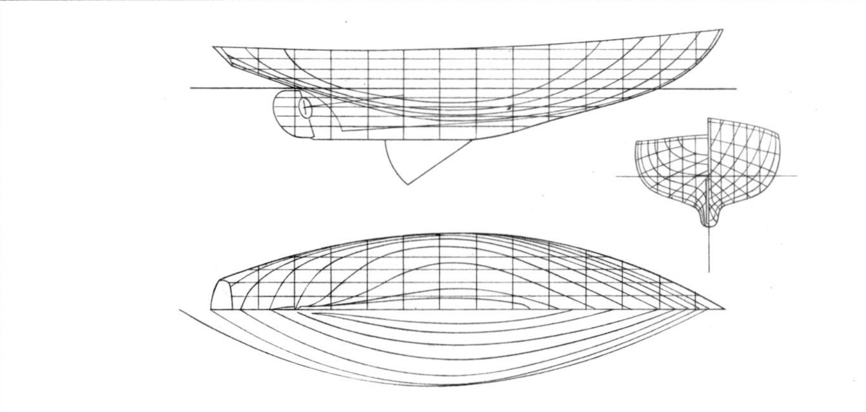

| | | | |
|---|---|---|---|
| **Length overall:** | 38′7½″ | **Draft, board up:** | 3′11″ |
| **Length waterline:** | 27′6″ | **Draft, board down:** | 7′7″ |
| **Beam:** | 11′3″ | **Sail area:** | 713 sq. ft. |
| | | **Displacement:** | 21,527 lbs. |

*Finisterre's yawl rig was similar to Dorade's, and was chosen for the same reasons: ease of handling and the low rating penalty. Her hull, however, could not have been more different. Whereas Dorade was long and lean, Finisterre was only two and a half times as long on the waterline as she was wide. Dorade's keel extended almost eight feet underwater; Finisterre, with her board up, drew less than four feet. Although centerboarders often perform best downwind, Finisterre did well close-hauled in a sea, when her weight helped keep her moving.*

*A class winner in the 1969 Southern Ocean Racing Conference, Melee, a Cal 40, picks up extra speed by riding a wave downwind. Before the Cal 40 emerged as a design, prolonged surfing was comparatively rare among ocean-racing boats. The fiberglass newcomer, relatively flat-bottomed and light for its length, could get up on a wave readily, and its well-balanced steering enabled it to stay there. As a result, while the boat did well going to windward, it scored some of its most notable successes in races that were long on leeward work.*

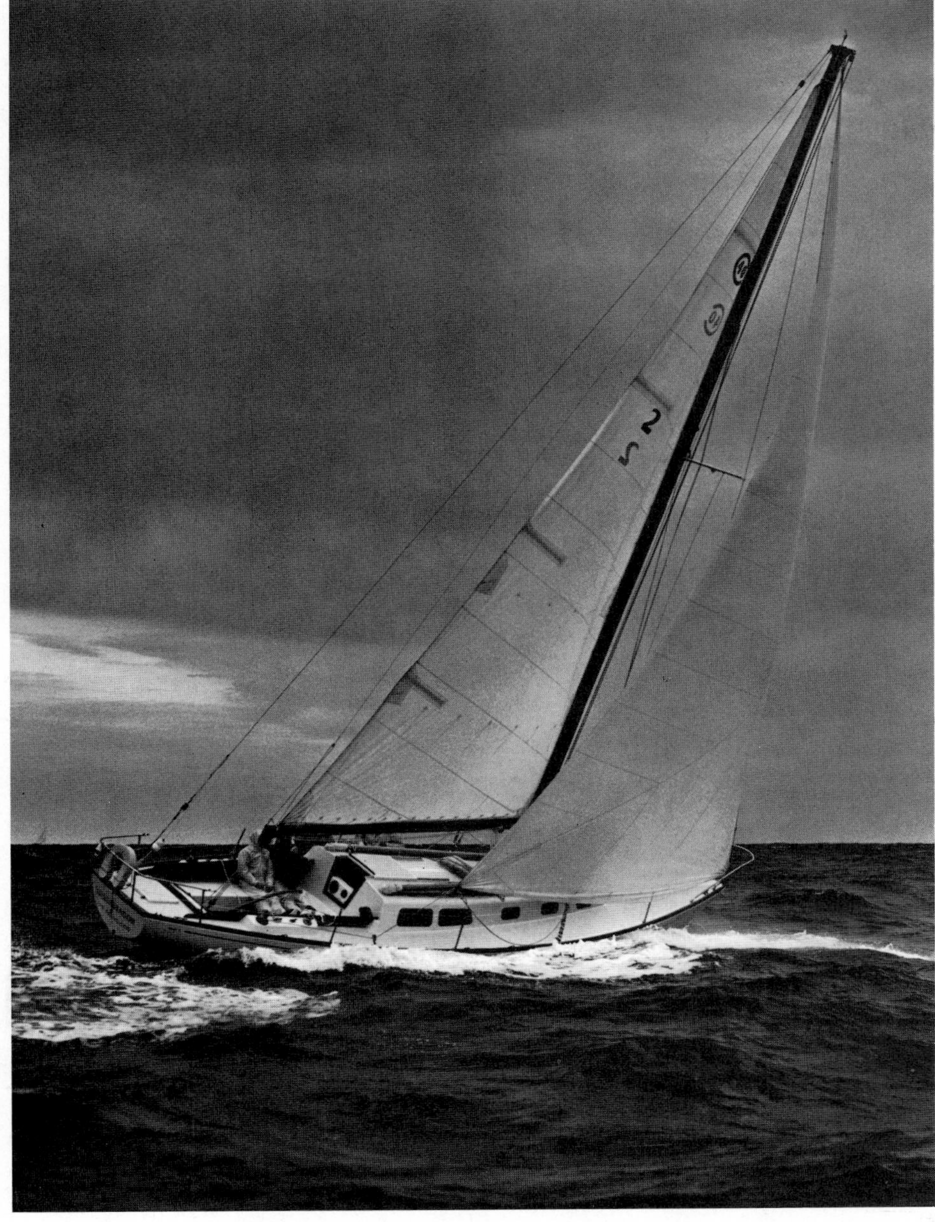

# The Cal 40

Before fiberglass was perfected for boat construction in the early 1950s, every ocean racer was custom designed, laboriously hand built, and tended to be restricted in its shape to forms that could be achieved with wood. Fiberglass, however, which assumes its shape in a mold, opened an almost limitless range of hull forms. Moreover, its vastly simpler construction requirements permitted mass production; and, also, fiberglass's excellent strength-to-weight ratio held out the promise of light but sturdy vessels with a fresh turn of speed.

The first designer to bring all these advantages together in a winning boat was Californian William Lapworth, when he unveiled his Cal 40 in 1964. The Cal 40's flat bottom and fin keel indeed made her fast: the second Cal 40 ever built, *Conquistador (left),* won the Southern Ocean Racing Conference in 1964. By the end of the decade, almost 200 more Cal 40s had been turned out.

In addition to this bonanza, Lapworth's design produced yet another dividend for ocean racers. Earlier efforts at reducing the area of keels had moved the rudder, traditionally attached to the back of the keel, farther and farther forward, until it tended to wildly oversteer the boat. Lapworth took the critical step of separating and moving the rudder all the way aft, where it supplied far better control.

Oddly enough, while Lapworth was busy conceiving the Cal 40 as a fine racing machine, he failed to produce a boat with a favorable handicap rating. But the design turned out to be so effective that Cal 40s went ahead not only to beat other boats head to head, but also to beat their own handicaps. Beginning in 1965, three consecutive Transpacific races were captured by Lapworth's masterpiece. And at the 1966 Bermuda Race, Cal 40s took five out of the top six places in their class and four out of the first nine in the fleet.

| | | | |
|---|---|---|---|
| **Length overall:** | 39′4″ | **Draft:** | 5′7″ |
| **Length waterline:** | 30′4″ | **Sail area:** | 700 sq. ft. |
| **Beam:** | 11′ | **Displacement:** | 15,000 lbs. |

*Designed as an all-out racer, the Cal 40 was sloop-rigged for minimal weight and wind resistance aloft. The boat's fin keel and spade rudder were quickly imitated by other boat designers and are now found on virtually every new blue-water racer.*

## One Tonners

Until recently, virtually all ocean-racing skippers, competing in the heterogeneous offshore fleets bred by the rating rules, tended to lose all track of their competitive positions by nightfall of the first day. Relief from this often-frustrating system was first offered in 1965, when the French sponsors of a longstanding trophy—originally for inshore boats rated at one ton under an abstruse 1892 rule—decided to offer their cup to offshore boats with a single new rating. Taking only their name from the old trophy, modern One Tonners rate at 27.5 feet under the current International Offshore Rule *(page 145)*. Evenly matched, they compete boat for boat.

The straightforward challenge of One-Ton racing has attracted many of the world's best sailors—and designers, too, all seeking a hull shape and sail plan that offer the ultimate in speed for the rating. One bold design theory—exemplified by *Robin,* at right—holds that a One Tonner should be as big as possible. *Robin's* creator, sailmaker and designer, Ted Hood, opted for a long waterline and a large sail area. At about the same time, the young California designer Doug Peterson took a radically different approach with his small, light *Ganbare (opposite).*

*Ganbare* won her very first regatta—the 1973 One-Ton North American Championships. At the One-Ton World Championships that year, *Ganbare* finished first in four out of five races. *Robin* struck back at the next North Americans, beating two of *Ganbare's* sister ships. But at the 1974 and 1975 Worlds, Peterson designs swept nearly every top position.

This spirited competition, both in racing and in design, has led to the formation of several derivative classes. And though the day may be a long way off, some blue-water men believe that the only real test for ocean-racing skippers will come when all boats—within a class if not a whole fleet—must go off at a single rating. And may the fastest man win.

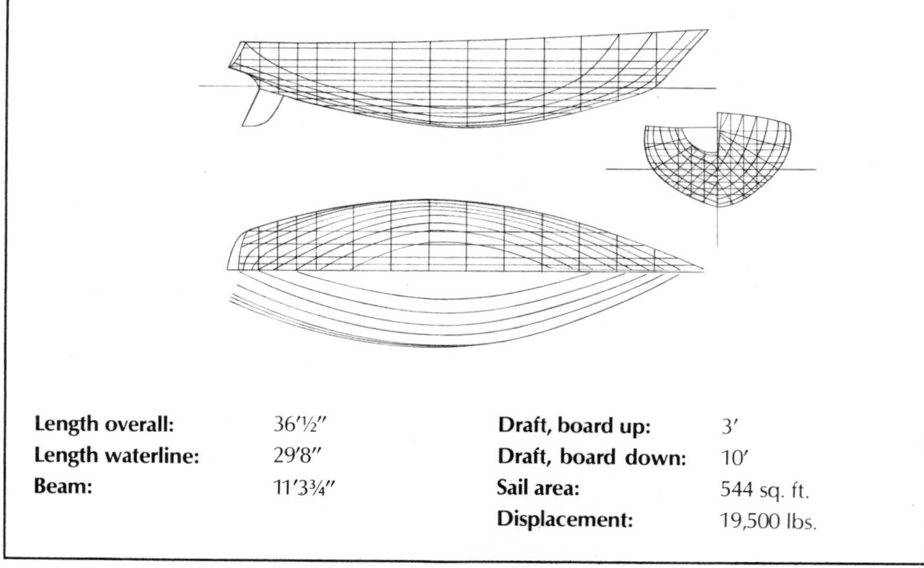

| | | | |
|---|---|---|---|
| **Length overall:** | 36′½″ | **Draft, board up:** | 3′ |
| **Length waterline:** | 29′8″ | **Draft, board down:** | 10′ |
| **Beam:** | 11′3¾″ | **Sail area:** | 544 sq. ft. |
| | | **Displacement:** | 19,500 lbs. |

*The 19,500-lb. centerboarder Robin, built in 1973, still ranks among the largest of the One Tonners. Her centerboard—less efficient upwind than a keel—and heavy displacement offset a long waterline and large sail plan, allowing her to meet the required rating.*

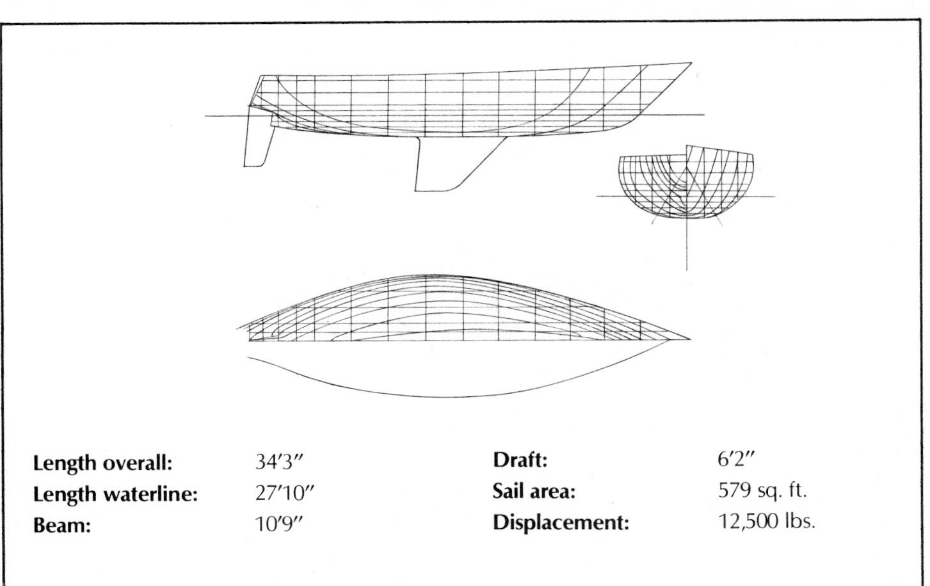

| | | | |
|---|---|---|---|
| **Length overall:** | 34′3″ | **Draft:** | 6′2″ |
| **Length waterline:** | 27′10″ | **Sail area:** | 579 sq. ft. |
| **Beam:** | 10′9″ | **Displacement:** | 12,500 lbs. |

*Almost two feet shorter on the waterline, and fully 7,000 pounds lighter than Robin, Ganbare changed the course of One-Ton design with her string of first-place finishes. Her light weight, comparatively small wetted surface and large sail area were expected to make her perform well primarily in light air. But she turned up at the front of the fleet even in heavy breezes.*

*With the wind backing aft, Charisma booms along under a freshly raised spinnaker in the 1975 Miami-Nassau Race as the crew takes down a genoa.*

# A MASTERPIECE OF MODERN TECHNOLOGY

In the fiercely competitive world of offshore racing, where great distances magnify the smallest speed differentials and sportsmen-tycoons will put up a bundle to win, the development of a boat has become a major exercise in modern technology. The artful and solitary marine architect, working mainly from instinct, has been replaced by a consortium of skilled specialists—experts in engineering, hydrodynamics and aerodynamics. Such a team was mustered by the firm of Sparkman and Stephens to create the eminently successful racing yacht *Charisma (left).*

*Charisma* first began to take shape in a series of discussions between the firm's managing partner, Olin Stephens, and his client, industrialist Jesse Phillips. Phillips was willing to spend upward of $400,000 for a medium-sized yacht that would rate well under the International Offshore Rule *(overleaf)* and that would perform under a wide variety of sailing conditions. They agreed on a 54-foot sloop with an aluminum hull.

After this basic notion had been translated into a set of preliminary lines, the team at Sparkman and Stephens settled down to some serious research and development. Experimental hull shapes, reproduced in the form of miniature wooden models, were analyzed at a 141-foot-long towing-tank facility at the Stevens Institute of Technology in Hoboken, New Jersey. As a result, the boat's basic lines were redrawn four times before her keel was laid. The rig received similarly sophisticated treatment: in an attempt to squeeze every ounce of power from the wind, the aerodynamic shape of the sails was drawn with the help of a Univac 1108 computer *(page 152).*

All these efforts paid off handsomely when the yacht captured nine offshore-class trophies and placed second in eight other events during her first year of competition. Despite the successes, however, the designers of *Charisma* continued to alter and perfect their creation. After her launching, the boat's hull shape was modified twice, including a major $20,000 change in the stern to improve both rating and performance *(page 154).*

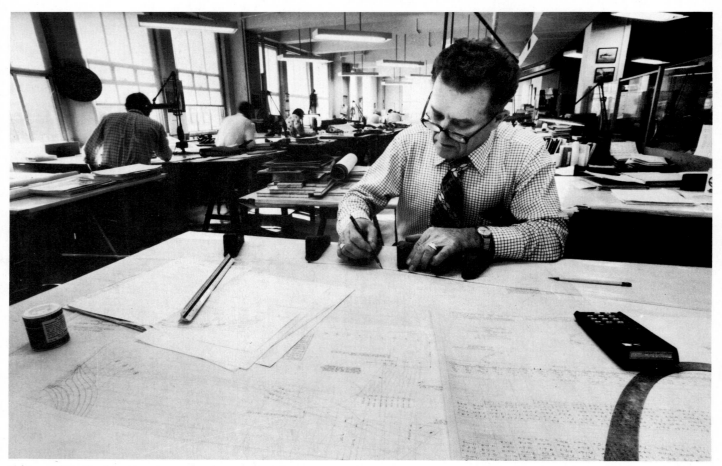

Designer Mario Tarabocchia, who previously supervised the creation of three America's Cup winners, uses a flexible clear plastic rod as a guide to trace a prospective curve of Charisma's quarter. The rod is held in place by four heavy lead weights, called bats, arranged by the designer according to his concept of how the lines of the racer should flow. As the dimensions take shape, Tarabocchia uses an electronic calculator (foreground) to weigh the consequences of his ideas against theoretical performance as projected by the IOR rating formula.

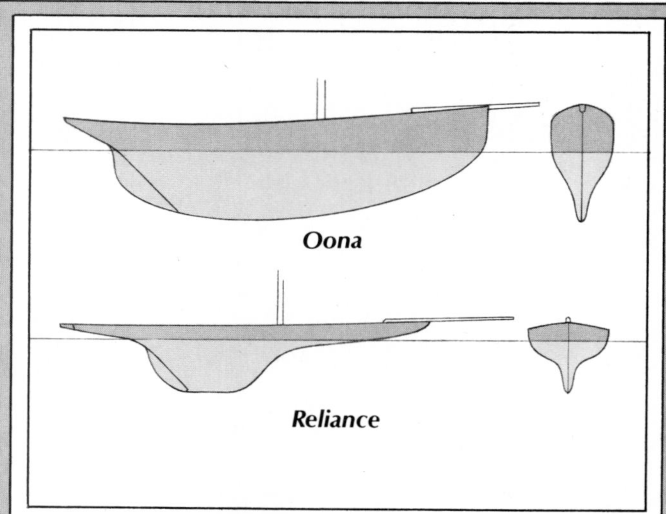


## Historic Rule-Beaters

Early rating rules contained glaring loopholes that produced a succession of freak boats, some very successful, others disastrous losers. The long overhangs of *Reliance,* the America's Cup winner of 1903, side-stepped a rule that penalized long waterlines. While *Reliance's* waterline was only 84 feet, she measured a whopping 143 feet overall—permitting a large increase in hull speed when the boat heeled. *Oona,* an earlier British yacht built to a rating rule that put a heavy tax on beam, was not so lucky. Forty-six feet overall but with a beam of 5 feet 6 inches, she had a spectacularly low rating—and was also hopelessly unseaworthy. The craft foundered in a storm in 1886, drowning her designer.

## Design by the Rule

In addition to the quest for high performance, a powerful influence on *Charisma's* design was the International Offshore Rule, which was adopted by the U.S. Yacht Racing Union in 1970 and is currently the most widely used yardstick for handicapping ocean racers. Like most previous rules, the IOR assesses the speed potential of boats according to a complex mathematical formula involving performance values for such factors as length, displacement and sail area.

More elaborate than its predecessors, the IOR requires over 150 measurements of a boat's dimensions. For example, length as defined by the IOR is not a boat's true, overall length at all but a measurement keyed to two arbitrary points called girth stations. The locations of the girth stations, in turn, depend on specified fractions of the boat's beam measurements; under this system, the forward girth station is positioned at a point where the girth is equal to one half of the beam. As a result of this aspect of the rating rule, many new ocean racers, including *Charisma,* are sharply pinched in at the ends to bring the girth stations closer together. Some speed is sacrificed by such lines, but the reduction in rated length more than makes up for the performance loss.

Another crucial design trade-off involves sail area. Adding sail area, either by raising the mast or lengthening the boom, tends to make a boat go faster—but also increases its IOR rating. Conversely, reducing sail area will lower a boat's rating but can seriously limit its performance: one engineer recently calculated that with no sails at all the IOR rating of his 35-foot racer would give it a time allowance of more than 13 minutes per mile. "This would be a desirable arrangement in a downwind race in 80 knots of wind," he noted, "but probably not otherwise."

Despite unmatched experience with the subtleties of the IOR, *Charisma's* design team at Sparkman and Stephens found few choices to be easy. In all, the architects spent more than 75 hours at their drawing boards before they were ready to put their ideas to preliminary tests under simulated sailing conditions in a towing tank *(overleaf).*

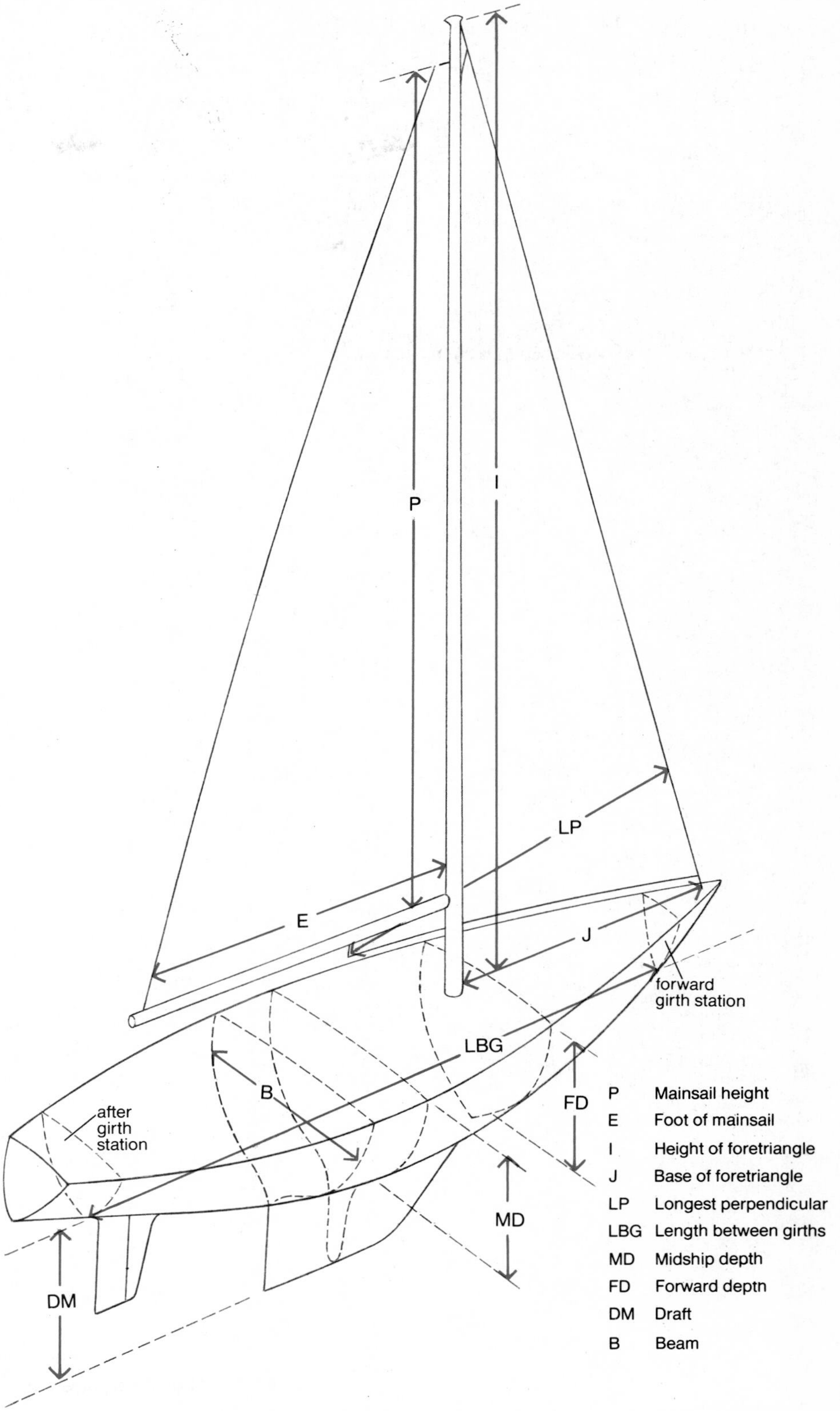

P
I
LP
E
J
forward girth station
LBG
B
FD
after girth station
MD
DM

P Mainsail height
E Foot of mainsail
I Height of foretriangle
J Base of foretriangle
LP Longest perpendicular
LBG Length between girths
MD Midship depth
FD Forward deptn
DM Draft
B Beam

*This diagram of a typical ocean racer labels in the arbitrary shorthand used in the IOR guidebook the vital measurements for rating a boat. Sail area is calculated from the height and base length of the mainsail (abbreviated P and E above), the height and base of the foretriangle (I and J), and the length of a perpendicular line from the luff to the clew of the largest genoa (LP). The boat's length is taken as the distance (LBG) between its two so-called girth stations. The boat's beam (B) is simply its width at the hull's broadest point; but another key figure, depth, is based on a set of equations that average the boat's contours by combining measurements at MD, FD and DM.*

## Insights from the Tank

*Peter de Saix, director of the testing-tank facilities at Stevens Institute of Technology, hooks up spring-activated sensors that will electronically record the forces exerted by the water on a perfect scale model of Charisma's hull. When the model is set in motion, statistical indications of hull resistance, and of the boat's tendency to roll and sideslip, will be displayed on the data bank at left. Brass weights (foreground) are used to adjust the model's displacement so it will float at the same level as the real boat.*

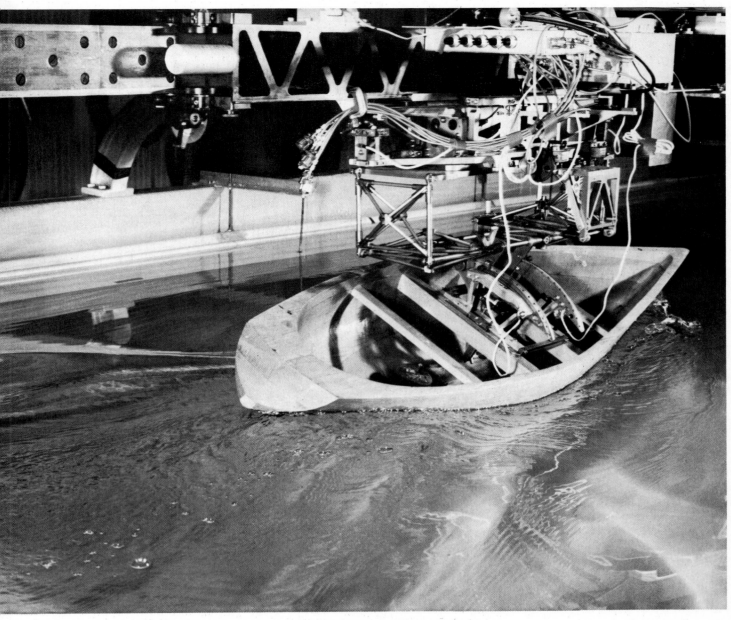

On an experimental run simulating a beat in a 16-knot wind, the model of Charisma is given a 20° angle of heel and a 4° yaw. During the towing process, while sensors are transmitting resistance data to the computer bank, engineers also examine visually the wave patterns that the model makes. On this particular run they noted an even and undisturbed wake, confirmation that the vessel's lines create little turbulence.

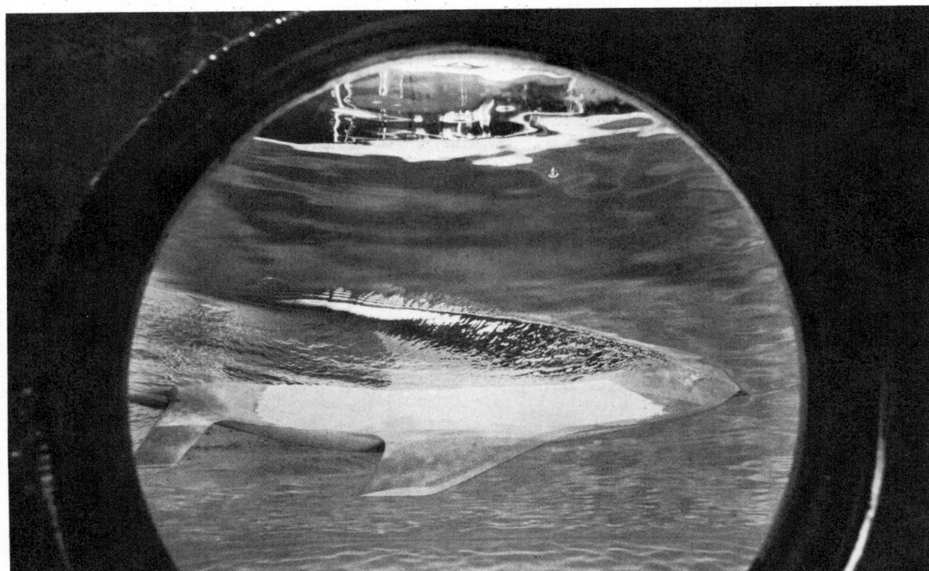

An underwater view from a porthole in the Stevens tank reveals the flow of water past the keel and rudder of Charisma's miniature prototype. The long, light area on the hull's midsection is waterproof putty applied experimentally to round out the boat's bilge. A sandpaper strip glued to the leading edge of the keel helps approximate the water turbulence that a full-scale boat experiences, but which does not register on small models.

*Charisma's finished aluminum hull gets a final check-out at Minneford Yacht Yard in City Island, New York, where the lines perfected in the towing tank and on the designer's board were translated into a full-sized boat. Viewed from the bow, the 40,000-pound vessel displays several design characteristics more typical of smaller day sailers than of traditional full-keeled ocean racers. Note, for example, the nearly vertical topsides that break sharply inward just below the waterline, a narrow stem for cutting through choppy seas and a relatively flat underbelly that keeps wave-making resistance to a minimum.*

# The Look of a Winner

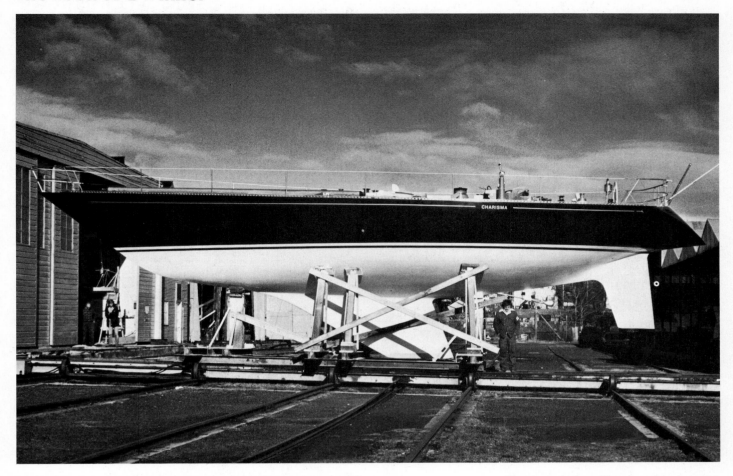

Charisma's sleek profile reflects her designer's intent to produce a fast boat at no sacrifice in handicap rating. Long overhangs at both bow and stern keep the waterline length of the 54-foot craft to a mere 41 feet. A swept-back fin keel, nine feet deep, supplies stability with minimal drag. The absence of a deckhouse cuts wind resistance and enables the crew to work freely during a race.

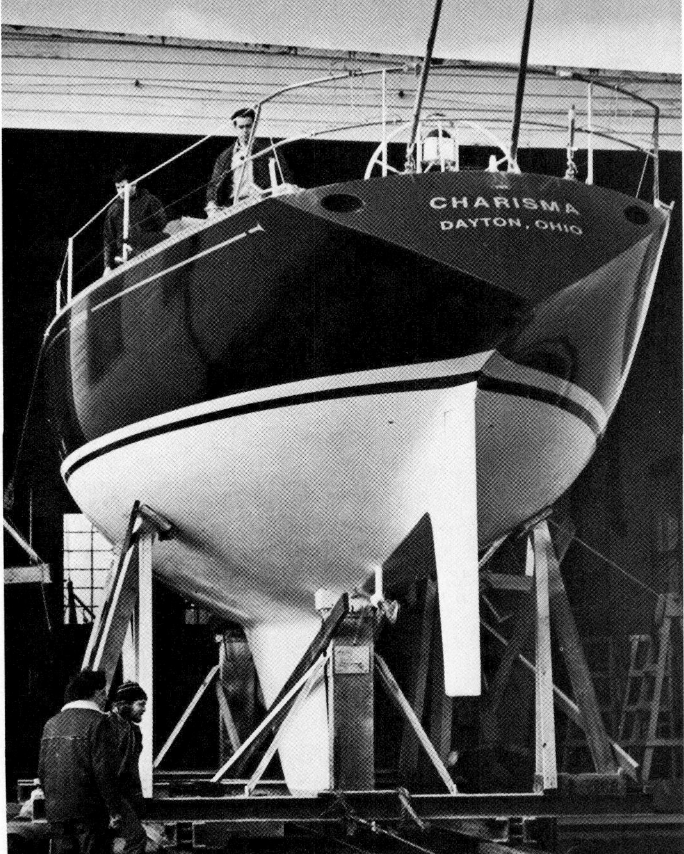


*This stern view of Charisma shows her full afterbody and deep spade rudder; the latter is located 14 feet aft of the keel and protrudes six feet below the waterline for precision steering. Above the waterline the reverse transom helps save weight and achieves a minor reduction in rating. Holes at either corner of the transom provide convenient stowage—and a quick-launching site—for 18-foot-long "man overboard" lighted marker buoys, required by the United States Yacht Racing Union on all offshore racers.*

## Rigged for Speed

In contrast to cruising-boat rigs, which are tailored for easy handling by casual crews, the abovedecks layout of a racing machine like *Charisma* is designed for high-speed maneuvering by a trained crew. The custom rig shown here, the most sophisticated type obtainable, cost *Charisma's* owner $50,000.

To keep windage and weight above decks at a minimum, *Charisma* carries a sloop rig *(right)*. Supporting the yacht's lightweight 67-foot aluminum mast are shrouds and stays of rolled stainless steel. These thin metal rods can sustain up to 23,000 pounds of tension, yet they weigh considerably less than the laid-up wire stays used on most cruising boats.

Two of *Charisma's* three forward stays support headsails; the third, a so-called baby stay near the mast, replaces a set of lower shrouds, normally angled forward to the rail. Eliminating these shrouds simplifies the foredeck crew's job of handling the boat's large genoa and sheets while tacking. Two grooves run the length of the headstay; both grooves can accommodate the luff rope of a jib, allowing the crew to raise a new sail before lowering its predecessor.

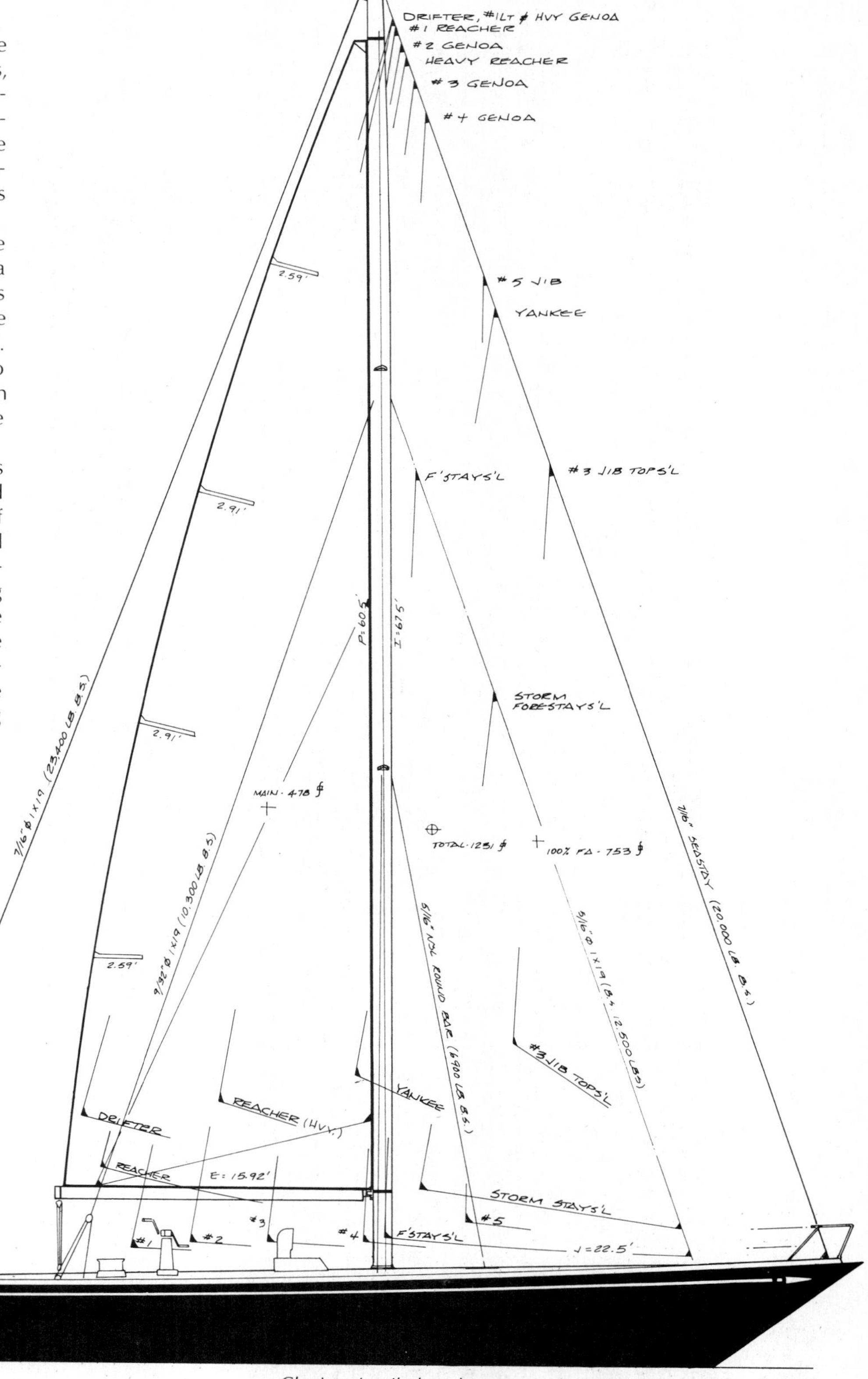


*Charisma's sail plan, drawn to scale at Sparkman and Stephens, meticulously details the rig's dimensions and gives the positions of each of her sails when set. In addition to a mainsail, the plan calls for 11 different racing headsails—nine flown from the headstay and two from the forestay. Each headsail's proper location is indicated by a trio of angles where the sail's corners would be. The designers have indicated total sail area—1,251 square feet—in the middle of the drawing, just forward of the mast. The computation for the area combines the size of the mainsail (which is 478 square feet) and the 753-square-foot foretriangle area (marked FΔ).*

*Deck hardware and electronic gear worth $30,000 are set in strategic locations on Charisma's deck. Dual boat-speed and wind-direction indicators flank the main hatch (foreground), providing quick reference for a helmsman seated to windward on either track. Amidships, two large jib-sheet winch drums, powered by variable-speed, pedestal-mounted handles, can multiply the sail-trimming strength of a crewman sixtyfold. A hydraulically operated boom vang installed on the mast can correct the shape of the mainsail in any breeze. Cabin windows, sail tracks and hatch covers are recessed into Charisma's flush deck, so crewmen will not stumble over them.*

*A constellation of paired winches, clustered symmetrically around Charisma's mast, comprises lightweight aluminum types (dark color) for handling rope and chromium ones that will accommodate wire halyards without scarring. Starting at the right foreground and moving counterclockwise are the winches used on port tack situations: an aluminum winch for adjusting jib Cunninghams or the spinnaker foreguy; a chrome winch for the spinnaker-pole lift; a spinnaker halyard winch; and a jib halyard winch. Partially hidden behind the mast is the main halyard winch. The winches to the left of the mast perform identical functions when on starboard tack.*

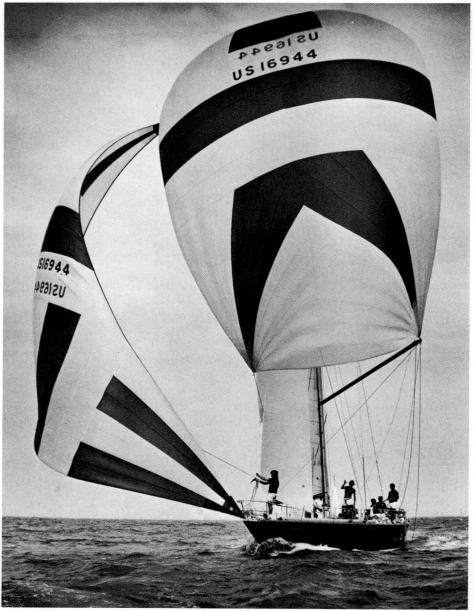

*Running downwind in a moderate breeze during an Admiral's Cup race off the coast of England, Charisma carries a mainsail, spinnaker staysail, spinnaker and a special racing sail called a blooper, here being trimmed by a crew member standing on the foredeck. The blooper, sewn from superlight nylon that weighs only 0.75 ounce per square yard, not only increases Charisma's speed but also helps control the boat by balancing the enormous forces of the wind in the spinnaker, set on the opposite side. The spinnaker's light and dark panels are sewn radially from all three corners to reduce stretching.*

## Customized Wardrobe

An ocean-racing yacht, like any other star performer, must have the right outfit for every occasion. *Charisma's* wardrobe of 28 sails—including duplicates of those most frequently used—is tailored to supply maximum effort on every point of sail and in virtually any weather imaginable *(diagram, right)*.

For these sails to function properly, they must hold their aerodynamic shape within close tolerances—no easy task, especially in heavy winds when the stress on the clew of the largest genoa may reach 4,000 pounds. To prevent stretching, each sail's seams were glued together before sewing, and the 478-square-foot main, in addition, was constructed from a double thickness of Dacron.

Even after *Charisma's* sails emerged from their loft at North Sails in Stratford, Connecticut, her wardrobe was still not complete. During the months after the boat was launched, a specialist from North shipped aboard as a crew member to observe the sails in action, to offer expert advice on trimming and setting *(right)*—and to carry an occasional imperfect sail ashore for alterations.

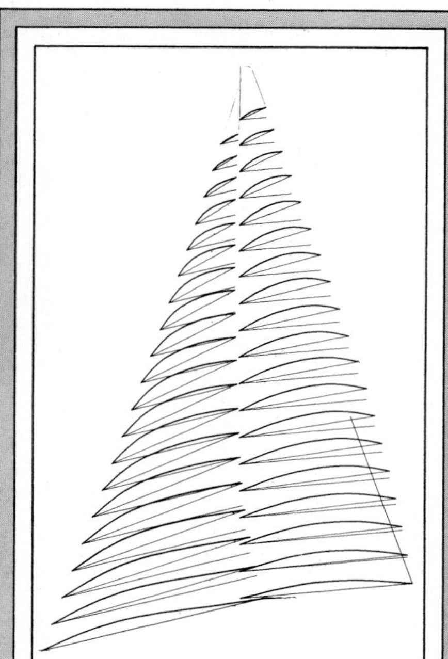

### Sail Shapes by Computer

To determine the optimal aerodynamic shape for *Charisma's* sails, North used a computer to generate cross-sectional curves for each set of sails. The printout above—based on such data as wind strength and angle of heel—shows a developmental design for the mainsail *(right)* and the even larger #2 genoa.

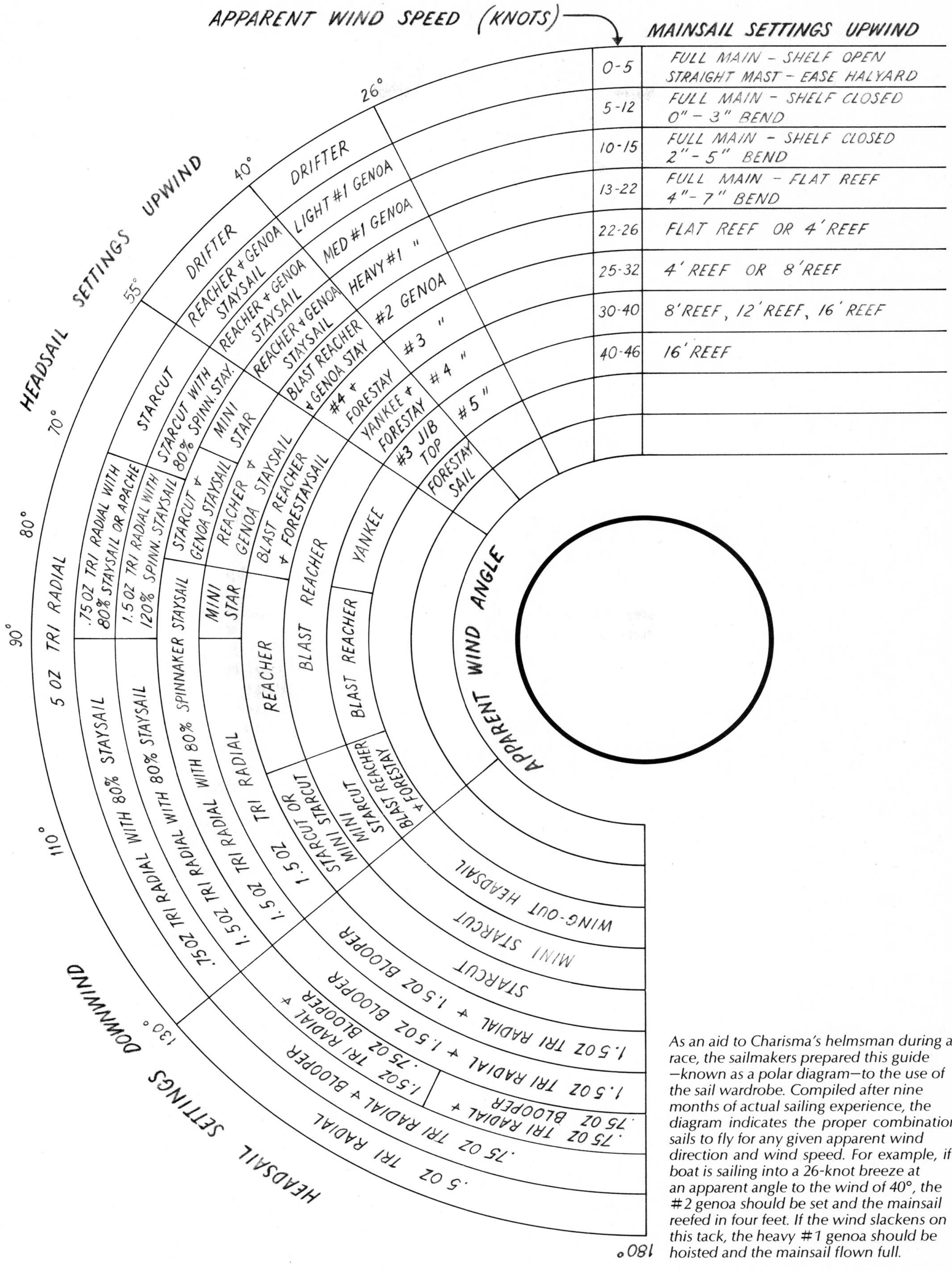

APPARENT WIND SPEED (KNOTS)

MAINSAIL SETTINGS UPWIND

| Apparent wind speed (knots) | Mainsail settings upwind |
|---|---|
| 0-5 | FULL MAIN – SHELF OPEN STRAIGHT MAST – EASE HALYARD |
| 5-12 | FULL MAIN – SHELF CLOSED 0" – 3" BEND |
| 10-15 | FULL MAIN – SHELF CLOSED 2" - 5" BEND |
| 13-22 | FULL MAIN – FLAT REEF 4"- 7" BEND |
| 22-26 | FLAT REEF OR 4' REEF |
| 25-32 | 4' REEF OR 8' REEF |
| 30-40 | 8' REEF, 12' REEF, 16' REEF |
| 40-46 | 16' REEF |

HEADSAIL SETTINGS UPWIND

26°
DRIFTER
LIGHT #1 GENOA
MED #1 GENOA
HEAVY #1 "
#2 GENOA
#3 "
#4 "
#5 "

40°
DRIFTER
REACHER + GENOA STAYSAIL
REACHER + GENOA STAYSAIL
REACHER + GENOA STAYSAIL
BLAST REACHER + GENOA STAY
#4 + FORESTAY
YANKEE + FORESTAY
#3 JIB TOP
FORESTAY SAIL

55°
STARCUT
STARCUT WITH 80% SPINN. STAY.
MINI STAR
REACHER + GENOA STAYSAIL
BLAST REACHER + FORESTAYSAIL
YANKEE

70°
.75 OZ TRI RADIAL WITH 80% STAYSAIL OR APACHE
1.5 OZ TRI RADIAL WITH 120% SPINN. STAYSAIL
STARCUT + GENOA STAYSAIL

80°
5 OZ TRI RADIAL
SPINNAKER STAYSAIL
MINI STAR
REACHER
BLAST REACHER
BLAST REACHER

APPARENT WIND ANGLE

90°
110°
.5 OZ TRI RADIAL WITH 80% STAYSAIL
.75OZ TRI RADIAL WITH 80% STAYSAIL
1.5OZ TRI RADIAL WITH 80%
1.5 OZ TRI RADIAL
1.5 OZ STARCUT OR MINI STARCUT
MINI STARCUT
STAST REACHER + FORESTAY

HEADSAIL SETTINGS DOWNWIND

130°
WING-OUT HEADSAIL
MINI STARCUT
STARCUT
1.5 OZ BLOOPER
1.5 OZ TRI RADIAL + 1.5 OZ BLOOPER
1.5 OZ TRI RADIAL + 1.5 OZ BLOOPER
1.5 OZ TRI RADIAL
.75 OZ TRI RADIAL + BLOOPER
.75 OZ TRI RADIAL + .75 OZ BLOOPER
.75 OZ TRI RADIAL
.75 OZ TRI RADIAL + BLOOPER
.5 OZ TRI RADIAL

180°

As an aid to Charisma's helmsman during a race, the sailmakers prepared this guide—known as a polar diagram—to the use of the sail wardrobe. Compiled after nine months of actual sailing experience, the diagram indicates the proper combination of sails to fly for any given apparent wind direction and wind speed. For example, if the boat is sailing into a 26-knot breeze at an apparent angle to the wind of 40°, the #2 genoa should be set and the mainsail reefed in four feet. If the wind slackens on this tack, the heavy #1 genoa should be hoisted and the mainsail flown full.

## Pursuit of Perfection

Modern construction techniques and new building materials have given the naval architect the freedom of a sculptor to continually reshape the contours of his creation—even after she has been launched and fully rigged for sea. When *Charisma* was six months old and in the midst of a successful racing season, designer Olin Stephens undertook a careful review of the boat's hull shape. He determined that by increasing *Charisma's* beam measurements her rating could be lowered without appreciably slowing her speed. This change was effected by simply applying to the sides of the boat a two-inch layer of microballoons—a strong, waterproof plastic putty suffused with tiny air bubbles that keep it light.

*Charisma's* stern received a more radical modification a few months later. In a tour de force of aluminum surgery, the tail section was sliced off and a new one, modeled to Stephens' specifications, was welded onto the hull. The restyling produced a faster boat more sensitive to the helm and with a better rating. A member of the design team put it another way. The alteration, he commented, would "make the rule think the boat is smaller and slower than it really is."

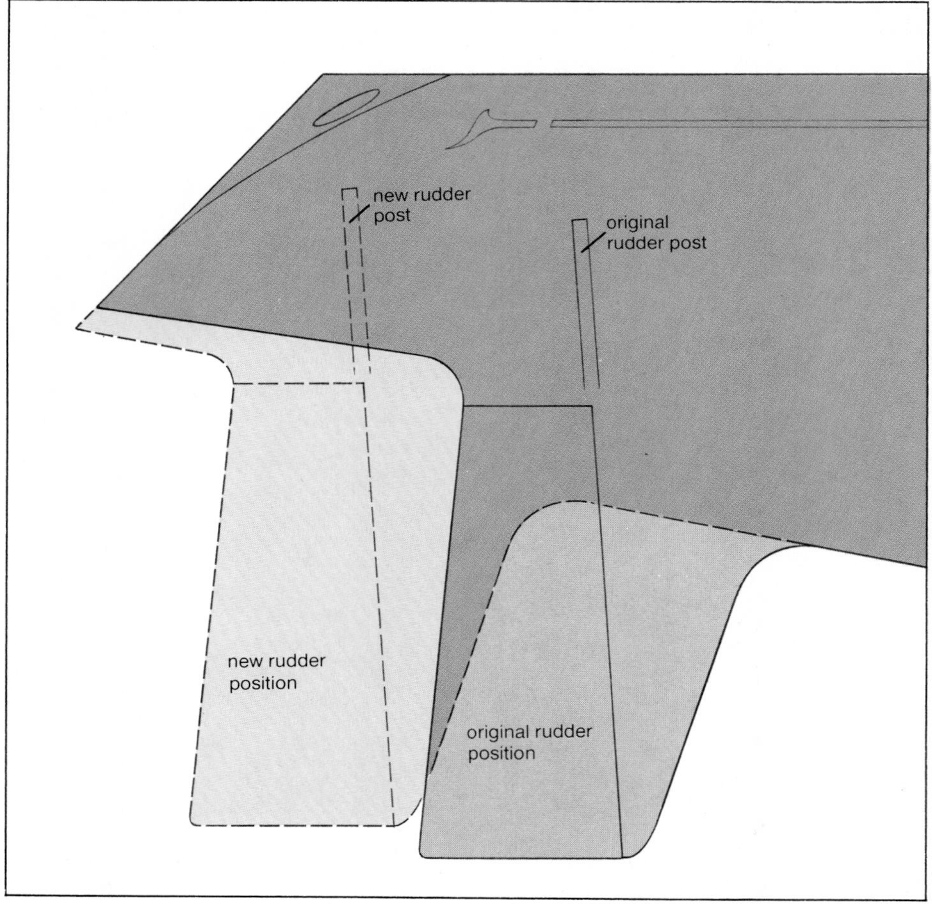


*The principal facet in the restructuring of Charisma's stern was the moving of the rudder 36 inches aft of its original position (gray). Because of a peculiarity of the IOR measurement system, the change did not raise Charisma's rating, even though the modicum of additional length allowed her to sail faster in strong winds. In fact, the rating turned out to be a fraction lower than before, since the new dimensions give a slightly larger displacement measurement.*

*The old 10-foot stern section of Charisma lies discarded on a spare track at the Minneford Yacht Yard. The excision was done in less than an hour with an acetylene torch. Installation of the new stern, complete with interior frames of aluminum, took about two weeks.*

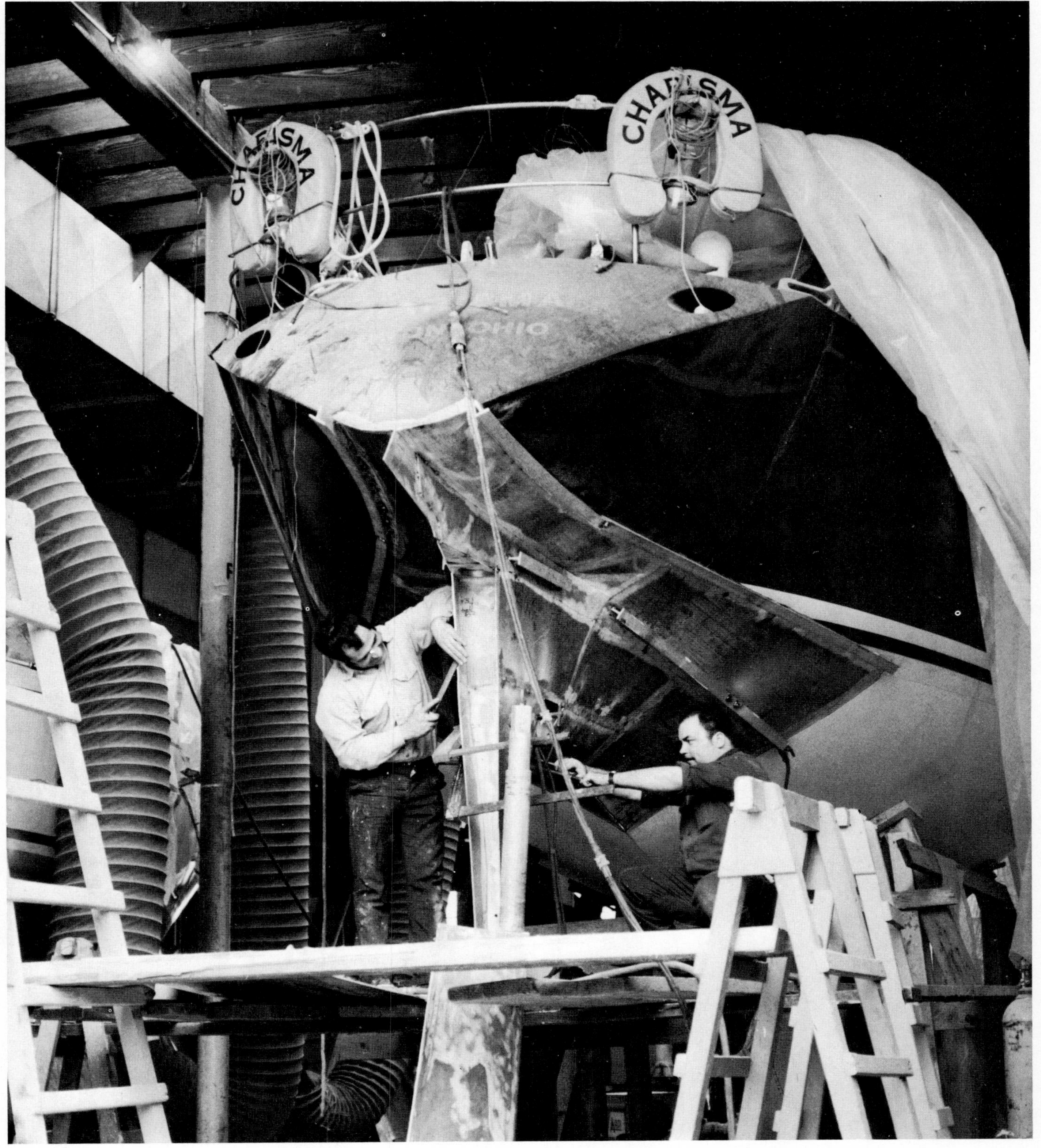

*During renovation, a workman (left) files down a 3/8-inch sheet of aluminum on the boat's new skeg structure, while his partner tightens a set of vises to keep the skeg in place until it is securely welded. The aluminum T-bars temporarily attached to the outside of the hull keep the new stern section from warping during installation; they will be removed when the welding is complete. The vessel's original rudder, resting at the workmen's feet, awaits reinstallation at its new location.*

# A ROSTER OF BLUE-WATER CLASSICS

No sport for the poor in spirit or in purse, offshore racing is nevertheless one of the fastest growing activities in boating, with a following of serious amateurs who go at their play with the dedication of professionals. In the years since World War II, the number of major offshore races in the United States alone has climbed to more than 40—about four times the prewar number. In addition, there are several international races of sufficient allure to draw entries thousands of miles from their home ports.

Whereas not long ago an ocean racer was likely to be little more than the family cruiser with a spinnaker and a couple of extra headsails tucked aboard, nowadays a competitive skipper will tend to build or buy a boat whose design and qualities suit the usual wind and sea conditions of races he wishes to enter. For example, the notoriously breezy Fastnet, run between England and Ireland, tends to favor boats of moderate sail area that have good stability and can be kept driving through rough seas.

Along with the Fastnet, the Bermuda Race *(right)* and the series of events in the Southern Ocean Racing Conference *(pages 164-165)* are considered to be particularly tough in terms of both the sea conditions and the competition they offer. But for those who like a good measure of ease with their racing, there are such downwind contests as the overnight Newport Beach, California-to-Ensenada race *(page 162)*.

In a league by itself is the grueling Whitbread Round-the-World Race, a 27,120-mile epic beginning and ending in Portsmouth, England. During its first running in 1974, three men were lost overboard during storms southeast of the Cape of Good Hope and in the southwest Pacific. The winner on corrected time spent a total of 152 days at sea, yet edged out the runner-up by only 43 hours.

*Closely bunched Class E competitors begin the 1970 race for Bermuda in the waters off Newport, Rhode Island. The contest proved a rough one: on the second night, squalls upward of 65 knots battered a large part of the 149-boat fleet, dismasting seven. The victor on corrected time was the Class C sloop Carina, skippered by three-time winner Richard Nye who, having chosen a course several miles east of the pack, slid smoothly home on a steady, less violent southwesterly wind.*

## Three Rigorous Tests

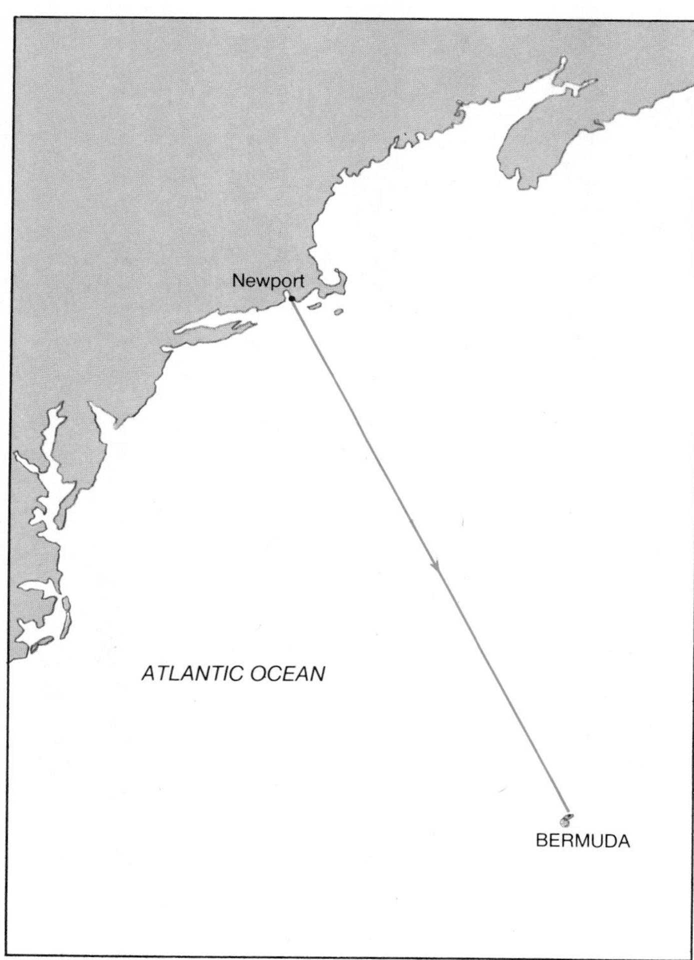


*The 635-mile Bermuda Race, staged in June of even-numbered years by the Cruising Club of America and the Royal Bermuda Yacht Club, ranks as the queen of offshore races. Since its 1906 inauguration, the event has attracted the world's hottest ocean-racing machines. To the competitive challenge is added the navigator's dilemma of crossing the Gulf Stream whose path may vary greatly from year to year—and even from week to week. Depending upon where a racer enters the Gulf Stream, he can add four or more knots to his speed, find himself pushed several miles east or be substantially set back.*

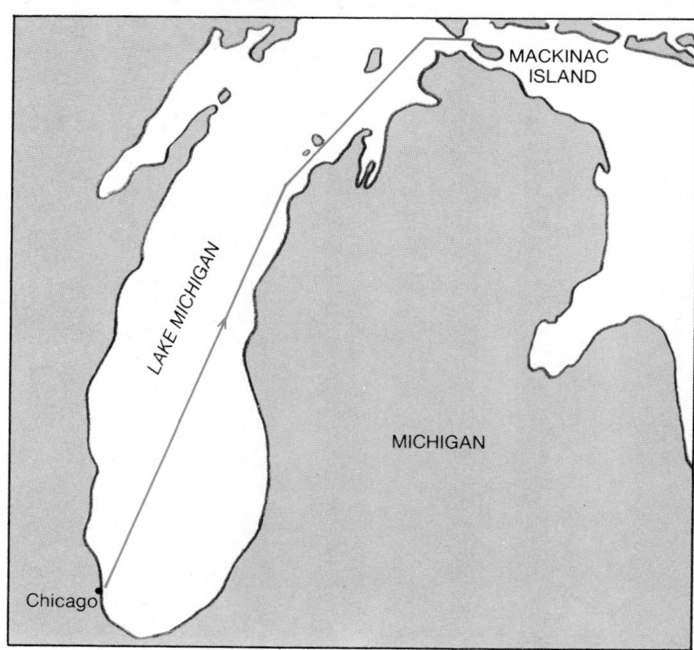


*The Chicago Yacht Club's Chicago-to-Mackinac fresh-water classic has been running since 1898. A five-boat affair that first year, the event now draws well over 200 yachts that are started in eight sections. Conditions along the 333-mile course are as unpredictable as any in racing: in 1911, winds of 80 mph catapulted the schooner Amorita to the finish in 31 hours—still a record—and also sent the sloop Vencedor to her destruction on rocks in northern Lake Michigan.*

With 15-knot winds kicking up the steel-blue waters of the English Channel, a portion of the 1975 Fastnet fleet sets off from Cowes. Over 250 yachts from 21 nations took part in the race's 50th-anniversary running—fittingly won by Noryema, a British entry.

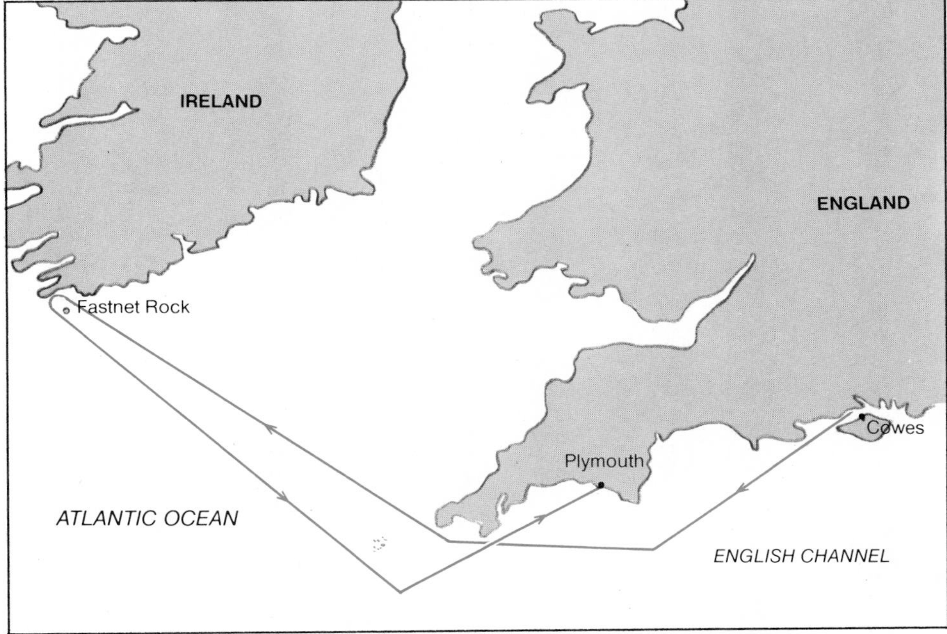


*The Fastnet, run biennially under the aegis of England's Royal Ocean Racing Club, is renowned as a supreme test of offshore seamanship. Its 605-mile course, from Cowes on the Isle of Wight to Fastnet Rock off the coast of Ireland and back to Plymouth, serves up the sort of adverse conditions of which racing legends are born: fog banks, whirligig currents and gales so fierce that, in one year, 29 out of 41 competitors were forced to drop out. The Fastnet is the main attraction in the four-race series called the Admiral's Cup, drawing three-boat teams representing countries around the world.*

*The 78-foot Canadian ketch Mir is knocked on her beam-ends by a sudden gust only 300 yards from the finish of the 1969 Transpacific Yacht Race. Moments after this photo was taken she righted herself, but not before the mainmast buckled. The wreckage was cut loose and the dismasted Mir gamely crossed the finish line—backward and under mizzen power alone—to take seventh place in her class. Heart-stopping knockdowns are not uncommon over the Transpac's final few miles, where the prevailing winds that provide idyllic sailing for most of the race are compressed between the mountainous islands of Oahu and Molokai, often producing gusts that approach gale force.*

# The Big One in the Pacific

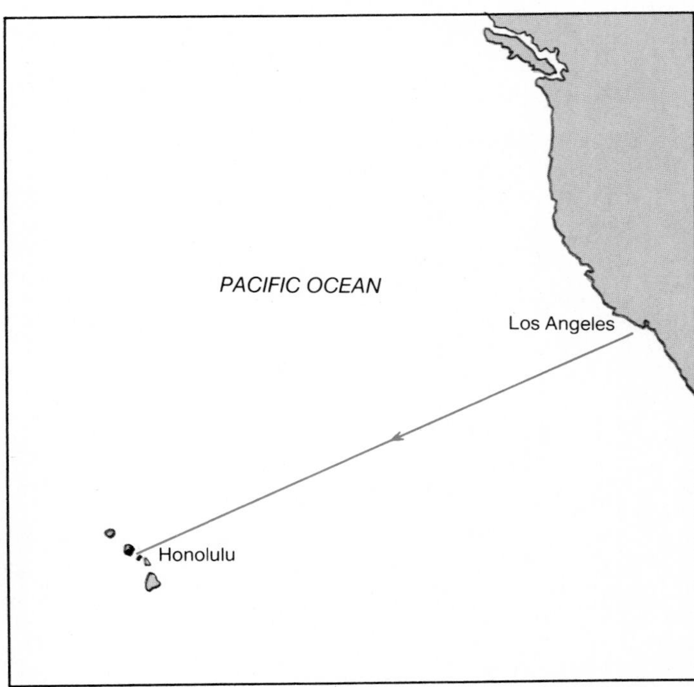


*The Transpacific Yacht Race, which covers 2,225 miles of Pacific Ocean between Southern California and Hawaii, is the longest regularly scheduled offshore race in the world and also one of the most prestigious. Inaugurated in 1906, it is currently held in July of odd-numbered years. Northeast trade winds have traditionally made for long downwind slides to the finish, with spinnakers billowing much of the way—though navigators are always wary of cutting too close to the dead air of an atmospheric high that generally sits on or just to the north of the straight-line course. Recent winners have clocked impressive elapsed times of less than nine and a half days.*

## Something for Everyone

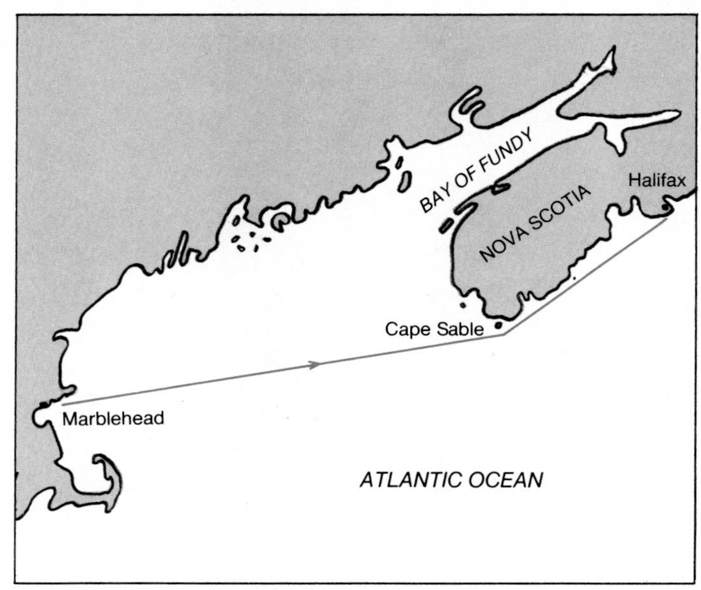


*The Marblehead-Halifax Race, run biennially in July by the Boston Yacht Club and the Royal Nova Scotia Yacht Squadron, has been a challenge to skippers since 1939. The course begins at Marblehead, Massachusetts, and proceeds 360 miles northeast past Cape Sable at the southern end of Nova Scotia and then on to Halifax. A dominant weather feature of the contest is usually pea-soup fog, brewed up by the meeting of the cold Labrador Current and the warm Gulf Stream. The key strategic decision is how close inshore to go on the final leg; a route brushing near Cape Sable is much shorter, but the risks of being caught in the Bay of Fundy's four-knot tidal current are high.*

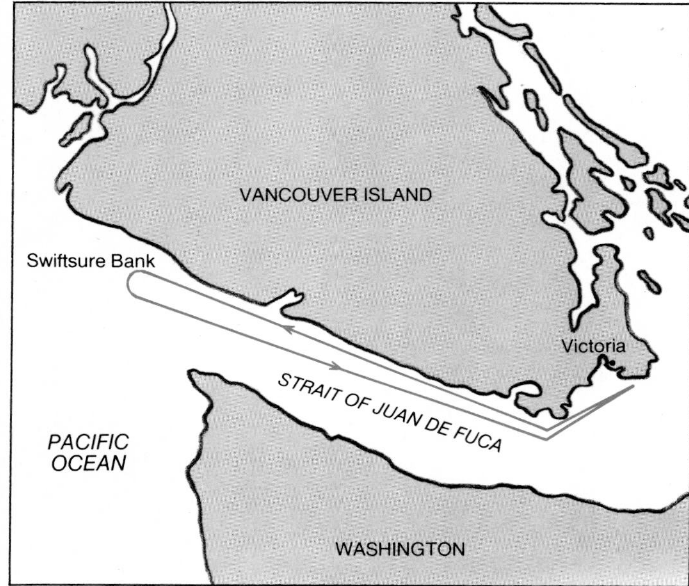


*A showpiece of Northwest racing since its inception in 1930, the Swiftsure Lightship Classic is run largely within Juan de Fuca Strait, between Vancouver Island and Washington. On Memorial Day weekend, the fleet starts outside the harbor of Victoria, British Columbia, heads into the Pacific for a course marker off the Swiftsure Bank (a lightship served as the mark until it was taken off station in 1961), then retraces the route—traveling a total of 136 miles. Along the way, competitors frequently meet heavy winds, choppy seas, rip tides and erratic currents flowing as fast as six knots around rocks.*

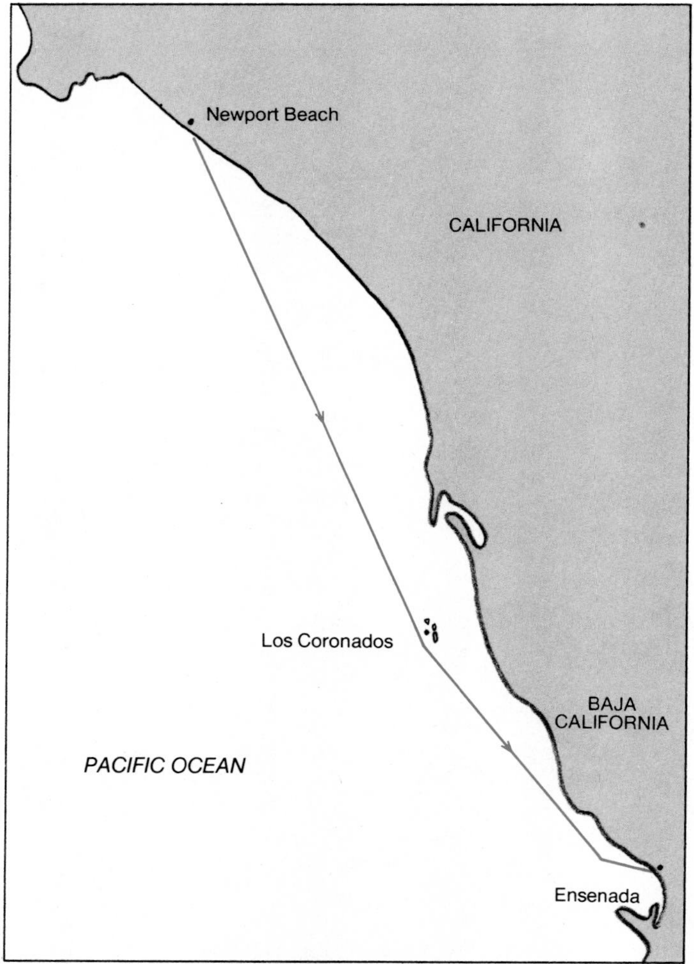


*The Ensenada Race, staged in late April between Newport Beach, California, and the Mexican seaport of Ensenada, is part sailing contest and part rambunctious rite of spring. Founded in 1947, the event has burgeoned until it boasts the largest race entry in the world, attracting armadas of 550 boats or more. The 125-mile-long course has just one tactical variable: if winds permit, vessels can cut inside of four towering rock outcroppings known as Los Coronados —rather than taking the normal outside passage—thereby saving several miles in overall travel distance to the finish line.*

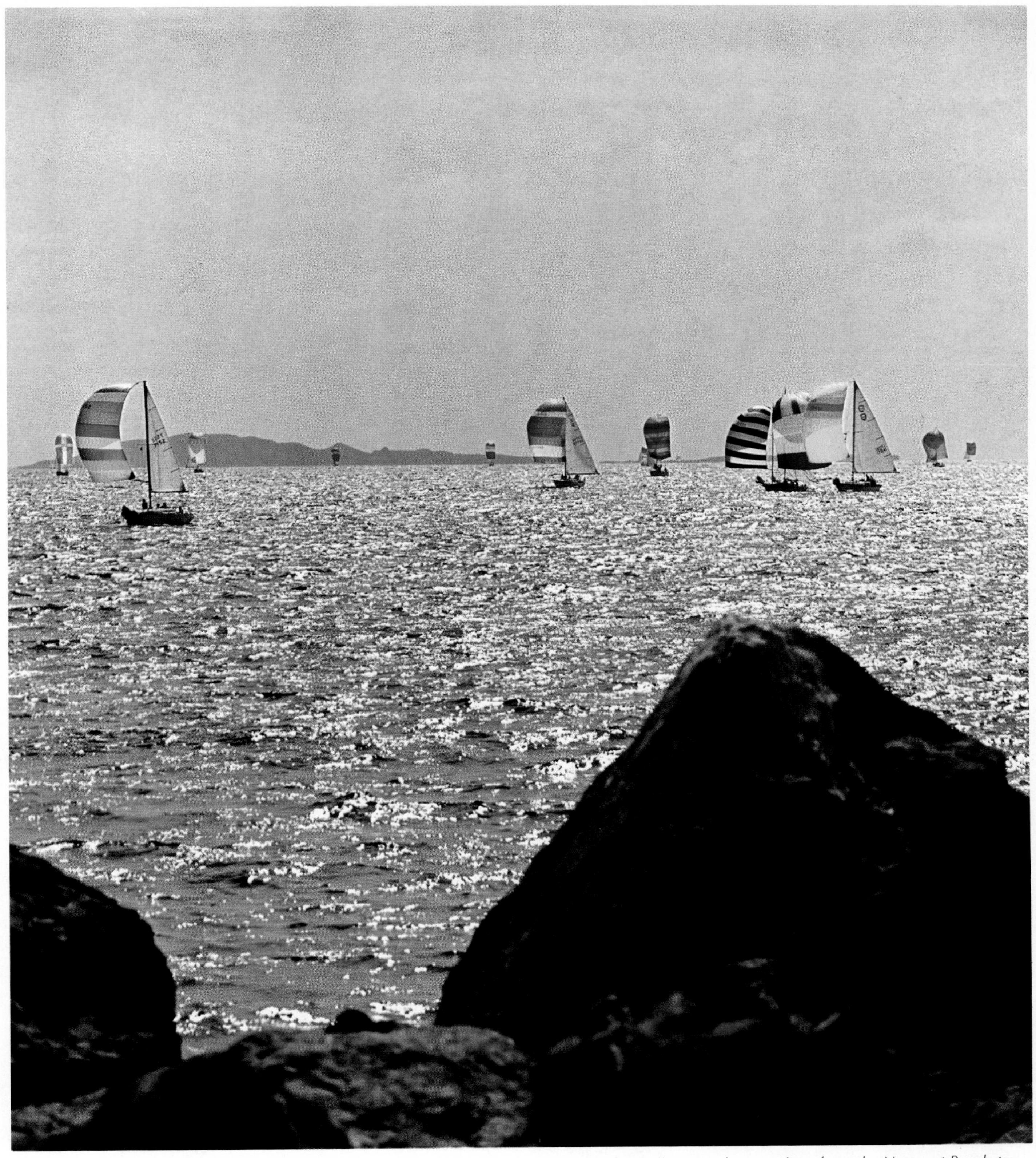

*A relatively small covey of competitors from the Newport Beach-to-Ensenada race fleet coasts under spinnakers to a sunny and sedate finish off Todos Santos Bay. Chaotic finishes—and starts—are more typical of the event, whose enormous entry list is often swelled by a complement of unofficial starters. In one race, scores of boats found themselves simultaneously closing in on a 100-yard-long finish line when the wind abruptly died, leaving all hands drifting and out of control at close quarters. By the time the melee had ended, 80 boats bore scrapes, gouges and other scars from collisions.*

*The sloop Phantom dips her boom and spinnaker in a wave as she flies along in 20-knot winds shortly after the start of the 1974 running of the notoriously gusty Miami-Nassau Race in the Southern Ocean Racing Conference. In this same race the 46-foot sloop Wimoweh struck a rock and went to the bottom off the Great Isaac lighthouse. Her 11 crewmen were rescued by another competitor, Osprey, which then continued on to Nassau. Osprey crossed the line in 89th place out of a fleet of 111—but the race committee decided to award her a two-hour allowance for lost time and extra weight, as a result of which she vaulted into first place in the final order of finish.*

# The Season in the South

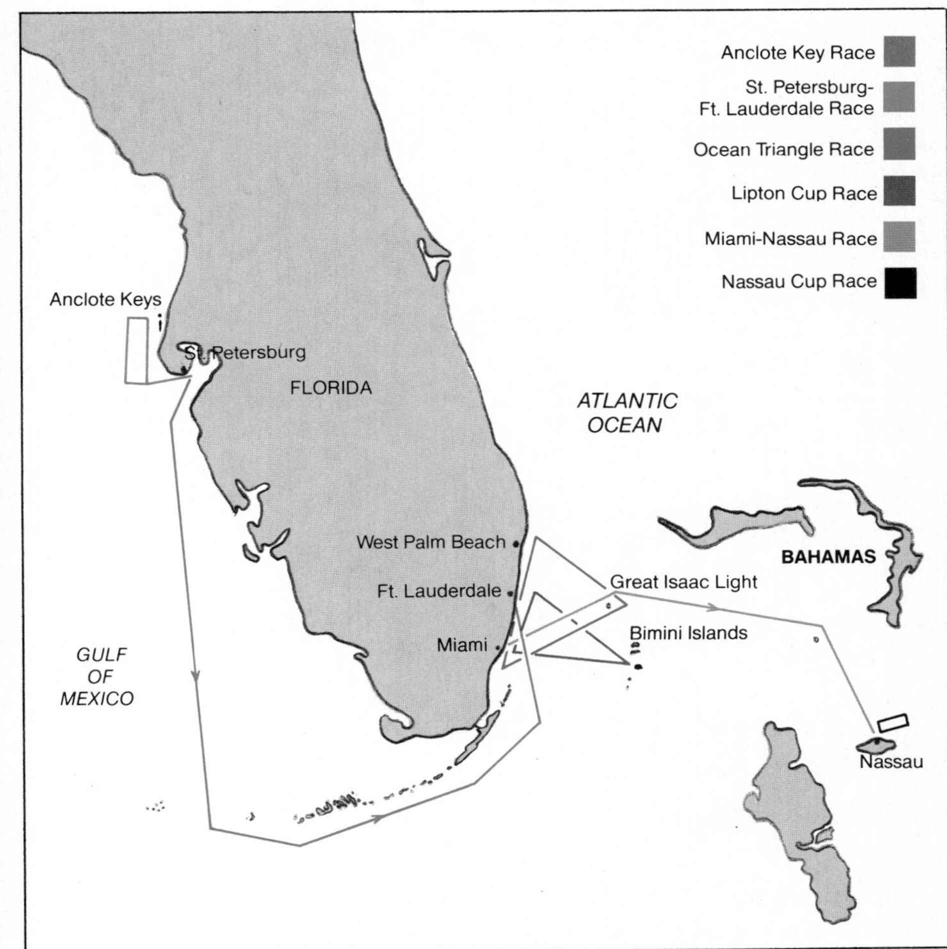


*The six events of the Southern Ocean Racing Conference provide a full measure of winter racing in Florida and Bahamian waters. The races, supervised by five mainland yacht clubs and one in Nassau, are run off at weekly intervals beginning with the Anclote Key Race in late January. Several of the contests existed as separate events for as long as two decades before the S.O.R.C. was organized in 1947. Scoring for overall standings is cumulative, with two long blue-water matches —the 407-mile St. Petersburg-Fort Lauderdale and the 176-mile Miami-Nassau races—accounting for nearly half of the point total.*

# Glossary

**Aft** Toward the stern.

**Altitude** The angular distance of a celestial body above the horizon as measured by a sextant.

**Apparent wind** A combination of the natural wind and the breeze created by the boat's forward motion.

**Azimuth or True azimuth** The horizontal direction of a celestial body's geographical position from a boat, expressed as true compass direction.

**Ballast weight** Usually iron or lead carried inside the boat or outside on the keel for trim or for stability.

**Beam** The width of the boat at its widest part. A boat is "on her beam ends" when heeled over 90°.

**Boomkin** A device extending from the stern—somewhat as a bowsprit extends from the bow—that carries a sheet block for the mizzen.

**Broach** To allow a boat to swerve and heel dangerously, especially in a following sea, so that the boat turns broadside to the waves and is in danger of capsizing or foundering.

**Bulkhead** Any wall in a boat.

**Cam cleat** A quick-release cleat having two side-by-side, spring-loaded cams with teeth. A line leading between the cams is held in the teeth but can be released by a quick upward pull on the line.

**Catamaran** A twin-hulled boat.

**Caulking** The waterproofing material that is packed into the seams of a planked boat to make it watertight.

**Celestial body** The sun, the moon, any planet or any star.

**Celestial sphere** An imaginary sphere concentric with the earth and on which all celestial bodies are considered to be projected.

**Center of effort (CE)** A theoretical point on a boat's sail plan that represents the focus or center of the total forces of wind on the sails.

**Chafing gear** A covering put around a short section of line to reduce wear, or on the rigging to protect the sails.

**Chain plate** A narrow metal plate attached to the hull as a fastening point for shrouds and stays.

**Chronometer** A highly accurate timepiece, set to Greenwich Mean Time and used for celestial navigation.

**Coast Pilots** Government publications giving information on domestic coastlines, harbors and aids to navigation.

**Come about** To steer a sailboat through the eye of the wind so that the sails shift from one side of the boat to the other, putting the boat on another tack.

**Companionway** A passageway through which a ladder or flight of stairs.leads from the deck down to the cabin.

**Comparing watch** A watch that is synchronized with a boat's chronometer to be used in conjunction with the sextant.

**Counter** The underside of the overhanging part of the stern above the waterline.

**Cringle** A circular eye—often formed by a metal ring, grommet or piece of rope—set in the corners or on the edges of a sail and used for fastening the sail to spars or running rigging.

**Cutter** A sailboat with one mast stepped more than one third of the way aft, capable of carrying two or more sails ahead of the mast; also, a Coast Guard boat.

**Dead reckoning** The process of projecting a ship's position based on the course steered and the distance run since the vessel's last known position—commonly abbreviated as DR.

**Deadrise** The angle at which the bottom rises from where it joins the keel to the turn of the bilge, or chine.

**Declination** Angular distance of a celestial body north or south of the celestial sphere's equator.

**Deviation** The error in a magnetic compass caused by magnetic influences on board a boat. Deviation is described as being easterly or westerly according to whether the ship's compass is deflected east or west of magnetic north.

**Dip** The vertical angle between the actual horizon and a navigator's line of sight to the visible horizon.

**Displacement** The weight of water displaced by a floating boat, equal to the weight of the boat.

**Draft** The depth a vessel extends below the waterline; the position and amount of maximum camber in a sail.

**Equinoctial** The equator of the celestial sphere.

**Equinox** One of two moments, occurring within a four-day period around March 21 and September 21 of each year, when the sun passes directly over the equator.

**Fin keel** A deep narrow keel found on most modern ocean-racing boats that creates less drag than do longer conventional keels.

**Fix** A boat's position as marked on a chart. In celestial navigation, a fix is established by making two or more sextant sightings of the sun, the moon, a planet or a star; in coastal piloting, it is obtained by taking bearings on two or more known landmarks (visual fix) or two or more radio sources (electronic fix).

**Forefoot** The forward portion of a boat's hull below the waterline.

**Foretriangle** On a sailboat, the triangle formed by the headstay, the front of the mast and the deck.

**Freeboard** The vertical distance measured on the boat's side from the waterline to the deck.

**Furl** To roll, fold or wrap an expanse of cloth—such as a sail, a flag or an awning—close to or around a spar, staff or stay.

**Gaff** A spar to support and spread the head of a sail of four generally unequal sides. A sail so rigged is said to be gaff-headed.

**Geographical position** The point at which a line drawn from a celestial body to the center of the earth would intersect the surface of the earth.

**Gimbals** Pivoted mounts that enable the object they support (a compass, stove, lamp, etc.) to remain level when the boat does not.

**Greenwich hour angle** The angle at the pole, measured westward through 360°, between the Greenwich meridian and any other meridian.

**Greenwich Mean Time** Time kept on a master atomic clock at the Royal Observatory in Greenwich, England, and used by offshore navigators around the world in computing their position.

**Greenwich meridian (also prime meridian)** The meridian designated as 0° that runs through Greenwich, England, and serves as the base line for measurements of longitude.

**Headsails** Sails set within the foretriangle, i.e., forward of the mast and usually on a stay. Headsails include jibs and staysails.

**Heave to** The general term for various methods of riding out a storm without attempting to travel through it; to lie almost stationary while still underway by heading up into the wind, by adjusting engine speed or by trimming the sails in such a way that the boat will head up and then fall off the wind.

**Horizon glass** On a sextant, the glass or lens through which the horizon is observed. The half of the glass nearer to the sextant frame is a mirror, the other half is clear.

**Intercept** The difference between the sextant altitude of a celestial body and the precomputed altitude of the same body as listed in the sight reduction tables.

**International Offshore Rule (IOR)** A formula for measuring the dimensions of a boat and extrapolating from those dimensions a handicap rating for ocean races.

**Jiffy reefing** A quick reefing system employing lines fixed on the boom.

**Jury-rig** A temporary or makeshift rig set up to substitute for some broken or lost piece of equipment.

**Ketch** A boat with a two-masted rig in which the larger, or mainmast, is forward, and the smaller mizzenmast is stepped aft —but forward of the rudder and, usually, of the helm.

**Latitude** Angular distance from the equator, measured northward or southward through 90°. Each degree of latitude subdivides into 60 minutes of arc, and each minute contains 60 seconds of arc.

**Length** The greatest length of a boat, not counting the bowsprit or other protuberances, is called length overall (LOA); length at the waterline (LWL), usually shorter, is measured at the designed waterline and excludes the bow and stern overhangs.

**Level racing** Racing among deepwater boats with a single rating, that is, with no time allowances.

**Light lists** Coast Guard publications giving the location and distinguishing characteristics of all aids to navigation.

**Limb** The circular outer edge of a celestial body, most commonly the sun. The half with the greatest altitude is called the upper limb and the half with the least altitude the lower limb.

**Local hour angle** Angular difference between the Greenwich hour angle and the boat's assumed longitude.

**Log** A ship's journal or written record of the vessel's day-by-day performance, listing speeds, distances traveled, weather conditions, landfalls and other information; also, a device for measuring the rate of a ship's motion through the water.

**Longitude** The angle at the pole, measured eastward or westward through 180°, between the Greenwich meridian and the meridian of any point on the earth. Like latitude, longitude is measured in degrees, minutes and seconds.

**Loran** A radio positioning system that allows navigators to make fixes by the reception of synchronized low-frequency radio transmissions. The word loran is an acronym for long-range navigation.

**Mainmast** Usually, the principal—and the heaviest—mast of two or more. In yawls and ketches, the forward mast is the mainmast; in schooners and vessels with more than two masts, it is the second mast from the bow.

**Marconi** The name of a three-cornered sail whose luff sets on a mast—as opposed to the four-sided gaff-rigged sail; also called a Bermuda or jib-headed sail.

**Mast step** A socket in which the heel, or bottom, of a mast is stepped.

**Meridian** A north-south reference line usually expressed as a longitude; also a great circle through the geographical poles of the earth.

**Mizzen** The sail set on the mizzenmast; the aftermast of a yawl or ketch.

**Nautical mile** A unit of distance, used in navigation, equal to the length of one minute of latitude.

**One Tonner** An oceangoing sailboat that rates at 27.5 feet under the current International Offshore Rule.

**Panel** A section of fabric in a sail.

**Parallax** The difference in the apparent direction of a celestial body due to a navigator's usual inability to view it from a point directly between the body and the center of the earth. In navigation, it is customary to apply a parallax correction to sextant altitudes of the sun, the moon, Venus and Mars.

**Pilot charts** Charts that give information on winds, weather and currents covering all the world's major oceans for each month of the year.

**Pitchpole** To somersault, as when a boat is thrown end over end by a wave.

**Plumb bow** A bow that is straight up and down, with no overhang.

**Plumb line** A line with a weight on the end, used to determine whether something is vertical.

**Quarter** Either side of a boat's stern; to sail with the wind on the quarter.

**Rating** A designation, expressed in feet and based on a boat's dimensions, that is used as an index for assigning a handicap or time allowance to that boat in ocean races.

**Reef** To reduce sail area without removing the sail entirely, by partially lowering the sail and securing loose fabric along the foot with lines called reef points.

**Refraction** The change in direction of a

ray of light as it passes obliquely into the earth's atmosphere.

**Rig** A noun indicating the arrangement of masts, rigging and sails that distinguishes a vessel by type, for example, ketch, yawl, etc.; also, a verb meaning to prepare a boat or some piece of nautical gear for service.

**Roving** Coarse cloth.

**Run** The part of the boat from the point of widest beam to the stern; to sail before the wind.

**Running fix** A position determined by creating an intersection of lines of position derived from sextant sightings of the sun (celestial navigation) or visual compass bearings (piloting) made at different times.

**Sailing Directions** Government-published loose-leaf volumes that give pertinent information for the mariner on coastlines, harbor approaches and aids to navigation in foreign countries.

**Schooner** A sailboat that generally has two masts (though some have had up to seven). The mainmast is aft of a smaller foremast, and the sails are either jib-headed or gaff-headed.

**Sheer** The curve of a boat's rail from stem to stern.

**Skeg** An underwater fin installed in the sterns of some boats lacking full keels to protect the rudder from damage by floating debris.

**Sloop** A sailboat with a single mast that is stepped not more than one third of the way aft from the bow. A sloop usually carries only one headsail.

**Snatch block** A block hinged on one side and latched on the other so that it can be opened to receive the bight of a line and then closed to hold the line securely.

**Spade rudder** An inboard rudder mounted separately from the keel and usually well aft.

**Spar** General term for any wood or metal pole—mast, boom, yard, gaff or sprit—used to carry and give shape to sails.

**Starcut** A type of spinnaker whose cloth panels are cut in a distinctive star shape. It is used by racing boats when reaching or when running in heavy air.

**Stem** The forwardmost part of the bow.

**Step** To step a mast is to place it in position.

**Stove in** Smashed inward. A boat whose hull has been broken in from outside is said to be stove in.

**Surfing** Traveling down the forward face of a wave so as to increase a boat's speed.

**Swage** A cylindrical metal shank that is cold-rolled onto the end of a wire as a terminal.

**Thwart** A crosswise seat in an open boat.

**Towing tank** A long, narrow tank of water in which scale models of boats are subjected to simulated sailing conditions to perfect their designs.

**Transducer** The sending-receiving device of a depth finder that transmits sonic pulses to the bottom and then picks up the echoes.

**Trim tab** A pivoting plate used to influence the performance of a hull or rudder, e.g., to turn the rudders of self-steering devices.

**Trimaran** A triple-hulled boat.

**True azimuth** See **Azimuth**.

**Turnbuckle** An adjustable fastening for attaching the standing rigging to the chain plates and for adjusting the tension on the standing rigging.

**Vernier scale** A scale used to obtain a precise reading of an instrument, particularly for mariners, of the altitude readings on a sextant.

**Watch** A period of duty to which part of a boat's crew is assigned; also, crew members assigned to that period of duty.

**Waterline** The level of the water on a floating hull.

**Wetted surface** The immersed area of a floating hull including keel and rudder.

**Whisker pole** A spar, usually with snap fittings on either end, that is extended more or less horizontally from the mast and used to hold out the clew of a jib or genoa, or to prevent the spinnaker guy from chafing on the shrouds.

**Winch** A machine around which a line is turned to provide mechanical advantage for hoisting or hauling.

**Yawl** A boat with a two-masted rig in which the mizzen, or jigger, is abaft the rudderpost and the helm. The yawl's mizzen is smaller than the ketch's, as well as being placed farther aft.

**Zenith** The point at which a line drawn from the center of the earth through a boat would intersect the celestial sphere.

# Bibliography


**General**

Baader, Juan, *The Sailing Yacht.* W. W. Norton & Company, Inc., 1965.

Beebe, Robert, *Voyaging under Power.* Seven Seas, 1975.

Borden, Charles A., *Sea Quest.* Ballantine Books, 1967.

Brown, Jim, *Searunner Construction.* Jim Brown, 1971.

Bruce, Erroll, *Deep Sea Sailing.* John de Graff, Inc., 1973.

Chapman, Charles Frederic, *Piloting, Seamanship and Small Boat Handling.* Motor Boating & Sailing Books, The Hearst Corporation, 1974.

Chichester, Francis, *Gypsy Moth Circles the World.* Hodder and Stoughton Ltd., 1967.

Coles, K. Adlard, *Heavy Weather Sailing.* John de Graff, Inc., 1972.

Fuller, Beverly, *Cooking on Your Knees.* David McKay Company, Inc., 1973.

Herreshoff, L. Francis, *The Common Sense of Yacht Design.* Caravan-Maritime Books, 1973.

Hiscock, Eric C., *Voyaging Under Sail.* Oxford University Press, 1974.

Hollingworth, Alan, *The Way of a Yacht.* W. W. Norton & Company, Inc., 1974.

Howse, D., and M. Sanderson, *The Sea Chart.* McGraw-Hill Book Company, 1973.

Illingworth, J. H., *Further Offshore.* Quadrangle Books, 1969.

Jenkins, Commander H. L., *Ocean Passages for the World.* The Hydrographer of the Navy, British Admiralty, 1973.

Johnson, Peter, *Yachtsman's Guide to the Rating Rule.* Nautical Publishing Company, 1971.

King, Commander William:
*Adventure in Depth.* G. P. Putnam's Sons, 1975.
*Capsize.* Nautical Publishing Company, 1969.

Kinney, Francis S., *Skene's Elements of Yacht Design.* Dodd, Mead & Company, 1962.

Letcher, John S., Jr., *Self-Steering for Sailing Craft.* International Marine Publishing Company, 1974.

Parker, David M., *Ocean Voyaging.* John de Graff, Inc., 1975.

Pearson, Everett A., *The Lure of Sailing.* Harper and Row, 1965.

Phillips-Birt, Douglas:
*The History of Yachting.* Stein and Day, 1974.
*Sailing Yacht Design.* International Marine Publishing Company, 1971.

Robertson, Dougal:
*Sea Survival: A Manual.* Praeger Publishers, 1975.
*Survive the Savage Sea.* Paul Elek Limited, 1973.

Robinson, Bill, *Legendary Yachts.* The Macmillan Co., 1971.

Ross, Wallace, *Sail Power.* Alfred A. Knopf, Inc., 1975.

Scharff, Robert, and the editors of *One-Design & Offshore Yachtsman, Encyclopedia of Sailing.* Harper & Row, Publishers, Inc., 1971.

Smeeton, Miles, *Once Is Enough.* Rupert Hart-Davis, 1959.

**Ocean Racing**

Antrobus, Paul, Bob Ross, and Geoffrey Hammond, *Ocean Racing around the World.* Prentice-Hall, Inc., 1975.

Cook, Peter, and Bob Fisher, *The Longest Race.* Stanford Maritime Limited, Member Company of the George Philip Group, London, 1975.

Illingworth, John, *The Malham Story.* Nautical Publishing Company, 1972.

Jones, Theodore A., *The Offshore Racer.* Quadrangle, The New York Times Book Company, 1973.

Loomis, Alfred F., *Ocean Racing.* Yachting Publishing Corp., 1946.

Phillips-Birt, Douglas, *British Ocean Racing.* Adlard Coles Ltd., 1960.

**Navigation**

Birney, Arthur A., *Noon Sight Navigation.* Cornell Maritime Press, 1972.

Blewitt, Mary, *Celestial Navigation for Yachtsmen.* John de Graff, Inc., 1964.

Bowditch, Nathaniel, LLD., *American Practical Navigator.* U.S. Government Printing Office, corrected print, 1966.

Crawford, William P., *Mariner's Celestial Navigation.* Miller Freeman Publications, Inc., 1972.

Dunlap, G. D., and H. H. Shufeldt, *Dutton's Navigation and Piloting.* Naval Institute Press, 1972.

Watts, Oswald M., *The Simplified Sextant.* Thomas Reed Publications, Ltd., 1973.

**Historical**

Cotter, Charles H., *A History of Nautical Astronomy.* American Elsevier Publishing Company, 1968.

Dodd, Edward, *Polynesian Seafaring,* Volume II of *The Ring of Fire.* Dodd, Mead & Company, 1972.

Frere-Cook, Gervis, *The Decorative Arts of the Mariner.* Little, Brown and Company, 1966.

Gladwyn, Thomas, *East Is a Big Bird.* Harvard University Press, 1970.

May, Commander W. E., *A History of Marine Navigation.* W. W. Norton & Company, Inc., 1973.

Needham, Joseph, *Science and Civilization in China.* Cambridge University Press, 1971.

Singer, Charles, E. J. Holmyard, A. J. Hall, and Trevor I. Williams, eds., *A History of Technology,* Volume III. Oxford University Press, 1957.

Taylor, E. G. R., *The Haven-Finding Art.* Hollis and Carter, 1956.

Taylor, E. G. R., and M. W. Richey, *The Geometrical Seaman.* Hollis and Carter, 1962.

Taylor, William H., and Stanley Rosenfeld, *The Story of American Yachting.* Appleton-Century-Crofts, Inc., 1958.

Waters, D. W., *The Art of Navigation in England in Elizabethan and Early Stuart Times.* Hollis and Carter, 1958.

**Articles**

Emory, Kenneth P., "The Coming of the Polynesians." *National Geographic,* December 1974.

Lewis, David, "Wind, Wave, Star and Bird." *National Geographic,* December 1974.

Roth, Hal (articles listed are from the *Yachting* magazine series "After 25,000 Miles"):
"Planning the Voyage." December 1972.
"Cost of Cruising." April 1973.
"Foreign Paperwork." November 1973.

# A Mariner's Library

*One of the special pleasures of offshore voyaging is reading about it, whether in the living room at home or snug in the cabin of one's own blue-water vessel. The following list contains a selection of true deepwater narratives; though some are out of print, they may be obtained at libraries or secondhand bookstores.*


Allcard, Edward:
*Single-Handed Passage.* Norton.
*Temptress Returns.* Norton.
*Voyage Alone.* Dodd, Mead.

Anderson, J. R. L.:
*The Greatest Race in the World: Solo across the Atlantic.* Hodder & Stoughton.
*The Ulysses Factor.* Harcourt Brace Jovanovich.

Bardiaux, Marcel, *Four Winds of Adventure.* De Graff.

Barton, Humphrey:
*Atlantic Adventurers.* Van Nostrand.
*Vertue XXXV.* (Mariners Library) Fernhill.

Belloc, Hilaire:
*The Cruise of the Nona.* Penguin.
*On Sailing the Sea.* De Graff.

Blyth, Chay, *The Impossible Voyage.* G. P. Putnam's Sons.

Carlin, Ben, *Half-Safe.* Morrow.

Chichester, Francis:
*Alone Across the Atlantic.* Doubleday.
*Along the Clipper Way.* Ballantine.
*Atlantic Adventure.* De Graff.

Coles, K. Adlard:
*Close Hauled.* Seeley Service.
*North Atlantic.* Norton.

Cook, Captain James, *Journal of a Voyage Round the World in H.M.S. Endeavor.* DaCapo.

Darwin, Charles, *The Voyage of the Beagle.* Bantam.

Davison, Ann:
*Last Voyage.* Sloan.
*My Ship Is So Small.* Sloan.

Dumas, Vito, *Alone Through the Roaring Forties.* Adlard Coles.

Ellam, Patrick, and Colin Mudie, *Sopranino.* Norton.

Garland, Joseph E., *Lone Voyager.* Little, Brown.

Gerbault, Alain:
*Fight of the Firecrest.* (Mariners Library) Fernhill.
*In Quest of the Sun.* (Mariners Library) Fernhill.

Gunn, John, *Barrier Reef by Trimaran.* Collins.

Guzzwell, John, *Trekka around the World.* Adlard Coles.

Hasler, H. G., *Roving Commissions.* R.C.C. Press.

Heyerdahl, Thor:
*The Kon-Tiki Expedition.* Rand.
*Ra Expeditions.* Doubleday.

Hiscock, Eric:
*Around the World in Wanderer III.* Oxford.
*Beyond the West Horizon.* Oxford.
*Sou'West in Wanderer IV.* Oxford.

Hughes, John Scott, ed., *MacPherson's Voyages.* Methuen.

Johnson, Irving, *Westward Bound in the Yankee.* Norton.

Johnson, Irving and Electa, *Yankee's Wander World.* Norton.

Kenichi, Horie, *Koduku.* Tuttle.

Kent, Rockwell, *N by E.* Brewer & Warren.

King, Commander William, *Adventure in Depth.* G. P. Putnam's Sons.

Lewis, David:
*Daughters of the Wind.* Gollancz.
*Dreamers of the Day.* Gollancz.
*Ship Would Not Travel Due West.* (Mariners Library) Fernhill.

London, Jack, *Cruise of the Snark.* Seafarer.

Long, Dwight, *Sailing All Seas in the Idle Hour.* Hart-Davis.

MacGregor, John, *The Voyage Alone in the Yawl Rob Roy.* Fernhill.

Manry, Robert, *Tinkerbelle.* Harper & Row.

Marin-Marie, *Wind Aloft, Wind Alow.* Scribners.

Martyr, Weston, *Southseaman.* (Mariners Library) Fernhill.

Maury, Richard, *Saga of Cimba.* De Graff.

Mitchell, Carleton, *Wind's Call: Cruises Near and Far.* Scribners.

Moitessier, Bernard, *First Voyage of the Joshua.* Morrow.

Morison, Samuel E., *Spring Tides.* Houghton Mifflin.

Nutting, William, *Track of the Typhoon.* Motor Boat.

O'Brien, Conor:
*Across Three Oceans.* (Mariners Library) Fernhill.
*The Small Ocean-Going Yacht.* Oxford.

Pidgeon, Harry, *Around the World Singlehanded.* Appleton.

Piver, Arthur:
*Trans-Atlantic Trimaran.* Underwriters.
*Trans-Pacific Trimaran.* Pi-Craft.
*Trimaran Third Book.* Pi-Craft.

Ransome, Arthur, *Racundra's First Cruise.* (Mariners Library) Fernhill.

Robinson, W. A.:
*Deep Water and Shoal.* Hart-Davis.
*To the Great Southern Sea.* De Graff.

Rose, Sir Alec, *My Lively Lady.* McKay.

Shackleton, Ernest H., *Heart of the Antarctic, Being the Story of the British Antarctic Expedition, 1907-1909.* Greenwood.

Slocum, Joshua, *Sailing Alone around the World.* Dover.

Smeeton, Miles:
*Because the Horn Is There.* Gray's.
*Misty Islands.* De Graff.

Snaith, William, *Across the Western Ocean.* Harcourt Brace Jovanovich.

Swale, Rosie, *Children of Cape Horn.* Walker.

Tabarly, Eric, *Lonely Victory.* Clarkson Potter.

Tambs, Erling, *Cruise of the Teddy.* (Mariners Library) Fernhill.

Tilman, H. W.:
*Mischief among the Penguins.* Rupert Davis.
*Mischief in Greenland.* Tilman, Hollis & Carter.
*In Mischief's Wake.* Transatlantic.

Tomkins, Warwick M., *Fifty South to Fifty South.* Norton.

Uriburu, Ernesto, *Seagoing Gaucho.* Dodd, Mead.

Voss, J. C., *The Venturesome Voyages of Captain Voss.* Lauriat.

## Acknowledgments

For help given in the preparation of this book, the editors wish to thank the following: Richard Boulind, Brown University, Providence, R.I.; Mrs. Yu-ying Brown, British Museum, London; H. M. T. Cobbe, British Museum; Bruce and Alexandra Crabtree, San Diego; B. A. L. Cranstone, British Museum; Dr. William Davenport, University of Pennsylvania, Philadelphia; Defensė Mapping Agency Hydrographic Center, Washington, D.C.; Dr. Kenneth P. Emory, formerly of the Bernice P. Bishop Museum, Honolulu; Moulton H. Farnham, Glen Cove, L.I., N.Y.; Beverly Fuller, New York, N.Y.; Gayle Griffiths, Little Harbor Boat Yard, Marblehead, Mass.; Alan Gurney, New York, N.Y.; Hammond Map Store, New York, N.Y.; Hewlett-Packard, Paramus, N.J.; Warren D. Hight, National Weather Service, Rockville, Md.; Ted Hood, Little Harbor Boat Yard, Marblehead, Mass.; Lt.-Comdr. H. D. Howse, National Maritime Museum, Greenwich, England; E. J. Huddy, British Museum; Darryl and Ruth Ann Johnston, Lafayette, Calif.; Henry Karlin, Great Neck, N.Y.; Commander William King, Galway, Ireland; William Lapworth, Newport Beach, Calif.; Andrew MacGowan, Sparkman and Stephens, New York, N.Y.; William McKee, National Weather Service, Garden City, L.I., N.Y.; F. R. Maddison, Museum of the History of Science, Oxford, England; John Marples, San Diego; John Marshall, North Sails Inc., Stratford, Conn.; Jacques Megroz, Mamaroneck, N.Y.; Samuel G. Mellor; Matawan, N.J.; Mrs. J. Moore, National Maritime Museum, Greenwich, England; Dr. Joseph Needham, F.R.S., Caius College, Cambridge, England; New York Nautical Instrument and Service Corporation, New York, N.Y.; Lowell North, North Sails Inc., Stratford, Conn.; Rudy S. Osti Jr., Islander Yachts, Irvine, Calif.; David and Joanne Parker, Topanga, Calif.; Douglas B. Peterson, San Diego; Jesse Phillips, Phillips Industries, Inc., Dayton, Ohio; Dr. Samuel H. Riesenberg, Smithsonian Institution, Washington, D.C.; Dougal Robertson, Piraeus, Greece; J. C. Robinson, Science Museum, London; Chuck Saddler, Minneford's Yacht Yard, City Island, N.Y.; Pete de Saix, Stevens Institute of Technology, Hoboken, N.J.; Miles and Beryl Smeeton, Cochrane, Alberta, Canada; Olin Stephens, Sparkman and Stephens, New York, N.Y.; A. N. Stimson, National Maritime Museum, Greenwich, England; Walter Stoddard, National Weather Service, New York, N.Y.; Lt.-Comdr. C. C. W. Terrell, National Maritime Museum, Greenwich, England; Jack Weston, Rye, N.Y.


## Picture Credits

*Credits from left to right are separated by semicolons, from top to bottom by dashes.*

Cover—John Zimmerman. 6,7—Erwan Quemeré. 9—John Zimmerman. 12—Christopher G. Knight. 14—John Zimmerman. 15,16,17—John Zimmerman, drawings by Whitman Studio, Inc. 18 through 31—John Zimmerman. 32,33—John Zimmerman (2)—drawing by Whitman Studio, Inc. 34,35—John Zimmerman. 36,37—Martin Schreiber. 38,39—Reproduced from British Admiralty Chart No. 5308 with the sanction of the Controller, Her Majesty's Stationery Office and of the Hydrographer of the Navy. 40 through 43—Drawings by Whitman Studio, Inc. 44,45—Henry Groskinsky. 46—Defense Mapping Agency Hydrographic Center. 47—Defense Mapping Agency Hydrographic Center—reproduced from British Admiralty Chart No. 5124 (12) with the sanction of the Controller, Her Majesty's Stationery Office and of the Hydrographer of the Navy. 48 through 53—Defense Mapping Agency Hydrographic Center. 54,55—Martin Schreiber—provisions list adapted from *Cooking on Your Knees* by Beverly Fuller, David McKay Co. Inc., 1973. 56—Chart by Whitman Studio, Inc. 58,59—Courtesy United States Department of Commerce. 60—From *Sailing Directions for the West Indies,* Volume II, Defense Mapping Agency Hydrographic Center. 61—Christopher G. Knight. 62,63—From *Gypsy Moth Circles the World,* Hodder and Stoughton Ltd., 1967. 64 through 72—Drawings by Dale Gustafson. 73,74,75—Drawings by Dale Gustafson based on drawings by Pam Littlewood from *Survive the Savage Sea,* by Dougal Robertson, Paul Elek Limited, 1973. 76—Paul A. Darling. 78 through 81—Drawings by Fred Wolff. 82—Al Freni. 83—Drawing by Fred Wolff. 84—Humphrey Sutton. 85,86,87—Al Freni, drawings by Fred Wolff. 88—Humphrey Sutton. 89—Paul A. Darling—drawing by Fred Wolff. 90—Drawings by Fred Wolff. 91—Humphrey Sutton—drawings by Fred Wolff. 92,93—Al Freni, chronometer and stopwatch courtesy Tiffany & Co. 94 through 104—Drawings by Fred Wolff. 105—Humphrey Sutton. 110,111—Paul A. Darling; Defense Mapping Agency Hydrographic Center. 112,113—United States Naval Institute Hydrographic Office. 115—Simex Star Finder and Identifier, courtesy Coast Navigation School, Santa Barbara, California. 118,119—Defense Mapping Agency Hydrographic Center. 120,121—Al Freni. 122,123—Derek Bayes, courtesy British Museum; courtesy British Library. 124,125—From G. Phillips' "Seaports of India and Ceylon" published in the Journal of the North China Branch of The Royal Asiatic Society, 1885 and 1886, reproduced by permission of the British Library Board, except bottom right copied by Frank Lerner from Academia Sinica/Chinese Journal of Archaeology, 1951, Volume 5, courtesy East Asian Library, Columbia University. 126—Courtesy National Maritime Museum, Greenwich, England. 127—From Rare Book Division, The New York Public Library, Astor, Lenox and Tilden Foundations. 128—Courtesy National Maritime Museum, Greenwich, England. 129—Courtesy National Maritime Museum, Greenwich, England, on loan from Ministry of Defence, Navy. 130—Eric Schweikardt for SPORTS ILLUSTRATED. 132—Morris Rosenfeld & Sons—drawing by Fred Wolff. 133—Fusanori Nakajima. 134—Morris Rosenfeld & Sons—drawing by Fred Wolff. 135—Morris Rosenfeld & Sons. 136,137—Stanley Rosenfeld, drawings by Fred Wolff. 138—Roland Rose, courtesy Bahama News Bureau. 139—Stanley Rosenfeld—drawings by Fred Wolff. 140,141—Eric Schweikardt, drawing by Fred Wolff. 142—Eric Schweikardt for SPORTS ILLUSTRATED. 144—Enrico Ferorelli—drawing by Dale Gustafson. 145—Drawing by Fred Wolff. 146,147—Enrico Ferorelli. 148,149—Stanley Rosenfeld. 150—Courtesy Sparkman & Stephens. 151—Stanley Rosenfeld. 152—Stanley Rosenfeld; courtesy North Sails. 153—Drawing by Fred Wolff, adapted from North Sails diagram. 154—Drawing by Fred Wolff—Enrico Ferorelli. 155—Enrico Ferorelli. 156,157—Dan Nerney. 158,159—Stanley Rosenfeld—drawings by Whitman Studio, Inc. 160,161—Lois J. Kennedy; drawing by Whitman Studio, Inc. 162—Drawings by Whitman Studio, Inc. 163—Lois J. Kennedy. 164,165—Stanley Rosenfeld; drawings by Whitman Studio, Inc.

# Index

*Page numbers in italics indicate a photograph or drawing of the subject mentioned.*

Printed in U.S.A.